ONTROLLING INDUSTRIAL ECONOMIES

ince the appearance of Keynes's *General Theory* macroeconomists have been reoccupied with controlling economies. In *Controlling Industrial Economies* articular attention is focused on some of the challenging problems faced by the vorld economy in recent decades. If anything, these problems are multiplying and re becoming more complex, particularly for the industrially advanced countries. 'he papers presented here deal partly with the responses to such problems and he adequacy of contemporary economic policies, and partly with some of the nore specific issues involved. The latter include key areas such as the future of ndustrial materials, the determinants of the direction and scale of inventive and scientific activity in contemporary Western industrialised societies, the raison d'être for trade among the industrial countries and for the industrialisation of the developing countries. Also investigated is the possibility of a capital constraint being one of the factors responsible for unemployment.

Further explored in *Controlling Industrial Economies* is the distribution of earnings, in particular the structure of industrial earnings in Western Europe, the dispersion of wages in the CMEA countries and the macroeconomic planning of oil revenue in industrialised countries. The latter provides a case-study of the United Kingdom. It covers the period 1976–2000 and applies the methodology of optimal control, a technique also used in a paper on stabilisation policies in West Germany and the Netherlands. Further papers are concerned with short-term forecasting, basic elements of British economic policy-making and the dynamic impacts of different modes of financing budget deficits on the level of aggregate income. The contents also provide an analysis of inflation in the USSR and Eastern Europe and a case-study of the Polish economy. The book is not without lessons for future policy-makers. Anyone interested in applied economics should find this book an indispensable guide to some of the most crucial economic issues of the day.

Christopher T. Saunders

Controlling Industrial Economies

Essays in Honour of Christopher Thomas Saunders

Edited by Stephen F. Frowen

MACMILLAN PRESS
LONDON

Director: Prof. Dr. Dr. F. Levcik

First published 1983 by
THE MACMILLAN PRESS LTD
London and Basingstoke
Companies and representatives throughout the world

ISBN 0 333 33035 8

Printed and bound in Great Britain at The Camelot Press Ltd Southampton

ACKNOWLEDGEMENTS

The publication of this volume was facilitated by a generous contribution of the *Creditanstalt-Bankverein*, Austria.

INTRODUCTION

Not for some time has the world economy been in such a turmoil as during the 1970s and early 1980s, and to a superficial observer it may have seemed as if the comfortable world of full employment and high rates of economic growth, basically built on Keynesian economic policies, had finally collapsed. The energy crises and inflation became the problems apparently in the forefront of the mind of many politicians in power (with money-supply targeting the principal instrument of monetary policy), while rapidly mounting unemployment and low growth rates in the industrial countries, not to speak of the very real problems of many of the developing countries and problems of world trade, seemed to rank much lower in importance. It would have been impossible, of course, to provide a comprehensive coverage of all these areas in the present volume, but it is hoped that the topics covered will throw some light on at least a few problems, on the solution of which the future of the world economy will in some way depend.

Part I of this book is concerned with some of the structural changes in the world economy, analysing problems arising from the 'Intra-Industry' specialisation and the foreign trade of industrial countries (P. B. W. Rayment), the industrialisation of the developing countries (A. Maizels), the supply of industrial materials (G. F. Ray) and the determinants of the direction and scale of inventive and scientific activity in contemporary industrialised societies (C. Freeman, V. Walsh and J. Townsend). This part also touches on the long wave theory as an explanation of the present economic crisis (the late L. H. Dupriez).

Part II deals with some of the economic pressures in East and West. The possibility is first discussed of a capital constraint on the realisation of full employment, i. e., an insufficiency of cooperating capital equipment to permit the full usage of labour resources in the developed economies resulting in 'Marxian Unemployment' (M. J. Artis). This is followed by an analysis of inflation in the USSR and the rest of Eastern Europe (Nita Watts) and by a discussion of Polish economic management during the 1970s and early 1980s (G. Blazyca).

The distribution of earnings is examined in Part III of the book. L. Needleman covers the structure of industrial earnings in seven of the West European countries, while the dispersion of wages in the CMEA countries and Austria is dealt with by B. Askanas and F. Levcik. Problems arising from the macroeconomic planning of oil revenue in industrial countries, with special reference to the British case, are analysed by Homa Motamen.

The fourth and final part of the book looks at stabilisation policies in industrial countries. This section deals with a post-mortem on British economic policy in the 1960s and 1970s by F. Blackaby. On fiscal policy there are two studies. One by S. F. Frowen and P. Arestis, on the impact of fiscal action on aggregate income using UK data, takes up the challenge by some economists to the Keynesian contention that an increase in government expenditure induces rounds of spending and thereby results in a multiple increase in national income. Their findings show that the results basically depend on how government expenditure is financed. The second study on fiscal policy is by N. Kloten and K. H. Ketterer and looks at problems of fiscal policy in West Germany. Optimal stabilisation policies in West Germany and the Netherlands are the subject of a paper by P. Arestis, S. Holly and E. Karakitsos. Quite appropriately, the final paper in Part IV of the book is by David Worswick, the successor of Christopher Saunders as Director of the NIESR. His essay on National Income Forecasting throws much light on the further development of forecasting techniques applied by the NIESR in recent years.

All the essays in this volume have been written in honour of Christopher Saunders to mark the occasion of his 75th birthday in November 1982. It is hoped that they will make some impact in those areas of economic policy to which Christopher Saunders himself has devoted so much of his time and thought.

Christopher Thomas Saunders, the son of a clergyman, was born on November 5, 1907, and educated at Craig School Windermere, St Edward's School and at Christ Church Oxford, where he obtained his B. A. in Philosophy, Politics and Economics in 1929. Before the Second World War he worked for the University of Liverpool on the Social Survey of Merseyside from 1930 - 33, in the Economics Research Department of the University of Manchester from 1933 - 35, and for the Joint Committee of Cotton Trade Organisations in Manchester, later coverted into the official Cotton Control, from 1935 to 1944, when he was seconded to the Combined Production and Resources Board in Washington for the rest of the war period. Then, in 1945, he began twelve years of Government service, first with the Ministry of Labour from 1945 to 1947, and subsequently with the Central Statistical Office, finally as Deputy Director, from 1947 to 1957. During this period, in 1953, he was awarded the CMG (Companion of the Order of St Michael and St George) for his services.

The work of Christopher Saunders on wider economic issues began in 1957 when he became Director of the National Institute of Economic and Social Research, London, a position he held until 1965. Soon after taking over the Directorship of the NIESR he took a leading part in launching the *National Institute Economic Review* and greatly enhanced the National Institute's work in forecasting and other fields. In 1965, at the age of 58, his interests in world and particularly European and East-West economic affairs took Christopher Saunders and his Dutch born wife Cora to Geneva, where he subsequently became Director of Research of the UN Economic Commission for Europe, a position he held until he retired at the age of 65 in 1972. But far from settling into a 'true' retirement, he continued to work as a consultant to the United Nations in both Geneva and New York, and as a Professorial Fellow at the Sussex European Research Centre of the University of Sussex, Brighton. This was also the time when Christopher Saunders became actively associated with the Vienna Institute for Comparative Economic Studies and its director, Friedrich Levcik – like him a former senior official of the UN Economic Commission for Europe. When the Vienna Institute (next to UN/ECE one of the important bridges for East-West European economic studies) initiated a series of East-West workshops, Christopher Saunders took a substantial part both as Member of the Steering Committee and as Editor of the series of published conference volumes (in the latter capacity assisted by Fred Prager of the Vienna Institute, whose help in the preparation of the present volume, too, has been invaluable). Christopher Saunders' association with the Vienna Institute in these two functions continues to the present day.

The deep-rooted interest and concern of Christopher Saunders in a wide range of economic issues is evident from the list of his publications. His work at the CSO was closely related to the development and use of national income statistics and it was thanks to him that the monumental volume on *National Income Statistics: Sources and Methods* could finally be published by the Central Statistical Office in 1956.

When he later concentrated more on some of the pressing economic problems of the day, in particular those which have emerged in some of the Western European industrial countries, he devoted much of his time to the study of incomes policies, earnings and pay patterns, and to the problems arising from concentration and specialisation in Western industrial economies. In this context he also paid attention to the structural problems of the world economy and to problems of East-West economic co-operation. On all these issues he has written books and numerous papers probing deeply into the essential nature of the problem and providing valuable guidance to policy-makers. These were published either under the auspices of the authorities and organisations he was associated with at the time, or, especially in later years, under his own name.

In view of Christopher Saunders's very special range of activities, it seemed appropriate that a volume of essays in his honour should be devoted to some of these and other issues which concern industrial countries throughout the world. Most of the contributors to the present volume have of course been close associates of Christopher Saunders during some phase or other of his professional life.

This impressive public record should be supplemented, however, by stressing the very special sort of person Christopher Saunders is to his friends and colleagues. His courtesy and kindness, his generous appreciation of others, and the painstaking care he has always taken in helping and advising younger economists both by commenting on their papers and by supervising their postgraduate work, is something generations of economists will remember with deepest gratitude.

Stephen Frowen

University of Surrey,
Guildford, Surrey.
April 1983

TABLE OF CONTENTS

PART I – STRUCTURAL CHANGES IN THE WORLD ECONOMY

PART II – ECONOMIC PRESSURES – EAST AND WEST

PART III – DISTRIBUTION OF EARNINGS

PART IV – STABILISATION POLICIES

PART I

STRUCTURAL CHANGES IN THE WORLD ECONOMY

Chapter 1

INTRA-'INDUSTRY' SPECIALISATION AND THE FOREIGN TRADE OF INDUSTRIAL COUNTRIES

P. B. W. Rayment

'... there is scarce a country or corner of Europe whose beams are not crossed and interchanged with others.'

Laurence Sterne

Introduction

In 1923, Alfred Marshall declared that the relative importance of manufactured goods in world trade was largely a temporary phenomenon due to countries being at different stages of industrial development. Eventually the spread of modern technology and economic growth would enable the lagging countries to acquire the same skills and aptitudes as the industrial leaders and then the relative importance of trade in manufacture would decline: '... those local inequalities of human faculty, which now afford a solid basis for such trade, seem likely on the whole to diminish' (1). Marshall in fact claimed that the proportion of world trade governed by differences in natural resources was already rising as a result of this process. Why Marshall was wrong or, at least, has so far proved to be so, is the underlying theme of this paper.

Marshall's argument was not original nor was he the last to advance it. The idea that the spread of technical progress and economic growth would reduce the international division of labour was the source of a spectre that had haunted all manufacturing nations since time immemorial, namely, that the export of the means of manufacturing production would lead to their self-destruction. Throughout European history, from the Venetian Republic to nineteenth century Britain, there were repeated and largely ineffectual attempts to prevent the emigration of skilled artisans and the export of machinery (2); and for those European powers with colonies, a major element of colonial policy was to suppress any emerging industrial activity which might threaten the traditional complementarity between the metropolitan country's export of manufactures and the colony's export of primary products (3). Most of the specific export controls to protect domestic manufacturing industry in England between the sixteenth and mid-eighteenth century may have simply reflected the fear of insurrection ensuing from unemployment in an age when both poor relief and the forces of law and order were rudimentary (4), but this fear was re-inforced by the conception that there was a fixed global quantity of trade and that one country's gain could only be at the expense of another (5). There was also, as post-Ricardians know, a failure to distinguish between absolute and comparative cost differences.

Marshall's prediction that natural resource differences would account for a growing proportion of world trade had also been made a century earlier by Robert Torrens, who argued that population pressures and the law of diminishing returns in agriculture in the primary product producing countries would eventually force all countries to produce most of their own primary products and manufactures, and that international trade would then be 'confined to those peculiar articles, in the production of which the immutable circumstances of soil and climate give one country a permanent advantage over another' (6). Viner thought that if the primary producing countries were in fact to industrialise on a major scale then 'Torrens' forecast will become true', but he doubted that industrialisation would in fact take place on a sufficient scale to make it even a reasonable forecast for the 'next century' (Viner, 1946, p. 8). Keynes, on the other hand, followed Marshall in accepting the equalising effect of technical progress and in assuming that it had occurred on a significant scale: 'the advantages of a high degree of national specialisation were very considerable' in the nineteeth century 'when there were enormous differences in degree in the industrialisation and opportunities for technical training in different countries'. In 1933 these advantages no longer seemed comparable with what they were. Since 'most modern processes of mass production can be performed in most countries with almost equal efficiency' the real costs of greater national self-sufficiency would not be very large: 'National self-sufficiency, in short, though it costs something, may be becoming a luxury which we can afford, if we happen to want it' (Keynes 1933, pp. 759 – 760). For Keynes the possibility of reducing the relative importance of trade in manufactures was thus an opportunity: a greater measure of national self-sufficiency might improve the prospects for peace ('the age of economic internationalism was not particularly successful in avoiding war' (7)) and would permit countries to experiment with alternatives 'to decadent international and individualistic capitalism' without outside interference. Robertson (1938, p. 2) also thought that it was 'fairly evident that [differences in comparative advantage] were tending to become narrower' and although he noted opposing tendencies, he concluded that on balance the outlook was for a permanently diminished relative volume of international trade.

Although Viner (1946) challenged the assumptions of Keynes and Robertson on empirical grounds, it was only with the classic studies of Hilgerdt (1945) and Maizels (1963) (8) that this long-standing pessimism (or optimism in the case of Keynes) as to the effects of the industrialisation of primary producing countries on world trade in manufactures was subject to detailed statistical analysis. Neither of these investigations, each covering periods of around seventy years, provided empirical support for the 'pessimistic' view; instead they found a positive relation between changes in world manufacturing production and changes in world trade in manufactures, and in their explanations they stressed the inter-relationships between growth and trade expansion, industrialisation simultaneously improving both the ability to export and the capacity to import. The real threat to the growth of trade in manufactures was not the spread of industrialisation but, as the 1930s were to demonstrate, the spread of restrictions on trade.

But what seems particularly curious to someone writing at the end of the 1970s is that throughout the long history of this 'pessimistic' view of the future of trade in manufacture intra-trade among the already industrialised countries is scarcely, if ever, mentioned (9).

Perhaps the most familiar features of world trade since the Second World War are its increasing domination by trade in manufactures and the increasing domination of world trade in manufactures by the industrialised countries of North America, Western Europe and Japan. (The share of manufactures in world trade rose from around 45 per cent in 1955 to just over 60 per cent in 1973; the share of the industrialised market economies in world trade in manufactures rose from about 48 per cent to 66 per cent over the same period (10).) But an equally striking feature is that the industrialised countries' exports of manufactures are dominated by their exports to one another, such that in 1973 about 60 per cent of world trade in manufactures was among the industrial countries themselves (compared with some 44 per cent in 1955). However, Maizels' data (which are only broadly comparable with those quoted above) show that trade among the industrial countries already accounted for some 54 per cent of world trade in manufactures in 1899 (Maizels 1963, Table A.3). This share subsequently declined between the two world wars but never fell below 40 per cent. It is therefore somewhat surprising that there could be so much concern at the possible effects of spreading industrialisation on trade in manufactures when large volumes of trade among the existing industrialised countries provided *prima facie* evidence that the effects might not be serious. Part of the explanation must be that this was very much a preoccupation of the English who were more concerned with the preservation of imperial markets and who exported a much lower proportion of their manufactures to other industrialised countries than did other European countries (38 per cent in 1899, compared with 68 and 55 per cent for France and Germany). Also when Marshall was writing UK exports to other industrial countries had been declining relatively (though not absolutely), while Robertson, writing in the 1930s, would naturally have been more impressed by the absolute contraction of trade in manufactures than by its proportionate distribution among various country groupings.

Bertil Ohlin, however, took a different view. He observed that customs statistics frequently showed individual commodities being simultaneously exported and imported and he explained this partly in terms of differences in regional transport costs giving rise to border trade and partly in terms of quality differentiation. But he also remarked that the advanced manufacturing countries exchanged among themselves highly specialised products 'in a surprisingly large volume' and he thought that Marshall had 'probably underestimated the importance of the fact that economies of large-scale production and specialisation increase rapidly ... An examination of the trade in machinery between the leading manufacturing nations brings out this fact clearly' (11). Ohlin was thus perhaps the first economist to suggest that intra-'industry' specialisation was an important characteristic of intra-industrial country trade in manufactures. There is a nice touch of irony in this when one considers how much time has been spent in the past thirty years in trying to resolve the Leontief 'paradox'.

Ohlin's observations appear to have had little or no impact on the empirical analysis of trade and none on the theoretical. Much of the post-war theoretical work was taken up with the development and refinement of the Heckscher-Ohlin-Samuelson model, while much of the empirical work has been devoted to trying to discover why it is not very successful in explaining trade among industrial countries. Attention did begin to focus on intra-'industry' specialisation at the beginning of the 1960s with the growing interest in the effects of customs unions. Following Meade's theoretical work (Meade 1955), it was thought that the formation of a customs union might be followed by severe adjustment problems since industries which had previously grown up behind national tariff barriers would be eliminated on their removal. But Verdoorn (1960) and Balassa (1963 and 1966) failed to find any significant increases in bankruptcies, structural unemployment or other signs of declining national industries. They concluded that the principal adjustments had taken place within industries (as defined statistically by their data) and this, presumably because of greater resource mobility within relatively narrow sets of activities (12), explained the lack of the more obvious signs of adjustment. Grubel (1967) then suggested a number of models for explaining intra-'industry' trade, mainly in terms of monopolistic competition theory. On the grounds that intra-'industry' trade was a phenomenon of aggregation, Grubel and Lloyd (1971) conducted a detailed analysis of the Australian trade data for 1968 – 69 and found that intra-'industry' trade persisted through successive degrees of disaggregation to even the 7-digit level. To explain the phenomenon they again suggested the need to incorporate elements of the theory of oligopolistic product differentiation into international trade theory, but they also suggested that diverse explanations, including specialisation in narrow product ranges, may be appropriate. Grubel's work has stimulated a number of papers on the subject (13), so that forty years on from Ohlin's original observations, it is now quite a flourishing sub-section of international trade analysis. Before considering the significance of intra-'industry' trade it is necessary to discuss first its measurement and then to present some estimates of its importance so that we can be clear as to what is under discussion.

Definitions of intra-'industry' trade

Intra-'industry' trade may be defined simply as the presence in national trade statistics of simultaneous exports and imports of a given product or by a given 'industry'. It is essentially a statistical phenomenon arising from the need to fit the enormous variety of traded goods into a manageable classification scheme. If each product category contained only identical products (14) then, except for seasonal and border trade (which would be in identical products except for their availability in space and time), intra-'industry' trade would disappear from the annual trade statistics. Intra-'industry' trade is therefore very much a phenomenon of statistical aggregation and quantitative estimates of its relative importance will not be meaningful unless accompanied by a specification of the product classification or level of aggregation employed. Intra-'industry' trade does not exist in trade theory: there, industries and products are usually coterminous and are homogeneous with respect to factor intensity and everything else that might upset the simplicity and rigour of the analysis; with omnipresent homogeneity two-way trade flows of a given product cannot exist, for a country cannot simultaneously have a comparative advantage and disadvantage in the same product. I have placed inverted commas around the industry of intra-'industry' trade as a reminder that this is a statistical construct which in most cases is likely to be very different from the concept encountered in trade and production theory (that is, an aggregate of enterprises producing identical products with identical factor ratios, etc.).

Some of the earlier studies of intra-'industry' trade inferred its increasing importance from changes in the variance of selected variables: of the ratios of bilateral product flows and of price differentials within individual 'industries' (Verdoorn 1960), or the variance of country product shares in total intra-EEC trade and of export-import ratios (Grubel 1967). The greater is the degree of intra-'industry' trade, the greater will be the similarity of the structure of imports and exports: thus the cosine of the export and import vectors provides another measure of the relative importance of intra-'industry' trade (15). However, the simplest and most flexible approach is to use the formula used by the League of Nations (16) to measure the extent of bilateral trade balancing in the 1930s. If X_i and M_i refer to exports and imports of 'industry' or commodity i (i = 1 ... n) from and into country j, then the proportion of intra-'industry' trade in total trade is given by:

$$T_j = \frac{\sum_i (X_i + M_i - |X_i - M_i|)}{\sum_i X_i + \sum_i M_i} \qquad \text{... (1)}$$

T_j (17) is a measure of the extent to which exports (imports) are matched by imports (exports) in the same industries at a given level of aggregation; its value lies between 0, indicating that exports and imports are entirely complementary (the case of the text-book trade model), and 1, indicating perfect similarity between exports and imports. Grubel and Lloyd (1971) use this measure, but they argue that if trade is imbalanced T_j will be biased downwards since it will then be impossible for T_j ever to reach 1; they therefore adjust the measure by subtracting the absolute trade balance, $|\sum_i X_i - \sum_i M_i|$, from the denominator of Equation 1. However, while their initial observation is arithmetically correct the adjustment they propose involves a highly arbitrary re-arrangement of the basic data and ignores the fact that the intra-'industry' flows are only one part of a three-part decomposition of total trade. If we take only the subset of trade in manufactures the decomposition is as follows:

(A) *Intra-'industry' flows,* for example, the exchange of machine tools for machine tools; the value of this is measured by the numerator of T_j above;

(B) *inter-'industry' flows* within the subset, for example, the exchange of textiles for machine tools. Calling this IT_j, it is given by:

$$IT_j = \sum_i |X_i - M_i| - |\sum_i X_i - \sum_i M_i| \qquad \text{... (2);}$$

(C) *inter-set flows,* for example, the exchange of manufactures for primary products, services and, if capital flows are included in the complete set of international transactions, for future goods and services. Calling this IST_j, it is measured simply by the trade balance of the subset in question:

$$IST_j = |\sum_i X_i - \sum_i M_i| \qquad \text{... (3).}$$

These three components (18) then sum to the total value of trade in the subset, that is:

$$\sum_i X_i + \sum_i M_i = T'_j + IT_j + IST_j \qquad \text{... (4),}$$

where T'_j is the numerator of Equation 1 above.

The Grubel-Lloyd adjustment simply suppresses the third component and inflates T'_j and IT_j. Indeed, if a country had an import surplus in all 'industries' or commodities, not an unlikely situation for some developing countries, the adjustment would always raise T_j to 100 per cent of total trade since in this case IT_j would always be zero (19). But if there is a surplus or deficit in total trade in manufactures, then by definition there must be an exchange of manufactures for non-manufactures and, by definition, trade in manufactures cannot consist entirely of intra- and inter-'industry' exchanges. It is difficult to see why this should be regarded as a bias in need of correction. The exchange of manufactures for primary products is in fact part of what Robertson (1938) called 'the Great Specialisation of the nineteenth century' – this pattern of exchange is still a component of international trade and I cannot see any useful purpose in suppressing it in order to inflate the relative importance of another type of exchange.

The data

The relative importance of intra-'industry' trade in manufactures is shown for 20 OECD countries in *Tables 1.1* and *1.2*, according to Equation 1 above. Manufactures are defined by the following sections of the Standard International Trade Classification (SITC): SITC 5, chemicals, SITC 6, manufactured goods classified chiefly by material but excluding non-ferrous metals (SITC 68); SITC 7, machinery and transport equipment; SITC 8, miscellaneous manufactured articles, synthetic rubber (SITC 231.2) and synthetic fibres (SITC 266). This is a fairly comprehensive definition and a fairly common one (it is more or less the same as Hufbauer's (1970), for example). Non-ferrous metals were excluded for the same reason as were processed foods, beverages and tobacco products, namely, that trade in them is heavily influenced by natural resource endowments (20); there are some obvious exceptions to this but in general their relative importance is small and did not justify the additional collection and separation of data. The basic data are current values of exports and imports converted into United States dollars at official exchange rates, as published in the official source. Exports are valued *f.o.b.* and imports *c.i.f.*, except for Canada and the United States where imports are also *f.o.b.* This difference in valuation will introduce some bias into the measurement of intra-'industry' trade in manufactures, but it is not possible to judge the direction of the bias since it will depend on whether the individual commodities or 'industries' are in deficit or surplus. Adjustment of *c.i.f.* values to *f.o.b.* is often made on the basis of some conventional ratio of *c.i.f.* to *f.o.b.* This may be acceptable at fairly high levels of aggregation but no attempt was made to apply such an adjustment procedure here. There would appear to be a fairly high inter-product variance of *c.i.f.* – *f.o.b.* ratios (21), and application of a simple rule of thumb seemed likely to introduce as much bias as it might remove. All one can do here is to signpost a source of error of unknown direction and magnitude.

The number of manufacturing 'industries' varies among countries at both the 3-digit and the 4-digit levels of aggregation. The variation at 3 digits is very small and is located in items of minor trade value. The variation is rather greater at 4 digits since non-availability of data increases considerably. When either exports or imports at 4 digits were not available sub-groups were aggregated until comparable export and import elements were obtained; in some cases disaggregation was impossible so that some of the elements in the calculations at 4 digits are in fact 3-digit groups. The average number of manufactures at the 4-digit level is about 350, but this varies, in 1969 for example, from 315 in the United States to 366 in Italy; over time there is a range of 292 to 352 in the United States and from 330 to 355 in Sweden and the United Kingdom. Most of this variation is located in fairly marginal items and so far as I can judge the effect on the coefficient of intra-trade at the 4-digit level is likely to be very small.

Table 1.1

Intra-'industry' trade as a percentage of total trade in manufactures, measured at the level of SITC 3-digit groups (a)

Country	1962	1963	1964	1965	1966	1967	1968	1969	1970	1971	1972	1973
Austria	55.4	57.3	58.3	58.8	59.8	63.4	63.9	65.0	66.6	66.5	67.2	69.9
Belgium	60.0	61.6	64.5	67.4	69.2	69.4	71.6	72.8	72.7	74.2	74.8	74.2
Denmark	54.8	57.4	57.8	59.7	61.6	63.7	64.4	61.8	62.4	63.1	64.8	63.7
Finland	..	..	20.4	21.6	23.2	28.1	30.7	35.0	34.9	35.1	38.6	32.9
France	66.7	70.6	74.0	74.1	76.7	78.5	79.9	82.0	79.4	80.1	80.8	82.2
Fed. Rep. of Germany	48.0	47.7	49.8	53.3	52.8	50.7	53.3	57.0	60.1	61.0	60.7	58.2
Greece	9.9	8.3	9.3	9.9	11.2	13.6	14.0	19.2	19.0	17.3	21.2	22.5
Italy	59.6	63.4	62.9	56.0	57.9	60.5	58.4	60.5	63.1	63.6	62.9	66.6
Netherlands	71.1	72.3	71.1	72.4	72.3	73.1	73.2	74.5	72.8	74.3	74.2	75.5
Norway	33.2	36.2	40.3	42.9	43.9	47.2	52.6	48.7	51.4	49.6	58.7	61.8
Portugal	25.1	26.9	31.3	33.9	34.5	36.7	35.4	40.9	38.9	40.5	40.0	41.2
Spain	23.3	22.7	26.4	26.5	28.3	32.3	37.1	38.8	41.0	45.2	42.2	45.6
Sweden	60.5	60.7	62.3	62.4	67.3	66.1	64.8	66.9	67.0	66.8	67.8	67.5
Switzerland	54.2	53.7	54.0	55.4	55.3	54.9	54.4	55.3	57.0	57.2	55.5	55.1
Turkey	1.0	1.0	2.4	2.8	2.2	2.5	3.1	6.9	6.5	5.6	5.6	6.3
United Kingdom	47.3	47.8	54.1	56.3	57.9	63.6	66.0	65.0	64.4	66.1	72.7	76.8
Yugoslavia	36.3	36.1	37.9	41.3	45.1	44.0	46.2	47.2	44.4	52.6	45.9	49.1
Canada	35.4	37.6	39.4	42.9	50.9	57.9	65.1	66.3	66.2	68.1	66.1	64.9
United States	41.5	43.0	44.4	49.3	56.7	58.2	58.4	59.0	56.8	55.4	57.6	60.3
Japan	26.6	29.4	30.4	25.0	25.8	30.3	29.7	30.1	32.3	28.4	28.3	38.1

(a) The proportion of intra-'industry' trade (Tj) is given by $\frac{\sum_i (2.\ \text{minimum of } Xi,\ Mi)}{\sum_i Xi + \sum_i Mi} . 100$

where Xi refers to exports (*f.o.b.*) and Mi to imports (*c.i.f.*) – except in Canada and the United States where imports are *f.o.b.* – and where i (= 1 ..... n) refers to a 3-digit group of the SITC, n being on average about 95.

Source: Basic data from OECD, *Trade by Commodities,* Paris: annual.

Table 1.2

Intra-'industry' trade as a percentage of total trade in manufactures, measured at the level of the 4-digit sub-groups of the SITC (a)

Country	1962	1963	1964	1965	1966	1967	1968	1969	1970	1971	1972	1973
Austria	45.8	47.3	49.3	49.9	51.8	54.3	55.0	56.3	58.8	59.2	58.1	61.1
Belgium	52.9	55.3	56.9	58.0	59.4	60.8	61.3	64.4	64.1	63.9	65.0	70.0
Denmark	46.2	48.3	49.3	50.9	52.8	54.2	56.3	53.5	53.8	55.0	55.7	55.0
Finland	..	..	16.8	18.4	18.4	22.9	24.3	28.7	30.2	31.0	32.3	32.4
France	60.3	63.6	67.2	66.9	69.2	70.6	72.3	74.3	76.6	80.2	80.2	81.1
Fed. Rep. of Germany	44.0	43.9	46.0	49.5	49.1	47.1	49.5	53.2	56.3	57.5	57.3	55.3
Greece	6.4	6.2	6.7	7.0	7.9	10.4	8.0	11.4	11.1	11.1	14.5	17.2
Italy	52.4	56.5	55.7	50.1	51.5	54.2	52.7	54.6	57.6	58.3	57.7	60.8
Netherlands	63.3	61.9	60.2	63.8	64.5	65.4	65.9	67.4	66.2	67.1	66.5	68.5
Norway	28.3	30.9	34.6	37.3	38.0	41.3	46.8	43.3	46.4	44.7	53.2	57.2
Portugal	15.1	16.3	21.7	24.4	25.8	28.3	21.9	23.2	24.2	24.2	25.4	27.3
Spain	15.8	15.8	17.8	17.7	20.7	25.0	28.0	30.8	33.2	37.3	33.9	36.6
Sweden	49.2	50.7	53.5	54.2	58.2	57.7	57.2	59.4	59.7	58.9	61.7	62.6
Switzerland	50.3	46.2	45.9	47.7	48.2	48.4	48.3	48.8	49.5	49.9	48.6	49.6
Turkey	0.6	0.7	1.2	1.5	1.1	1.7	1.3	3.3	3.6	3.8	3.3	3.9
United Kingdom	42.8	44.0	49.6	52.5	54.2	59.6	62.2	61.8	61.8	62.3	67.8	70.2
Yugoslavia	26.9	27.1	28.3	32.4	36.0	36.7	37.1	38.0	37.6	35.7	37.5	40.1
Canada	31.0	32.6	33.8	39.2	45.0	49.1	52.7	55.3	55.4	59.5	60.3	61.0
United States	30.1	31.2	33.3	39.2	43.5	44.7	44.5	45.9	52.5	52.7	55.2	57.9
Japan	19.9	21.1	22.4	19.9	20.7	24.5	24.6	24.9	26.4	23.8	23.7	32.6

(a) The number of sub-groups is, on average, approximately 350.

Source and note: as for table 1.1

Intra-'industry' trade in 20 countries, 1962 – 1973

The data in *Tables 1.1* and *1.2* show clearly that intra-'industry' trade flows account for a major proportion of total trade in all the major industrialised countries. In 1973, at the 3-digit level of the SITC, the most widely used in current international trade analysis, intra-'industry' trade accounts for more than 50 per cent of total trade in manufactures in 13 of the 20 countries shown: the only major manufacturing country not in this group is Japan. The relatively lower ratios are otherwise found in the countries of Southern Europe and Finland, the inclusion of forest products most probably accounting for the low proportion in the latter. There is hardly any intra-'industry' trade in Turkey, the least industrialised country among the twenty.

Disaggregation (22) to the 4-digit sub-groups of the SITC involves nearly a quadrupling in the number of commodity or 'industry' groups but, as is clear from a comparison of *Tables 1.1* and *1.2*, the impact on the measure of intra-trade is small. Apart from Portugal, the fall in the share of intra-trade is nowhere more than 10 percentage points. All the countries with intra-trade of more than 50 per cent of total trade at 3 digits retain 50 per cent and more at 4 digits. The proportionate fall in the intra-'industry' trade ratio tends to be larger in the relatively less industrialised countries of Southern Europe. However the rank order of countries with respect to the relative importance of intra-'industry' trade remains pretty much the same at both levels of aggregation (23).

A noticeable feature of the intra-'industry' trade ratios is that they have been rising since the early 1960s, in some cases quite rapidly, at both levels of aggregation. Exponential trends were fitted to the time series and the regression coefficients were nearly all significant at 1 per cent (t-test): the exceptions at 3 digits are Italy (not significant at 5 per cent), Switzerland and Japan (both significant at 5 per cent); and at 4 digits Italy (significant at 5 per cent) and Switzerland (not significant). The trend growth rates of the shares of intra-'industry' trade in total trade in manufactures are as follows:

	3 digits	4 digits		3 digits	4 digits
Austria	2.0	2.6	Portugal	4.3	3.8
Belgium	2.0	2.2	Spain	7.2	9.4
Finland	7.0	8.5	Sweden	1.1	2.0
Denmark	1.3	1.5	Switzerland	0.4	0.4
France	1.6	2.7	Turkey	18.9	19.1
West Germany	2.3	2.6	U.K.	4.1	4.4
Greece	9.8	9.2	Yugoslavia	2.4	3.5
Italy	0.7	1.1	Canada	6.7	7.0
Netherlands	0.5	0.9	United States	3.2	6.2
Norway	5.0	5.8	Japan	1.7	3.1

For most countries the growth of intra-'industry' trade at 4 digits has been growing faster than at 3 digits, which of course means that the impact of disaggregation on measured intra-'industry' trade has been declining over the eleven-year period. There has also been some convergence of intra-trade ratios in that the ratio has tended to grow faster in those countries where the ratios were relatively low at the beginning of the period: the Spearman rank correlation coefficient between the rank orders of intra-trade ratios in 1962 and of trend growth rates (at 3 digits) between 1962 and 1973 is – 0.66 (significant at 1 per cent, for a one-tailed test).

Clearly intra-'industry' flows are a major feature of world trade in manufactures which can be added to those mentioned already. Weighting the intra-trade ratios (at 3 digits) by the total trade values of the 20 individual countries gives an average share of intra-'industry' trade in 1973 of some 63 per cent. Given that the share of the industrialised market economies in world trade in manufactures is about two-thirds, this implies that at least 40 per cent of world trade in manufactures is intra-'industry'. Grubel and Lloyd's (1971) findings for Australia suggested that intra-'industry' trade is not confined to the most industrialised countries and so a figure nearer 50 per cent may not be unreasonable.

For the total trade of the 20 OECD countries considered here, the three-part decomposition described above is as follows (in percentages of total trade, at 3 digits):

	20 countries		Industrial Europe (a)	
	1962	1973	1962	1973
1. Intra-'industry' flows	48	63	55	68
2. Inter-'industry' flows	21	20	19	16
3. Inter-set flows	31	17	26	16

(a) Excluding Spain, Greece, Turkey, Portugal and Yugoslavia.

The 'Great Specialisation' of the nineteenth century (inter-set trade above), which still corresponds to many popular notions of what international trade is about and which is reflected in most text-book expositions of the '2 x 2 x 2' trade model, has continued to decline quite sharply in relative importance and, for industrial market economies, is now completely over-shadowed by the exchange of manufactures for manufactures. Within the latter the importance of intra-'industry' trade has increased while inter-'industry' exchanges have fallen. Between 1962 and 1973 two-thirds of the increase in the value of total trade for the 20 countries as a group occurred within the 3-digit groups; for the more industrialised European economies, the contribution was nearer three quarters. The disaggregation of commodity groups will shift the relative shares of intra-'industry' and inter-'industry' trade in favour of the latter, but in practice the move from 3 to 4 digits has only a small effect: at 4 digits, the share of intra-'industry' flows in total trade in 1973 is 58 per cent for the 20 countries (compared with 63 per cent at 3 digits) and 64 per cent for the more industrialised Europeans (compared with 68 per cent at 3 digits).

Interpretations

Attempts to provide a theoretical interpretation of intra-'industry' trade need to proceed with considerable care. In the first place, the mere existence of such trade says nothing about the validity of the Heckscher-Ohlin theory, although some writers have concluded that intra-'industry' trade is inconsistent with it. If factor-proportions vary more within the commodity or 'industry' groups than between them, then the factor-proportions theory may very well be consistent with the presence of intra-'industry' trade: what is wrong in this event is the classification system. Only if the individual commodity groups are homogeneous with respect to factor intensity will intra-'industry' trade be inconsistent with Heckscher-Ohlin. For the United States in 1963 Finger (1975) has shown that 40 per cent of the variation among 400 SIC (24) industries in physical and human capital intensity is within the corresponding 3-digit groups of the SITC. It is virtually impossible to repeat this test for other countries because of the lack of equally detailed production data. Finger's calculation confirms that a proportion of intra-'industry' trade may be explained by the factor-proportions theory. Just how large a proportion is difficult to determine: although the patterns of trade in individual products are extremely complex, it is possible in some cases to establish inter-country patterns of specialisation (25) (though not always with great precision); but having done so, at the expense of considerable statistical work, it is difficult to pursue the analysis in any depth because production data (employment, wage and salary bill, value added, capital stock, etc.) are simply not available to the corresponding degree of detail. However, although Finger's calculation is important and must hover over all discussions of intra-'industry' trade, I find it difficult to believe that all or even most of such trade can eventually be accounted for by the Heckscher-Ohlin theorem (26). In many cases investigation of the detailed trade data reveal extremely fine distinctions of national specialisation in the trade flows among, for example, the industrialised European countries. Steel of a certain thickness is exported from Germany to France and of another thickness from France to West Germany: the basis for this pattern of specialisation is unlikely to be significant differences in factor proportions. United Kingdom trade in scientific instruments provides a specific example of the complexity involved. At the 3-digit level of the SITC, 'scientific and measuring instruments' constitute a single group (SITC 861) in which intra-'industry' trade was 90 per cent of total United Kingdom trade in this group in 1974. Using data published by SIMA (27) and arranged according to the Brussels Tariff Nomenclature, the intra-trade ratio was calculated for three successive degrees of disaggregation as follows: 16 product groups, 78.5 per cent; 166 groups, 70.8 per cent; and 188 (28) products, 68.3 per cent. In other words a twelve-fold increase in the sub-division of the industry yields only a 13 per cent fall in the intra-trade ratio. Most of this intra-trade (about two-thirds) is with other industrial market economies and again it seems to me unlikely that differences in factor proportions are likely to be very significant, particularly among the countries of Western Europe.

In what follows I shall discuss some of the explanations of intra-'industry' trade and then suggest a general approach to the phenomenon of increasing specialisation among manufacturing countries. Given the complexity of the basic patterns of specialisation as revealed (or merely suggested) in the trade statistics and that there is little hope of comprehensive testing of many of the propositions, the approach is necessarily rather tentative and certainly not very rigorous. Nevertheless by putting together various types of evidence in the spirit of Wittgenstein's 'assembling reminders for a particular purpose' one may at least suggest that theory and empirical analysis should begin to move in one direction rather than another.

One of the main attempts to provide a theoretical account of intra-'industry' trade has involved the incorporation of elements of monopolistic competition theory into the analysis of trade flows. The main inspiration for this approach is Linder's theory of trade in oligopolistically differentiated products among countries at similar levels of income per head (Linder 1961, esp. Ch. 3). Linder argues that a necessary condition for a product to be exportable is that it be consumed in the exporting country; of the set of all exportables it will tend to export those with the relatively most advantageous production functions, which in turn will tend to be those which cater to 'representative demand' which corresponds, somewhat loosely, to 'majority' tastes or to those of the modal income group. Imports will meet 'minority' tastes and will tend to come from countries where such tastes are more representative. For any product there will be a range of qualitative variations, different income groups demanding different qualities. For any pair of countries potential trade will lie in the range of quality variations for which their domestic demands overlap. The less the difference in income per head between the two countries the greater the range of overlapping demands and the more intensive their mutual trade. The narrowing of income differences could diminish trade since the two countries would have their comparative advantages in the same goods, but this ignores entrepreneurial initiative: when entrepreneurs raise their trade horizons 'the almost unlimited scope for product differentiation – real or advertised – could in combination with seemingly unrestricted buyer idiosyncrasies, make possible flourishing trade in what is virtually the same commodity. Ships bringing European beer to Milwaukee take American beer to Europe' (29).

Linder thus provides an explanation of why trade in manufactures among the rich industrialised countries should be relatively important and also suggests why intra-'industry' specialisation should be a significant component. If rising incomes per head are accompanied by a fall in their inter-country variance, then we also have an explanation for a rising trend in intra-'industry' trade.

Drèze's standardisation theory (Drèze 1960 and 1961) also suggests the possibility of intra-'industry' trade since his basic distinction between nationally differentiated goods and internationally standardised goods may often occur within the standard product categories of the SITC: simple tableware may qualify as internationally standardised, but national tastes may be more important for other items in the group. Because of economies of scale, the smaller country will export the standardised product and import the more differentiated items from larger countries. Drèze's emphasis on the longer production run is similar to Linder's emphasis on 'representative' demand, but Drèze stresses the relationship between standardisation and the long production run and does not argue that an exportable must first be demanded at home (30). However, the prediction of intra-'industry' trade is less strong under Drèze's model than Linder's: internationally standardised goods generally tend to be intermediate goods while nationally differentiated products tend to be consumer goods. Thus Drèze's model may encourage inter-'industry' as much as intra-'industry' specialisation.

Linder's model has not in fact stood up particularly well to theoretical criticism or to empirical testing (31), but it was clearly attractive to those who had assumed that the 3-digit groups of the SITC corresponded reasonably well to theoretical conceptions of an industry. Given that assumption, it was inevitable that two-way trade flows in the same commodity group would be regarded as trade in close substitutes and that oligopolistic product differentiation would appear to be a useful source of explanation. Kreinin (1969) has stated strongly his view that future developments in trade theory should be in the direction of incorporating the role of consumer preferences. He argues that supply models may be useful for explaining trade in homogeneous goods but for differentiated goods they only set the limits within which the commodity composition of trade responds to demand: those limits may be rather wide and within them only consumer preferences can explain the booming trade in differentiated products. But it is not very clear how one distinguishes differentiated goods from homogeneous goods if one does not accept that only close substitutes are grouped within the SITC categories. However, a major objection to this recommended direction for trade theory is that international trade in final consumer goods is not very important. An unambiguous definition of consumer goods is difficult to formulate statistically, but adding consumer durables (32), passenger cars and parts (33) and other consumer goods (34) gives a share of 19 per cent in total OECD imports of manufactures in 1969 and 27 per cent in total exports. These shares are certainly overstated since it is impossible to exclude a number of 'investment' goods (sewing machines), and components. But the actual proportion of consumer goods for which oligopolistic theories of product differentiation might be relevant is even smaller. A fairly large proportion of such trade can probably be explained in traditional Heckscher-Ohlin terms (clothing and footwear, for example), as can a certain amount of the flows in components and semi-finished products (which are included here). Moreover, the potential domain for oligopolistic product differentiation will be exaggerated by measuring trade in gross values: the exchange of Fiats for Volkswagens may indeed reflect the influence of capricious consumer preferences, but underneath the differentiated exterior of products such as cars one frequently finds a large proportion of internationally standardised parts with a variety of national origins. The actual characteristics which differentiate close substitutes may account for only a small part of total value added. It is also relevant to point out that the relative importance of finished consumer goods in world trade in manufactures has been falling throughout most of the present century (35).

Closer inspection of the SITC definitions also casts doubts on the extent to which intra-'industry' trade might be explained in terms of product differentiation among products which are supposed to be close substitutes in production or consumption or both. It would be somewhat surrealist to argue that a bicycle wheel is a reasonably close substitute for a bicycle saddle, that printed circuits are substitutes for electronic calculators, and even the most myopic of consumers would reject 'domestic refrigerators, electrical' as a substitute for 'electric shavers and hair clippers' – yet these are all examples of pairs of products contained within the 3-digit groups of the SITC (36). This already begins to suggest that an alternative view of intra-'industry' trade is that it is more a matter of exchange in complementary and otherwise non-competitive products than of trade in oligopolistically differentiated consumer goods. Intra-'industry' trade in components and semi-finished goods is an obvious example of complementarity, and the broadness of many SITC categories ('machine-tools for working metals' is a single (37) sub-group at 4 digits) suggests considerable scope for trade in highly specialised but distinct products, most of which would appear to be intermediate and other producer goods.

The scope for theories of oligopolistic product differentiation and consumer preferences in explaining the patterns of trade in manufactures thus appears to be rather narrow. Making a somewhat rough and summary estimate, the set of final consumer goods to which such theories would apply seems unlikely to be much more than 10 per cent of both total OECD exports and imports of manufactures (38). The central fact that the analysis of trade has to grapple with is that world trade in manufactures is dominated by trade among the advanced industrial economies in intermediate and capital goods. The purpose of such trade is of course to shift outwards each national production bloc for final consumer goods, but from this one cannot infer that consumer preferences are a major direct determinant of trade.

The most promising explanations of intra-'industry' and of intra-industrial country trade would therefore appear to be those which concentrate on the economies of specialisation and scale; much of the recent literature lists these among the probable explanations, but, having discounted the importance of oligopolistic product differentiation, I would argue that they are likely to provide the principal explanation. This is not the place to review the voluminous literature on economies of scale, but it is relevant to note that the focus of recent attention has been much more on the size of plants and the length of individual production runs than on the size of firm. Most of the research in this area has concentrated on inter-firm, inter-plant or inter-industry comparisons within individual countries and the data on scale economies is rarely, and then only with great difficulty, linked with trade performance, although Owen (1976) has reported a positive relationship between scale economies at the plant level and relative export performance. However, what I want to do here is to discuss briefly the outlines of a dynamic theory of specialisation which may serve as a general framework for the discussion of intra-'industry' trade. Since international trade is simply the extension of the division of labour across national boundaries, it is simpler and more useful to start the discussion in terms of the individual enterprise.

Adam Smith's analysis of the division of labour is typically presented in terms of functional specialisation within a single factory and thence as a source of internal economies of scale. But he also makes it clear that the division of labour is also a source of external economies through industrial differentiation which, as we all know, is limited by the extent of the market. However, although the proposition that 'the division of labour is limited by the extent of the market' is probably one of the most famous in the entire literature of economics, its impact on economic analysis (and economic history) has been remarkably small. Among the few papers owing any serious intellectual debt to it, the best known is Allyn Young's analysis of externalities and that has suffered more or less the same fate as Smith's proposition: ritual reference in all the text-books but almost zero impact on the actual analysis. Apart from the possibility that, *ex post,* basic insights may mimic truisms and therefore risk being ignored, the main reason for this neglect appears to be that Adam Smith's analysis of the division of labour is incompatible with the static equilibrium models that have dominated economic theorising since the 1880s. Another reason, I believe, is that the recognition that economic growth may be intimately associated with increasing industrial differentiation gives rise to extremely difficult problems of measurement due to the changing definitions of industries and enterprises over time: and statistical and other problems of measurement provide a powerful incentive to ignore certain questions, as we know for example from the long time that it took for technical change to become an important subject for analysis.

Young saw the process of industrial differentiation as the principal type of change associated with economic growth: 'notable as has been the increase in the complexity of the apparatus of living, as shown by the increase in the variety of goods offered in consumers' markets, the increase in the diversification of intermediate products and of industries manufacturing special products or groups of products has gone even farther' (Young 1928, p. 537). The crucial point concerning the division of labour is that it reduces complex processes into simpler ones which can then be performed by machines (or by more specialised machines), but Young emphasises two features: first, that the principal economies of scale are derived from roundabout methods of production for which *large* production is more important than large-scale production, in the sense of being carried out by large firms or industries; and, secondly, that the economies of roundabout methods of production depend even more than others on the extent of the market.

This analysis emphasises the importance of the long production run or of cumulative output, but there is also the important distinction between the effect of the market on the rate of production in a given plant or from a given machine, and the effect of the potential market on investment decisions. A larger planned output is produced in a different way from a smaller planned output – different, more specialised machines, different methods of assembly and so on, and, as will be clearer from the discussion below, even a different set of activities performed within the enterprise or, rather, the plant. In terms of the similar argument put forward later by Alchian (1959), marginal costs may rise with increases in the rate of output but, for a constant rate, they will fall with increases in planned output.

The process of industrial differentiation occurs because of an increase in the number of specialised activities engaged in in the entire chain of transforming raw materials into finished manufactures. Young's example was the printing industry which in its earliest stages included not only the specialist printers as we know them today, but also the producers of pulp, paper, inks, machinery and so forth. In this process the representative firm and the industry lose their identity – their internal economies dissolve into the external and internal economies of their more specialised successors.

The argument and its relevance to intra-'industry' specialisation become clearer, I think, if we revise our notion of a 'product'. Most production and trade theory implicitly assumes that all products can be defined with the precision and simplicity of, say, 'Malayan RSS No. 1 rubber'. Lancaster (1966) has proposed a much more illuminating approach on the consumption side by regarding a product as a bundle of characteristics, a given set of characteristics being obtainable in different proportions from different goods or combinations of goods. The demand for goods is thus a derived demand for sets of characteristics. We can pursue an analagous approach to production. Adam Smith noted that even the woollen coat of the day labourer was in fact the '... produce of the joint labour of a great multitude of workmen' (39). He goes on to suggest the idea of industrial differentiation increasing with the growth of the market, and he gives the example of the country carpenter who formerly had to make a range of products from cabinets to cartwheels. Smith's example is of increasing final product specialisation; but once we regard production as a joint set of activities, another source of differentiation clearly arises from the possibility of the increasing disintegrability of the activity set for any final product. If each activity in the set is homogeneous with respect to factor proportions, economies of scale etc., and if all producers within the 'industry' are faced with identical conditions, then there would be no incentive for disintegrating the activity set as the market grows, and the production function will be a legitimate simplification of the complexity of the production process. But in practice the individual firm or plant will tend to be better at doing some things rather than others; returns to scale will vary from one activity to another, partly because of indivisibilities but also because the possibility of applying further specialised equipment will vary among the different activities as the market expands, which in turn may be due to localised technical progress; and relative factor intensities may also vary within the activity set. For a given 'extent of the market' and a given technology or, rather, set of technologies, a given product is the result of a set of activities which must be jointly performed within a given plant or establishment or by the entrepreneur undertaking to supply the final product. The set of activities must be performed jointly either because the total market is not large enough to support specialists who could carry out parts of the activity set for the industry as a whole or because the costs of co-ordinating a set of activities spread over many specialists and sub-contractors is too high. As is well known, the growth of the total market for the product will lead to the installation of more specialised plant for some activities, which may or may not remain under the control of the original enterprise, and to the emergence of outside specialists who may replace all the previous performers of a given activity (40). Changes in technology, particularly in communications, may have a similar effect not only by geographical extension of the market but also by reducing the relative costs of co-ordination. (A notable consequence of the latter since the mid-1960s has been the peeling off of unskilled labour intensive activities from a number of predominantly skilled labour and capital intensive industries in developed countries and their re-location in developing countries.) This view of production as a joint activity set implies that when we speak of producers in a given country as having a comparative advantage in the production of 'x' we mean that *on average* or on balance they have a comparative advantage in those activities whose joint performance is necessary to produce the final product 'x'. As the market expands so the relatively more disadvantageous activities can be peeled away and the original producer will compromise less with his greatest comparative advantage. Another way of expressing this is that as the extent of the market increases (and other things being equal), the producer is able to reduce the variance of the cost functions in his activity set.

The effect of the length of the production run on costs and productivity has been approached somewhat hesitantly by economists: at the beginning of the 1960s Scitovsky noted that it had taken economists fifty years to realise that the size of firm was not the same as size of plant and it was then being 'suggested that size of plant is not the main factor, but the scale on which each single product is produced' (41). This neglect of the long run by economists stems partly from theoretical traditions and partly from the lack of data. What data have been used have generally been obtained from engineers' estimates, from sample surveys and case studies and these perhaps have suffered from a lack of generality. However, the importance of the length of run has been constantly stressed in empirical studies since the Second World War. In their studies in the 1940s and early 1950s, the Anglo-American Productivity teams identified differences in the length of production run and in the number of product varieties as a major source of productivity differences between the United States and the United Kingdom. And in the late 1950s a number of case studies by the European Productivity Agency (1958) brought out the considerable cost reductions that could result from increases in the production run through standardisation and variety reduction. Pratten's (1971) recent work again brings out the importance of the long run as a source of scale economies.

The economies of the longer production run are usually related to a reduction in set-up and set-down times for machinery and a reduction in the number of tool changes. But the case studies mentioned above generally indicate a more comprehensive impact on costs. An increase in the run through a reduction in the variety of inputs or of end-products affects the entire production process: marketing, invoicing, stock and distribution costs may all be reduced, operator training simplified and management control improved. The search for the longer production run is therefore likely to occur within a larger and more extensive rationalisation of all sections of an individual enterprise, although a *leitmotif* of the Anglo-American Productivity team report is that among the more successful enterprises this type of rationalisation is almost a continuous process.

The search for the long run generally means increasing the standardisation of components or of end-products or of both. In this context product diversification in a single enterprise may be quite superficial. Certain consumer goods are supplied in highly competitive markets where the ability to supply a range of products and to meet frequent fashion changes may be crucial for competitiveness. In such circumstances firrns will concentrate on standardising inputs for as many end-products as possible. The degree to which this is possible will depend on the relative importance of the differentiating characteristic in the total characteristics set of the end-product and the extent to which its production is separable in the activity set. If the principal differentiating characteristic of a consumer durable is the colour and style of the outer casing then the economies of the long run in the production of its main components may scarcely be affected; but in the case of tailor-made clothes, for example, such possibilities are greatly restricted because the differentiating characteristics are relatively dominant and the activity set is not highly disintegrable. Most manufactured goods, however, are likely to be more like the former than the latter. Attempts to lengthen the production run for individual products leads to disintegration of the individual producers' activity set through two routes: reduction of the number of final products, particularly when the advantages of diversification (spread of risks etc.) may be offset by the loss of economies from the reduction in the length of individual product runs; and secondly through a reduction in the number of intermediate processes performed by the producer himself.

An example of these changes is given by the pottery industry. Firms have generally sought long runs by reducing their product range and 'specialist firms now supply already-prepared materials, clays, flints, bones, colours, glazes, lithographs, etc., and machines, kilns, driers and even buildings can readily be purchased or hired on the market' (Smyth 1971, p. 92). The same study by Smyth also provides the example of a supplier of machinery to the pottery industry who is now able to modify his machines for a wide range of other industries: the firm's filter presses 'treat, in addition to clay, sugar, starch, yeast, sewage sludge, chemicals, works effluent and paints' (Smyth 1971, p. 92). The declared motive of the firm for such diversification may have been to reduce dependence on a single industry, but it is clearly an example of how the production run can be expanded by increasing the degree of diversification within strictly controlled limits. One might say that the firm was simply exploiting its basic area of competence (to modify a phrase of Professor Penrose) or, simply, its greatest comparative advantage in its activity set.

It is important in this context not to equate the advantages of specialisation simply with the economies of the *very* long run, or to suppose that economies of scale only emerge at 'very large' or massive levels of production (42). Mass production is simply a very large volume of specialised output; but most engineering cost curves show unit costs falling sharply over the lower ranges of output, particularly in engineering and tool-making. All that matters to an individual producer is that he realise sufficient of the potential economies of scale (internal and external) to remain competitive in his own industry.

From the point of view of international trade it is clearly of basic interest to ask whether the disintegration of activities will have predictable effects on trade, which activities will be peeled off, which imported. Insofar as joint sets do contain activities with significant differences in factor requirements this would not be too difficult, if the data were available: if value added was available for each activity then Lary's factor intensity criterion could be used as a guide to which activities are likely to be shipped off to developing countries, for example. But if, as seems most likely, the differences in cost functions are due to differences in scale economies, and particularly dynamic scale economies, where what the enterprise has learnt from its production experience is significant, then history is important and factor endowment theories will provide little guidance. Prediction is also difficult because the producer is no longer the myopic producer of most production theory: given likely developments in relative prices, demand, technology, intensity of competition etc., he must decide where his future comparative advantage is likely to be (or even what he would like it to be). This will not, of course, be a completely free choice (43), since the range of feasible options will be heavily influenced or constrained by his present set of specialisations, and by what he has learnt. This view of the production process recalls Herbert Spencer's account of the process of evolution in which matter passes from indefinite incoherent homogeneity to a definite, coherent heterogeneity, which in turn disintegrates under exogenous or environmental influences (44). 'Coherent heterogeneity' is probably a more realistic summary description of even the simplest productive enterprise than anything in the world of general equilibrium analysis.

As specialisation becomes finer and finer, both in respect of final products and of intermediate processes, so industries become less easily distinguishable from one another. Most of the generally available statistical series fail to reflect these changes (45). But the disintegration of industrial activity sets, it seems to me, is picked up in the trade statistics where it is largely responsible for what we are calling intra-'industry' trade. If the division of labour evolves as suggested above then each succeeding stage is of course a finer subdivision of the previous one and if the statistical categories are not disaggregated *pari passu* then there is likely to be an increase in intra-'industry' transactions or, when conducted across national boundaries, intra-'industry' trade. It has also been argued above that this increasing sub-division turns less and less on differences in traditional factor endowments and more on ephemeral factors such as learning curves and the other constituents of dynamic economies of scale. It is therefore probable that the evolution of the international division of labour will proceed faster among countries with similar industrial structures and, therefore, similar levels of income per head; international specialisation in capital and skill intensive machine tools can only proceed among capital abundant countries with machine tool industries. If we combine this simple point with Allyn Young's model of cumulative causation – that the enlarging of the market for any one commodity produced under increasing returns, generally has the net effect of enlarging the market for other commodities – then we have an explanation not only of rising intra-'industry' trade but of why world trade in manufactures should be increasingly dominated by trade among the developed industrial economies. This does not however help us to explain the particular patterns of specialisation within the developed industrial economies; as suggested already, much will depend on history, past investments in human skills and so on, and, maybe, even a certain amount of pure historical accident. Past and present patterns of domestic demand may also be important since inter-country variations in these imply that national industries will have 'learnt' different things, which in turn will give rise to comparative cost differences and to potential international trade. This appears to have brought us back to the Linder explanation of intra-'industry' trade among industrial countries. But the differences are crucial: instead of complementarity being abandoned or relegated to a minor role it remains the mainspring of international trade; and international trade in manufactures is dominated by intermediate and capital goods (46), not by beer and toothpaste.

There is a current popular argument which regards trade among the industrial countries as of marginal or even zero benefit since they are simply trading the 'same' goods with one another, merely 'taking in one another's washing' (47). Such a view would have some foundation if this trade were in fact dominated by consumers' idiosyncratic tastes for beer and foreign baubles, as suggested by Linder-type models of trade in oligopolistically differentiated products; it also echoes Keynes' conclusion of the 1930s insofar as one of its implications is that a reduction in such trade would not involve very great costs. On the argument of this paper, however, this view is based on a fundamental misconception of what has actually occurred in the world economy. Keynes appears to have seen technological innovation and diffusion as supplying the means for each individual country to become self-sufficient in all manufactured goods, but the actual tendency has been to increase international interdependence at the intermediate stages of production. Keynes was right in seeing interdependence as a cost and not as a benefit to the individual nation (48), but any attempt to reduce it would most probably involve very considerable losses of external and internal economies.

Much has been written in the last few years on the increase in international economic interdependence, and the 'discovery' of intra-'industry' trade has sometimes been interpreted as indicating a major change in the nature of the international division of labour. But interdependence, particularly among the industrial market economies, has been growing, with a brief setback in the 1930s, since the mid-nineteenth century (and probably earlier). Intra-'industry' trade, or specialisation within narrow activity sets, cannot be measured over very long periods because of the data problems, but specific examples abound: Charles Babbage noted in 1851 that British bootmakers imported superior French uppers to be joined to superior British soles (49), while international trade in bicycle components and parts of motor cars was already flourishing in Europe before 1914. Given the fact that intra-trade in manufactures among the industrial countries was already of considerable importance before the Second World War, and that intra-'industry' trade was already a high proportion of total manufactures trade in the developed industrial countries by the beginning of the 1960s, it seems reasonable to surmise that this too is a long and well-established trend, though it is likely that there has been an acceleration since the 1960s (50). But as often happens, major changes in the 'real world' frequently turn out to be the product of contradictions, hidden assumptions, and other defects in the apparatus with which we try to observe and interpret it. The most commonly used classification of international trade for empirical analysis is the SITC at 3 digits, but for the purpose of eliciting patterns and changes in international specialisation among industrial countries it is a crude and hopelessly inadequate instrument: yet we go on using it, trying to overcome its deficiencies by assuming, for example, that the groups correspond 'reasonably well' to theoretical concepts of an industry, and so on. The resulting account of 'reality', however, may often be little more than a reflection of such initial assumptions. It is salutary to conclude by recalling the words of the French historian Braudel (1972, p. 18): 'The question of boundaries is the first to be encountered; from it all others flow. To draw a boundary around anything is to define, analyse, and reconstruct it, in this case select, indeed adopt a philosophy...'. Unfortunately the 'question of boundaries' is hardly ever raised in empirical economics, the failure to do so being a major source of dubious conclusions.

Footnotes

(1) Marshall (1923), p. 106.

(2) In Britain the schedules of prohibited machinery exports in the Customs Regulation Acts of 1825 and 1833 were repealed in 1843; and the law forbidding the emigration of skilled artisans was repealed in 1825.

(3) Although this policy was an important factor leading to the American revolution it was still in force elsewhere more than a century later, for example, under Lord Cromer in Egypt.

(4) Cf. Mathias (1969) chapter 4.

(5) As Coleman (1977, p. 131) points out, in pre-industrial economies the slow growth of aggregate income meant that merchants could in general only hope to increase their sales by capturing their rivals' share of the market.

(6) Torrens (1821). The relevant passage is quoted in full by Viner (1946).

(7) *Loc. cit.*, p. 758.

(8) Maizels' work originated in the Board of Trade where, in the early 1950s, officials were concerned at the possible effects of overseas industrialisation on UK export prospects.

(9) Hilgerdt and Maizels of course clearly recognise and establish statistically its importance, although the basic orientation of their studies is nevertheless towards the probable effects of overseas industrialisation on the trade prospects of the older industrial economies.

(10) Statistics calculated from data in UNCTAD (1976). The definition of manufactures is SITC Sections 5 to 8 *less* non-ferrous metals.

(11) Ohlin (1933), chapter VI. Marshall (1923) had also noted what is defined below as intra-'industry' trade but which he calls 'cross-trade' (*ibid*, p. 128). Most of his examples relate to border trade (for example, Germany importing English coal along the northern sea coast and the lower Rhine while exporting it over nearly every inland frontier); but he thought that the more common case was of commodities which 'differ a little from one another, though called by the same name' — his example was Belgium and England exporting steel to one another, though he suggests this may have been due to restrictive practices (*ibid*, p. 104). However, Marshall does not attach any broader significance to these examples.

(12) Possibly even within the same firm or enterprise.

(13) For example, Gray (1973). For a sceptical view of the need for a theory of intra-'industry' trade see Finger (1975).

(14) That is, where elasticities of substitution are infinite within categories and zero between them.

(15) The cosine of country j's exports and imports is given by

$\text{Cos } X_i M_i = (\Sigma X_i M_i) \cdot (\Sigma X_i^2 \cdot \Sigma M_i^2)^{-1/2}$, where X_i and M_i are total exports of commodity i, $(i = 1 \ldots n)$. It has been used in a gravity model of trade by Linnemann (1966, pp. 140 - 145) and by Hufbauer (1970): the leading diagonal of Hufbauer's Table A-3 is an indicator of the relative importance of intra-'industry' trade in manufactures for each country at SITC 3-digits.

(16) See League of Nations (1936), pp. 181 - 182, for a verbal explanation.

(17) The numerator in the equation may be written as $\sum_i (2. \text{ minimum } X_i, M_i)$ which is simpler for computation.

(18) Analogously the League of Nations (1936) divided a country's total trade balance into (i) triangular trade, i.e. the sum of balances with opposite sign, (ii) bilaterally balanced trade and (iii) the total trade balance, which is offset by invisibles and capital transactions.

(19) For example, if a country exports three goods to the extent of 10, 5 and 2 dollars respectively and imports to the extent of 100 dollars each, intra-'industry' trade is 34 dollars or 10.7 per cent of total trade; the Grubel-Lloyd adjustment raises it to 100 per cent. In Table 1 below, the proportion of intra-'industry' trade in Turkey in 1969 is about 7 per cent; the Grubel-Lloyd adjustment raises it to 68 per cent, which is about the same proportion as in Sweden.

(20) On the same grounds forest products should also have been excluded. In the tables below this mainly affects Finland.

(21) See Hal B. Lary (1968), pp. 91 – 93 and Appendix E.

(22) In principle, different levels of aggregation represent increasing degrees of fineness in the specification of products: thus the 3-digit 'Universals, plates and sheets of iron and steel' (SITC 674) is divided into 5 sub-groups at 4 digits. But not all products are disaggregated to the same degree of fineness and so the extent to which disaggregation leads to a fall in measured intra-trade will partly depend on a country's broad pattern of specialisation at 3 digits.

(23) In 1973 the Spearman rank correlation coefficient between the country rankings at 3 and 4 digits is 0.98.

(24) The United States Standard Industrial Classification.

(25) Christopher Saunders (1978) has made some detailed investigations of inter-country differences in specialisation as part of a study of the engineering industry.

(26) As already noted, international trade in manufactures is not most intense between countries where the differences in relative factor endowments are generally presumed to be largest.

(27) Scientific Instrument Manufacturers Association of Great Britain (1976).

(28) This is the equivalent of the BTN at 8 digits but with an additional breakdown of parts and accessories. At this level of aggregation, 40 per cent of the intra-'industry' trade consists of 'other, n.e.s.' and 'parts and accessories', cf. footnote 46 below.

(29) Linder (1961) p. 102. This picturesque example, worthy of John Masefield, has been quoted by many succeeding writers and has almost become the symbol of intra-'industry' trade. However, in 1969, beer was less than one-tenth of one per cent of total OECD exports and imports. Probably more beer flowed along the trade routes in the eighteenth century when it was used as quasi-ballast (along with bricks) in ships carrying textiles.

(30) Actually Drèze's internationally standardised goods have very similar characteristics to those which Linder suggests as likely exceptions to his own theory. See Linder (1961), p. 90.

(31) Basevi (1970) rejects on theoretical grounds the argument that it is necessary for a good to be in demand domestically before it can qualify as an exportable. For an empirical test, see Hufbauer (1970).

(32) SITC 714.1, 717.3, 724.1-2, 725, 719.4, 729.1-2, 732.9, 733.1, 861.4-6 and 864.

(33) SITC 732.1, 732.5-8, 729.4.

(34) SITC 821, 831, 841, 842, 851, 891-897, 899.

(35) Cairncross (1955).

(36) It is not very clear what is meant by their being close substitutes in production other than that their factor-input ratios do not differ significantly.

(37) Schedule B of the United States Tariff Classification lists 46 4-digit items as belonging to this single SITC sub-group. It has been stated that in the United Kingdom there are more than 3000 types and sizes of machine tool (*Financial Times,* 16 June 1975).

(38) Nevertheless the study of the direct impact of consumer tastes on international trade promises to be fascinating; but it may also prove to be very complex: for example, in the eighteenth century Europeans were importing the work of Chinese weavers who were 'producing fabrics adorned with the now famous "tree of life" design, based on Indian patterns, derived from English originals which were an expression of the European vision of the Orient'. Honour (1961), chapter 2.

(39) Smith (1970), Book 1, chapter 1, p. 116.

(40) This does not necessarily mean that there will be a general tendency towards monopoly among specialist producers. Not only is an expanding market likely to attract new entrants, but there is always the threat of re-entry by the enterprise or enterprises that formerly performed the function as part of a joint-set. The Anglo-American Productivity Council (1949) in fact noted that intense competition among specialist producers was common in the United States.

(41) In Robinson (1960), p. 360.

(42) Some such confusion would appear to be behind the curious view that Henry Ford discovered or invented the principle of interchangeable parts and mass production. Given his well-known views on history, Ford would presumably not have known of, or would have excused himself from drawing attention to, his predecessors in the Venetian Arsenal of the sixteenth century and in the Dutch shipyards of the seventeenth (to name but two).

(43) The choice set will of course remain within the broad limits set by relative factor endowments.

(44) I am not resuscitating the nineteenth century propagandist 'theory' of enterprise which described entrepreneurial behaviour in simple terms of 'the survival of the fittest'. Spencer was not responsible for the theory, although he did coin the phrase which inspired it.

(45) Changes in the ratio of intermediate transactions to final sales might do so, but for most countries the run of input-output tables is still small and their comparability over time is generally weak.

(46) This distinction between intermediate and capital goods is becoming weaker with the increased trade in components and parts. With M.C. Pont-Vieira, I have estimated for West Germany that, in 1969, 23 per cent of total intra-'industry' trade in 'machinery and transport equipment' was accounted for by items specifically described in the national trade statistics as 'parts' or 'components'. If 'ball-bearings', 'pumps and centrifuges' and a few other items are included (SITC 719.1-.2, 719.7 and 729) the proportion rises to 41 per cent. Comparisons over time were difficult to make but these ratios appear to have nearly doubled since 1962. When one moves to SITC 4 digits there is scarcely any disaggregation of items designated as 'parts' at 3 digits. This is probably a major reason why intra-'industry' trade remains important even when the trade classification is highly disaggregated. (cf. footnote 28.)

(47) Tether (1975). The same view surfaces from time to time in the correspondence columns of *The Times*.

(48) People such as Jean Monnet, however, would regard such increased interdependence as a world benefit.

(49) Quoted in Clapham (1932), p. 15.

(50) Apart from the growth of incomes per head, the fall in relative communications costs, and reductions in trade barriers, witness the growth of sub-contracting agencies, of international technical and other standards, of increasingly specialised trade fairs, etc. These activities may be

seen in the context of reducing the relative costs of co-ordination (including information) entailed by industrial disintegration. Increased productivity in these fields may be both cause and effect of increasing intra-'industry' specialisation.

References

Alchian, A. (1959) 'Costs and Outputs' in Moses Abramovitz and others, *The Allocation of Economic Resources* (Stanford University Press) pp. 23 - 40.

Anglo-American Productivity Council (1949) *Simplification in Industry* (London).

Balassa, B. (1963) 'European Integration: Problems and Issues', *American Economic Review,* vol. 53, May.

Balassa, B. (1966) 'Tariff Reductions and Trade in Manufactures among the Industrial Countries', *American Economic Review,* vol. 56, June.

Basevi, G. (1970) 'Domestic Demand and the Ability to Export', *Journal of Political Economy.*

Braudel, F. (1972) *The Mediterranean and the Mediterranean World in the Age of Philip II* (London: Collins), vol. 1.

Cairncross, A.K. (1955) 'World Trade in Manufactures since 1900', *Economia Internazionale,* vol. VIII.

Clapham, J.H. (1932) *An Economic History of Modern Britain — Free Trade and Steel 1850 - 1886.* (Cambridge: Cambridge University Press).

Coleman, D.C. (1977) *The Economy of England 1450 - 1750* (Oxford: Oxford University Press).

Drèze, J. (1960) 'Quelques réflexions sereines sur l'adaptation de l'industrie Belge au Marché Commun', *Comptes Rendus des Travaux de la Société Royale d'Economie Politique de Belgique,* no. 275, December.

Drèze, J. (1961) 'Les exportations intra-CEE en 1958 et la position Belge', *Recherches Economiques de Louvain,* no. 8.

European Productivity Agency (1958), *Simplification, Standardisation and Specialisation,* (Paris: OEEC).

Finger, J.M. (1975) 'Trade Overlap and Intra-Industry Trade', *Economic Inquiry,* vol. 12, December.

Gray, H. Peter (1973) 'Two-way International Trade in Manufactures: A Theoretical Underpinning', *Weltwirtschaftliches Archiv,* vol. 103, no. 1.

Grubel, H.G. (1967) 'Intra-Industry Specialisation and the Pattern of Trade', *Canadian Journal of Economics and Political Science,* XXXIII.

Grubel, H.G., and Lloyd, P.J. (1971) 'The Empirical Measurement of Intra-Industry Trade', *The Economic Record,* vol. 47, December.

Hilgerdt, F. (1945) *Industrialisation and Foreign Trade,* (Geneva: League of Nations).

Honour, H. (1961) *Chinoiserie, The Vision of Cathay* (London: John Murray).

Hufbauer, G.C. (1970) 'The Impact of National Characteristics and Technology on the Commodity Composition of Trade in Manufactured Goods' in Raymond Vernon (ed.), *The Technology Factor in International Trade,* (New York: NBER).

Keynes, J.M. (1933) 'National Self-Sufficiency', *The Yale Review,* vol. XXII, June.

Kreinin, M.E. (1969) 'The Theory of Comparative Costs – Further Empirical Evidence', *Economia Internazionale,* vol. XXII.

Lancaster, K. (1966) 'Change and Innovation in the Technology of Consumption', *American Economic Review,* LVI, Papers and Proceedings.

Lary, Hal B. (1968) *Imports of Manufactures From Less Developed Countries* (New York: NBER).

League of Nations (1936) *World Economic Survey 1935/36* (Geneva).

Linder, S.B. (1961) *An Essay on Trade and Transformation,* (Stockholm: Almqvist and Wicksell).

Linnemann, H. (1966) *An Econometric Study of International Trade Flows,* (Amsterdam: North Holland).

Maizels, A. (1963) *Industrial Growth and World Trade* (Cambridge: Cambridge University Press).

Marshall, A. (1923) *Money, Credit and Commerce* (London: Macmillan).

Mathias, P. (1969) *The First Industrial Nation* (London: Methuen).

Meade, J.E. (1955) *The Theory of Customs Unions* (Amsterdam: North Holland).

Ohlin, B. (1933) *Interregional and International Trade,* (Harvard University Press).

Owen, N. (1976) 'Scale Economies in the EEC – An approach based on intra-EEC trade', *European Economic Review,* 7.

Pratten, C.F. (1971) *Economies of Scale in Manufacturing Industry,* (Cambridge: At the University Press).

Robertson, D.H. (1938) 'The Future of International Trade', *The Economic Journal,* XLVIII, March.

Robinson, E.A.G., ed. (1960) *Economic Consequences of the Size of Nations* (London: Macmillan).

Saunders, C.T. (1978) 'Engineering in Britain, West Germany and France: Some Statistical Comparisons' *Sussex European Papers,* No. 3, (Brighton: Sussex European Research Centre, University of Sussex).

Scientific Instrument Manufacturers Association of Great Britain (1976) *SIMA 1974 and 1975 Statistics of the United Kingdom Instrument Industry* (London).

Smith, Adam (1970) *The Wealth of Nations* (London: Penguin Books).

Smyth, R.L. (1971) 'Theories of Competition and the British Pottery Industry', *Scottish Journal of Political Economy,* XVIII.

Tether, C.G. (1975) *The Great Common Market Conspiracy* (London: Get Britain Out Referendum Campaign).

Torrens, R. (1821) *Essay on the Production of Wealth* (London).

UNCTAD (1976) *Handbook of International Trade and Development Statistics* (New York: United Nations).

Verdoorn, P.J. (1960) 'The Intra-Bloc Trade of Benelux', in E.A.G. Robinson, ed., *Economic Consequences of the Size of Nations* (London: Macmillan).

Viner, J. (1946) 'The Prospects for Foreign Trade in the Post-War World', *Transactions of the Manchester Statistical Society,* Session 1945 - 46.

Young, A. (1928) 'Increasing Returns and Economic Progress', *The Economic Journal,* vol. XXXVIII, December.

Chapter 2

THE INDUSTRIALISATION OF THE DEVELOPING COUNTRIES*

A. Maizels

Introduction

It is generally acknowledged that industrialisation is the major path to the economic development of the underdeveloped regions of the world. However, in spite of strenuous efforts to foster the growth of manufacturing industry in a wide range of developing countries over the postwar period, very few of these countries have so far been able to develop a substantial and diversified industrial base. The majority of developing countries remain heavily dependent on exports of primary commodities to the markets of developed countries for their supplies of manufactured goods.

This 'vertical' exchange of primary commodities for manufactures is, to a large extent, a hangover from the period of Colonial domination of the majority of countries in the underdeveloped regions. It contrasts sharply with the mutual trade of the present developed countries, which has come increasingly to consist of an interchange of different types and qualities of manufactured goods (1), a pattern of exchange which can be termed 'horizontal'.

The postwar period has also witnessed a number of significant developments in the process of industrialisation in underdeveloped countries. First, industrial growth has been extensively fostered on the basis of importsubstitution, usually behind high tariff and non-tariff barriers to imports of competing manufactures and often, also, accompanied by severe pressure on the balance of payments. For countries with large internal markets, the process of importsubstitution has resulted in the creation of a large and, in some cases, diversified industrial sector. This is so for the three large countries of Latin America – Argentina, Brazil and Mexico – and for India, which in aggregate accounted for almost one-half of the total value of manufacturing production in developing countries (excluding China) in 1974, and about one-fifth of the total value of their manufactured exports. It would seem that for the large developing countries, the earlier phase of importsubstitution on a high-cost basis can give way to a later phase in which economies of scale allow for the successful development of an export trade in manufactures on a competitive basis.

A second development of note is that a number of small countries have succeeded in achieving rapid industrialisation based on exports of manufactures. Countries such as

* Acknowledgements are due to R. Hellberg, P.B.W. Rayment, G.P. Sampson and A.J. Yeats for helpful comments on an earlier draft.

South Korea, Hong Kong and Singapore — these three countries alone accounting for some 45 per cent of all manufactured exports from developing countries in 1976 — are often held up as 'success stories', whose example in encouraging exports of manufactures as the basis for industrialisation should be followed by other developing countries (2). The exports of this group of countries have become increasingly diversified over the past decade, from consisting exclusively of labour-intensive manufactures (particularly textiles, clothing, leather, footwear and other 'light' manufactures) to a wider range of products, including more capital-intensive goods such as steel, ships and engineering and electronic products. However, labour-intensive manufactures still account for the bulk of manufactured exports from these countries (representing about 70 per cent of the total in 1976).

The argument for considering these successful exporters as examples for other developing countries to follow has become much less convincing in recent years because the import markets of developed countries for manufactured goods have become increasingly subject to protection, particularly against low-cost goods produced in developing countries. It now seems doubtful whether, without a radical change in current protectionist policies, the rapid penetration of the markets of the industrialised countries achieved by the successful exporters can be readily emulated by other developing countries.

A third development, of pervasive character, has been the increasing importance of transnational corporations of developed countries in the production and external trade of developing countries. The transnational corporations have in fact generally played a key role in both the import-substitution and the export-expansion phases. Particularly in the earlier phases of industrial development, reliance necessarily had to be placed on the transnationals for the required technology and know-how. Typically, however, production of import-substituting consumer goods was accompanied by greater imports of capital equipment and intermediate products from the transnational company involved. A recent UNCTAD review states that currently 'the bulk of manufactured goods imported into developing countries originate with TNCs in developed countries' (UNCTAD, 1978a).

Transnational corporations have become increasingly important in the production and export of manufactured goods from developing countries, particularly in electronic and other products requiring labour-intensive assembly or processing, a development which has been greatly stimulated by the provision of free-port manufacturing zones in a number of developing countries, and by tariff concessions on the import of such products into certain developed countries, notably the United States (Finger, 1975). The 'traditional' manufactured exports of developing countries — textiles, leather goods, clothing and metal goods — are still, however, very largely produced by domestically-owned enterprises, though transnational corporations have made some inroads in recent years by takeovers of some of these enterprises and by the introduction of new technologies, particularly as regards the use of synthetic textile fibres. Moreover, an increasing range of manufactures produced by domestically-owned enterprises is finding export outlets through the marketing and distribution networks of transnationals, often corporations which specialise in marketing operations.

While there is insufficient information available to make any precise assessment of the role of transnational corporations in the manufacturing production and export of developing countries, it would appear unquestionable that these corporations now have a major influence on the pace and pattern of industrialisation in probably the majority of developing countries. Moreover, these corporations have established effective control over a large – and probably growing – proportion of the export trade in manufactures from developing countries. This general trend has been accentuated over the past decade by the growing network of trade barriers imposed by developed countries on the 'traditional' manufactured exports of developing countries, which – as mentioned earlier – have remained largely the preserve of domestically-owned enterprises.

The industrialisation of the underdeveloped countries to anywhere near the levels already attained by the present developed regions will inevitably involve vast changes in resource use, in the patterns of production, consumption and trade, and in the socio-economic structures of developing countries. It will also most probably involve large changes in relative prices and in the terms of trade between developed and developing countries. In any event, it would involve complementary changes in the economic structures of the present developed countries, and supporting changes in the institutional framework of economic relations between the two groups of countries.

The question which arises in this context is whether the existing international economic system which, as mentioned earlier, has been built up on a 'vertical' exchange of commodities for manufactures between developed and developing countries can adjust to the requirements of a 'horizontal' exchange of a two-way flow of manufactures. Certainly, such an adjustment would not seem likely as a result of the 'normal working of market forces' (i.e. essentially a continuation of the existing dominance of transnational corporations). Rather, it calls for positive and complementary policies by both developed and developing countries to achieve this objective. A central element in such policies on the part of developed countries would need to be the promotion of structural change in their own economies to facilitate the expansion of their markets for the manufactured exports of developing countries. The developing countries, for their part, would need to mobilise their own resources to meet the elementary needs of the majority of their populations, and to exploit the latent complementarities of their economies by closer economic co-operation among themselves. Development on the basis of such an essentially 'self-reliant' strategy would also strengthen the countervailing power of developing countries in their negotiations with transnational corporations, and help to ensure that the activities of these corporations promote the kind of economic development which accords with the needs and cultures of the developing countries.

These considerations raise major issues of economic analysis and of economic and social policy, which fall well beyond the scope of the present chapter. Here, only one particular, though crucial, aspect of the economic interchange between developed and developing countries is considered, namely the structural changes that will be required in the industries of developed countries to accommodate and facilitate the industrialisation of the present underdeveloped regions.

Manufacturing production, trade and consumption of developing countries: the present situation and prospects for the future

Manufacturing industries in the underdeveloped regions are, as indicated earlier, largely concentrated in a relatively few countries. However, even the poorest countries undertake some manufacturing activities. If developing countries are grouped according to the relative importance of manufacturing in total output, then about 70 per cent of their total population live in substantially under-industrialised countries (taken here as those where manufacturing represents under 15 per cent of GDP). This can be seen from Table 2.1, which includes the production and trade data of 84 countries in 1974. These 84 countries account for about 95 per cent of the total population of the developing countries (excluding China), and about 90 per cent of the total value of their manufacturing production.

The gross value of manufacturing production in all 84 developing countries in 1974 averaged about \$ 160 per head, or only six to seven per cent of the corresponding output per head in the developed market-economy countries in that year (about \$ 2,500) (3). Among the developing countries, there is a wide dispersion in the degree of industrialisation. The least industrialised group, where manufacturing represents under 5 per cent of GDP, has an average manufacturing production per head of only \$ 20 a year – less than 1 per cent of the developed country average. At the other extreme, the countries most industrialised, with over 20 per cent of manufacturing in the GDP, have an average manufacturing production per head of \$ 520, or about one-fifth of the developed country average. The countries included under the heading 'Major oil exporters' include some with substantial industrial sectors, the average manufacturing production per head for this group (\$ 465) being not far short of one-fifth of the developed country average.

The great majority of developing countries are heavily dependent on exports of primary commodities for the foreign exchange needed to purchase capital equipment, intermediate products and other manufactures from developed countries. Their export earnings, supplemented by aid and external borrowings, have to pay for essential imports of food and fuel, as well as manufactures, and in addition have to cover interest and amortisation of foreign debt and the cost of services, such as shipping and insurance, purchased from foreign sources. Nonetheless, it is the import of manufactured goods which is the key element in the real gain from trade, and is generally of most significance for the development process.

Table 2.1

Production, trade and apparent consumption of manufactures in developing countries, 1974

Manufacturing production as proportion of GDP	Number of countries	Population	Production (a) total	Production (a) per head (d)	Exports (b) total	Imports (b) total	Apparent consumption (c) total	Apparent consumption (c) per head (d)
Per cent		*Million*	*$ bill.*	*$*		*$ billion*		*$*
Non-oil exporters:								
under 5	9	87	1.8	20	0.3	1.5	3.0	35
5 – 9	14	321	11.6	35	0.4	6.9	18.1	55
10 – 14	27	756	45.6	60	3.0	9.7	52.3	70
15 – 19	13	291	70.8	240	4.3	15.3	81.8	280
20 and over	13	221	115.3	520	12.7	22.9	125.5	570
Total	76	1 677	245.1	145	20.7	56.3	280.7	165
Major oil exporters (e)	8	84	39.1	465	1.2	15.5	53.4	635
Total	84	1 761	284.2	160	21.9	71.8	334.1	190

(a) Gross output of manufacturing industries (including both intra-industry and inter-industry deliveries). – (b) SITC 5–8 (less 67 and 68); exports f.o.b., imports c.i.f. – (c) Gross output plus imports minus exports. The figures are inflated to the extent that imports include intermediate products for use by domestic industry. – (d) Rounded to the nearest $ 5. – (e) Algeria, Iran, Iraq, Kuwait, Libya, Saudi Arabia, Trinidad and Tobago and Venezuela.

Sources: UNCTAD *Handbook of International Trade and Development Statistics, Supplement 1977* (New York: United Nations, 1978); *Monthly Bulletin of Statistics,* and *Yearbook of National Accounts Statistics, 1976* (New York: United Nations, 1977).

As can be seen from Table 2.1, imports of manufactures added substantially to the volume of domestic supplies (production plus imports) in all groups of developing countries. The import content of supplies was as high as 45 per cent for the least industrialised group, declining to 37 per cent for the next group, and to 17 to 18 per cent for the last three – more industrialised – groups. For the oil exporters, the corresponding proportion was 28 per cent. Thus, foreign trade acted to reduce the differences, among the various groups of developing countries, in the production of manufactures per head – but only marginally so. The differences in apparent consumption per head were still very great. For the least industrialised group, apparent consumption per head, at some $ 35 a year, was less than one-fifth of the average for all developing countries, and only 1 ½ to 2 per cent of the average for the developed market-economy countries. For the three groups of developing countries distinguished in Table 2.1 as having less than 15 per cent of GDP in manufacturing industry, the average per capita apparent consumption of manufactures, at $ 65, was only one-sixth of the average for the two more industrialised groups ($ 405).

In terms of the absolute contribution made by foreign trade to domestic availabilities of manufactures, this amounted to only some $ 10 to 20 per head for each of the three least industrialised groups of developing countries. For the fourth group, with manufacturing representing 15 to 19 per cent of GDP, per capita imports averaged about $ 55 per capita, and net imports $ 40. For the most industrialised group, per capita imports rose to $ 105 on average, but as this group includes some of the principal exporters of manufactures, per capita net imports were reduced to about $ 50. By comparison, the contribution of foreign trade to domestic availabilities of manufactures was considerably greater for the oil exporters (about $ 170), and this contribution was greatly enhanced in subsequent years as a result of the rise in oil prices.

This analysis would seem to indicate that the benefits accruing to the majority of developing countries from the existing 'vertical' division of labour are relatively small, if measured in terms of the absolute contribution of foreign trade to their supplies of manufactures for domestic consumption.

The Lima target

The concern of the international community, and especially of the developing countries, at the slow and uneven progress of industrialisation in these countries, was expressed in the Lima Declaration and Plan of Action on Industrial Development and Co-operation, adopted at the Second General Conference of UNIDO in 1975. This Plan sets an ambitious target of 25 per cent for the developing countries' share of world industrial production by the year 2000, compared with a share of only some 9 to 9 ½ per cent in 1972 (see also UNIDO, 1979). The rate of industrial growth in developing countries required to achieve this target will, of course, depend on the corresponding rate of growth in the developed parts of the world. If the developed countries (4) are able to maintain their average 1960–1972 growth rates over the succeeding period, 1972–2000, then industrial production in developing countries over this period will have to rise by over 11 per cent a year (a dramatic increase compared with the previous average growth rate of 6 ½ per cent a year for 1960–1972) to attain the Lima target (UNCTAD, 1976 a) (5).

Assuming, however, a reduction in the previous growth rate in developed countries, from about 6 per cent a year over the period 1960 to 1972 to about 5 per cent a year for 1972 to 2000, as a more realistic starting point, the required growth rate in industrial production in developing countries would be some 9 ½ per cent a year – still a major acceleration from past rates. On this basis, and using the results of cross-country regressions of per capita manufactured output and imports in relation to per capita GDP, as well as a number of specific assumptions, an UNCTAD study (1976a) estimates that the volume of manufactured goods imported by developing countries from the rest of the world would expand by about 7 ½ per cent per annum between 1972 and 2000, whereas the flow in the reverse direction – assuming that developing countries will increase their share of the imports of developed countries at a slightly higher rate than previously – is estimated to rise by almost 10 per cent a year. The UNCTAD estimates also allow for a more rapid rise in the mutual trade of developing countries – by nearly 12 per cent a year – than in their trade with developed areas (see Table 2.2).

As regards the trade in manufactures between developed and developing countries, two main conclusions can be drawn from the UNCTAD estimates. First, in order to achieve the Lima target, the flows of imports and exports should be much less unbalanced. Whereas, in 1972, developing countries' imports of manufactures from developed countries were over 2½ times the reverse flow, by the year 2000 the ratio could be reduced to under 1½ times. Second, the volume of trade in both flows will need to expand at a much faster rate than the probable rate of industrial growth in the developed countries. In other words, the developing countries – on the assumptions of this exercise – are likely to become a very substantial export market for the industrial products of developed countries but, at the same time, developed countries will have to accept a significantly higher share of imports from developing countries in their domestic supplies of manufactured goods.

The UNCTAD study also gives a quantitative assessment of the changes required in the relationship between manufacturing output and trade of developed market-economy countries in order to make it possible for the developing countries to reach the Lima target (Table 2.3). Four broad groups of industries are distinguished: those showing an export surplus for developing countries in both 1972 and 2000 (Group I); those changing from an import surplus for developing countries in 1972 to an export surplus in 2000 (Group II); and those showing an import surplus for both years (Group III for non-metal, and Group IV for metal industries).

Table 2.2

Manufacturing output and trade of developing countries: 1972 and 2000

	1972	2000 (a)	*Growth rate*
	($ billion at 1972 prices)		*(Per cent per annum)*
Manufacturing output			
Value added	108	1,411	9.6
Gross output	273	3,261	9.3
Manufacturing trade			
Total trade:			
Imports	61.6	567	8.3
Exports	27.5	447	10.5
Net imports	34.1	120	..
Intra-trade	7.5	170	11.8
Trade with developed countries:			
Imports	54.1	397	7.4
Exports	20.0	277	9.8

(a) Hypothetical figures based on results of cross-country regressions for per capita output and imports in 1970, and on a number of specific assumptions.

Source: The dimensions of the required restructuring of world manufacturing output and trade in order to reach the Lima target (TD/185/Supp.1) (Geneva: UNCTAD, April, 1976).

While the individual percentages shown for the year 2000 are essentially hypothetical and illustrative, being based on a number of assumptions, the changes compared with the position in 1972 are of some significance. In particular, imports from developing countries, which in 1972 accounted for only about 1 per cent of consumption of manufactures in developed market-economy countries, would – on the assumptions made – represent some 4½ per cent by the year 2000. For the first two industry groups in Table 2.3

Table 2.3

Trade of developed market-economy countries with developing countries: 1972 and 2000 (a)

Industry group	Imports		Exports		Net trade (b)	
	1972	2000	1972	2000	1972	2000
	(Per cent of gross output)					
I. Food processing; clothing, etc.; wood products; petroleum products	2.2	7.1	1.2	3.2	+1.0	+3.9
II. Textiles; rubber and plastic products; miscellaneous light industry products	1.9	5.4	3.6	3.4	−1.7	+2.1
III. Paper and printing; chemicals; non-metallic mineral products	0.3	3.1	3.0	6.9	−2.8	−3.9
IV. Basic metals; machinery; electrical machinery; transport equipment	0.6	3.7	3.8	7.5	−3.2	−3.9
Total	1.1	4.4	2.9	6.2	−1.8	−1.9

(a) The percentages for 1972 are estimates; those for 2000 are hypothetical figures based on a number of assumptions (see text).

(b) Net imports (+) or net exports (−).

Source: As for Table 2.2

— by and large the labour-intensive industries (apart from petroleum refining) — the share of developing countries would rise from about 2 per cent to 5½ to 7 per cent. The rise in share for the more capital-intensive products is also noteworthy. As regards the reverse flow of trade, exports to developing countries would become significantly more important as market outlets for the industries of developed countries in three of the four industry groups.

Such changes in the patterns of production and trade would necessarily imply greater intra-branch specialisation between the two groups of countries, and this would be an important step towards transforming the present 'vertical' division of labour towards a more 'horizontal' one, that is, one consisting largely of intra-branch trade such as characterises the present trade among developed countries (Rayment, 1982).

The question has already been raised as to whether the existing international economic system can adjust to the requirements of a 'horizontal' exchange of manufactures between developed and developing countries. Clearly, the kind of changes in the relationship of trade to production in the developed countries which are indicated by Table 2.3 will imply substantial shifts in industrial structures in these countries, as well as policy changes to encourage such shifts.

Changes in industrial structures in relation to comparative advantage

The relationship between changes in industrial structure and in overall economic growth has been the subject of numerous quantitative studies since the first systematic analysis made by Chenery in 1960 (Chenery, 1960). It is well known that the relative importance of certain industries — particularly chemicals and engineering — increases with per capita real income, while that of others — particularly processed foods, beverages and tobacco, textiles, clothing, leather and footwear — decline in relative importance (6). At the same time, there is a well-defined positive association between relative rates of growth of different industries and relative changes in their rates of productivity growth. This can be seen from Table 2.4, which gives the results of simple linear regressions of growth rates in manufacturing output per person employed on the corresponding growth rates in total output for nine broad industry groups for the developed market-economy countries as a whole (7).

The goodness of fit of the regressions varies considerably for the three periods covered (8), but the co-efficient of total output is reasonably stable, and indicates that, on average, an increase of 1 percentage point in the rate of growth of output is associated with an increase of 0.5 to 0.7 percentage points in the relevant growth rate of output per person employed. This relationship is generally consistent, also, with the corresponding cross-country result of 0.5 percentage points found by Kaldor (1966), and with an elasticity of productivity with respect to output of 0.6 calculated by Beckerman et al (1965) for British industry. Earlier investigations by Salter (1966) had also found a close correlation between changes in the volume of output per head and in the volume of output in selected United Kingdom industries between 1924 and 1950. These results are all variants of the relationship first elaborated by Verdoorn (1949).

In the present context, the interesting question is whether, and to what extent, the output and productivity patterns of developed countries are changing in a way which is

Table 2.4

Regressions of productivity growth on output growth in manufacturing industries of developed market-economy countries, 1953–74

Period	Regression equation (a)	D.W.	$\bar{R}^2$
1953 – 63	$P = -0.173 + 0.653\,X$ (3.303)	1.66	0.609
1963 – 70	$P = 0.264 + 0.736\,X$ (5.689)	2.60	0.822
1970 – 74	$P = 1.852 + 0.525\,X$ (2.719)	1.79	0.514

(a) Based on annual rates of growth in output per person employed (P) and in total output (X) in nine broad industry groups. Figures in brackets are t values.

Source: Based on data in UNCTAD, 1978 b.

complementary to the pattern of comparative advantage of the manufacturing industries of developing countries.

There are various ways in which indicators of comparative advantage can be constructed. One approach, developed originally by Hal Lary (1968) is to use value added per employee as an indicator of the capital-intensity of production, 'capital' being interpreted as covering the flows of services from both human skills and physical assets. This kind of analysis is useful since it can be assumed that developing countries have a relative abundance of unskilled and semi-skilled labour, so that they should generally have a comparative advantage in labour-intensive products. Another approach, pioneered by Bela Balassa (1965), is to compute coefficients of 'revealed comparative advantage' based on the relationship of a country's imports to its exports of particular products. A recent study by Donges and Riedel (1977) for 12 industrialising developing countries, covering 119 different manufactured products showed that, on the basis of Balassa-type coefficients, the industries exhibiting the strongest comparative advantage according to 1972–1973 data were all labour- and/or raw material-intensive products (cotton fabrics, footwear, textile clothing, leather, wood products, etc.), but that these countries had also developed a comparative advantage in a number of 'product cycle' goods (in particular, electrical equipment, metal containers and telecommunications equipment). Other possible indicators of comparative advantage are the shares held by developing countries in the imports or consumption of developed countries in particular manufactured goods. Shares of imports or consumption are, however, likely to be significantly distorted by the structure of tariffs and other trade barriers, so that this approach is less to be preferred. However, a recent study by Tuong and Yeats (1978) has shown that a strong association exists between capital-intensity, as measured by value added per employee, and changes in the share of developing countries in total imports into developed countries.

Indicators of comparative advantage based on three alternative criteria are shown in Table 2.5 for ten broad industry groups. The available figures for the share of developed countries' consumption provided by imports from developing countries are, however, incomplete or not otherwise comparable with the industry groups listed. Nonetheless, the broad picture emerging is very similar, whichever indicator is used: developing countries have a substantial comparative advantage in the clothing, leather and footwear group, and a less-pronounced, though still significant, comparative advantage in textiles and in other generally labour-intensive industries. Within these and most other industry groups there will be sub-sections of industry, and also individual products, in the production of which developing countries can be expected to have a comparative advantage. As Rayment (1976) has pointed out, the fact that 'industries' as defined for statistical purposes are usually heterogeneous with respect to factor-intensity indicates that the potential set of labour-intensive products on which developing countries could specialise is very much wider than is suggested by an analysis of the statistics for industries or industry group.

A more precise relationship between the various indicators can be derived from regression analysis. Linear and quadratic regressions for the year 1976 of the share of developing countries in developed countries' imports (S) on value added per employee (V) gave the following result (t values shown in brackets):

$$(1)\quad S = 32.8 - \underset{(-3.504)}{0.229\,V} \qquad D.W. = 0.84 \qquad \bar{R}^2 = 0.606$$

$$(2)\quad S = 63.6 - \underset{(-3.584)}{0.881\,V} + \underset{(2.707)}{0.003\,V^2} \qquad D.W. = 1.67 \qquad \bar{R}^2 = 0.807$$

The quadratic form gives a substantially better fit than does the linear regression (9). Both equations are consistent with Lary's hypothesis that developing countries can be assumed to have a comparative advantage for industries with value added per employee under 110 per cent of the average for all manufacturing industry (Lary, 1968, ch.4). Putting V = 110 in the above equations, the corresponding import share of developing countries is 7½ per cent on the linear and 4½ per cent on the quadratic equation.

Table 2.5

Indicators of comparative advantage of industries of developing countries

	Value added per employee (a)		Share of consumption (b)		Share of imports (c)	
	1972	1976	1971–72	1975	1970	1976
	(All manufacturing = 100)		*(Per cent)*			
Generally labour-intensive						
Clothing, leather and footwear	53	48	4.06	8.63	21.2	32.8
Processed food, beverages and tobacco	94 (d)	105 (d)	1.51	2.16	15.3	14.4
Textiles (e)	70	64	2.63	3.25	11.6	14.8
Wood products and furniture	75	71	. . .	. . .	12.5	14.2
Miscellaneous light manufactures	99	96	. . .	. . .	10.4	11.1
Generally capital-intensive						
Basic metals	100	102	. . .	. . .	3.2	4.7
Engineering and metal products	115	112	0.11	0.21	1.6	3.4
Chemicals	164	164	1.26	1.73	3.2	3.0
Non-metallic mineral products	106	101	0.13	0.25	2.3	2.9
Paper products	108	121	. . .	. . .	0.7	1.5
Total	100	100	. . .	. . .	4.9	7.3

(a) In the United States.

(b) Imports into the European Economic Community (original 6), United Kingdom, United States and Japan from developing countries as percentage of estimated apparent consumption of the former group of countries.

(c) Imports from developing countries as percentage of total imports into 21 developed market-economy countries.

(d) Fish products, processed fruit and vegetables, confectionery products, pickles, etc. and cigars.

(e) Excluding synthetic textiles.

Sources: H.D. Tuong and A.J. Yeats (1980); UNCTAD (1976 b, 1978 b and 1978 d).

To throw some light on the relationship, if any, between the pattern of output change in developed countries and the pattern of comparative advantage of developing countries, an index of structural change has been calculated for certain developed countries for which comparable output statistics by industrial branches were available. For the period 1958–1960 to 1968–1970, a special analysis by the UN Economic Commission for Europe (1977) provides comparable figures of value added at 1963 factor cost for 18 industrial branches for 10 European countries. For a later but overlapping period 1965 to 1974, comparable output figures were extracted for 13 industrial branches for 4 European and 3 non-European developed countries (10). An index of structural change was then computed for the 7 largest European countries for the earlier period, and for the 7 European and non-European countries for the later period. The index was derived by weighting the value added for individual branches (expressed as percentages of total value added for the relevant country and year) by the percentage of imports into developed countries from developing countries, in the corresponding branch, in 1970.

Thus, the index of structural change is defined as:

$$I_j = \frac{\sum_{I}^{i} v_{ij_1} w_i \Big/ \sum_{I}^{i} w_i}{\sum_{I}^{i} v_{ij_o} w_i \Big/ \sum_{I}^{i} w_i}$$

where v_{ij} = share of value added in industry i in total manufacturing in country j, w_i = corresponding share of developing countries in imports into developed market-economy countries, and 0 and 1 relate to different time periods. Since the w_i's are much higher for the labour-intensive than for the capital-intensive industries, a shift in the pattern of output towards the latter industries will reduce the index, and *vice-versa* (11).

The results of this calculation are summarised in Table 2.6, which also shows the annual rate of growth in the volume of manufacturing production as a whole. For convenience of comparison, the reciprocal of I_j has been taken (to keep changes in the figures positive) and expressed as an annual rate (to standardise for differing time periods).

For both periods the pattern of structural change in all the countries shown has shifted in favour of the capital-intensive industries. The relative magnitude of the shift was by far the greatest in Japan and least in the United Kingdom, and in the United States and Italy (in the later period). This general shift in structure is complementary to the needs of developing countries to expand their exports of labour-intensive manufactures. However, the structural change has been very small in some developed countries, particularly the slow-growing ones. Indeed, it might be expected on *a priori* grounds that substantial changes in the pattern of output will occur only at high overall rates of growth.

Table 2.6

Changes in industrial structure in certain developed countries: 1958–60 to 1974

	1958–60 to 1968–70		1965 to 1974	
	Total manufacturing production	Index of structural change (a)	Total manufacturing production	Index of structural change (a)
	(Per cent per annum)			
France	6.4	1.4	. . .	. . .
Germany, Fed. Rep.	6.3	1.4	. . .	. . .
Italy	8.3	1.0	6.1	0.4
Netherlands	6.9	1.5	. . .	. . .
Norway	5.3	1.5	3.7	0.9
Sweden	6.9	2.0	4.6	1.5
United Kingdom	3.4	0.8	2.2	0.2
Canada	. . .	. . .	5.2	1.1
United States	. . .	. . .	3.8	0.4
Japan	. . .	. . .	11.2	3.2

(a) See text for definition.

Sources: UN Economic Commission for Europe (1977); UNCTAD (1978 b).

Yet for the first period, 1958–1960 to 1968–1970, there does not appear to be any significant relationship between the pattern of industrial change in Europe and the pattern of comparative advantage of the developing countries (as indicated by their share of imports into developed countries). However, bringing non-European developed countries into the comparison, as for the later period, makes a considerable difference. In the decade up to 1974, Japan experienced by far the greatest rate of industrial growth of the countries covered and, as already mentioned, this was accompanied by the greatest shift by far in output structure. In 1965, the generally labour-intensive industries (as defined in Table 2.5) accounted for 41 per cent of total value added in Japanese manufacturing industries, whereas by 1974 the proportion had fallen to 27 per cent. At the other extreme, the corresponding proportions for the United Kingdom declined only marginally, from 36 to 35 per cent.

The relationship between structural change and comparative advantage can conveniently be expressed in terms of regression equations (see Table 2.7). The lack of statistically significant results for the earlier period seems to result largely from the combination of high growth in Italy with very little structural change; one reason for slow structural change in Italian industry was that the supply of labour to the unskilled labour-intensive industries was maintained by an inflow from the overpopulated agricultural sector. For the later period, however, about three-quarters of the variance in the structural change indices can be explained by differences in the rates of growth of manufacturing output, the proportion so explained falling to three-fifths for the combined period.

Table 2.7

Regressions of indices of structural change on rates of output growth in manufacturing industries of certain developed market-economy countries: 1958–60 to 1974

Period	Regression equation	D.W.	$\bar{R}^2$
1958–60 to 1968–70	$S = 0.823 + 0.088\,X$ (0.836)	2.02	0.123
1965 to 1974	$S = -0.540 + 0.312\,X$ (4.043)	2.44	0.766
Combined periods	$S = -0.279 + 0.264\,X$ (4.467)	2.19	0.625

Source: As for Table 2.6.

It seems reasonable to conclude that the change in industrial output pattern in the developed market-economy countries over the past two decades was essentially a resultant of changing demand patterns associated with rising real income, combined with the effects of technological progress in the various manufacturing branches. Moreover, the structural shift was effected in all cases entirely as a result of more rapid growth in the output of the capital-intensive, than in that of the labour-intensive, branches. From 1965 to 1975, the expansion in the volume of output in the latter branches of industry ranged from nearly 20 per cent in the United Kingdom to some 70 per cent in Japan.

A similar result was found by ECE (1977) in the analyses already quoted. For the decade of the 1960s, the ECE study showed that 'the process of structural change is associated much more strongly with the growth of total manufacturing employment than with the shift of labour out of the manpower-releasing branches of manufacturing' (ECE, 1977, page 39). The ECE analysis also shows that for the 10 countries covered the volume of production rose over the decade for each of the manpower-releasing branches — being generally also the labour-intensive branches — as well as for the manpower-absorbing ones (UN ECE, 1977, Tables A.11 and A.12).

Given the comparative advantage of developing countries generally in labour-intensive industries, the small relative shifts in industrial structure and the absolute expansion in the output of the labour-intensive industries in developed countries would appear at first sight as something of a paradox. Since, as shown earlier, productivity growth is generally associated with relative output growth, it is the labour-intensive industries of developed countries which should, *ceteris paribus,* exhibit relatively slow improvements in productivity, so that over time their relative competitive position *vis-a-vis* the export products of developing countries should stimulate a shift of resources in the developed countries from labour-intensive to capital-intensive industries.

That this has not generally happened may perhaps be attributed to the inability of the economic systems of most developed countries to adjust sufficiently rapidly, or to a sufficient extent, to the rapid changes in comparative advantage that have been such a notable feature of the world market over the past two decades. Difficulties of structural adjustment — which involve large private and social costs of relocation of industries and families — are particularly acute in slow-growing countries, such as Britain, when confronted with a major loss of competitive position in export markets or with a major deterioration in the terms of trade. As a result, a widespread network of government measures has been evolved in order to protect domestic industries from import competition, and to finance the rationalisation of less competitive industries in order to protect their employment and market position.

Policy implications

The commercial policies of the developed market-economy countries since the end of the war can be divided broadly into three phases. There was, first, the immediate postwar phase of bilateral trade and payments agreements operated in the context of widespread shortages of essential primary commodities and of many industrial products. Then, second, a new expansionary phase was begun with the Marshall Plan, the creation of the OECD in 1947, and the implementation of its programme of phased reductions in import restrictions, supported by credits provided by the European Payments Union. The OECD programme, together with the various rounds of tariff reduction negotiated in the framework of GATT, stimulated an unprecedented expansion of trade among the industrialised countries concomitant with their postwar recovery and rapid economic growth.

Even in this expansionary phase, however, many developed countries were having difficulties in adjusting to increasing supplies of low-cost cotton textiles from Japan and certain Asian developing countries. In 1961, a Long-Term Agreement on Cotton Textiles was negotiated under GATT auspices as a temporary method of regulating imports to allow time for the necessary readjustment of domestic textile industries. That Agreement proved not to be temporary; it continued in modified and extended form until 1973, when it was replaced by a Multifibre Arrangement of much wider scope. In this expansionary phase, too, the various rounds of GATT tariff reductions were oriented essentially to the trade needs of the industrialised countries; they brought relatively small trade benefits to developing countries (see UNCTAD, 1968).

By the early 1960s, the emergence of a large number of newly-independent developing countries, and their growing pressure for changes in trade policy to promote the development process, led in 1964 to the creation of UNCTAD, and by 1968 this pressure had induced the developed countries to accept the principle of preferential treatment for the manufactured exports of developing countries. The resultant Generalised System of Preferences (GSP), which consists of separate preferential systems administered by the different developed countries is, however, subject to innumerable restrictive conditions which have severely limited its potential benefit for the manufactured exports of developing countries (UNCTAD, 1979) (12).

Nonetheless, these exports made great strides during the period of economic expansion in the developed countries, albeit from a relatively small base. As a proportion of total exports from developing countries, manufactures rose from 16 per cent in 1955 to 22 per cent in 1965 and to 28 per cent in 1973. In volume terms, their growth rate reached 10.3 per cent per annum from 1965 to 1973, as against 5.0 per cent per annum for primary commodity exports (other than petroleum). However, exports of manufactures from developing countries have remained only marginal in the total consumption of developed market-economy countries, representing little more than 1 per cent of that total by 1972 (see Table 2.3).

A third phase of commercial policy appears to have set in with the onset of the economic crisis in the mid 1970s. The retardation in economic growth has adversely affected production and employment in very different degrees in different industries. The weaker industries in developed countries, which are also generally the labour-intensive ones, have been hardest hit. As a result, many developed countries have resorted to additional protectionist measures which affect, in particular, the low-cost products of labour-intensive industries in which developing countries have a comparative advantage.

The new protectionism evades the existing GATT rules by the use of so-called 'agreed' or 'voluntary' trade restrictions on a widening range of individual products. These restrictions may be negotiated among governments, or they may be left to be agreed by the industries of the trading countries concerned. The growing use of this latter type of 'voluntary export restraint' has generally led to cartelisation of the export trade in both developed and developing countries (UNCTAD, 1978 c). According to GATT estimates (Long, 1977) new import restrictions introduced by developed market-economy countries in the three years 1975–1977 affect some $ 30–50 billion of international trade (or 3 to 5 per cent of the total). Since the new restrictions are aimed primarily at protecting employment in labour-intensive industries, a disproportionate part of the resulting burden has fallen on the export industries of developing countries.

It is indeed ironic that even while the GATT multilateral trade negotiations – the 'Tokyo Round' – were under way with the aim of achieving major reductions in existing trade barriers, new protectionist measures were being introduced which effectively bypass the GATT rules. As far as the developing countries are concerned, the situation regarding barriers to their manufactured exports appears on balance to have seriously deteriorated.

It seems very probable that the new protectionism will become an integral part of economic policy in the developed market-economy countries, at least for as long as the current phase of persistent 'stagflation' and external payments disequilibria lasts. If so, there will be considerable adverse long-term effects on the economies of both developed and developing countries. For one thing, these additional barriers to trade will seriously limit the export earnings of a number of developing countries and this, in turn, will place a limit on their demand for imports of capital goods and other high-technology products. To this extent, the new protectionism will safeguard employment in the labour-intensive industries of the developed countries at the expense of lost employment opportunities in their capital-intensive industries. This, again, is likely to result in lower overall growth in output and in productivity, and in an increase in inflationary pressures in these countries. More generally, the new phase in commercial policy will retard the process of structural change in the industrialised countries at a time when the long-term need is for more flexibility in resource allocation and an acceleration of structural change.

The retardation of structural change is also a resultant of the various adjustment assistance programmes which most of the developed market-economy countries have been operating for many years. These programmes generally aim to rationalise and modernise uneconomic branches of industry – even where these branches are unlikely to become cost-competitive in relation to potential imports. The consequent decline in employment in the rationalised industries, though it makes some contribution to the process of structural change, is necessarily smaller than would have occurred without such adjustment assistance. To promote faster structural change, a new orientation will be needed in adjustment assistance programmes so that they facilitate the movement of resources from uneconomic lines of production to other, viable, activities. An effective industrial readjustment policy would also allow a progressive dismantling of protectionist barriers against imports of manufactures to be undertaken. With the progress of industrialisation in developing countries, and the emergence of new types of manufactures (including both skill- and capital-intensive products) in which some developing countries have a comparative advantage, the dismantling of existing protectionist barriers will need to be on a broad front, covering a wide range of both labour-intensive and capital-intensive products, if the needs of developing countries for export markets are to be adequately accommodated. Such a reorientation in domestic industrial policies would yield long-term benefits to the developed countries themselves. Certainly, without such reorientation, these countries will not be able to provide the expanding export markets for the manufactures of developing countries on which the Lima target is predicated.

Footnotes

(1) See P.B.W. Rayment (1982) for a detailed analysis of the intra-trade in manufactures of the industrial countries.

(2) There is now a large literature on the reasons for the successful export drives of South Korea, Hong Kong, Singapore and Taiwan, the main conclusion reached being that export success followed the application of a variety of specific fiscal and other incentives to exporters, coupled with the absence of significant protection for manufacturing production for the domestic market and adequate incentives for foreign investment. For a major theoretical and empirical analysis of the issue, see Little, Scitovsky and Scott (1970).

(3) This comparison is based on official exchange rates, which generally exaggerate the differences between output in real terms between developed and developing countries: see Kravis and Lipsey (1971).

(4) In this context, 'developed countries' include the socialist countries of Eastern Europe as well as OECD countries.

(5) To further industrial production in developing countries on the scale required to attain the Lima target, UNIDO has proposed the setting up of an International Bank for Industrial Development – see UNIDO (1981) and Frowen (1981).

(6) For a detailed analysis of changes in the relative outputs and employment in European industries over the 1960s, see UN Economic Commission for Europe (1977).

(7) A similar close relationship between changes in labour productivity and changes in output in British industries was found by Beckerman et al (1965), and for nine countries of Western Europe by the UN Economic Commission for Europe, *op. cit.*

(8) The lower value of $\bar{R}^2$ for the period 1970–1974 is due mainly to the relatively high rate of productivity growth in the textile industry (reflecting the substantial rationalisation and re-equipment undertaken) in relation to output growth.

(9) Similar results were obtained from regressions using the 1970–1972 data. The better fit obtained from the quadratic form is due to the high value added per employee in the chemical industry in relation to the corresponding import share held by developing countries. Excluding chemicals, the linear equation for 1976 becomes $S = 42.7 \underset{(-4.565)}{-0.347V}$, with D.W. = 1.28 and $\bar{R}^2 = 0.749$.

(10) The industrial output statistics of France, the Netherlands and the Federal Republic of Germany for the years selected were not available in the classification used here.

(11) This is, of course, only one out of many possible indices of structural change that could be constructed; employment-weighted indices, for example, would no doubt reveal a smaller structural shift than would value-added indices. In any case, the present calculation would have been greatly improved if it had been based on a much more detailed industrial classification, allowing for the variation in comparative advantage among different products within individual industry groups, but the resources required for such a detailed analysis were beyond the scope of the present chapter.

(12) According to UNCTAD estimates, preferential imports into the EEC, Japan and the United States under the GSP in 1976 would have been greater by \$ 4 to 5 billion (or some 50 per cent), had there been no *a priori* limitations – by tariff quotas, import ceilings, maximum country amounts and administrative procedures – and competitive need exclusions (see UNCTAD 1979).

References

Balassa, B. (1965) 'Trade Liberalisation and "Revealed" Comparative Advantage', *Manchester School of Economic and Social Studies,* vol. 33.

Beckerman, W. *et al* (1965) *The British Economy in 1975* (Cambridge: Cambridge University Press).

Chenery, H. B. (1960) 'Patterns of Industrial Growth', *American Economic Review,* vol. 50, no. 4, September.

Donges, J.B. and Riedel, J. (1977) 'The expansion of Manufactured Exports in Developing Countries: An Empirical Assessment of Supply and Demand Issues', *Weltwirtschaftliches Archiv,* vol. 113, no. 1.

Finger, J.M. (1975) 'Tariff Provisions for Offshore Assembly and the Exports of Developing Countries', *The Economic Journal,* vol. 85, June.

Frowen, S.F. (1981) *The Economic Rationale for a New International Institution in the Field of Industrial Financing* (UNIDO Document v.81–28056).

Kaldor, N. (1966) *Causes of the Slow Rate of Economic Growth of the United Kingdom* (Cambridge: Cambridge University Press).

Kravis, I. and Lipsey, R. (1971) *Price Competitiveness in World Trade: Studies in International Economic Relations,* no. 6, National Bureau of Economic Research, New York.

Lary, Hal B. (1968) *Imports of Manufactures from Less Developed Countries,* National Bureau of Economic Research, New York.

Little, Scitovsky and Scott (1970).

Long, O. (1977) *The Future of World Trade,* GATT Press Release 1199, November.

Maizels, A. (1963) *Industrial Growth and World Trade* (Cambridge: Cambridge University Press).

Rayment, P.B.W. (1976) 'The Homogeneity of Manufacturing Industries with respect to Factor Intensity: The Case of the United Kingdom', *Oxford Bulletin of Economics and Statistics,* vol. 38, August.

– (1982) 'Intra-Industry' Specialisation and the Foreign Trade of Industrial Countries', Chapter 1 in the present volume.

Salter, W.E.G. (1966) *Productivity and Technical Change* (Cambridge: Cambridge University Press).

Tuong, H.D. and Yeats, A.J. (1980) 'On Factor Proportions as a Guide to the Future Composition of Developing Country Exports', *Journal of Development Economics,* vol. 7, October.

UN Economic Commission for Europe (1977), *Structure and Change in European Industry,* United Nations, New York.

UNCTAD (1968) *The Kennedy Round estimated effects on tariff barriers* (TD/6/Rev.1), United Nations, New York.

– (1976 a) *The dimensions of the required restructuring of world manufacturing output and trade in order to reach the Lima target* (TD/185/Supp.1), mimeo, Geneva.

– (1976 b) *Handbook of International Trade and Development Statistics,* United Nations, New York.

– (1978 a) *The role of transnational corporations in the marketing and distribution of exports and imports of developing countries* (TD/B/C.2/197), Geneva, March.

– (1978 b) *Recent trends and developments in trade in manufactures and semi-manufactures of developing countries and territories: 1977 Review,* Geneva, (TD/B/C.2/190), March.

– (1978 c) *Growing protectionism and the standstill on trade barriers against imports from developing countries,* (TD/BC.2/194), Geneva, March.

– (1978) d) *Handbook of International Trade and Development Statistics: Supplement 1977,* United Nations, New York, 1978.

– (1979) *Review and evaluation of the generalised system of preferences* (TD/232), mimeo, Geneva.

UNIDO (1979) *Industry 2000 – New Perspectives* (New York: United Nations).

UNIDO (1981) *A Proposal for Setting up an International Bank for Industrial Development* (UNIDO Document ID/B/261/Add. 7).

Verdoorn, P.J. (1949) 'Fattori che regolano lo sviluppo della del lavoro', *L'Industria.*

Chapter 3

THE LONG WAVE THEORY CONFIRMED BY THE PRESENT CRISIS*

L. H. Dupriez †

Since 1945, the long waves in economic life have been a subject very scantily treated in economics if not even rejected in economic literature published in English. Interest in the long-wave theory is reviving as a result of economic trends since 1974. But many still look askance at the problem, as it appears in a garb very different from the original association of the long wave with gold which many remember as being linked with the name of N.D. Kondratieff: indeed so associated with that name that Schumpeter once called the long wave the Kondratieff movement (see Kondratieff, 1925).

During the Second World War, I made an extensive study of the long wave, not only as a monetary, but also as a real phenomenon (Dupriez, 1947, Part III). This study led me to abandon the former search for a mechanistic explanation of a special monetary phenomenon; instead, the long wave appeared as a full-fledged general economic movement, implying an integrated association of monetary, fiscal and 'real' phenomena. Looked at from this perspective, the explanation of long waves in terms of gold movements appeared to be determined by incidental events in the earlier movements; it vanished gradually in the light of a much broader explanation combining not only real with monetary phenomena, but also considering psychological and theoretical trends.

My contention is therefore not that the original Kondratieff explanation, and still less the alternative Cassel-Kitchin explanation, remembered in textbooks on the history of economic thought, should guide our present thinking. Instead, I shall examine in how far the structured monetary-financial-real explanation, which is advocated in my book, can be developed so that it can be applied to post-war phenomena and particularly to more recent events.

The long wave is thus construed as a general economic movement embracing monetary phenomena. Thus, the original relationships applicable to some of the contingent situations of the 19th century such, as 'real phenomena' and psychological attitudes, and including Schumpeter's own long search for swings in inventions and innovations, seem applicable. My own principle is to analyse the complex evolution of the long waves within an integrated 'real-monetary' theory which rejects any dichotomy (Dupriez, 1976, ch. I).

* Attention is drawn to the following new study on long waves published after the completion of this paper: C. Freeman, J. Clark and L. Soete, *Unemployment and Technical Innovation: A Study of Long Waves and Economic Development* (London: Frances Pinter, 1982). A selected annotated bibliography on long waves by K. Barr appeared in *Review,* vol. 11, no. 4, Spring, 1979, pp. 675–718. ED.

In order to recognise a present swing in the long wave, it is necessary first to ascertain an upswing covering approximately a period from 1945–1948 to 1972–1974. This period seems rather extended, but is not unusual for our phenomenon, as we must be able to state that the long wave has not ceased to exist after the Second World War under the impact of new doctrines and policy. I refer here to all intellectual and political statements regarding the level of employment as the direct result of full employment policies – and therefore no more subject to any natural and spontaneous economic developments. If such policies were really masters of events, traditional long waves should disappear with economic cycles and leave room only for either success or the erratic consequences of errors of policy.

In the 1940s and 1950s it was quite fashionable to consider that employment policies through monetary injections easily produced near-full employment; they thus covered not only cyclical conjunctural conditions for which they were meant, but also the long waves and trends, which short-term employment equilibria were obviously not meant to cover.

My own position has been that a structured historical development was not prevented simply by virtue of the new school of economics. If the phenomena of a long upswing were recognisable after the war, the existence of long waves could not be dismissed. Long waves as such must therefore be recognised as long as they do not disappear.

The period 1948–1972 was obviously a period of easy and spontaneous economic development, to the point of loosening all sorts of economic controls which governments would have been unable to dismiss under adverse economic conditions. The obvious fact dominating all implications was the elongation of prosperity and the exceptionally strong shortening of phases of depression. This phenomenon was even more typical than in former upswings.

Under such conditions, production and commerce grew quantitatively and at very high rates: rates higher than in the past, and so fast that their logarithmic development over time must necessarily break rather soon, i.e. at the end of the long swing. In fact, the quantitative development was so great that it implied a high rate of technical progress, which meant, correlatively, a persistent increase in real wages. This increase surpassed all historical experience. Thus, nominal wage indices rose fast, while wholesale prices increased only at the typical average rate of 1 to 2 per cent per annum. The growth of the economy dominated the entire conjunctural situation to such an extent that economists considered rapid growth a natural phenomenon not subject to any setback; they developed an 'economics of growth' in which qualitative progress was only an underlying requirement.

This 'real' expansion of the economy was accompanied by a very high rate of 'credit expansion': much faster than either the real development or even the rapid rise in the quantity of money, stimulated by Keynesian thinking. This increase in the credit system, both relatively to the real national product and to the quantity of money, was stressed by professor C. Rist before the war and by myself in 1947 (Dupriez, 1947), where it was substantiated by strong statistical evidence. It had never occurred in previous discussions.

Concretely, this means that the upswing in the long wave starts when recourse to credit is low in relation to disposable funds and when interest rates are obviously low, especially on short-term funds. As recourse to credit grows, rates move up. Tensions develop within the credit system and, beyond it, within the monetary system, i.e. in its international implications. This growing tension had become noticeable as early as 1958, and continued until 1967, when sterling was devalued; it ended when the entire monetary system of Bretton Woods crashed in 1970–71.

As a whole, the credit and monetary situation continued – in its commercial implications – in a typical upswing mood until 1970 and even until 1974. Notwithstanding underlying tensions, it worked smoothly on the surface; there were as yet no abnormally high interest rates.

I cannot go beyond this very summary description of facts; but details all confirm that until 1972–74 the world economy was enjoying an upward swing in the long wave, in a very typical manner – perhaps in an even more unmistakeable way than in the past.

Let us now consider 1972–74 in the light of past experience of downturns.

It should first be recognised that we need not have recourse to any specific long wave explanation of the sequence of events involved in the crisis leading to a downturn. The long wave is an underlying complex of trends working through ordinary business cycles. Obviously, in such a case, the upward movement breaks precisely with and through an ordinary conjunctural crisis, just as the lower point is associated with a severe and protracted depression. We must therefore reject any temptation to search for a mechanistic and special explanation of the downturn of the long wave. This downturn can occur only within a crisis of the ordinary type. But it tends to aggravate it, as in 1872 and 1920. Obviously, it is correct to describe the 1974 crisis as drastic.

The downturns of the 19th and 20th centuries have been associated with war or, more precisely, with the end of postwar monetary inflations; they have thus corresponded to moments of return to sound financial practices. Is this fact intimately linked with the long wave itself or is it contingent?

N.D. Kondratieff himself, in a typically deterministic and marxist approach, placed the main wars within the long wave, i.e. at the end of a period of prosperity following a great accumulation of armaments. As viewed in 1925, facts could not serve to contradict this type of argument. But the relation does not hold any more; the war of 1939 broke out at the end of a long downswing and in 1972 no major war broke aut, notwithstanding the tremendous accumulation of armaments which accentuated the upward trend. For the first time we are therefore faced with the necessity of explaining the downturn itself without recourse to the aftermath of war.

It is now obvious to anyone scrutinising the facts that the smooth upward trend since the war has been broken, and that this occurred after a period of adequate length to allow the upward wave to spend itself. We are suddenly faced with huge problems which imply a break from past developments, and these problems are interrelated.

It is less clear what type of new trend in economic affairs we are facing after the break, because the pattern of events has been shaken. The first and most obvious difference from historical experience is an unusual acceleration of price inflation, to a point where we are engaged in a process of declining money values. This has become common international experience. But although the theory of money does not integrate the process of declining money values in its system of thought, price rises of 6 per cent to 10 per cent do not appear disturbing to most commentators on economic conditions. The taxation process through inflation has taken on enormous proportions, but, notwithstanding Keynes, nobody seems to have taken cognizance of the apparently fantastic writings of Silvio Gesell. Without any attention to long-run developments and their already present implications for the business world, the international monetary system is engaged in a process which becomes common and necessary practice.

The international monetary crisis, which developed through successive accidental developments, from the fall of sterling in 1967 and the institution of a free gold market in 1968, through the inconvertibility of currencies into US dollars and the inconvertibility of the US dollar into gold (1970–1971), to the formal dethronment of gold as the unit of measurement by the International Monetary Fund and the generalisation of floating exchange rates, has upset all previous thinking about monetary standards.

Gold, although no longer a determinant of monetary developments, it is still an important part of international reserves; however, its functional value has been repudiated by the I.M.F. This new attitude has been due to inordinate developments in the world monetary and credit system rather than to any insufficiency of gold, according to the criteria used by the Gold Delegation of the League of Nations in 1930. Gold production has been pushed up to high levels in South Africa through concentration on high grade ores to offset the handicap of frozen prices; however, commercial gold has been in high demand at soaring prices and accumulation of gold reserves by central banks has been small, while United States reserves were almost depleted.

Inconvertibilities suppressed institutional links between domestic monetary systems through reserve fluctuations. Many nations nevertheless had to practice restraint in order not to depreciate their currencies in the foreign exchange market. But this form of restraint did not work in the case of the US dollar; in 1973, the United States felt free to expand their monetary system in an effort to curb a mild depression, in accordance with typical Keynesian doctrines; excess money overflowed the world and drove prices upwards, contributing to the 1974 world crisis.

A rift is now developing among the member states of the I.M.F. on how best to deal with these exceptional circumstances. On the one hand, the idea of pump-priming the economy by means of a full-employment policy is not abandoned, but the predicament is that it does not work when price inflation is the immediate result of monetary inflation. On the other hand, governments get frightened by excessively high inflation rates and advocate anti-inflationary policies. But they dare not push them to their limits on account of the higher immediate unemployment risks. The antithesis between price and quantity reactions of monetary policies has dominated politico-economic thinking, but the problem, which was so clear in the 1930s, has been blurred by complications and ideological differences.

Owing to the high rates of price inflation, interest rates have moved up rapidly since 1970; they have attained levels far above any experienced since the industrial revolution. In many of the industrial countries consol rates move around the rate that the Bank of England practised for discount of short-term paper on Black Friday in 1866! And in London they went much higher.

Markets must therefore reorganise to face uncommon circumstances. Creditors realise that, even at those rates, they cannot maintain the real value of their capital; but borrowers must, at the margin and in the short run, meet conditions which are crucial for the working and even the survival of their enterprise. The economic calculus relative to capital is completely upset; both creditors and debtors are frustrated in their aims. Rates have continued to rise to unprecedented levels and are linked in their causes and consequences to the process of declining money values; the process is worldwide and due to unprecedented international borrowing and cannot just be construed as an effect of United States lending habits on the internal market.

The price, money and credit situation of 1982 still presents an overall picture of a protracted period of hardship associated with an economic downturn which does not break through. The 'real' phenomena nevertheless exhibit a downswing in long-period developments.

Logarithmic growth has been easy for twenty-five years in nearly all types of activities: economists developed a type of 'growth economics' completely determined by these easy economic developments; rates of growth were extrapolated without any inhibition and believed to show a true perspective for the future. But these trends were unequivocally broken in 1974. Global results started to fluctuate without any sign of underlying expansion; more dramatically, several basic industries suffered from severe structural setbacks; intellectually, the growth trends were replaced by a mood of zero growth, to face the suddenly blatant lack of resources for logarithmic growth.

An acceleration in the rate of application of technical progress has always been associated with the downturn of the long wave in the first decade of its development. Capital investment, which had been mainly directed to increases of capacities, has suddenly been switched to increases of productivity; at the same time, the obsolescence of older equipments is intensified and these are eliminated from the production process. This phenomenon has taken on fantastic proportions. Research already procured high rates of productivity increase during the upswing phase; organised research has become a secular development, and electronics have brought about changes in methods of production similar to those which Schumpeter associated with the invention of railways and, later, with electricity. Started in the upswing, they are very far from having spent their influence; on the contrary, appliances have been multiplying. A tremendous backlog of possibilities is now being exploited to rationalise industry, most strongly in the basic industries.

Broken trends in quantities produced, associated with rapid technological progress, inevitably bring about high rates of unemployment and there seems to be no hope that they will soon diminish. Basic industries have all cut their personnel, often drastically, and necessary developments in tertiary activities are hard to organise; they are inhibited by the fact that labour has become very expensive and that labour-intensive products and services rank high in price increases.

Wages have moved in accordance with these changes in productivity; they have also received the impetus of a high secular trend of progress and, after 1970, they grew both in monetary and in real terms to an unprecedented degree.

The amount of progress in real terms may seem surprising but it is implied, in some way, by the very changes in the modes of production in basic industries: marginal productivity of labour has increased; otherwise, the movement would have been broken; but actual moves went somewhat ahead of productivities and induced strong pressures towards further improvements.

An increase in the real wage of employed labour is not contradicted by past experience of downswings: in the past prices tumbled more rapidly than wages were reduced, but social trouble resulted from the increase in unemployment. With rising nominal wages, this same type of relationship still holds good, notwithstanding contrary movements in nominal wages.

The inflationary development of the world price system as a whole should not obscure the fact that the economic system is living under pressure of necessary adjustments in relative prices, both national and international; all these are associated with the requirements of adjustment following a long period dominated by growth.

International commodity prices rank high in this respect. They have moved rather erratically since 1974, but remained below the level they would have reached if there had been a systematic increase in wages and domestic prices. Metals and textile raw materials rank lower than the average price increase and seem under no pressure of immediate scarcity; food prices have been most erratic and efforts to stabilise them have yielded little results; petroleum is, of course, the big winner. Owing to its importance, there has been a tendency to interpret business conditions as a consequence of the oil crisis, considered as an exogenous variable, owing to the monopoly practices involved. I would not agree with this. Oil is the first raw material faced with the scarcity problem involved in long-term overdevelopment and it happened that producers were able to use restraint. Other such cases are bound to happen in due course. North-South discussions show that the problem has been perceived by low-cost producers, but in many cases there is still enough elasticity of production in many countries to render restraint unfeasible.

The downward trend of the long wave has suddenly increased the pressure to adjust average wages between countries to their comparative levels of technique and organisation. Since the war, wage levels in Europe were slowly moving towards North American levels; after 1970, they rose to unexpectedly high levels: in several continental countries, wages in the basic industries even surpassed the corresponding North American levels. Japan is following suit and now Korea, Taiwan and Brazil, among others, are doing the same. An overall wage increase in underdeveloped countries is inhibited by overpopulation and political disorganisation. The claims for more equal real income cannot be met without corresponding advances in methods of production.

The present concentration of problems largely ignored or forgotten in periods of upswing is remarkable in two directions: the fear of scarcity of natural resources and the growing understanding of pollution. These problems were hardly mentioned before 1970, not only among laymen and journalists, but also in economic literature. They have suddenly become a major concern.

Scarcity of natural resources is a problem of secular trends, but industrialists have usually been satisfied with a perspective of two or three generations. In the optimistic mood of long-term upswings, concern over scarcity has been dismissed in economic literature. It is not by accident that W.S. Jevons in the 1860s wrote a chapter on 'the natural law of social growth' in his study on *The Coal Question,* nor that A. Hansen was concerned with the exhaustion of the 'frontier', i.e. the end of the period of empty land in the United States during the 1930s. On the contrary, in 1955, experts of the European Coal and

Steel Community accepted trends which were obviously impossible in the long run, but proved correct in the short-run. Following this example, many of the exponential trends calculated for the year 2000 were until quite recently based on past experience over relatively short periods. But the Club of Rome's propositions for a policy of zero-growth are a phenomenon of the 1970s. Our intellectual mood is clearly dominated by the downturn in the long wave.

Pollution is the obverse side of the problem of scarcity of natural resources; it is associated with their altogether too lavish use and an insufficient economic concern about the disposal of their waste products. In the past the problem remained specific and localised, but now our big reserves of life are menaced. It is again typical of the long wave that there was no general discussion of pollution in the 1960s, while it became a major concern early in the 1970s, to the point of provoking strong political movements of ecologists.

The list of problems associated with the downturns and the new conditions traditionally linked with the receding wave should certainly be worked out in detail; a clear understanding of this association would be very useful for policy purposes. But I cannot go into further details. Let me only stress that the objective economic conditions are not the only ones involved; there are far-reaching impacts on mental attitudes. These now comprise the attitudes in the scientific and theoretical field, government and policy, and in the business and entrepreneurial worlds. The phases of the long wave are thus truly a general economic phenomenon. Specific explanations are just a part, even a modest part, of the picture.

It is difficult to perceive what should be the outcome of the passing of the phase of growth economics and the development of a long phase dominated by reorganisation, rationalisation and damaging pressures of the factors of production on the national product. It would be wishful thinking that the problems facing us today will not be protracted.

We are still beset by a number of contradictions. The first is the continuance of price increases at a rate which implies, in fact, 'melting money'. Next, we have inordinately high interest rates in accordance with rising prices; they conflict with the very low average productivity of old capital and require very high efficiency for new capital. Most crucially, technical progress is proceeding at a rapid rate while growth trends in the production of physical products are broken; unemployment is the price of inadequate and too slow adaptation.

The history of long waves teaches us that they subside as the great problems causing them are progressively solved. These problems are unusually big today. Let us therefore strengthen our efforts to meet them with a clear insight into their interrelationships.

Postscript

The present study was written in December 1977 and was subject to only minor corrections. The year 1974 was already then perceived as a major turning point in all the 'real phenomena' of the Kondratieff waves and their implications for the attitudes of all economic agents. It was also clear that the regulated monetary system of the world had crashed in 1970–71.

Events since then have shown unprecedented pressure on employment, stimulated by extraordinary technological progress; the clash between progress and security remains acute and is not reducible to insufficient national planning, as some political manifestos seem to suggest. The monetary problem too remains worldwide, as uncontrolled international credit expansion continues. It is myopia to attribute it simply to errors of judgment in the domestic monetary policy of the United States.

References

Dupriez, L.H. (1947) *Mouvements Économiques Généraux*

Dupriez, L.H. (1976) *La Monnaie dans l'Économie* (Paris: Cujas)

Kondratieff, N.D. (1925) 'The Major Economic Cycles', *Voprosy Konjunktury,* 1, pp. 28–79. A German version under the title 'Die langen Wellen der Konjunktur' was published in the *Archiv für Sozialwissenschaft und Sozialpolitik,* vol. 56, no. 3, 1926, pp. 573–609; an English translation of this paper under the title 'The Long Waves of Economic Life' first appeared in the *Review of Economic Statistics,* vol. 18, 1935, pp. 105–115 and was reprinted in *Lloyds Bank Review,* no. 129, July 1978, pp. 41–60.

Chapter 4

INDUSTRIAL MATERIALS: PAST, PRESENT AND FUTURE

G. F. Ray

Introduction

There are three signs that indicate the coming of age of any subject in terms of the thinking and interest of economists: the proliferation of literature, the choice of the topic for one of the celebrated lectures, and a survey of the academic publications in the *Economic Journal.* Using this standard, the 'problem' of industrial materials, or resources, has definitely come into the forefront: the number of reports, articles, monographs and books dealing with the adequacy of resources, whether in the area of energy or other materials, has been mushrooming in the academic, trade and popular press; it was chosen by eminent speakers for discussion in their major lectures in the early 1970s (1) and eventually the *Economic Journal's* survey also saw the light of day (Petersen and Fisher, 1977).

Why the present preoccupation of academics, politicians and industrialists with the future supply of industrial materials? The impetus probably came from the warnings given by the well publicised works of Forrester (1971) and Meadows (1972) whose frightening exponential demand curves tended to cross the much more moderate supply curves within a relatively short-time horizon. Relative scarcity of many materials at various times during the 1972 – 74 boom gave a further stimulus to these warnings which were strongly supported by both the OPEC action in 1973 – 74 and by the endeavours of the primary producing countries to introduce a new international economic order. Producers' associations, with the inherent possibility of being transformed into a cartel, began to burgeon.

These, and possibly other factors, gave rise to views that foresaw a total change from the 25-year postwar period of abundance and surpluses, when the producers' problem was access to markets, to an era of relative scarcity, when the main problem would be that of the consumers' access to supplies. Or in other words: a shift from a buyers' to a sellers' market. These views (e.g. Brown, 1974) have probably been modified in the meantime in view of the relative plenty created by the deep world recession, in 1975, and the following slow pace of recovery; however, a few years of relatively slow demand, though postponing the problem, cannot essentially remove the cause of preoccupation.

The subject of this essay therefore is the future adequacy of supplies. The discussion will be restricted to industrial materials. The limitation is solely due to the scope of this paper. It is not intended to belittle the importance of food or energy, which is obvious. The significance of energy should be particularly stressed because, apart from its all-pervasive importance, there has always been a unique relationship between energy and industrial materials: past material shortages were usually overcome by technological advance — by innovation, that is, the introduction of some new material, product or process — but always, without exception, at the cost of using more energy for the novel solution. We assume here, perhaps heroically, that energy — in whatever form — will be forthcoming.

Industrial materials are either produced by agriculture and forestry or extracted by the mining industries; they are renewable or non-renewable. Although the first group also presents some problems, more attention will be devoted to the non-renewable ones — that is, minerals and metals — since they are the prime object of the general pre-occupation.

The desirability of looking ahead does not make it any easier. Science advances, technology changes, as do economic and social conditions over a longer future period. A concrete forecast of the supply position of any of the major industrial materials is not the aim of this paper; rather, it is believed that a round-up of the available relevant information, and a logical approach, may suggest the shape and direction of likely developments.

We need a starting point for looking ahead, and for this purpose a brief sketch of the past history and of the present situation will be useful before turning to an assessment of the future.

The past

This ist the period ending in 1972, the start of the recent commodity boom. A simple, but enlightening approach for surveying a long period in the past is to study the movement of prices of industrial materials. Any material in short supply becomes immediately more expensive; its price can easily double, or rise even more, within a short time. An indicator which reflects the aggregate movements of materials prices is therefore a good starting point for a first assessment.

Such an indicator has been compiled since 1845 by *The Economist* in London. It includes the major materials, but excludes coal and petroleum. Prior to 1972 it shows three major peaks (Ray, 1977). The first was in 1864; this was the outcome of the American civil war which led to the 'cotton famine' (2). The second, around 1920, was the culmination of a long period of rising prices which started in 1914 and ended in shortages after the Great War. Though prices were rising during World War II as well, the next peak came in 1951 under the impact, on world markets, of the Korean war.

Prices fell heavily after each of these three peaks, including the Korean period. No major increase followed – especially in real terms – until 1973.

These peaks were caused by wartime disruption and indicated abrupt rises in the general price level of materials. Markets for many individual materials fluctuated much more than the aggregate indicator, signalling shortages; most of them were caused by natural disasters, political troubles, disruption of transportation facilities, major strikes, adverse weather conditions, bottlenecks in primary processing (e.g. smelters), or a sudden upsurge of real or speculative demand exceeding the expansive potential of existing capacity. Except for one or two isolated and minor cases they were not generally due to the exhaustion of non-renewable resources. Generally speaking shortages were temporary.

Thus, this past period did not vindicate the major earlier advocates of doom: the Malthusian trap was avoided in the area of materials (and in that of food, too), there was no trace of the Ricardian stagnation due to land shortage, nor of the Marxian demand shortage (Pavitt, 1973).

One of Ricardo's arguments, in a nutshell, was that growing population leads to higher production of manufactures, hence the price of food and raw materials will rise; consequently the rents accruing to owners of land and mines will absorb an ever larger proportion of the national income (Cooper, 1975a). His theory was right in one sense: that production of industrial materials, as well as of food, had to be extended geographically, often to faraway lands, and also to areas where production costs were gradually higher because of poorer natural endowment such as soil, climate or the leaner ore content of mines. Technological developments in transportation and production, however, much more than offset these handicaps. Indeed, it can be seen from *Table 4.1* that prices of minerals and metals, as related to wages in manufacturing, fell almost uninterruptedly from 1900 to 1970. A detailed analysis of the relative price of copper and of the metal content of copper ores mined indicates that this relative fall of the former coincided with the gradual but very significant reduction of the latter (*Chart 4.1*). The real cost of producing copper from ore with a metal content of half a per cent is significantly lower today than a century ago, when the average ore content was many times higher. The same is true of most other minerals (3).

In the past, there has been no lack of forward-looking exercises. Many of them painted a gloomy picture of the future, expecting the exhaustion of material resources: most of them have been proved wrong. The scarcity of British coal, feared by Jevons (1865) did not materialise, nor was the anxiety of President Roosevelt concerning the rundown of the USA's mineral resources, aired in 1908, well enough founded (Page, 1973). Leith's estimates (1975), made in the mid-1930s, which predicted the early exhaustion of certain US reserves, did not come true – with one exception, which provides an interesting

Table 4.1

Change in relative (a) prices of selected minerals/metals

Per cent (compound) a year

	1900 to 1940	1941 to 1950	1951 to 1970
Aluminium	– 5.8	– 5.3	– 2.5
Coal	– 2.2	+ 1.0	– 3.6
Copper	– 4.6	– 2.0	0
Iron	– 3.6	– 2.5	– 0.6
Lead	– 3.3	+ 1.1	– 4.0
Molybdenum	..	..	– 1.7
Petroleum	– 4.0	+ 0.7	– 3.7
Phosphates	..	..	– 1.3
Sulphur	..	..	– 3.8
Zinc	– 2.6	– 0.6	– 4.6

(a) Related to (US) average hourly wage rate in manufacturing.

Source: Nordhaus W.D., 'Resources as a Constraint on Growth', *American Economic Review,* vol. LXIV, no. 2, May 1974.

example of replacement of an exhausted resource by another (4); Pehrson's 1945 assessment of the USA's mineral position (Pehrson, 1945) fared no better either. Nor were resource needs more accurately foreseen; this was the subject of the best known of similar exercises, the 1952 Paley report (Paley, 1952). Cooper (1975b) produced a careful post-mortem on the Paley report, with the result that, although USA national output (GNP) was growing considerably faster than the Paley Commission expected, the consumption of most minerals was overestimated, in some cases by a very large amount (*Table 4.2*).

Cooper also searched for an explanation for these large deviations from the projections in the 'thoughtful report, done with care'; relative price movements help to explain the differences in the case of about half the minerals but 'the relationship is weak'; improved secondary recovery of metals and the changed pattern of imports (i.e. finished goods rather than metals) do not sufficiently account for them. He, therefore, concludes that the falling ratio of material input to output reflects 'technical and managerial changes'. Since many of the managerial changes presumably consisted of innovations of various natures, technology appears paramount in having reduced the relative needs. The rest of this section therefore deals with technological aspects in some detail.

Chart 4.1

Copper: the average metal content of ore produced and the relative price of refined copper (a)

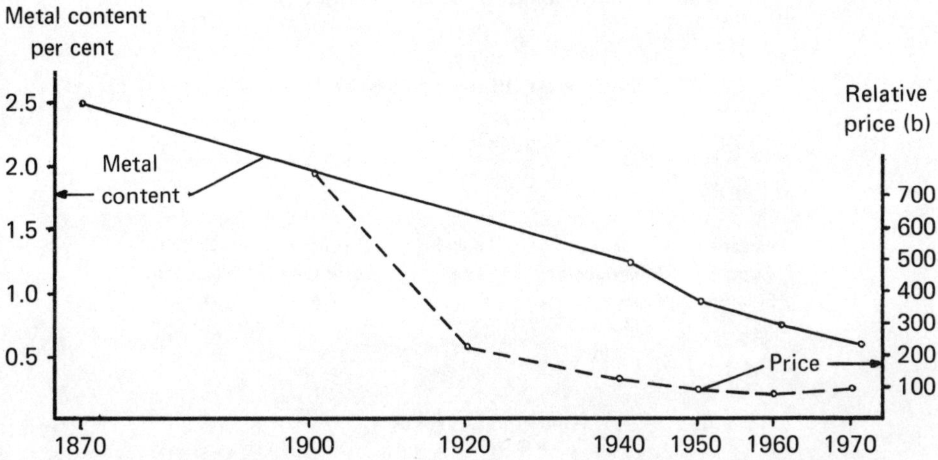

Data:	1870	1941	1951	1961	1971		1900	1920	1940	1950	1960	1970
Ore:	2,5	1,22	0,97	0,82	0,65	Price:	785	226	121	99	82	100

(a) All data concern the USA except for 1870 which indicates the ore content of Anglesey (UK) copper, the price leader at the time. In the first half of the 19th century Cornwall (UK) was the leading producer: the Cu content of Cornish ore was about 13 per cent.

(b) Price per ton of copper divided by the (US) average hourly wage rate in manufacturing, 1970 = 100.

Source: for ores, Sir Kingsley Dunham, 'How Long Will Our Minerals Last', *New Scientist,* 17 January 1974; for prices, W.D. Nordhaus, 'Resources as a Constraint on Growth', *American Economic Review,* vol. LXIV, no. 2, May 1974.

The exponential growth of demand for industrial materials, whether renewable or not, could not have been satisfied but for the rapid advance in science and technology (5). Progress on all fronts has characterised the past long period in the area of industrial materials. Exploration methods have been improving through advances in geology, in geophysical techniques and, more recently, in the use of satellites (6). New materials have become 'resources' as a result of scientific and technological advance discovering and

Table 4.2

The Paley Commission's projections assessed

Per cent deviation of actual from projected (a)

Overforecast (16 commodities) by

0-10	11-20	21-50	51-100	over 100
3	5	2	3	3
Manganese Copper Sulphur	Pig iron Molybdenum Tungsten Mercury Zinc	Nickel Lead	Chromium Antimony Tin	Cobalt Magnesium Titanium

Underforecast (5) by

0-10	11-20	21-50	over 50
1	2	1	1
Fluorspar	Aluminium Phosphate	Potash	Platinum

(a) The projections were for 1950 – 1975, the actuals are for 1972. They concern US consumption.

Source: Cooper, R.N., 'Resource Needs Revisted', *Brookings Papers an Economic Activity,* no. 1, 1975, Washington. Coal, petroleum and natural gas omitted.

developing their use (7). The natural resource base has also been significantly widened by process innovations (8). Methods of both underground and opencast/strip mining have changed almost out of recognition (9). Product development reduced the material content of the final product (10) and technologies aimed at re-using materials were improved and introduced (11). New requirements produced new uses for materials (12) and a long list of synthetic materials — the results of the 'molecular architecture' of modern chemistry (13).

The present

Spectacular developments characterise the 'present' which is defined here as the period 1972 – 80. Money prices of industrial materials generally doubled during the 1972 – 74 boom. It started with the upswing in the 'textile cycle' of wool prices; other commodities rapidly followed. The anatomy of this boom has been studied by several scholars (14). The very strong upswing of real consumption was coupled with a sudden upsurge of speculative demand fuelled by the rapidly rising rate of worldwide inflation and various adverse influences on the supply side (such as natural disasters, weather, sudden bottlenecks) – these were, briefly, the factors that sparked off the boom, which was exceptional in having occurred in peacetime. All the earlier peaks were the outcome of war. In earlier times – as far as documented history and information go – peaks were always followed by prices returning to somewhere near their starting level prior to the boom. This time, although there was a fall in 1975, caused by the deepest economic recession in the Western world since the war, it was rather modest, leaving the price of most commodities in 1975 still well above their level before the boom and already the weak recovery in 1976 – 77 pushed them back near their peak. A marked rise to 1980 followed, but that was due to worldwide inflation. In real terms the story was different: real prices of minerals and metals declined from the low 1975 level a little to 1978 and then improved to 1980, whilst those of materials of agricultural origin rose markedly in 1976 and fluctuated around that higher level to 1980.

The struggle for access to resources, mentioned above, did not materialise: practically any quantity of any material was available in the period 1975 to 1980 – at a price. There were even considerable surpluses, which were either taken up by stockholders, often government-backed and hence financially strong, in order to avoid a price collapse (e.g. in wool), or depressed the market to the extent of prices being reduced below the production costs of the less well endowed producers (e.g. copper). These eventually started slowly to pull down aggregate prices, but they remained at a historically high level. All this happened in an atmosphere characterised by three phenomena. The first was the example of OPEC – a clear case of an association of producers successfully raising its income. (The higher energy prices, of course, contributed to the higher price level for industrial materials.) Second, there were the attempts of primary producing countries to introduce a 'new international economic order' in the course of the various 'North-South' dialogues, within UNCTAD and elsewhere (and which, so far, have not led to any agreed solution). Third, as the outcome of the previous two factors, there was a proliferation of producers' associations.

Although most of the latter were not – or not admittedly – founded as price-raising cartels, the possibility that sooner or later they would attempt to become one is obvious. OPEC's example is too tempting despite obvious differences between oil and any other commodity in terms of importance in world trade and many other factors which have been analysed in detail elsewhere (15). There are many conditions for a cartel to be successful. Among them are high concentration of exports among a few countries; inelastic demand for the commodity; inelastic supply from non-cartel sources; lack of substitutes or their inelastic supply; crudely comparable costs of production among the cartel members (16) and a high degree of homogeneity in more general terms among exporters (17). The degree of reliance on the export of the cartelised product can make a difference (18); the extent of control over production can influence producing countries' governments whose political and social stability also play a part in their decisions (19), the nature of the product and the possible reaction of consumers or consuming countries to any producer action can also vary, the reactions — apart from the price effect — being political or economic or both (20); and so forth. There are very few commodities whose producers can successfully fulfil these conditions. This, presumably, is the main reason for the relatively limited success of recent cartelisation attempts in the face of the large number of producers' associations, with mostly, but by no means exclusively, LDC membership. The latter range from iron ore to bananas and number about a dozen, but only those concerning bauxite (21) and phosphates (22) have so far had partial and limited success in raising prices.

The chances of success for new commodity cartels are not highly rated (see e.g. the appended references [8] and [9]). Nevertheless, it cannot be denied that in a few cases potential monopoly gains for a limited period may make 'attempts at cartelisation a worthwhile gamble' (appended reference [9]). This, in turn, would not necessarily lead to interruption of supply; rather, it can mean increased costs to consumers, at least for a while, until new resources can be tapped or substitutes developed. A recent thorough study of the experience of previous international commodity cartels seems to support this cautiously negative attitude, as opposed to the view that cartels may become a predominant feature of commodity markets in the foreseeable future (23).

The future

Some recent developments will have implications for the future. First, many branches of primary production have become more expensive relative to other activities because increasingly restrictive environmental regulations hit, for obvious reasons, extraction and other primary activities more than other sectors; because royalty charges and taxes on primary production have increased sharply, as host countries understandably endeavour to enlarge their piece of the cake; and because primary production carries more of the burden of higher energy costs since it tends to use more energy than secondary or tertiary activities (Tilton, 1977b). Second, costs of exploration are increasing and the chances of success decreasing (24). Third, since the location of new projects tends to be more and more remote, the cost of allied infrastructural investment has been growing gradually, especially in developing areas where, apart from the productive equipment itself, water and power supply, transport and community facilities, etc. all have to be created (25).

Finally, there are doubts concerning the ability of the mining industry to supply abruptly rising requirements in the medium term (i.e. in the mid-1980s) because of the relative lack of investment during the recent recession and the following years, when metal prices, and hence profitability, were low; since the opening of a new mine may take up to six to eight years a sudden upturn of demand could find some branches of the primary industries unprepared. Furthermore, it is questionable whether capital and skills will continue to flow into the development of primary resources in non-industrial countries under threats of nationalisation, or of irresistible pressure by host governments to change the financial conditions (taxation, royalties, participation) which provided the basis for investment. At present there is no institutional arrangement for reducing this risk to the investor. There has already been a noticeable movement away from the LDCs: 'it is not geological endowment alone that have made Australia and Canada especially, and Brazil and South Africa to a lesser extent, the principal recipients of OECD mineral investment outside the US in the last ten to fifteen years' (Manners, 1977). Whilst it is true that the LDCs in recent years exported only a little more than one third of all the ores and minerals entering international trade (Fried, 1976) and (Landsberg, 1976), the further development of their mineral wealth is nevertheless necessary to meet future global needs. The nationalisation of primary production also influences future development in another, more complex, way: hitherto the lion's share of prospecting and exploration, and of the production of minerals was concentrated in the hands of large, mostly transnational companies, which ensured a high degree of geographical flexibility for exploration and investment capital. The international mining industry was therefore largely self-financing: profits earned in one country would easily be moved to finance exploration and investment in another. With nationalisation, however, that flexibility has been diminished, since no nationalised industry in any country can provide funds for exploration elsewhere. Whilst this is understandable and proper, it narrows the capital base for further development on an international scale.

Thus, acts of man — from cartelised cutbacks to lack of investment in productive facilities — can cause interruptions in supply in the future, but these are likely to be of short duration. Acts of God — such as adverse weather, floods, earthquakes and other natural disasters — are essentially unpredictable and unpreventable, but again they are unlikely to cause very long-lasting disturbances; also, they are a greater risk for industrial materials of agricultural origin than for mining products, though of course the latter are not exempt.

We come now to the vexed problem of the more remote future and, inescapably, to that of reserves — resources of non-renewable materials and the future production potential for renewable materials. *Table 4.3* analyses various relevant pieces of information for 36 major minerals (coal, oil and gas are omitted, but uranium is included); it shows (a) 1975 reserves, (b) avarage production in 1972 — 74, (c) their postwar growth rate of production, (d) their life expectancy assessed in three ways: taking the 1972 — 74 rate of production as static, assuming production continues to rise at postwar rates, and assuming it rises at 70 per cent of the rate (26). The addition to reserves between 1950 and 1975 is

Life expectancies of world

Mineral/metal (a)	Unit (b)	1975 reserves (b)	1972-74 average annual production (b)	1947-74 growth rate of production p.c.
(i)				
Antimony	000	4301	70	2.4
Arsenic AS_2O_3	000	4536	46.8	– 0.6
Asbestos	000	87090	4000	6.5
Barite ($BaSO_4$)	mn	181.4	4.3	4.1
Bauxite ore (e)	mn	17280	69.7	9.8
Bismuth	000	88.5	4.2	4.4
Cadmium	000	1270	17.0	4.7
Chromium ore	mn	1724	6.5	5.3
Cobalt	000	2449	25.3	5.8
Copper	mn	408.2	7.0	4.8
Diamond industrial	mn (b)	680.0	31.4	5.4
Fluorspar 90 % CaF_2	mn	106.1	4.5	7.5
Gold	000	42.0	1.3	2.4
Ilmenite conc.	mn	526.2	3.4	9.5
Iron	mn	90718	500	7.0
Lead	mn	145.1	3.5	3.8
Manganese	mn	1905	10.1	6.5
Mercury	000	181.0	9.4	2.0
Molybdenum	000	5987	71.6	7.3
Nickel	mn	53.98	0.7	6.9
Phosphate rock	mn	16066	99.4	7.3
Platinum group metals	000	17.45	0.2	9.7
Potash K_2O	mn	99790	22.2	9.0
Silver	000	189.7	9.3	2.2
Sulphur	mn	2032	46.8	6.7
Tin	000	10364	200	2.7
Tungsten	000	1769	39.0	3.8
Vanadium	000	9707	15.7	11.1
Zinc	mn	136.1	5.6	4.7
(ii) (f)				
Columbium	000	10000	11.6	5.0*
Germanium	tonnes	1815	87.5	4.0*
Rutile	000	12400	320	7.0*
Selenium	000	170	1.2	4.0*
Tantalum	000	59	0.45	3.0*
Uranium U_3O_8 (g)	000	2175	24.0	15.0*
Zirconium	000	29935	454	4.0*

(a) Reserve figures relate to the metal content unless otherwise stated. – (b) Metric tons except for diamonds (carat). – (c) After 1950 - 75 extraction. – (d) See text, A = substitution very difficult or unsolved. D = easy substitution. – (e) Only ores containing more than 50 % aluminium. – (f) Life

Table 4.3

reserves of selected minerals

Life expectancy in years: at 1972-74 rate of consumption	at past growth continuing	at 70 % of past growth rate	Addition to reserves 1950-75 p.c. (h)	1975 reserves, 1950 = 100 (c) (h)	Substitutability (d)
61	38	43	60	120	C
97	145	124	..	..	C
22	14	15	280	120	A
42	25	28	..	..	A
248	35	44	1100	120	D
21	15	16	..	..	D
75	33	38	..	..	C
265	53	65	1700	170	D
97	34	40	260	310	C
58	28	33	400	400	C
22	15	16	160	120	D
24	14	16	700	480	A
32	24	26	120	130	B
155	30	38	..	..	C
181	39	48	400	470	A
42	25	28	430	360	C
189	41	51	310	380	A
19	16	17	190	140	B
84	28	33	50	150	B
77	28	33	280	380	B
162	36	45	450	620	A
87	24	29	2500	2200	C
4495	70	92	1500	2000	A
20	17	18	140	120	D
43	21	24	550	500	A
52	33	36	140	170	D
45	27	30	–	75	B
618	40	52	..	..	C
24	17	18	210	190	C
862		78	..	..	C
21		15	..	..	C
39		19	..	..	B
142		48	..	..	C
131		54	..	..	D
91		19	..	..	A
66		33	..	..	B

expectancy based on *projected* rate of extraction, as shown in col. 5, marked *. – (g) Reserves at US $ 30/1 b, consumption for 1974–76. – (h) Rounded.

Source: Commodity Data Summaries 1976, US Bureau of Mines; Tilton (1977b) and Crowson (1977).

then shown and the 1975 reserves are compared with those in 1950 (after extraction in the intervening 25 years). Finally, the minerals listed are classified into four groups, based on information collected from published sources and from the trade, which gives an arbitrary indication of their substitutability.

Before further discussion of the concept of reserves (27) (and of why the figures in the table should be treated with caution), it already appears that there are only three minerals with a life expectancy of less than 25 years *and* very limited possibilities of substitution: asbestos, fluorspar and uranium. In the first two cases, the addition since 1950 to the reserves then known was significant, whilst for uranium, reserves are assessed at a given price level and it is known that at higher prices more are (already now) available. Among other minerals with an expected reserve life of less than twentyfive years, we find some for which comparable synthetic substitutes are in commercial use (diamonds, quartz, rutile), some for which technological change has reduced demand (e.g. mercury), others which are known to be available in much larger quantities at higher prices (e.g. silver) or for which eventual resources are estimated to exceed by many orders of magnitude the reserves as recorded now (e.g. zinc). Again others are subject to intensive research and it can be hoped that eventually complete substitutes will be found (bismuth, germanium).

The substitution of one mineral for another has, of course, to be regarded with some caution, because of the 'domino effect' which can be encountered when one scarce product is replaced in its major use by another, which will then itself become scarce in turn. There are, however, factors to be borne in mind which point in the other — more optimistic — direction.

First, no one has as yet found it necessary to know the absolute limit of resources and no one has been motivated to try to find out. Producers of any mineral are, as a rule, quite satisfied if the known reserves cover ten to twenty years' requirements and are not easily persuaded to spend money and scarce resources on prospecting and exploration for excess reserves which would not come into production for over twenty years. 'Reserves' therefore are a dynamic concept: as the known reserves are exploited, further areas are explored and new deposits found which add to the reserves. The relevant columns of *Table 4.3* provide powerful evidence for this argument.

Secondly, a very large part of the earth has not yet been explored. Even in the United States, which can be supposed to be in the forefront of this activity, major finds of mineral deposits have been announced practically every year. Elsewhere exploration is much further behind; for example, three quarters of Argentinia has been geologically classified as rich in minerals, but only one third has been explored (Surrey and Page, 1975).

Thirdly, reserves depend on price. At higher prices it becomes worthwhile to exploit reserves which at lower prices are not considered commercially viable (28). Estimates made a few years ago, and reproduced in *Chart 4.2,* indicate the relationship between reserves and price for four important metals: for example, a 40 per cent increase in the price of iron ore would double the reserves which are commercially exploitable. The relationship between price and reserves may change, but for most minerals its tendency

Chart 4.2

Commercially recoverable resources of four major ores under selected price assumptions

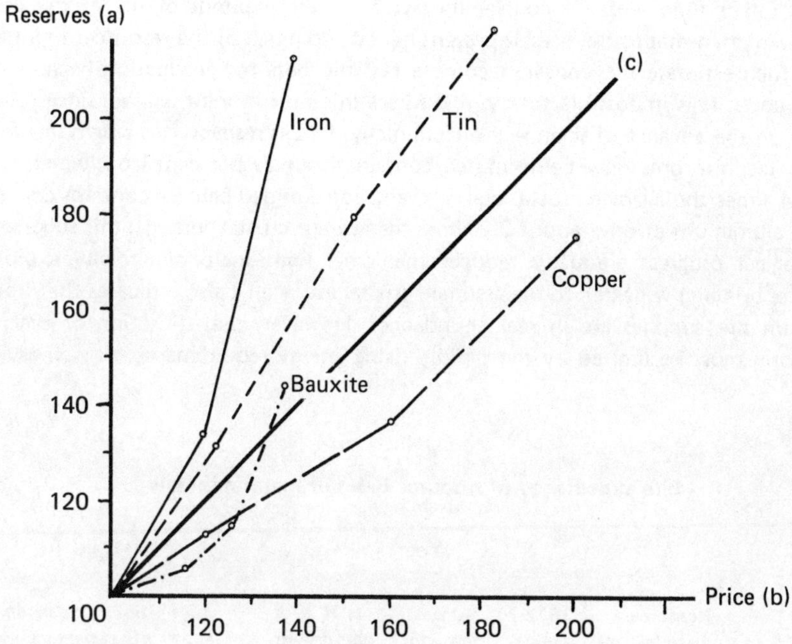

Data:

Bauxite					*Iron ore*				
price	100	115	126	137	price	100	119	138	
reserves	100	104	113	143	reserves	100	133	212	
Copper					*Tin*				
price	100	120	160	200	price	100	122	152	183
reserves	100	112	136	174	reserves	100	131	179	218

(a) Estimated reserves at given price levels, 1969 = 100
(b) 1969 = 100; in constant 1969 dollars
(c) 1 : 1 relationship.

Source: Bosson and Varon (1977), page 226.

is such that in Houthakker's view (Houthakker, 1976) 'the world will never run out of any non-renewable resource provided prices are allowed to adjust'. This and similar views are based on the crustal abundance of the earth: Manners (1977) writes, for example: 'A cubic kilometer of the earth's crust contains some 200 million tons of aluminium, 100 million tons of iron ore, 800 thousand tons of zinc and 200 thousand tons of copper'. A crude comparison of the life expectancy of some of the major metals based on crustal abundance with that calculated on present reserves is given in *Table 4.4.* On this basis, life expectancy is many times that of the present reserves; it is to be counted in hundreds of years rather than tens. Of course, the average metal content of the earth's crust is much lower than that of the ores at present mined and much of the resources represented by any such estimate may never become a realistic base for production because of increasing costs. It is impossible to say now where this cut-off point will be, since it largely depends on the advance of science and technology. In this respect, it is worth mentioning that the taconite ores now being mined contain about 27 per cent iron, which is only some 3.4 times the average crustal content, and some mined bauxite contains concentrations of aluminium at only about 2.2 times the average crustal content; this suggests that technological progress gradually reduces the lower limit for commercially exploitable resources, bringing it nearer to the assumed crustal average (it also indicates that iron and aluminium ore supplies are in real abundance). However, the utilisation of ever more diffuse ores must be limited by the rapidly rising energy requirements, as well as by the

Table 4.4

Life expectancy of resource bases of major minerals

Years

	Resource base (a)	At 1972-74 rate of consumption (b) (i)	At past growth rate continuing (b) (ii)	At 70 % of past growth rate (iii)	*For comparison:* life expectancy of 1975 *reserves* (c) (i)	(ii)	(iii)
Aluminium (d)	2.0×10^{18}	166×10^{9}	275	388	248	35	44
Copper	1.5×10^{15}	214×10^{6}	408	579	58	28	33
Iron	1.4×10^{18}	2.8×10^{9}	320	454	181	39	48
Lead	290×10^{12}	83×10^{6}	529	752	42	25	28
Tin	40.8×10^{12}	204×10^{6}	717	1021	52	33	36
Zinc	2.2×10^{15}	393×10^{6}	430	610	24	17	18

(a) The figures represent the estimated quantity of minerals found in the earth's crust (i.e. elemental abundance per metric ton times the total weight of the crust). — (b) The 1972 - 74 rate of consumption and the past (1947 - 74) rate of growth are given in *Table 4.3.* — (c) As in *Table 4.3.* — (d) The last three columns concern bauxite ore (containing more than 50 % aluminium) only.

Source: Tilton, John E., *The Future of Non-fuel Minerals* (Brookings, 1977).

environmental problems posed in dealing with the waste materials produced, and the disturbance caused to nature by the extension of mining. This is the point when 'backstop' technologies must come in, taking a number of forms from straightforward substitution to the transformation of the final product. If it is allowed to work, the price mechanism will always give the signal — although it is important to remember that in some cases the material cost of the final product is relatively small (29); then the importance of the signal may be belittled and the adjustment may require a long lead time.

The likelihood is that long before reserves, exploitable at a cost considered commercially viable, near exhaustion, science and technology will point to new solutions of the problem which emerges. This at least has been the case in the past. Whilst history does not necessarily repeat itself and thus there is no absolute guarantee of such an outcome, there is plenty of evidence for trusting that if mankind is in danger of running out of some non-renewable industrial material it will learn how to live without it.

Table 4.5

Scrap recovery in major consuming areas, 1976

	Recovery in per cent of domestic consumption					
	UK	EEC (a)	USA	Canada	Australia	Japan
Aluminium	46	37	30	10	15	35
Copper (c)	19	16	18	13	25	9
Lead	22	28	46	68	(b)	27
Tin	41	37	27	4	8	14
Zinc (d)	28	(b)	24	3	9	13

(a) Including UK. — (b) Not available. — (c) Excluding scrap directly used by manufacturers. — (d) All types; crude estimates.

Source: Metal Statistics, Metallgesellschaft AG.

One obvious means of helping to prolong the lifetime of reserves as known at present is the recovery of scrap — recycling. *Table 4.5* indicates the great differences between the major consuming areas in scrap recovery, showing how much can be done in this relatively simple matter by dissemination of best practice techniques (which, of course, concern technological, institutional and many other aspects, including the pricing of scrap).

Little has been said so far of renewable materials, that is those originating in agriculture and forestry. Being reproduceable, their problems are different and the main constraint on their production is the availability of land in suitable climates. Since industrial materials such as cotton or rubber compete for the land with basic food, it is a constraint of some importance, especially in developing countries where population growth is rapid and pressure to produce more food may be overwhelming. There are, however, considerations on the other side too. First, many of these materials are replaceable by manmade materials (30). Second, there still are areas where production is possible that are not yet utilised; they may be less suitable than the land already under cultivation but there will come a time when, with rising price levels, it becomes economic to draw them into production. Third, yields can be raised; indeed, differences in yields are very large and we are far from even considering the application of best practice techniques everywhere. Fourth, agricultural technology is also advancing, resulting in high-yield and more resilient varieties which also mature more rapidly — often helped by scientific progress in other areas (31). Finally, whilst many developing countries have in the past devoted insufficient attention to agriculture, there are signs now in some of their future plans of more emphasis on agricultural development; this may help the future supply of industrial materials as well.

Conclusions

Nothing can be said with absolute certainty about the future, but insofar as one can predict at all, the supply of industrial materials, whether renewable or not, does not seem to be jeopardised by the exhaustion of resources in the foreseeable future. This is the view for the rest of this century, and probably for much longer. The possibility of man-made shortages — caused by political upheavals, or artificial cutbacks for any reason — cannot be wholly excluded, but they, as well as other adverse influences, are unlikely to affect the normal flow of supplies more than temporarily. In the more remote future, new discoveries will add to the present reserves of non-renewable materials, and at higher prices more and more mineral deposits will become commercially exploitable. Even further, in the next century or later, production costs of some minerals may become prohibitively high, but on past experience there is reasonable hope for trusting that by then, or possibly long before, science and technology will find the way to bypass this problem.

Thus, while preoccupation with the future of non-renewable resources is right for a number of reasons — to draw attention to them, and to encourage 'intergenerational equity' — there appears to be no reason for immediate anxiety.

Footnotes

(1) Examples being an inaugural lecture at University College London (Beckerman, 1972), the Richard T. Ely Lecture to the annual meeting of the American Economic Association (Solow, 1974), or the Chester Beatty lecture to the Royal Society of Arts (Manners, 1977).

(2) *The Economist* indicator is a 'chain' index, reweighted annually according to the most recent pattern of trade; cotton had a very big weight in the 19th century (Ray, 1977).

(3) In their careful study Barnett and Morse found that the index of labour-plus-capital input per unit of mineral output in the United States fell from 210 in 1870 (1929 = 100) to 47 in 1957 (Barnett and Morse, 1963).

(4) It concerns Lake Superior iron ore, which did indeed become exhausted as foreseen by Leith (although somewhat later than he expected), but was replaced by taconite, an iron ore bearing rock which in Leith's time was not considered ore at all and certainly could not have been considered an economic proposition because of its much lower iron content (Anderson, 1977).

(5) For more details, see — among other works — Rosenberg (1973 and 1976), Hueckel (1975) and Beckerman (1974).

(6) These helped greatly in the discovery of the bulk of iron ore and nickel deposits in Australia, bauxite in Brazil, copper in Papua-New Guinea, all of them unknown until around 1960. Recent photographs taken by satellite have uncovered a large copper deposit in the US, in an area where previous geological searching had found nothing worthwhile (Perlman, 1974). Offshore exploration is another relatively new departure, made possible by a long chain of innovations in various areas of technology.

(7) Originally, there was only neutral matter in nature; a material became a natural resource when man began to use it for any particular purpose. Coal was a useless black rock until man, having discovered that it gave warmth, started to burn it. Bauxite did not even have a name before it was discovered that it could be processed into aluminium. Other clays also are being used now in the USSR for the same purpose.

(8) One example is taconite, as already mentioned, replacing the much richer Lake Superior iron ore. The rich coal reserves of Pennsylvania could not be used in ironmaking because of their low gas content until the 'hot blast' furnace was introduced in 1828 (Rosenberg, 1972). The Thomas-Gilchrist process enabled the French to use, from about 1880, the high-phosphoric iron ore — 'minette' — of Lorraine in their iron industry (Landes, 1969).

(9) The idea of strip mining was born out of experience gained in digging the Panama Canal; developments, which yielded the huge 150 — 200 ton truck or the 15 cubic yards shovel used now in strip mines, made possible the economical use of low-grade ores. The various phases of underground mechanisation led to the remote control of face operations.

(10) The miniaturisation of many products was a great help in this direction. Improved processes helped to reduce the amount of tin required for the production of tinplate, by about 25 per cent, in the 1960s.

(11) Methods of recycling metals were greatly improved, but in other areas there have been advances as well — e.g. the de-inking of newspaper for re-pulping.

(12) Titanium is one example: it accounted for only 2 per cent of the airframe structure weight of both the Trident and the Boeing 727, but made up 9 per cent of the Boeing 747 some ten years later (Ray, 1975).

(13) The best known examples are synthetic rubber and man-made fibres. The first — rubber — indicates how rapidly technology can respond to pressing shortages: from very small beginnings the German Reich almost covered its total requirements during World War II with synthetic rubber and, similarly, when the USA was cut off from the usual sources of supply, an industry was built up, producing, after the small experimental output in 1940 of about 3000 tons, 944,000 tons

only four years later (Hölscher, 1972). Without man-made fibres world production of cotton, wool and jute would have to be more than doubled; whilst this may perhaps not be inconceivable, it certainly could not be done without producing on submarginal land and at a heavy cost to basic food production in all climatically possible areas, including countries that could ill afford it. The various 'plastics' materials, with wide ranging properties, hardly need detailed mention. Moreover, there are less well known examples of more recent vintage, such as synthetic cryolite (to replace this material used in aluminium smelters, the unique source of which in Greenland was exhausted); man-made radio-isotopes to replace radium; synthesised polycrystalline diamonds which are now perfectly competitive with natural stones in many industrial applications; and 'cultured' quartz crystals to supplement the limited resources of natural quartz crystals of a grade suitable for electronic use.

(14) The most detailed is probably that of Cooper and Lawrence (1975).

(15) Among others, Connelly and Perlman (1975), Landsberg (1976), Tilton (1975) and Fried (1976).

(16) For a long time, the high cost producer (Bolivia) was reluctant to join the International Tin Agreement – which is not a cartel – for want of higher price ranges.

(17) E.g. Sweden and Mauretania are unlikely partners in an iron ore cartel because of their very different political, economic and cultural heritage, attitudes and institutions.

(18) It determines whether the exporting country is able to sustain a loss in revenue stemming from production cutbacks.

(19) Banks (1977) writes: 'perhaps the most important factor to prevent the effective functioning of commodity cartels is the extensive nationalisation that has taken place in many of the less developed of the raw material producing countries; these ... have come to mean that – for political reasons – production must be maintained at as high a level as possible, regardless of profitability and of the level of investment'. The case of the depressed market, low price and enormous stocks in the copper industry in 1975 – 78 seems strongly to support this thesis.

(20) Brown (1974) points to the fact that the US and Canada control a greater share of the world's exportable supplies of grain than the Middle East does of oil. See also Fried (1976).

(21) This gave rise to Jamaica's huge increase in the tax/levy on exported bauxite, which was followed by other producers (Bergsten, 1976).

(22) The trebling of the price by the price leader, Morocco, had to be considerably reduced – although to a level still far in excess of the earlier price – under market pressure.

(23) Eckbo's study (1975) analysed 51 cartels in 18 industries for 'efficiency', defined in terms of the ability of the cartel to raise prices at least 200 per cent above the unit cost of production and distribution. He found that 19 of the 51 organisations (some of them not literally cartels) were efficient in these terms, but they were not long-lasting (4 – 6 years). In cases which were efficient, production was highly concentrated, demand inelastic, the cartel's market share was high, the members had cost advantages over outsiders, and governments were not involved in the cartel's operations. Eckbo's research covered a very long period and many of the conditions favouring cartels, or those leading to their breakdown, are not applicable in the modern world. (E.g. 'In 1838 the UK broke the Sicilian sulphur monopoly by sending gunboats'.)

(24) According to Banks (1977) it was estimated in 1973 that the cost of locating a single mineral deposit of copper, lead or zinc could range up to $ 0.5 million (by 1978 it was nearer $ 1 million) in an area of good mineral potential, and even then there was only a 1 :50 chance that it would prove to be worth exploiting.

(25) For example, in the ten years ending 1970, 65 per cent of the capital investment in eleven major projects in Western Australia was for infrastructural facilities — and this is not an unusually high proportion (Bosson and Varon, 1977). See also (Takeuchi and Thiebach, 1977).

(26) Based on the general expectation of economic growth in the next decades possibly lagging behind postwar rates.

(27) For detailed discussion, see (G.J.S. Govett and M.H. Govett, 1974), (Tilton, 1977a) and (Vogely, 1977).

(28) Typical examples are the Cornish tin mines or King Solomon's copper mine in the Negev. Exploitation of both started in ancient times, but costs of production rose and they came to a standstill until (well after World War II) prices of tin and copper again reached a level which made their reopening profitable.

(29) For example, the cost of bauxite ore accounts for only a small percentage of the aluminium metal and even less of the final product. Pick (1977) demonstrates that an engineering component worth £ 700 contains no more than £ 13, i.e. less than 2 per cent, worth of iron ore.

(30) More than half of the textile fibres and rubber consumed in recent years was man-made and the amount of wood replaced by a variety of other, mostly man-made, materials has also been increasing.

(31) For example, delaying the clotting of blood is a well known technique in medicine. Exactly the same technique is now used on Malayan rubber plantations; by applying the right preparation to the rubber tree clotting is delayed and the flow of latex increased.

References

[1] Anderson, R. (1977). 'Resource Conservation and Pricing', *Resources Policy,* vol. 3, no. 2, pp. 78 - 86.

[2] Banks, F.E. (1977), 'Natural Resource Availability: Some Aspects', *Resources Policy,* vol. 3, no. 1, pp. 2 - 12.

[3] Barnett, H. J. and Morse, C. (1963), *Scarcity and Growth* (Baltimore: Johns Hopkins University Press, for Resources for the Future) p. 8.

[4] Beckerman, W. (1972), 'Economists, Scientists and Environmental Catastrophe', *Oxford Economic Papers.*

[5] Beckerman, W. (1974), *In Defence of Economic Growth* (London: Jonathan Cape) pp. 215 - 240.

[6] Bergsten, C.F. (1976), 'A New OPEC in Bauxite', *Challenge,* pp. 12 - 20.

[7] Bosson, R. and Varon, B. (1977), *The Mining Industry and the Developing Countries,* (Oxford: Oxford University Press, for World Bank) p. 47.

[8] British-North American Committee (1976), *Mineral Development in the Eighties: Prospects and Problems* (London) pp. 7 - 9.

[9] Brookings Institution (1974), *Trade in Primary Commodities: Conflict or Cooperation? (Washington) pp. 26 - 33.*

[10] Brown, L.R. (1974), 'The Global Politics of Resource Scarcity', *Development Paper,* no. 17 (Washington: Overseas Development Council) p. 5 and 24.

[11] (US) Bureau of Mines, *Commodity Data Summaries, 1976* (Washington: US Dept. of the Interior).

[12] Cole, H.S.D., Freeman, C., Jahoda, M., Pavitt K.L.R. (eds), *Thinking About the Future* (London: Chatto & Windus, for Sussex University Press, 1973).

[13] Connelly, P. and Perlman, R., *The Politics of Scarcity* (Oxford: Oxford University Press, for Royal Institute of International Affairs, 1975).

[14] Cooper, R.N. (1975a), 'Natural Resources and National Security', *Resources Policy,* vol. 1, no. 4, pp. 192 - 203.

[15] Cooper, R.N. (1975b), 'Resource Needs Revisited', *Brookings Papers on Economic Activity,* no. 1, pp. 238 - 245.

[16] Cooper, R.N. and Lawrence R.Z. (1975), 'The 1972 - 75 Commodity Boom', *Brookings Papers on Economic Activity,* no. 3, pp. 671 - 723.

[17] Crowson, P. (1977), *Non-fuel Minerals and Foreign Policy* (With 'Data Base' by Crowson P. and Francis S.) (London: Royal Institute of International Affairs).

[18] Sir Dunham Kingsley (1947), 'How Long Will Our Minerals Last?', *New Scientist,* London, pp. 129 - 245.

[19] Eckbo, P.L. (1975), *OPEC and the Experience of Previous International Commodity Cartels.* Paper (mimeo) prepared for the US Department of the Interior, Washington.

[20] Forrester, J.W. (1971), *World Dynamics* (Cambridge, Mass.: Wright-Allen Press).

[21] Fried, E.R. (1976), 'International Trade in Raw Materials: Myths and Realities', *Science,* vol. 191, no. 4228, pp. 641 - 646.

[22] Gordon Scott (1973), 'Today's Apocalypses and Yesterday's', *American Economic Review,* vol. 63, no. 2, pp. 106 - 110.

[23] Govett, G.J.S. and Govett, M.H. (1974), 'The Concept and Measurement of Mineral Reserves and Resources', *Resources Policy,* vol. 1, no. 1, pp. 46 - 56.

[24] Hölscher, F. (1972), *Kautschuke, Kunststoffe, Fasern,* BASF, Ludwigshafen, p. 32.

[25] Houthakker, H.S. (1976), 'The Economics of Nonrenewable Resources', Harvard Institute of Economic Research, *Discussion Paper,* no. 493, p. 10.

[26] Hueckel, G. (1975), 'A Historical Approach to Future Economic Growth', *Science,* vol. 187, pp. 925 - 931.

[27] Jevons, W.S. (1865), *The Coal Question* (London: Macmillan).

[28] Landes, D.S. (1969), *The Unbound Prometheus: Technological Change and Industrial Development in Western Europe from 1750 to the Present* (Cambridge: Cambridge University Press) p. 460.

[29] Landsberg, H.H. (1976), 'Energy and Materials: How they Differ in the International Context', *Engineering and Mining Journal,* pp. 63 - 71.

[30] Leith, C.K. (1935), *Science,* reprinted in McKenzie G. and Utgard R. (eds), *Man and his Physical Environment* (Minneapolis: Burgess, 1975) and quoted in Anderson (1977).

[31] Leontief, W. (1977), *Structure, System and Economic Policy* (Cambridge: Cambridge University Press).

[32] Manners, G. (1977), 'Three Issues of Minerals Policy', *The Royal Society of Arts Journal,* vol. CXXV, no. 5251, pp. 386 - 396.

[33] Meadows, D.L., Meadows, D.H., Randers, J. and Behrens, W.W. (1972), *The Limits to Growth* (London: Earth Island).

[34] Metallgesellschaft AG, *Metal Statistics,* 64th edition, 1966 - 1976, Frankfurt am Main 1977.

[35] Nordhaus, W.D. (1974), 'Resources as a Constraint on Growth', *American Economic Review,* vol. LXIV, no. 2, pp. 22 - 26.

[36] Page, R.W. (1973), 'Non-renewable Resources Subsystem', in [12], pp. 33 - 42.

[37] (Paley) *Resources for Freedom* (1952), A Report to the President by the Materials Policy (Paley) Commission (Washington: USGPO) (five volumes).

[38] Pavitt, K.L.R. (1973), Malthus and other economists, in [12], pp. 137 - 158.

[39] Pearce, D.W., Rose, J. (eds) (1975), *The Economics of Natural Resource Depletion* (London: Macmillan).

[40] Pehrson, E.W. (1945), 'The Mineral Position of the United States and the Outlook for the Future', *Mining and Metallurgy Journal,* no. 26.

[41] Perlman, R. (1974), 'Is the World Running out of Raw Materials?', *International Affairs* (Chatham House), vol. 50, no. 3, pp. 416 - 424.

[42] Petersen, F.M. and Fisher, A.C. (1977), 'The Exploitation of Extractive Resources: A Survey', *Economic Journal,* vol. 87, no. 348, pp. 681 - 721.

[43] Pick, H.J. (1977), 'Materials, Resources and Production: An Engineer's View', in [31], p. 146.

[44] Ray, G.F. (1975), 'Raw Materials, Shortages and Producer Power', *Long Range Planning,* pp. 2 - 16.

[45] Ray, G.F. (1977), 'The "Real" Price of Primary Products', *National Institute Economic Review,* no. 81, pp. 72 - 76.

[46] Rosenberg, N. (1972), *Technology and American Economic Growth* (New York: Harper & Row).

[47] Rosenberg, N. (1973), 'Innovative Responses to Materials Shortages', *American Economic Review,* vol. 63, no. 2, pp. 111 - 118.

[48] Rosenberg, N. (1976), *Perspectives on Technology* (Cambridge: Cambridge University Press).

[49] Solow, R.M. (1974), 'The Economics of Resources or the Resources of Economics', *American Economic Review,* vol. LXIV, no. 2, pp. 1 - 14.

[50] Surrey, A.J. and Page W. (1975), 'Some Issues in the Current Debate About Energy and Natural Resources', in [39], p. 64.

[51] Takeuchi, K., Thiebach G.E., Hilmy S. (1977), 'Investment Requirements in the Non-fuel Mineral Sector in the Developing Countries', *Natural Resources Forum,* no. 1, pp. 263 - 275.

[52] Tilton, John E. (1975), 'Cartels in Metal Industries', *Earth and Mineral Sciences,* Univ. Park, Pa., vol. 44, no. 6, pp. 41 - 44.

[53] Tilton, J.E. (1977a), 'The Continuing Debate over the Exhaustion of Nonfuel Mineral Resources', *Natural Resources Forum,* no 1, pp. 167 - 173.

[54] Tilton, J.E. (1977b), *The Future of Non-fuel Minerals* (Washington: Brookings).

[55] Vogely, W.A. (1977), 'The State of our Mineral Position: A Provocation', *Technology Review,* pp. 65 - 68.

Chapter 5

THE DETERMINANTS OF TECHNICAL CHANGE IN THE CHEMICAL INDUSTRY: DEMAND-PULL OR TECHNOLOGY-PUSH?*

C. Freeman**, V. Walsh and J. Townsend

For many years now controversy has continued over the determinants of the direction and scale of inventive and scientific activity in contemporary industrialised societies. Participants in the debate have included economists, sociologists and scientific administrators as well as engineers, inventors and scientists. A related but more specialised controversy has raged among historians of science, between 'internalists' and 'externalists'.

The debate has been rather a confused and ill-structured one but crudely speaking there have been two poles, usually characterised as 'demand-pull' and 'science-push' (sometimes 'technology-push'), or more simply as demand theories and supply theories. Proponents of the first theory cite evidence purporting to demonstrate that market demand is the dominant influence determining the direction and scale of inventive activity (and in some versions, even of scientific activity). Proponents of the second theory hold that it is changes on the supply side, i.e. internal developments within science and technology, which mainly determine (or in weaker versions, permit) changes in the composition of output and the way in which it is produced.

As with the analogous theories of inflation in economics (cost-push and demand-pull), it is quite possible to subscribe to both theories or to elements of both theories. Most of those involved in the debate could in fact be described as 'hybrid' participants, or would at least disclaim the more extreme polarised viewpoints. Nevertheless, there are major contributors who are clearly identified with one or other pole in the debate, or who at least place the major emphasis on one side.

* This paper is based upon the results of a recent project carried out at the Science Policy Research Unit of the University of Sussex and supported by the Social Science Research Council, but it also draws upon the results of several earlier projects, most of which were carried out at the National Institute of Economic and Social Research at the time when Christopher Saunders was Director of the Institute. I should like to take this opportunity of expressing an enduring debt of gratitude and personal affection and respect for his continuous encouragement and for first orienting my applied research in the direction of the topic which has since become my main sphere of work.

** I should make it clear that although I was mainly responsible for this particular analytical summary of our project, my co-authors, Dr. Vivien Walsh and Mr. Joe Townsend were responsible with Dr. Basil Achilladelis for almost all the investigation upon which it is largely based. A fuller version of the detailed results is available in mimeographed form from the Science Policy Research Unit and will be published later.

As with the debate on inflation this is by no means a purely hairsplitting academic controversy. It clearly has major implications for industrial policy, investment decision-making and research policy. If the demand theories are valid, then social and market forecasting are fundamental for all these activities, but if the supply theories are correct then technological forecasting may be even more important. If the hybrid theories are substantiated then there is no escape from the difficult and complex task of combining social and technological forecasting. In view of the strong implications for government policy it is not surprising that some of those most actively involved in the discussion have themselves had responsibility for decision making. Nor would it surprise a sociologist of science to find that studies sponsored by agencies responsible for basic science (such as the National Science Foundation or the former Council for Scientific Policy in Britain) have tended to come up with findings which by-and-large might justify a 'science-push' interpretation, whilst studies sponsored by 'mission-oriented' departments, such as the Department of Defence, have come up with rather a different emphasis.

This does not necessarily justify a cynical view of the debate, although it does provide additional evidence of the extent to which the choice of subject matter and the emphasis of interpretation may be influenced by interest groups affected. The complexity of the issues and the poor information base mean that it is quite legitimate as in many branches of social science, to entertain the possibility of several different interpretations until further evidence shows more conclusively which of them (if any) has the greatest substance and justification.

However, during the 1960s it became rather fashionable to assume that the debate was over, and that it had ended in a clear victory on points, if not a technical knock-out, for the 'demand' school. This tendency was nourished above all by Schmookler's (1966) book but also by the findings of a series of empirical studies of industrial innovation, particularly in the USA and the UK, notably those by Myers and Marquis (1969), Langrish et al. (1972) and the US Department of Defence (Project Hindsight) (Sherwin and Isenson, 1967). In fact, as Mowery and Rosenberg (1979) have recently shown, few if any of these studies point unambiguously to the simple conclusion that market demand is the sole or even the principal determinant of the scale and direction of inventive or innovative activity (still less of scientific activity). Nevertheless, the results are often cited as though they did justify such a simple interpretation, and for this some of the authors of these studies must take part of the responsibility.

One of the reasons that these studies were so influential in strengthening the 'demand' school of interpretation was that they gave an appearance for the first time of quantitative, statistical support for this viewpoint, whereas previously it had been argued mainly on purely logical theoretical grounds or on the basis of individual case studies or anecdotes. The Myers and Marquis (1969) (Harvard) study was an analysis of 567 different innovations, the Langrish (1972) (Manchester) study was based on 84 industrial innovations. Project Hindsight (DOD) (Sherwin and Isenson, 1967) was a study of 30 major weapons projects involving several hundred new technical developments. The studies were in fact very different in scope and methodology, and none of them made any claims to be statistically representative. Nevertheless, they were frequently (if unjustifiably) jointly cited as providing firm evidence that demand was the mother of innovation, if not of invention.

Mowery and Rosenberg (1979) here pointed to several serious fallacies in the simple demand theories. Some confusion has been caused in the debate by the failure to distinguish clearly between 'need' and 'market demand'. It is only with the benefit of hindsight that we are able to classify an unmet social need or a potential demand as 'demand'. Another fundamental criticism is that they make little or no distinction between an 'autonomous' increase in market demand based on a change in consumer incomes or preferences (Figure 5.1), and an induced increase in demand based on a shift of the supply curve to the right and a movement along the demand curve (Figure 5.2). Clearly the latter case could frequently be based on technical inventions permitting a reduced cost of production and lower relative prices.

Figure 5.1

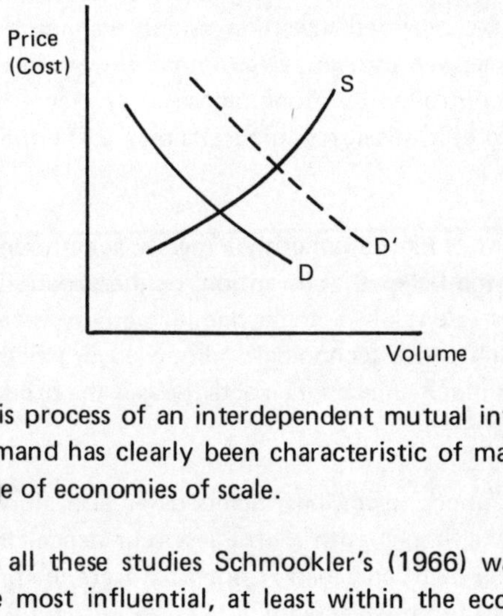

Figure 5.2

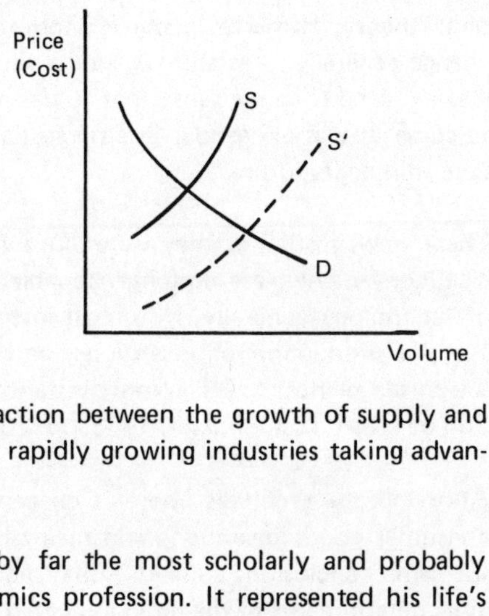

This process of an interdependent mutual interaction between the growth of supply and demand has clearly been characteristic of many rapidly growing industries taking advantage of economies of scale.

Of all these studies Schmookler's (1966) was by far the most scholarly and probably the most influential, at least within the economics profession. It represented his life's work, being the result of more than 15 years' patient research with patent statistics, assisted by the contribution of a number of able postgraduate students. His own premature death so soon after the publication of his major book was a tragic loss and greatly diminished the quality of the subsequent debate. No economist or historian before or since has had the patience or the imagination to make use of patent statistics in the interpretation of long-term trends in economic development and technical change with anything approaching the same success.

He summarised his own conclusions as follows:

'. . . the most striking and most significant result of the entire study . . . concerns the relation of capital goods output to the number of capital goods inventions. The relation is evident in time series involving a single industry, and in cross sections relating to several industries. When time series of investment (or capital goods output) and the number of capital goods inventions are compared for a single industry, both the long-term trend and long swings exhibit great similarities, with the notable difference that lower turning points in major cycles or long swings generally occur in capital goods sales before they do so in capital goods patents.

. . . The possibility that the results reflect the effect of capital goods inventions on capital goods sales is grossly implausible. In the time series comparisons, trend turning points tend to occur in sales before they do in patents and long swing troughs in sales generally precede those in patents. Moreover, trends and long swings in investment in the industries examined are adequately explained on other grounds.

. . . The fact that inventions are usually made because men want to solve economic problems or capitalise on economic opportunities is of overwhelming importance for economic theory. Hitherto, many economists have regarded invention — and technological change generally — as an *exogenous,* and some even thought, an *autonomous,* variable. It was exogenous in the sense that it was not controlled by economic variables. According to some, it was exogenous in a particular sense, it was autonomous, its own past entirely determining its future.

These views insofar as they were of a substantive nature rather than merely a methodological convenience, are no longer tenable . . . the belief that invention, or the production of technology generally, is in most instances essentially a non-economic activity is false . . . the production of inventions, and much other technological knowledge, whether routinised or not, . . . is in most instances as much an economic activity as is the production of bread' (Schmookler, 1966, pp. 204–208).

Although the emphasis above is on capital goods inventions, Schmookler also studied consumer goods inventions and maintained (although with a little less vehemence) that the same conclusions applied — that market growth and market potential were the principal determinants of the direction and scale of inventive activity.

Nevertheless, despite his remarkable achievement, he would have been the last to discourage critical debate on his findings and his interpretation. As in every branch of science the successors of a major theorist have the dual responsibility of building on past achievements without being so dazzled that they fail to see weaknesses or check the validity of received propositions in new or different circumstances. Consequently, although all of us very much respect Schmookler's achievements and regard his work as the major contribution to the post-war debate, we are equally convinced that the best way to demonstrate this respect is to attempt to go beyond his work, and to re-assess some of his conclusions.

Schmookler's study concentrated mainly on four major industries (railroads, petroleum refining, agricultural machinery and paper-making), but he also assembled data on 'all other' industries and could reasonably lay claim to a fairly comprehensive statistical coverage of the entire United States economy over the period 1840–1950. The exact terminal and starting points of his various statistical series varied a little, but most of them covered a period of about a century, ending usually some time in the 1950s.

The fact that his coverage was so comprehensive, that he spanned an entire century and that he was so careful about his method and definitions meant that his work was far less vulnerable to criticisms of bias and selectivity than several of the other contemporary studies which focussed on innovations rather than inventions. We share with him the belief that patents do provide the most useful, systematic and comprehensive set of information about inventive activity which is available over a long period; and on the whole we accept his defence of the legitimacy of using time series of patent statistics, with qualifications which will become apparent.

We differ from Schmookler in not accepting that aggregate trends in patent numbers (or scientific papers) are a wholly satisfactory surrogate for a more specific investigation of the relative importance of various discoveries, inventions and innovations and the complex way in which these interact. However hard it may be to measure, we believe that there is a real distinction between 'radical' and 'incremental' innovations and between 'master' patents and 'improvement' patents. From earlier work on the history of invention and innovation all of us were very much aware of the dangers of simplistic use of aggregated statistics, which may obscure as much as they reveal.

More recently, together with other colleagues, we have been involved in further work on trends in basic innovations in relation to long waves in economic development, which clearly brings out the importance of these distinctions (Clark, Freeman and Soete, 1981). Schmookler was well aware of the strength of this counter-argument and was at pains to justify his view that total numbers of patents and inventions gave a more representative picture of the main trends in industry than 'key' inventions, 'master' patents or basic scientific discoveries. (Schmookler, 1966, pp.18–19 and chapters 3 and 4).

Nevertheless his own evidence on 'important inventions' compared with patented inventions showed that in all the four major industries which he researched in depth the 'important invention' time series led the patent statistics in each field at the outset (Schmookler, 1966, p. 81). Although he dismissed this mainly on the grounds that the 'important' inventions were not really so 'important' as they appeared to those who listed them, most of his critics would certainly argue that this was one of the most vulnerable aspects of his entire theory.

This does not mean that we reject the value of Schmookler's technique of using the time trend of aggregate statistics of inventions (and in our case also of scientific papers), but we believe that this approach must be complemented by a more concrete type of historical investigation and particularly by an effort to gain a qualitative understanding of the major discoveries and inventions affecting the entire development of an industrial sector or product group. To be fair to Schmookler he also used this type of analysis in his own approach but he did so not in order to complement his purely statistical approach but in order to dismiss the whole idea that 'important' inventions really were so important after all. We remain convinced that it is necessary to make distinctions and in pursuit of this objective we have used some alternative measures. For example, in the drug industry we thought it particularly useful to discuss the category of 'new chemical entities' as well as simple patent numbers, and we believe that the divergence between these two series is particularly revealing.

Nevertheless, despite these important reservations we have preferred to take Schmookler's work as the point of departure for our own study, rather than the more numerous studies of innovation, which lacked any comparable data base. Like Schmookler we have made extensive use of patent statistics and tried to relate these to various indicators of production, investment and market growth. Our coverage, however, is less comprehensive, being confined to one industry — the chemical industry — and within that industry to a few major sub-sectors: plastics, dye-stuffs, pharmaceuticals and petrochemical intermediates.

We chose this industry for a variety of reasons, but perhaps the principal one was that we wished to test Schmookler's hypothesis not only for a more recent period — the post-war period — but also for an industry which could be described as 'R and D-intensive' or even as 'science intensive'. Although in their own time all of the four industries on which Schmookler concentrated his attention were certainly the field of considerable inventive efforts, none of them (with the possible exception of petroleum refining after 1920) could be described as 'science-intensive'. Yet the view that technology has recently come to depend to a greater extent than hitherto on new development in science is usually justified with respect to a few industries, notably chemicals and electronics.

We would ideally have liked to investigate several such industries; our more restricted coverage was due primarily to limitations of time. As Schmookler and his assistants found, the extraction, classification, enumeration and analysis of patents is an extremely time-consuming business. However, in one respect, we have gone beyond what Schmookler attempted. We have not only made use of longtime series of patent statistics, we have also attempted to use parallel time series of statistics of the publication of scientific papers. The use of these statistics was pioneered by an historian of science, Derek de Solla

Price; and again, whilst we recognise that there are serious methodological problems which have been raised by his critics, we nevertheless believe that for certain purposes their use has been vindicated and can provide valuable insights into long-term trends.

Our main purpose has been to use longtime series of scientific papers, patents, production and investment in several sectors of the chemical industry in order to throw some light on the 'push-pull' controversy, and to relate these series to a descriptive historical account of the same periods.

In our analysis we are taking Schmookler's theory as the most consistent and articulate exposition of a 'strong' market-leads-technology view and Hessen's (1931) standpoint as a strong representation of the view that technology also leads science. These theories are represented in an oversimplified schematic way in Diagrams 5.1 and 5.2.

Diagram 5.1

Schematic representation of Schmookler's model of demand-led invention

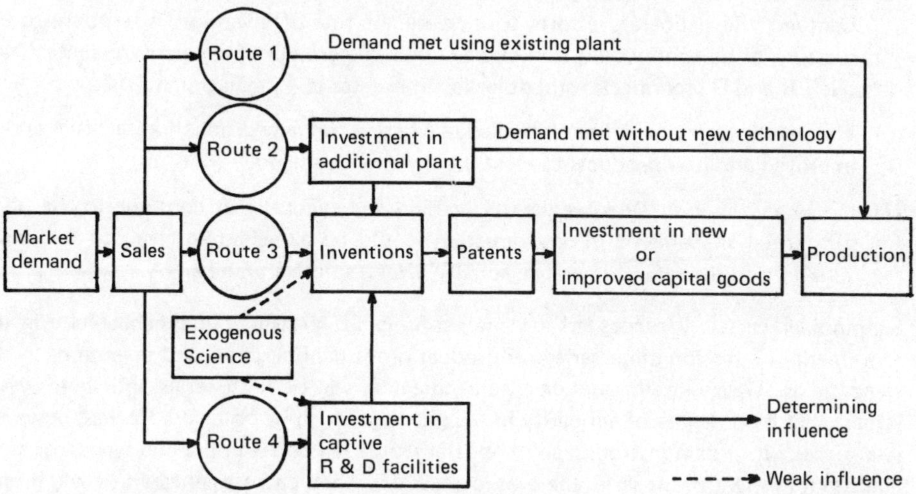

Diagram 5.2

Schematic representation of Hessen's model of technology and demand-led science

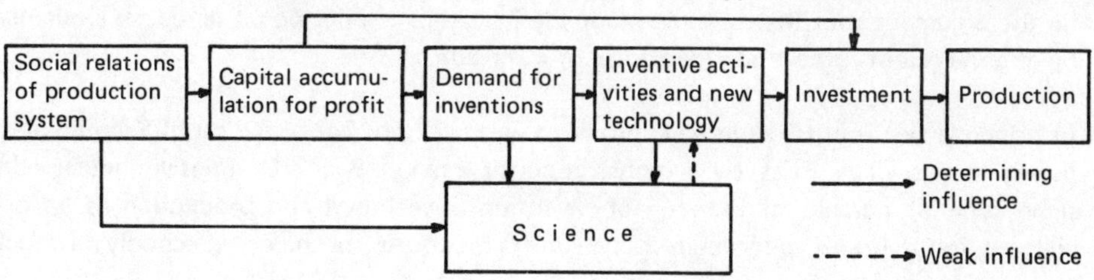

If Schmookler's view were correct then we would expect the following patterns to emerge from the type of analysis which he and we have made:

(1) Growth of market demand gives rise to increased production and investment to satisfy that demand.

(2) Initially, the increased demand may be met by using mainly, or entirely, existing knowledge (Routes 1 and 2 in Diagram 5.1).

(3) Within a few years, however, the strength of demand and the technical problems arising within the industry will generate increased inventive activities both within existing firms and outside them (Route 3). These increased efforts will generate a more or less proportionate increase in the rate of invention.

(4) This increased flow of inventions will be reflected in statistics of the number of patents (and other measures of inventive and innovative activity if they are available).

(5) On a very small scale in the 19th Century but much more generally in the 20th Century, the deliberate efforts to increase the rate of invention in response to the pressure of demand would find expression in the growth of company-financed ('captive') R and D laboratories and other facilities (Route 4 in Diagramm 5.1).

(6) The new inventions will be embodied in existing and new production facilities and in improved and new products to meet the increased demand.

(7) If demand should fall subsequently or fluctuate cyclically or continue to rise, then substantial movements in any direction would be expected to give rise to similar variations in the rate of inventive activity after a suitable time-lag.

Schmookler certainly succeeded in demonstrating a high degree of synchronicity in the movements of his longtime series on production of capital goods and inventions in the same fields. Wave-like fluctuations were characteristic of both series and there was a remarkably high degree of similarity in the patterns which he obtained. He was, however, less successful in demonstrating any consistent time lag between the two series, for as he admitted, in most of his series there were occasions when patents appeared to lead investment, as well as the (slightly more frequent) cases of investment leading patents. He rested his case therefore not on a general consistent lead of the investment series but on the argument that investment usually led the upswings from the low points (troughs), and on the argument that the movements of the investment series could be better explained by external events other than the course of invention.

In principle our results could have provided an important confirmation of Schmookler's theory in two ways. Frist, by demonstrating for a major R and D-intensive industry the same type of parallel movements of invention, investment and production as he discovered for railroads, petroleum, paper and agricultural machinery. Secondly, a much more powerful vindication would have been a demonstration that the investment and production series clearly led the inventions series.

The even stronger theory of market-demand leadership propounded by Hessen and some of his colleagues (1931) was of course advanced many years before Schmookler's work. Nevertheless it still represents a clear and forceful statement of a widely held view.

Hessen was concerned mainly to demonstrate the profound influence of the economy not only on technology but also on the most fundamental kind of science (Newtonian physics). Although he did not attempt the type of analysis which Schmookler undertook nor indeed use any quantitative indicators of scientific and technical activities, his argument ran on very similar lines to that of Schmookler with respect to technology. But whereas Schmookler had little to say about the technology-science relationship, Hessen was a firm proponent of the view that technology leads and science follows. His ideas are represented schematically in Diagram 5.2.

We do not know whether he would have accepted numbers of scientific papers as constituting evidence of the intensity of scientific effort in a particular field. But on the assumption that he might have done so, then our work could in principle provide a means of testing his theory. If he was correct then a time series of numbers of scientific papers could be expected normally to *follow* at least several years behind the series for inventions, although it might not follow *downward* movements to the same (or to any) extent.

Although Schmookler's work (and to some extent Hessen's) was our starting point, we also wished to test the alternative view that exogenous science and technology were the principal determinants of the introduction of new products and processes. It is in principle more difficult to test than Schmookler's view, since it does not necessarily rest on evidence that waves of inventions (or of scientific papers) preceded growth of demand, production or productive investment. Such evidence would indeed be an extremely powerful validation of science-technology push theories. But many proponents of these theories would themselves not expect to find it, since they would argue that what matters for the birth of a new product or a new industry is not a mass of inventions or scientific papers, but a few key inventions or discoveries, which provide the starting point for all subsequent developments.

This was an additional reason for our desire to complement a purely statistical analysis of the Schmookler-type with an historical narrative type of investigation, which would pay particular attention to the major discoveries, inventions and innovations and the interplay between them and the growth of the specific sector in question.

Although Schmookler's ideas were our own starting point and have had a powerful influence, they have certainly never been universally accepted by economists. Rosenberg

(1976) has been a very powerful critic and in earlier times Schumpeter (1911) expounded a very different approach to the relationship between invention and the market. Perhaps more than any other single economist Schumpeter strove to incorporate invention and innovation into his theories of economic development, and any discussion of these themes must surely take his views into account. Since his death his ideas on technological competition have had a strong indirect influence both on the theory of the firm and on the theory of international trade. We have therefore chosen to take his theories as representative of the view that exogenous science and technology have had a fairly powerful influence on entrepreneurial activity and through this on the growth of productive investment and markets, indeed on the very creation of new markets.

There are two major difficulties in attempting to test Schumpeterian ideas on the growth of industry. The first is that even his firmest adherents would agree that the quantitative elaboration and test of his own models was not the strongest aspect of his work. Perhaps he would have argued that such an attempt would be futile because of the intractability of the measurement problems and the subtlety of the issues involved. However, although we have certainly not solved the measurement problems we do believe that the evidence which we have assembled does provide at least a partial vindication of his views.

The second difficulty is different in nature. As Almarin Phillips (1971) has so cogently pointed out there is not one Schumpeterian model but two. The first is that developed by the young Schumpeter already before the first world war and expounded in his *Theory of Economic Development* (1911). The second is that advanced by the mature economist in his last great book *Capitalism, Socialism and Democracy* (1942).

Diagrams 5.3 and 5.4 are a schematic representation of these two models which we shall designate as Schumpeter (I) and Schumpeter (II). They are based essentially on the diagrams used by Phillips (1971) to illustrate his view of the two Schumpeterian models, but they have been modified to take account of the specific purposes of this study. [The original Phillips diagrams (5.5 and 5.6) are also included to show the derivation.]

The pattern postulated by the Schumpeter (I) model and illustrated in Diagram 5.3 may be summarised as follows:

(1) There is a (discontinuous) flow of important inventions related in an unspecified way to new developments in science. These are largely exogenous to existing firms and market structures, and hence to any measurable type of 'market demand', although they may certainly be influenced by the belief in a potential demand or concept of unmet need.

(2) A group of entrepreneurs (who in Schumpeter's view are responsible for the main dynamic thrust in capitalist economies) realise the future potential of these inventions and are prepared to take the risk of developing and innovating. We owe to

Diagram 5.3

Schematic representation of Schumpeter's model of entrepreneurial innovation (I)

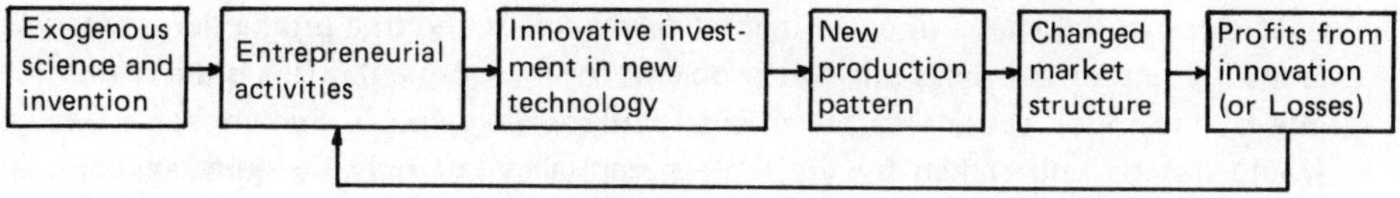

Diagram 5.4

Schematic representation of Schumpeter's model of large firm managed innovation

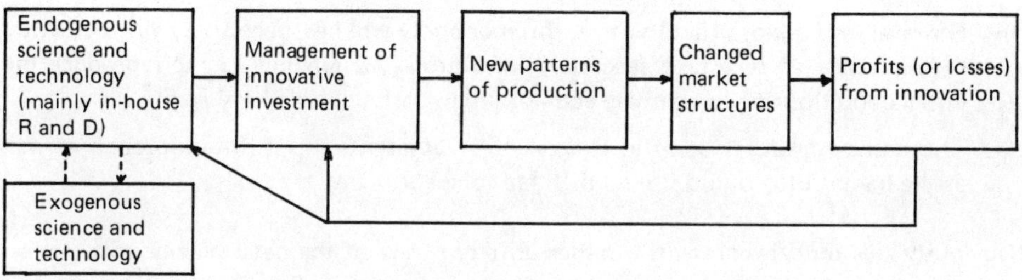

Diagram 5.5

Relations between science, technology, and market structure in Schumpeter's Theory of Economic Development

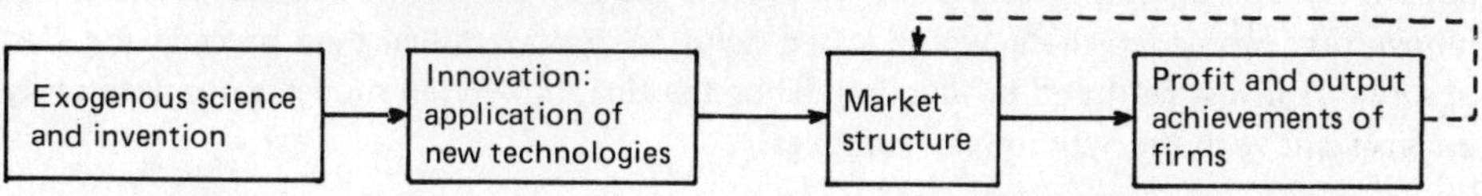

Diagram 5.6

Relations between science, technology and market structure in Schumpeter's *Capitalism, Socialism and Democracy*

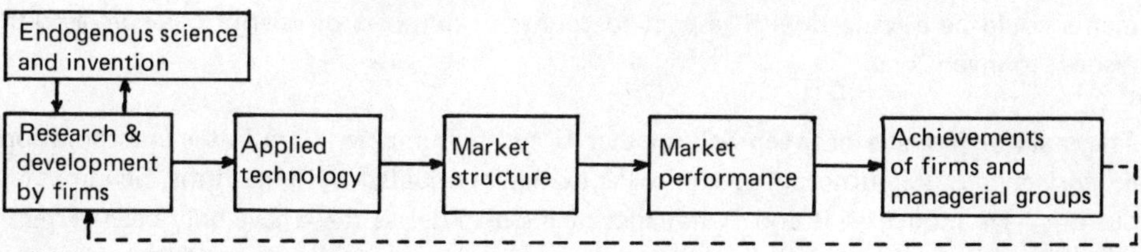

Source: A. Phillips (1971)

Schumpeter the clear and extremely important conceptual distinction between 'invention' and 'innovation', which has since been taken over by almost all economists concerned with this field. Many inventions (in fact most inventions) never reach the point of commercial application. The hazardous process of bringing the successful ones through the stages of experimental development and trial production to market launch is one of the most difficult problems for management. [This is the reason for one of the modifications to the original Phillips diagrams. In Schumpeter's view it would not be undertaken by the average capitalist but only by quite exceptional entrepreneurs. Sometimes this might be the inventors themselves (Inventor-Entrepreneurs).]

(3) Once a radical innovation had been made it would completely disequilibrate existing market structures and reward the successful innovator with exceptional growth and temporary monopoly profits.

(4) However, as Phillips (1971) puts it, this monopoly will be 'successively whittled away by the entry of swarming secondary innovators . . . tending . . . to reproduce the initial conditions of competitive equilibrium in particular markets' (p.5).

The dashed feedback loop in Diagram 5.5 represents this diffusion process as well as the bankruptcy of old firms which fail to adapt.

Obviously this model represents a rather different view of the determinants of technical change and economic development than that propounded by Schmookler. However, it is important to note that in terms of Schmookler's statistical analysis the results might sometimes look the same. Since no distinction is made between the original radical inventions and innovations and all subsequent inventions in Schmookler's method, it is highly probable that in terms of simple patent counts, there would be far more inventions and patents by the 'swarming' secondary innovators than by the original radical inventors and innovators. Moreover these would often tend to follow rather than precede the first upsurge of investment and production. Thus the Schumpeterian model is not necessarily inconsistent with the Schmookler statistics.

Neither in his early model nor his later model did Schumpeter attempt to develop the distinction between science and technology or discovery and invention, and we have therefore not attempted to illustrate this distinction in Diagrams 5.3 and 5.4. However, it should be noted that in relation to a strong 'science push' theory, essentially similar arguments could be advanced with respect to counts of numbers of scientific papers as with respect to inventions.

The main differences between Schumpeter II and Schumpeter I are in the incorporation of *endogenous* scientific and technical activities conducted by large firms. Schumpeter did not have industrial R and D statistics at his disposal as these have only been systematically collected since the Second World War. However, he was undoubtedly aware of the rapid growth of these activities and of the extent to which innovative activity was generally becoming institutionalised within large corporations. Indeed, he was so impressed by these tendencies that he foresaw the innovative entrepreneur as ultimately being completely superseded by a 'bureaucratised' type of innovation. He had actually foreshadowed this change in the emphasis of his theory in an article as early as 1928 (Schumpeter, 1928). In *Capitalism, Socialism and Democracy* he went even further and saw this tendency as the main force which would ultimately lead to the disappearance of capitalism itself.

In Schumpeter II therefore there is a strong feedback loop from successful innovation to increased R and D activities setting up a 'virtuous' self-reinforcing circle leading to renewed impulses to increased market concentration. What has happened in fact is that Schumpeter now sees inventive activities as increasingly under the control of large firms and constantly reinforcing their competitive position. The 'coupling' between science, technology, innovative investment and the market, once loose and subject to long-time delays is now much more intimate and continuous.

Whilst some economists have seen Schumpeter's models as essentially two different views of the world, we prefer to regard them as complementary and reflecting not so much a different analysis, as a different world which was being analysed. Model I was based on 19th Century history as seen in the early years of the 20th Century. Model II was based on what had been happening in the world war and the inter-war period.

From the standpoint of our analysis what we would expect to find if Schumpeter's views are to be vindicated or refuted is evidence relating to Model I primarily before 1914 and evidence relating to Model II primarily since then. However, since we do not take the view that Schumpeter II made Schumpeter I totally and suddenly obsolete, we would still expect to find instances of Schumpeter I down to the present time, although with diminishing frequency.

At first sight it might appear that Model II is more difficult to test. However, we shall postulate that if it is correct this would be shown in the following ways:

(1) In an increased share of large firms R and D and in numbers of inventions and a decline of individual patents. Schmookler himself accepts this and indeed presents a wholly convincing argument on the reason that US patent statistics do not fully reflect this shift (Schmookler, 1966, ch. 2). We were not able ourselves to develop an analysis of patent statistics or R and D statistics by size of firm but we return to this issue later.

(2) To a lesser extent in the increased contribution of industrial research to science as well as technology. We would not expect this to be reflected so fully in statistics of

publications, because whereas firms often have a strong commercial incentive to patent, the opposite is true of scientific papers.

(3) In a tendency for statistics of production, investment, patenting and scientific publication to move together with rather small or blurred time lags reflecting the self-reinforcing virtuous circle of endogenous scientific and technical activities closely linked on the one hand to sales growth and profitability, and on the other hand to links with the exogenous sources of scientific and technical advance.

Before summarising the main results which emerge from our study it is necessary to clarify a few major points about our sources of information and methods. Our sources were standard national statistics of production, trade and investment, complemented in some cases by more detailed information provided by individual firms and from historical sources and published papers. Mont-Edison (Montecatini) and ICI were particularly helpful with respect to plastics and dyestuffs, but many other individuals and firms were generous in giving us time and information. We are grateful to them all and particularly to Professor Colombo, formerly Research Director of Mont-Edison, who enabled Dr. Walsh to make a detailed case study of polypropylene with full access to the relevant records and statistics. This case was chosen as the major new plastic invented and innovated since the Second World War.

Most of Schmookler's work concerned the demand for capital goods in particular industrial sectors, which he related to the trend of patenting in those same capital goods. This is a defensible technique in his case since inventive activity in such industries as building, railroads, agriculture, petroleum refining and paper was heavily concentrated on the supply of equipment and machines, and there was very little product innovation reflected in the patent statistics, particularly in the 19th Century. He therefore based his work on the time series for capital formation in the chosen sectors or other indications of demand for the various relevant capital goods by the user industries. He compared these with his own re-classification of the relevant patent statistics.

Our case was very different. The inventive efforts of the chemical industry have been mainly concentrated on *product* innovation and improvement, but *process* innovation has also been very important and the two are often intimately connected. Inventions in the mechanical equipment, such as pumps, valves and filters, supplied to the industry, are also relevant but far less so than the two main categories. Moreover, it would be extremely difficult, if not actually impossible, to obtain time series of the mechanical equipment inventions relevant to the chemical industry, separated from those which are used in many other process industries, such as food and drink. Sometimes the most relevant and important equipment inventions will in any case be included in our series of chemical inventions since they are a part of the process inventions classified to the chemical industry.

Consequently for our purposes the most sensitive indicators were (1) the production and sales of various categories of chemicals, and (2) the patents and papers relating to the products and processes in each of these categories. It is the demand for the chemicals themselves which is the most relevant in our analysis rather than the derived demand for plant and equipment. In Schmookler's case too, of course, it was the final demand for products and services of the sectors that he studied, which gave rise to the indirect demand for various types of plant and equipment. But while he was quite justified in looking at the derived demand rather than the final demand, this would not be justifiable in our case.

Another difference between our approach and his relates to the coverage of national statistics. His work was entirely confined to the United States and again for his purposes and for the time period which he covered this was understandable and had many advantages. Foreign invention and foreign demand probably did have rather minimal influences on US developments in the industries which he examined. In the case of the chemical industry, however, this would not be a defensible procedure, as worldwide science and invention affect the activities of chemical firms in every country. In particular it is generally agreed that for long periods the German chemical industry led the world in many respects, both technically and economically.

We therefore preferred to work with statistics of world patents and world scientific publications (derived from *Chemical Abstracts*), complemented in specific cases where the national trend was particularly important with national data for one or more key countries, and a detailed historical narrative of several countries where this was relevant. In practice our data relates mainly to the USA, Germany, the UK, and Italy. These countries were responsible during almost all the period under consideration for more than eighty per cent of inventions, patents and scientific papers.

One of the most difficult issues in the interpretation of the data relates to the question of time lags. It is generally agreed that there is a lag between the performance of inventive work and the recorded manifestation of this work in the form of a patent. If therefore we are postulating an influence of demand upon measured invention, then the lag between the two series ought to be one of several years for the evidence to be convincing as the growth or decline of the market is measured almost immediately by the production series. If, however, we are postulating the reverse case of an influence of invention on production and demand (technology-push) then an apparent lag of only a year or so could actually represent a much longer real time-lag, as the inventions could have been embodied in production or even in new equipment during the time in which patents were being generated and applied for. It is generally agreed that for a variety of reasons, but mainly because of pressures on national patent offices, time-lags grew longer in the 1950s and 1960s and may sometimes have been as long as three or four years. There is no means of knowing how long the average or typical lag may have been for the many different kinds of chemicals and processes which we are considering, but the fragmentary evidence points to the conclusion that it varied between one and four years. This must be taken into account in considering the plausibility of the various theories of 'demand-pull and technology-push'.

The difficulty does not arise to the same extent in the case of scientific papers. Whereas firms may sometimes have an interest in delaying patent application or publication, as for example in the case of I.G. Farben with caprolactam and nylon 6, most scientists have a strong interest in publication as soon as possible. They are delayed only by the journals and the requirements of writing up the papers. Such delays are rarely likely to be much more than a year.

Taking these important qualifications and explanations into account we now consider our main results in relation to the various theories which we have discussed. Taking first of all Schmookler's model of market demand leading and determining the scale and direction of inventive activity, there is some support for a weak version of this theory but little to justify a strong version. At the major turning points in economic activity we found only limited evidence to support the view that either the expansion of the market (or its contraction) clearly *preceded* (pre-dated with a significant time-lag) a change in the scale of inventive activity. Some of our evidence directly contradicted Schmookler's theory in that an upsurge of inventive (and occasionally even scientific) activity clearly preceded the growth of the market. This was the case with both plastics and dyestuffs in the period 1925–1935, and it was also the case with drugs in the 1930s. However, a weaker version of the theory could be justified on the grounds of intelligent long-term *anticipation* of future market demand stimulating inventive activity in these cases.

A weaker version of the Schmookler theory could also find support from the post-war evidence of similar long-term relationships between the various time series. There was a powerful upward movement of production and investment in all the main product groups we are considering and this was accompanied in every case by an upward surge of similar scale and duration in the number of patents and scientific publications. To this limited extent the statistical evidence provides some support not only for Schmookler but for all the four models which we are considering. There is clearly some fairly close association between scientific activities, inventive work, production and investment in each of the various sectors.

This certainly does not mean that *annual* fluctuations in the various series corresponded to annual fluctuations in the other series, whether with or without time-lags, and indeed Schmookler made no such claim. There was some bunching of patents associated with particular products or processes in certain years, and similarly in the case of scientific papers, leading to minor annual fluctuations within an overall upward trend. There is no evidence that such minor perturbations were associated with short-term fluctuations in the economy.

One difficulty in the interpretation of our data as compared with Schmookler's is that there were very few 'long swing' turning points during the period we were considering. For the period which he reviewed there were several major peaks and troughs in what he called the 'Kuznets' cycles of United States development and he endeavoured to show some association between the movement of demand and inventive activity associated with the turning points in these long cycles. He was especially concerned to try and demonstrate that the upturns from the troughs of these long cycles were led by demand rather than invention.

However, in the case of drugs, plastics and intermediates for plastics and fibres, these industries did not really exist before the First World War, so that the only major trough which could be considered in our time series was that of the early 1930s. The behaviour of the statistical indicators in this period was the opposite of that predicted by the Schmookler model. There was actually a strong upward movement in the numbers of patents for dyestuffs, plastics and drugs at a time when production was declining or stagnant and investment fell even more sharply.

In the case of one product group — dyestuffs — it was possible for us to extend our analysis back to the period in the 19th Century which was the main focus of Schmookler's work, and this did indeed provide some support for his theory. Here we did find one clear-cut case of demand leading invention. Paradoxically this is an instance which is usually cited by supporters of science-push, and even supporters of demand theories have made an exception in this case. Our re-examination of this period shows that the original growth of dyestuffs patenting clearly followed the growth of demand from the textile industry and especially the UK textile industry (then by far the largest in the world).

Following upon the growth of demand for dyes in the first half of the 19th Century which was reflected in rapidly increasing imports of natural dyestuffs, there was a later increase in patenting and inventive activities. To begin with this was entirely in the field of natural dyestuff patents and the first synthetic patents were simply a part of this upward movement. Even in the 1860s the pattern still remained essentially 'Schmooklerite' in that the severe recession in the textile industry associated with the American Civil War was followed by a downturn in dyestuffs patenting. It was in fact not until the 1880s and 1890s that the German dyestuffs industry clearly emerged as the new world leader which had by 1914 captured eighty per cent of the entire world market for synthetic dyestuffs. The synthetic products had by then almost entirely superseded the natural products.

This astonishing success thus followed on an earlier 'normal' Schmookler pattern of development. However, we would not disagree with those historians, notably Beer (1959) and Haber (1958 and 1971), who have emphasised that the German expansion did represent a major change from this earlier pattern. It did appear to owe at least as much to supply factors as to demand factors in that the big difference was not so much the larger, or more rapid growth of demand in Germany at that time, as in the availability of first-rate research chemists and their efficient organisation on a long-term basis in 'captive' industrial R and D laboratories. The enormous German chemical trust I.G. Farben ultimately emerged from the combination of these three dyestuffs firms, and it was able again to 'reverse' the Schmookler pattern of development through its surge of inventive activity in plastics, dyestuffs and intermediates in the inter-war period.

There is an additional explanation of these apparently 'counter-Schmookler' developments. This is in terms of the German drive for national self-sufficiency prior to the First and Second World Wars, and particularly to overcome excessive dependence on imported natural materials of all kinds. This far more plausible explanation would account also for the intense efforts to develop a synthetic materials and synthetic rubber industry before the First World War. But at the very least this implies a considerable modification of the original strong form of the Schmookler model. This model attempted to explain the trend of invention as an activity which *followed* on the expansion of the market, not as an activity which attempted to *anticipate* future changes in the market.

However, a weaker and much more acceptable version of the Schmookler theory loses its deterministic character as the *anticipated* future developments are necessarily far more uncertain and the interplay of new science, new technology and conjectural future markets becomes far more the realm of imaginative entrepreneurship and/or very long-term strategic planning. Schumpeter's models seem to have much more to offer here, but before we go on to consider them, we first briefly review what we have described as the 'Hessen' model.

This appears from the statistical indicators to come off rather better than the Schmookler model, particularly if we allow fairly generously for the lag with which patent statistics record inventions by comparison with the analogous lag in scientific publications. There does seem to be evidence in the case of plastics, dyestuffs and intermediates for a *derived* or secondary demand for a certain kind of scientific activity following upon the invention and innovation of a new product or process. In terms of *numbers* of scientific papers, moreover, this is quite a large-scale activity. Thus it is difficult to escape the conclusion that the rather large numbers of scientific papers concerned with acrylonitrile or caprolactam in the 1950s and 1960s were the direct result of the large-scale manufacture of these materials and the efforts to invent new and better processes.

However, before simply accepting the Hessen deterministic theory of technology and the economy leading basic science, we have to consider counter-evidence which seems to upset the simpler versions of the model.

There are cases in which the evidence contradicts both Hessen and Schmookler. Drugs in the 1920s and 1930s is the most clear-cut case. A major surge of scientific publication preceded by several years both the inventive activity and the production activity. In general, the drug industry appears to provide a case of invention which has often been 'science-led'.

There are in any case other good reasons for not accepting the over-simplified Hessen-type approach to the relationship between science and technology. Advances in fundamental science (which *permit* both the inventive activity to succeed and the derivative 'gap-filling' science following these inventions) would not necessarily be measured at all by the indicators which we have used. The relevant papers would simply not be classified by product group or even appear in chemical abstracts. Moreover, they might be very few in number yet essential to the whole process in the sense that few if any of the technical and industrial developments could have taken place without them. There are also cases when important discoveries were made by scientists working on a completely different problem — the so-called 'chemical miracles'. A number of the early dyestuffs discoveries fall into this category including the original Perkin 'mauve'.

Although therefore some of the statistical data appear superficially to support a crude version of the Hessen theory, we cannot support it in its simple form on the grounds of its incompatibility with a number of specific cases and with the logical evidence of the actual historical development of chemistry and physics.

Whilst our evidence would not support a purely deterministic view of demand leading invention or technology leading science, it would certainly be consistent with a theory which postulated an interdependent or shifting relationship. There do appear to be some periods when technology leads and some when science leads, and others when the indicators move very close together. In these circumstances we would expect not only similar patterns (although with varying leads and lags), but also that publications themselves would reflect a degree of convergence of science and technology. This is indeed the case. Derek Price (1965) himself, while maintaining in general that technologists did not seek to publish like scientists, but to patent or to design, made an exception for chemistry and electronics, where there is substantial publishing activity by technologists, much of it linked directly or indirectly to fundamental science. In an interesting citation study of science-technology coupling in electronics Liebermann (1978) found that for industrial authors publishing in the *Transactions of the I.E.E.E.* references to the basic science literature from *Physical Review* were slightly more recent than those of university authors. He concludes from his study that in electronics the 'science-technology coupling has remained strong over the past two decades, as a consequence of the continued birth of new science-related technologies within the solid-state field. Thus it appears that the coupling between the scientific and technological sectors proceeds over time like a series of overlapping waves, as various ties form and then gradually die out' (Liebermann, 1978, p. 13).

These findings are remarkably similar to our own, and the institutional mechanism which Liebermann suggests is one in which the links between the most fundamental research and applied technology are made by intermediaries who are able to communicate with both. Our own study and his suggest that such people are to be found mainly within industry and especially within industrial R and D departments.

Our study showed several other ways in which this two-way linkage and interdependence has been fostered in the chemical industry. Since the 1870s the German chemical firms regularly employed leading academic chemists as consultants. Both Staudinger and Ziegler were consultants with the chemical industry when they made their remarkable discoveries, which led rapidly to many new products, processes and patents, as well as publications.

The leading German chemical firms also regularly awarded prizes for outstanding achievements in university research and spent a great deal of money supporting research projects in universities. This is one obvious mechanism which would explain the tendency for a surge of secondary academic interest and publication to follow the growth of industrial interest and patents in such products as acrylonitrile or polypropylene. But it also worked the other way – the academic interest in the molecular structure of benzene or cyclohexane preceded rather than followed industrial exploitation.

Chemical firms in other countries followed the German example of stimulating and financing academic research projects and also of encouraging movement in both directions with leading industrial scientists holding chairs in universities and technological institutes, and academic scientists spending periods in industry as consultants or full-time employees. The best known example of this was of course Carothers, deliberately recruited by Du Pont as an outstanding academic researcher to lead their programme of work on macro-molecular structures, which ultimately led to nylon.

This case has often been cited and to investigate more closely the intimate links between science, technology and industrial exploitation we preferred to take the case of polypropylene. Thanks to the generous support of Mont-Edison (Montecatini) we were able to show in some depth how closely Professor Natta's original work at the Milan Polytechnic interacted with Montecatini's own R and D, and also how rapidly the American petrochemical companies moved in with their own secondary patenting and publishing activities in an area of such great commercial importance for them. This was a clear case of the 'swarming' secondary inventors and innovators pushing up the aggregate patent numbers after the first breakthrough.

This evidence of two-way linkages with strong reciprocal influences is inconsistent with deterministic theories of demand-led invention or of technology-led science. It is however fully consistent with Schumpeter's models, and especially with the later development of his theory. Before turning finally to a fuller consideration of this theory it is important to point out that the example of polypropylene does indicate another extremely important economic mechanism for driving invention. The large oil and chemical companies often have a problem of disposing of by-products, such as propylene and ethylene. Their vertical integration and their multi-product basis gave rise to an important new type of invention and innovation : that based not on 'pull' of 'demand' but on the desire of a large firm to make use of what would otherwise be a 'waste' or 'surplus' product or by-product. This is certainly an economic incentive to invent and innovate but it is hardly the market-demand leadership mechanism postulated by Schmookler. Our studies show that it was a very important mechanism in the case of organic intermediates both in relation to coal-tar and acetylene chemistry and in relation to petro-chemical intermediates.

All of this is far more consistent with Schumpeterian theories than with Schmookler or Hessen. Schumpeter stressed the active striving of the firm to generate new markets and change existing market structures on the basis of its own technical innovations, not simply as a response to existing market signals.

But what of the links with 'exogenous' basic science? Here again our evidence is much more consistent with both the Schumpeterian models than with the other theories. Schumpeter Mark I suggested that exceptional creative entrepreneurs deriving ideas from an exogenous science background undertook risky innovative developments to launch new products and change existing market structures. They often anticipated rather than followed demand.

Schumpeter Mark II postulated that 'endogenous' science and technology, mainly within the R and D laboratories of the large firms had increasingly substituted for the mechanism of the 'exogenous' inventor setting up in business. He did not however rule out the possibility of the Mark I mechanism continuing to operate within a climate increasingly dominated by large-scale corporate R and D. According to our findings, this is almost exactly what has happened in the chemical industry since the 19th century. Men like Perkin and Baekeland coming from an academic background were able to make a fortune from their own discoveries by establishing their own firms. Sometimes these chemist-inventors worked with partners who had greater commercial experience, sometimes they acquired this knowledge themselves, but they laid the foundations for the modern chemical industry, whilst at the same time, as Schumpeter argued, they completely disequilibrated the previous market structures and destroyed some traditional trades in older materials.

However, as the new chemical firms grew up and consolidated their new markets they made an extraordinarily important social innovation – the captive industrial R and D laboratory. This meant that they were no longer so vulnerable to the 'creative destruction' brought about by exogenous science and technology through new entrepreneurs. They themselves learnt the trick of institutionalising this process. By earning exceptional profits on their major innovations they were able to finance scientific and technical activities on such a scale as to retain the ability to generate successive new waves of invention and innovation, or at least to keep fairly close behind the leaders. Nylon accounted for more than half the corporate profits of Du Pont for many years, and such products as polyethylene and PVC made a similar contribution to ICI and the German chemical firms. The original growth and strength of the German chemical industry was based on the profits from synthetic dyestuffs. The evidence of our studies on dyestuffs, plastics and organic intermediates confirms the view of those who have argued that in these sectors the largest chemical and oil firms have dominated the inventive and innovative process over the past fifty years whilst strengthening their own market leadership. Not only did the German chemical firms BASF, Bayer and Hoechst rise to their pre-eminent position in the world through their dyestuffs inventions in the 19th Century, but it was also I.G. Farben and ICI who were responsible for most of the major dyestuffs inventions since the 1920s.

Similarly in the case of plastics and synthetic fibres it was the leading chemical firms in each country (I.G. Farben in Germany, Du Pont in USA, ICI in Britain, and Montecatini in Italy) who were able to dominate the technical developments leading to the introduction of most of the major new materials and their application in a great variety of novel end uses. They were also usually the first to imitate or license each others' major innovations (nylon 66, nylon 6, polyethylene, PVC, acrylics etc).

The drug industry does not differ essentially from this pattern. There were new entrants at the time of the birth of the modern drug industry in the 1930s and one major new entrant corresponding to the Schumpeter Mark I model since the war (Syntex). But since the 1950s the pattern of growth has mainly been one of the R and D leaders reinforcing their own position (Merck, Hoffmann Laroche, Wellcome, Bayer, ICI etc.). The pattern was upset a little in the 1960s and 1970s by the social efforts at regulation affecting mainly the US industry. Reekie (1969) has pointed out that the only new entrants to the British industry since the war have been multi-nationals establishing branch operations in Britain.

This self-reinforcing 'virtuous-circle' mechanism enabled the large chemical firms to change the market structures not only in the chemical markets themselves but in many other industries which they penetrated through technological competition, such as textiles, packaging, building components and even some sectors of metal products and engineering.

Although our evidence appears to support the Schumpeterian model (and those theorists like Rosenberg and Nelson who have followed largely in his tradition) there is one important line of research and argument which might appear to refute Schumpeter II whilst continuing to vindicate Schumpeter I. This is the argument that large firms tend to rest on their monopolistic laurels, to stagnate and to become less innovative, thus providing continuous new opportunities for the small innovative firm to undermine the large monopolistic firms despite the scale of their R and D and other technical resources.

In the 1950s it was often argued that the process of industrial concentration had slowed down or ceased, and also that the largest firms tended to be relatively less R and D-intensive than small or medium-sized ones. Scherer (1965a and 1965b) and Hamberg (1964) in particular argued from the statistical evidence then available that there was no association between firm size and relative scale of research and inventive activities, or if there was such an association then it was one in which R and D efforts tended to diminish in the largest firms (a 'hump-backed' distribution).

Whilst the evidence of growing industrial concentration is now seldom disputed, the Schumpeterian explanation is often ignored or contradicted, usually on the basis of Scherer's work. However, his data were based on the statistics of the 1950s which were unsatisfactory and provided no time-trend. In a recent D. Phil. thesis and in a major paper on the subject Soete (1979) has made use of the most recent statistics of the National Science Foundation and other US sources to show that Schumpeter was essentially correct. In most branches of US industry, including chemicals, it is the largest firms which are the most R and D-intensive. Another study for the Bolton Committee showed that large firms accounted for a disproportionately large share of post-war British innovations, and that in the chemical industry, scarcely any significant innovations came from small firms.

Consequently, the main conclusion of our study is that the results are fully consistent with the Schumpeterian theory of invention and innovation, but not with the Schmookler or other demand theories.

It is essential to emphasise that the rejection of a pure market-demand theory does not mean the denial of the influence of the market. Indeed, part of the debate on market demand is largely 'tautological'. If 'innovation' is defined (as it usually is, following Schumpeter) as the commercial introduction and exploitation of an invention, then acceptance by the market is a condition which must be met for all innovations, irrespective of their origins. Our own project SAPPHO, which was a comparison of success and failure, showed that the most successful industrial innovators are those who take a great deal of trouble to learn about the needs of potential users, that is to study the future market in all its complexity. It does not follow that the market is the only or the determining factor influencing the outcome. The fascination of invention and innovation lies in the fact that both the market-place and the technology and science 'frontiers' are continually changing. This creates a kaleidoscopic and almost infinite succession of new possibilities and combinations.

The advance of scientific research in many different fields is constantly throwing up new discoveries and opening up new technical possibilities, which are to a large extent independent of any particular market pressure. It follows from this that a firm, or a country, which is able to monitor this advancing frontier by one means or another may be able to gain both a technological and a market lead over its competitors by the speed of its response. Strong in-house R and D would usually be needed to convert the first awareness of the new potential into a competitive advantage, as well as close contact with potential future users and markets.

Innovation is a 'coupling' process and this coupling first takes place in the minds of imaginative people. An idea 'gels' or 'clicks' somewhere at the ever-changing interface between science, technology and the market. But the coupling process is usually far more than an imaginative 'leap' or an intuitive flash. It is a continuous creative dialogue over a long period of research, experimental design and development. That is why Schumpeter was so right to insist on the rare quality of 'entrepreneurship'.

This interpretation of innovation behaviour in the firm is very different from conventional theory, but it has recently found recognition and more precise formulation in the work of Nelson and Winter (1973 and 1978), and in the more general theories of firm behaviour propounded by Herbert Simon.

Our conclusions also have some relevance for national policies as well as firm strategies and theories of firm behaviour. If we are right in emphasising supply factors as well as demand factors in explaining the rate and direction of invention and innovation, then it follows that aggregate demand management is a quite inadequate tool for economic policies whose objective is to maintain a competitive position in a world market dominated by technological competition.

Technology and science policies designed to improve the efficiency of the supply side are just as important as Keynesian demand management. So too are those policies designed to improve the 'coupling' throughout the system. It is for this reason that we have stressed in our detailed historical studies the revival of the British dyestuffs industry during and after the First World War based on an active long-term 'supply' strategy both on the part of industry and on the part of government.

If simple 'demand-pull' or 'science-push' theories are not supported by the evidence, then there is no substitute for the deliberate and difficult effort in government, industry and academic life to bring together those concerned with science, technology and with the market to endeavour to anticipate future trends in all three and formulate appropriate long-term policies and strategies, accordingly.

References

Beer, J. J. (1959) *Emergence of the German Dyestuffs Industry* (Illinois University Press).

Byatt, L. and Cohen, A. (1969) *An Attempt to Quantify the Benefits of Scientific Research,* DES, London, Science Policy Studies, no. 4.

Clark, J., Freeman, C. and Soete, L. (1981) 'Long Waves, Inventions, and Innovations', *Futures,* vol. 13, no. 4, August, pp. 308–322.

Freeman, C. (1974) *Economics of Industrial Innovation* (London: Penguin).

Haber, L.F. (1958) *The Chemical Industry during the Nineteenth Century* (Oxford: Oxford University Press).

Haber, L.F. (1971) *The Chemical Industry 1900–1930* (Oxford: Oxford University Press).

Hamberg, D. (1964), 'Size of Firm, Oligopoly and Research: The Evidence', *Canadian Journal of Economic and Political Science,* February, pp. 62–75.

Hessen, B. (1931) 'The Social and Economic Roots of Newton's "Principia" ', in *Science at the Crossroads,* papers from the second international Congress of the History of Science and Technology (1931), re-printed and published by Cass, London, 1971.

Langrish, J. et. al. (1972) *Wealth from Knowledge* (London: Macmillan).

Liebermann, M.B. (1978) 'A Literature Citation Study of Science – Technology Coupling in Electronics', *Proceedings of the I.E.E.E.*, vol. 66, no. 1, January, pp. 5–13.

Mowery, D. and Rosenberg, N. (1979) 'The Influence of Market Demand upon Innovation: A Critical Review of Some Recent Empirical Studies', *Research Policy,* vol. 8, no. 2, April, pp. 102–154.

Myers, S. and Marquis, D.G. (1969) *Successful Industrial Innovations,* NSF (Washington).

National Science Foundation, Illinois Institute of Technology Research Institute (1969) *Technology in Retrospect and Critical Events in Science,* (TRACES), NSF 0535 (Washington).

Nelson, R.R. and Winter, S.G. (1973) 'Neo-classical Versus Evolutionary Theories of Economic Growth', Yale Growth Center, (mimeo).

Nelson, R.R. and Winter, S.G. (1978) 'Factors Generating and Limiting Competition under Schumpeterian Conditions', *Bell Journal of Economics,* vol. 9, no 2.

Phillips, A. (1971) *Technology and Market Structure* (London: Lexington Books).

Price, D.J. de Solla (1965) 'Is Technology Historically Independent of Science?', *Technology and Culture,* no. 4.

Reekie, W.D. (1969) 'Barriers to Entry and Competition' in (ed.) G. Teeling Smith, *Economics and Innovation in the Pharmaceutical Industry* (London: Office of Health Economics).

Rosenberg, N. *(1976) Perspectives on Technology* (Cambridge: Cambridge University Press).

Scherer, F.M. (1965 a) 'Firm Size, Market Structure, Opportunity and the Output of Patented Inventions', *American Economic Review,* pp. 1097–1123.

Scherer, F.M. (1965b) 'Size of Firm, Oligopoly and Research: A Comment', *Canadian Journal of Economic and Political Science,* May, pp. 256–266.

Schmookler, J. (1966) *Invention and Economic Growth* (Harvard).

Schumpeter, J.A. (1911) *The Theory of Economic Development* (Harvard).

Schumpeter, J.A. (1928) 'The Instability of Capitalism', *Economic Journal,* pp. 361–386.

Schumpeter, J.A. (1942) *Capitalism, Socialism and Democracy* (New York: Harper and Row).

Seal, V. (1975) *The Relationships and Links between Academic Research in Steroid Chemistry and the Industrial Development of Steroid Drugs.* PhD Thesis, Manchester University.

Sherwin, C.W. and Isenson, R.S. (1967) 'Project Hindsight', *Science,* vol. 156, 23 June, pp. 1571–1577.

Soete, L. (1979) 'Size of Firm and Inventive Activity: The Evidence Reconsidered', *European Economic Review.*

Townsend, J. (1976) *Innovation in Coalmining Machinery: The Anderton Shearer-Loader,* SPRU Occasional Paper, no.3, Sussex.

PART II

ECONOMIC PRESSURES – EAST AND WEST

Chapter 6

THE CAPITAL CONSTRAINT ON EMPLOYMENT

M.J. Artis

Introduction

The possibility that there is a capital constraint on the realisation of full employment, that there may be an insufficiency of co-operating capital equipment to permit the full usage of labour resources, resulting in what may be (loosely) termed 'Marxian Unemployment', whilst not new in application to less developed economies, is rather a novel idea in relation to developed economies such as that of the United Kingdom. Nevertheless, this hypothesis has something of a hearing today, recurring, in particular, in continental European reflections on the unemployment problem. It had a brief, but somewhat dismissive airing in the McCracken Report (1977) but has been pursued by, among others, Malinvaud in a series of contributions (Malinvaud 1978, 1980a, 1980b)(1).

In order that the hypothesis should have a fair hearing, it is obviously required that *aprioristic* definitions of 'developed' and 'less developed' countries which prevent its application to the former category of economy should be abandoned.

Less obviously, but equally important, it is essential to remember that the explanation of unemployment need not be exclusive, and that unemployment may be overdetermined. To illustrate these points briefly, consider the following two possibilities:

i) There is a fixed coefficients technology in the economy such that the maximum employment of labour is given as

$$L_K^* = \beta \bar{K}$$

where $\bar{K}$ is the fixed stock of capital equipment, ß the labour-capital ratio and L_k^* the maximum employment of labour permitted. A capital constraint may be said to exist if

$$L_k^* < L_s^*$$

where L_s^* is the 'full employment' labour supply.

However, there may also exist an aggregate demand constraint on employment such that

$$L_D^* = \gamma \bar{Y}.$$

Actual employment is then the minimum of full employment labour-supply and the two constraints, or

$$L_A = \min (L_s^*; L_k^*; L_D^*).$$

Now it may be observed that in fact

$$L_A = L_D^* < L_k^* < L_s^*$$

in which event the capital constraint is not binding; nevertheless, *some* unemployment $(L_s^* - L_k^*)$ is 'over-determined', since if the aggregate demand constraint were not binding, the capital constraint would be. Moreover, it would be important to recognise the potential capital constraint in designing policy for a 'return' to full employment since the presence of L_k^* lowers the inflation and balance of payments barriers to a policy of 'pure' demand reflation.

ii) Alternatively, the co-existence of capital-constrained and demand-constrained employment may be motivated by the consideration that in an economy producing several goods, some sectors may encounter the one constraint and other sectors the alternative one.

In either case, fair hearing of the capital constraint hypothesis does not imply that it should be held responsible for all of observed unemployment, or of its observed increase(2).

It appears also from the above that the motivation for a capital constraint rests on some rigidity in the capital/labour ratio. The first section of this paper is devoted to clarifying the analytical basis for an assumption of this kind. The second section then reproduces, very briefly, some of the macroeconomic analytics relevant to this case, as expounded recently by Malinvaud (1978, 1980a, 1980b). The third section introduces the question of empirical verification and presents some evidence for the United Kingdom. The final section draws the argument together, tentatively suggesting the relevance of a dual sector theory to the analysis.

I

The statement of the capital constraint hypothesis given above indicates a dependence on some assumption of a fixed labour-capital ratio. This, as indicated in more detail below, may be viewed as a physical constraint, yielding Marxian unemployment and can be thought of appropriately as the 'strong form' of the capital constraint hypothesis. Alternatively, ß, the labour-capital ratio, may be viewed as the profitable ratio for going costs of production, without the implication that this is technically fixed. In this case, we could term the unemployment 'classical', following Malinvaud's categorisation and regard this as the 'weak form' of the capital constraint hypothesis. In the former case, additional new capacity is a necessary condition for the elimination of the associated unemployment; in the latter case, it is not, for there may be idle capacity on hand whose use would be profitable in some alternative production cost conditions. In this light, descriptions of the 'strong form' of the capital constraint may be viewed as parables to be appropriately reinterpreted for a world in which capacity is limited not by past accumulation but by present profitability.

Once again, however, the 'strong' and 'weak' forms of the capital constraint hypothesis are not exclusive, provided that *some* limit is envisaged for aggregate substitutability of labour for capital, and we shall concentrate below on the 'strong form' of the hypothesis.

It would obviously be too strong to assert that production is carried out with a single fixed coefficients technology, but an approach that is more flexible and yields a comparable result is provided by the vintage capital model. In such a model, the stock of capital is regarded as being composed of several 'vintages', dated according to the time at which the investment was made. Each separate vintage is characterised by a fixed coefficients production technology, which differs as between vintages. It is common to suppose that technical progress through time makes the more recent vintages relatively more capital intensive in production, and raises labour productivity on the later vintages as compared with earlier ones. A feature of these models is that the length of life of capital equipment can become an economic decision and endogenous to the wider model rather than technically determined by physical factors; for a regime of perfect competition in which the only variable factor is labour, the decision to scrap equipment is taken at the point where the real wage just exceeds the average (and marginal) productivity of labour (Salter, 1960). In a growth economy where technical progress endows the newer vintages with higher labour productivity than older ones, this rule determines the scrapping of equipment on which the quasi-rent has fallen to zero. Meanwhile, the intra-marginal vintages earn positive quasi-rents increasing inversely with the age of the equipment. Under imperfect competition, maintenance of the wedge between price and marginal cost indicates that equipment will be scrapped while the quasi-rent is still positive.

Capital/labour substitution may be allowed for in aggregate (single product) models of this kind by permitting 'ex ante' substitutability: that is, the technology of the current vintage is variable up to the point at which it is actually installed, thereafter being frozen. This is the so-called putty-clay model; where *ex ante* substitution of this type is infeasible, we have the clay-clay model in which production techniques are given both *ex ante* and *ex post.*

In a growth equilibrium, it can be shown that with Harrod-neutral technical progress there is a constant investment rate which will yield a capital stock of constant life and full employment of labour, in which real wages grow at a constant rate equal to the (constant) rate of increase in labour productivity between vintages while aggregate output grows at a rate equal to the sum of labour force growth and the rate of Harrod-neutral technical progress. At any point of time in such an economy there is a fixed capital/labour ratio which can be viewed as an appropriately weighted average of the capital/labour ratios of the vintages in existence in the capital stock, and the real wage is the average labour productivity of the oldest vintage of equipment still in use (see Solow *et.al.* (1966)).

An exogenous increase in the real wage would disturb such an equilibrium. Immediately, it would accelerate the scrapping decision and reduce the capital stock and employment. In a putty-clay model, new investment would become more capital intensive. An exogenous disturbance to demand prospects would amplify the problem. The incentive to adopt more efficient technologies by investing would not necessarily be impaired by this prospect, and if it were not, the capital intensity of average production would tend to rise. If the investment rate slackened, on the other hand, apart from the substitution bias, capital intensity would tend to fall and the equilibrium rate of increase of real wages would tend to fall. This could exacerbate the problem if real wage demands are not abated and would magnify the effects of the initial real wage disturbance.

It is to an articulation of this kind that we look for the emergence of a capital constraint. It is familiar enough that in a world of infinitely substitutable capital a rise in real wages will reduce employment. In such a world, however, there is no difficulty about restoring a higher level of employment provided that real wages can be forced to adjust downwards. This is the picture suggested by the 'neo-classical synthesis' version of Keynesianism ('classical unemployment') where an excessive real wage can be corrected by price increases induced by demand-reflationary monetary and fiscal policies. From this perspective, the strong form of the capital constraint hypothesis may be viewed as a kind of *extremum* of classical unemployment, in which the excessive real wage is accompanied by an accelerated scrapping of equipment, thus removing the opportunity for a decline in the real wage to result in the immediate restoration of a higher level of employment for lack of cooperating capital(3).

Since there seems no reason why real wages should, in relevant not-so-long runs, behave in the way required to maintain the kind of equilibrium which would prevent it, the emergence of a capital constraint on employment seems to be something which it is quite possible to envisage(4).

It is also clear that, in a world of multiple commodities and associated capital-labour ratios, changes in demand conditions may interact with changes in cost conditions(5) to create capital constraint problems, although by the same token, changes in the pattern of demand re-introduce a degree of substitutability between capital and labour not available in the single-commodity model.

The disequilibrium dynamics of a vintage capital model are extremely difficult to describe rigorously; the principal analytical results available are derived for equilibrium conditions. Nevertheless the heuristic use of the vintage approach to motivate the capital constraint hypothesis does not seem difficult to follow. There is no guarantee that real wages will follow the path required to maintain equilibrium, and no guarantee that demand pattern flexibility is sufficient to avoid the constraint arising.

A writer who has previously deployed the heuristic properties of the vintage capital approach in application to the United Kingdom, though with a rather different disequilibrium in mind, is J. R. Sargent (1968). In this contribution Sargent described the growth of real wages in the 1960s as responding to a disequilibrium presented by the low, and falling, costs of investment. The encouragement provided by increasing fiscal incentives and low-turning-negative real rates of interest on borrowing was seen as 'over-expanding' investment, resulting in rapidly rising productivity and a bidding up of real wages. The halting and possible reversal of this trend in borrowing costs can be seen, subsequently, as having slowed investment and the attainable increase in productivity, thus implying an attenuation of real wage growth. Employment need not be affected, provided that real wages find their new path. The proviso is a significant one, however.

II.

Malinvaud (1978, 1980a, 1980b) has drawn attention to the difficult policy implications ensuing from a situation where unemployment is overdetermined by deficient demand and deficient capacity.

In terms of the diagrammatic presentation made familiar by Malinvaud (1977), with the additional simplifications (a) that the supply of labour is fixed independently of the real wage and 'real wealth' (or non-labour income) and (b) that production is by fixed coefficients, Figure 6.1 shows that if $L_K^* < L_S^*$, then unemployment is over-determined. Above the line (w/p), no production would be scheduled, for none would be profitable. Below it, there are two regions: Marxian unemployment with repressed inflation (MU + RI) and Keynesian unemployment with a Marxian underlay (MU + KU).

Figure 6.1

Macroeconomic régimes

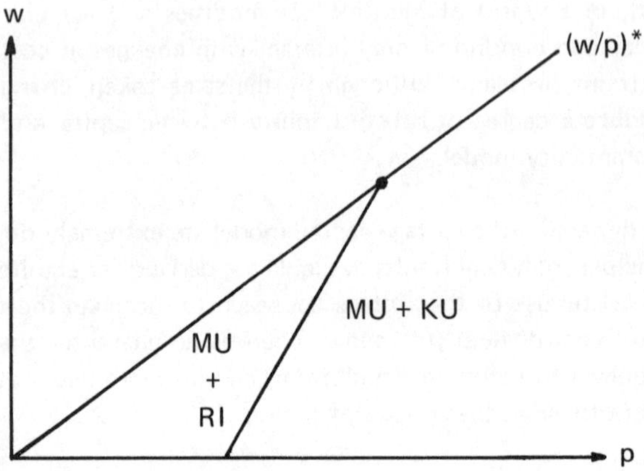

Thus, the lowest level of unemployment that can be achieved (in MU + RI) is $L_K^* - L_S^*$; for with Keynesian unemployment (MU + KU), the limited aggregate capacity is not fully utilised(6). The separating line between the two regimes thus traces out a locus of w,p combinations which exactly match aggregate demand to capital-constrained 'notional' aggregate supply, its slope being governed by a positive partial derivative of demand with respect to real wages and a negative partial derivative of demand with respect to real money balances (the nominal stock of money being given).

Investment, the creation of new capacity, is required to relieve the system of over-determined unemployment here, since the elimination of Keynesian unemployment in itself is insufficient. The policy prescription is difficult, however. It is plausible to suppose that the investment function has a positive sign on capacity usage (accelerator) and a negative sign on real wages. But a reduction of real wages in the Keynesian region increases the deficiency in demand, or may cause repressed inflation to be eliminated in favour of demand deficiency. A policy of demand reflation can remove Keynesian deficient demand and unemployment but at the risk of raising real wages and increasing the probability of Marxian unemployment in ensuing periods; but equally, not to remove deficient demand is to invite the onset of Marxian unemployment in later periods. The difficulty of the policy response required is described by Malinvaud (1978) as the difficulty of combining fiscal expansion designed to relieve Keynesian unemployment with an 'austerity' incomes policy, designed to reduce real wages and favour investment.

In a recent contribution, Malinvaud (1980a) has explored the analytics of this situation with greater rigour, but the 'awkward' policy implications remain much the same, with the difference that classical (or Marxian) equilibria are found to have a greater probability of transience than Keynesian equilibria(7).

These speculations are illustrated in Malinvaud (1980a) by a heuristic simulation of the oil price shock. The dual character of this shock is its depressing effect on demand and its depressing effect on capacity. The result of the simulation is a period of Keynesian unemployment followed by a period of 'classical' (Marxian) unemployment as capacity is further reduced, eventually giving way again to a period of Keynesian unemployment.

III.

The Vintage Capital Model approach

Granted what was said in Section I, it would seem that empirical verification of the capital constraint hypothesis could proceed by way of estimating a vintage capital model, and on the basis of the results obtained, proceeding to carry out the test $L_k^* \gtreqless L_s^*$.

Unfortunately, although some vintage capital models have been estimated both for the UK (e.g. Stamler *et. al.* 1978) and for other economies, the approach does not readily lend itself to the exercise. It turns out that, because there are a number of unobservables in play, vintage models have generally to be calibrated on the basis of 'plausible' but not directly observable values for some of these factors, leading to a situation in which the test for a capital constraint hypothesis cannot be carried out other than in a context of joint hypothesis-testing.

We first draw attention to some of the principal difficulties with the approach and then refer to an influential Dutch model which has claimed to detect a capital constraint for the Dutch economy although in fact, because of the problems referred to, it seems doubtful whether these claims can be substantiated. It is difficult to disagree with the conclusion drawn by Dreihuis (1977) that 'attempts to operationalise the vintage concept must be seen as heroic efforts with seemingly attractive results, which should not make us blind (to) their enormous problems'.

The two most serious specification problems are probably those concerning the specification of the scrapping condition and the question of the determination of new investment. On the first issue, the simplest and easiest to specify of the scrapping conditions is the Salter (1960) zero-rent perfect competition condition; but it seems fair to assume that the positive quasi-rent imperfect competition condition is the more 'realistic'. This is important because, as Dreihuis (1977), drawing on Malcolmson (1975) has shown, the critical comparison determining the scrapping decision is no longer that of wage costs versus product prices but that of wage costs versus the user cost of capital. Estimated vintage models also generally assume that the history of gross investment can be taken as exogenous; whilst this seems all very well for the quasi-mechanical computation of the labour requirement associated with the imputed pattern and size of vintages of capital, it is not a very reasonable assumption to make in a context where the level and path of real wages is to be shown to be 'responsible' for determining the age distribution of surviving vintages and, thence, the aggregate labour 'requirement'. For, had the history of the real wage been different, so too, would have been the rate of gross investment. Nor is it possible to be sure of the sign of the effect of a different real wage history on the gross investment history(8). Whilst the two particular problems mentioned seem the most important, there are in practice numerous other more detailed but also important difficulties in specifying an empirical vintage model in the face of unobservable data – e.g. lack of information on technical lifetimes, capacity utilisation etc.

The distinctive predictive qualities of the vintage approach are those pertaining to the age distribution of the capital stock and the associated employment. But data on the former are far from adequately comprehensive and it goes without saying that capital stock data generated by perpetual inventory methods are inappropriate to the vintage approach, for perpetual inventory methods assume scrapping to be determined by exogenous technical lifetimes rather than endogenous economic decisionmaking. Data on employment are less imperfect, although they still require distinctions to be drawn, on a largely arbitrary basis, between 'overhead' and 'production' workers.

For these sorts of reasons, the application of the vintage approach requires that a series of linked assumptions must be made to calibrate the model and its predictions are accordingly conditional on all of them(9).

Nevertheless, by making a plausible set of assumptions (including 'starting values' for the age distribution of capital equipment already in existence), gross investment data can be used in an empirical vintage model, together with scrapping conditions, to predict labour requirements. A basis of this sort is used by the Dutch model of den Hartog and Tjan (1976), a clay-clay model which in a brilliant, but breath-taking, way indicates a history in which the rise in real wages resulted in accelerated scrapping of equipment, a reduction in the mean age of capital equipment and – during the mid 1960s and after – a growing discrepancy between labour supply and labour requirements. The vulnerability of the model to detailed criticism has, however, been clearly demonstrated by Klerk *et. al.* (1977).

Enough has been said to suggest that the results of fitting empirical vintage capital models, whilst perhaps indicative, are too tentative to be firm in their implications. In any event, we have no comparable demonstration to that of den Hartog and Tjan (1976) for the British economy.

The Business Survey approach

The striking predictive quality of the vintage capital model is that it endogenises the mean life of capital equipment; as already mentioned, this effectively rules out the use of perpetual inventory estimates of the capital stock even supposing that these could be used in some way to cast light on the capital constraint hypothesis(10). However, evidence that it is in the spirit implied by the predictions of the vintage approach may be gleaned from business surveys, and in particular from the response of businessmen to questions concerning their capacity to produce, and limitations upon it. The agents concerned are, after all, uniquely well-placed to know what their capacity is, how much has been scrapped, what is standing idle, and so on; and provided the relevant questions are correctly framed, their responses should be informative on the issue in hand.

We therefore turn to the CBI's *Industrial Trends Survey.* The quarterly returns(11) of this survey are based on responses to a questionnaire in which two questions of interest in the present context appear. The first of these asks: 'Is your present level of output below capacity (i.e. are you working below a satisfactory full rate of operation)?' The aggregate responses to this question, recorded as 'percentage working below capacity', are a weighted average of the yes/no answers received to the question, with net output as the weighting factor. There must be some uncertainty, as in any questionnaire, about the way in which responses to this question are formulated; in particular, the use of the word 'satisfactory', though qualifying 'full rate of operation' may be thought to imply a relativity in responses such that the concept of full capacity is itself procyclical. It is also not clear what factors firms abstract from in answering the question – e.g. do they assume that they could get hold of key skilled labour of which they may currently be experiencing a shortage? In an attempt to settle such doubts, the CBI ran a 'survey of the survey' (Price, 1977), from which it emerged that a substantial proportion (two-thirds) of the firms concerned employed a physical notion of capacity in responding to this question. Others no doubt employ current profitability criteria and may disregard spare capacity which it would not be profitable to utilise even if the demand (at going prices and costs of operation) existed. Still others may answer the question in a manner which gives more weight than would be ideal to the short-run costs of bringing capacity on stream. Nevertheless, there seems a good chance that responses to this question will capture the 'capital constraint' if one exists.

Figure 6.2 plots the 'percentage working below capacity' against unemployment (GB, *per cent*). The observations are numbered sequentially from 1 = 1960 Q1 to 86 = 1981 Q2. The plot is consistent with (a) a general sympathy between the two variables so that they rise and fall together; and (b) a tendency for the 'percentage working below capacity' to *fall* against unemployment in the later cycles. Thus, assuming that the CBI question has been answered consistently in an appropriate way, the data plot is consistent with the hypothesis of a capacity/capital constraint(12).

Figure 6.2

Unemployment and spare capacity 1960–1981

Quarterly, 1960 QIII = 1

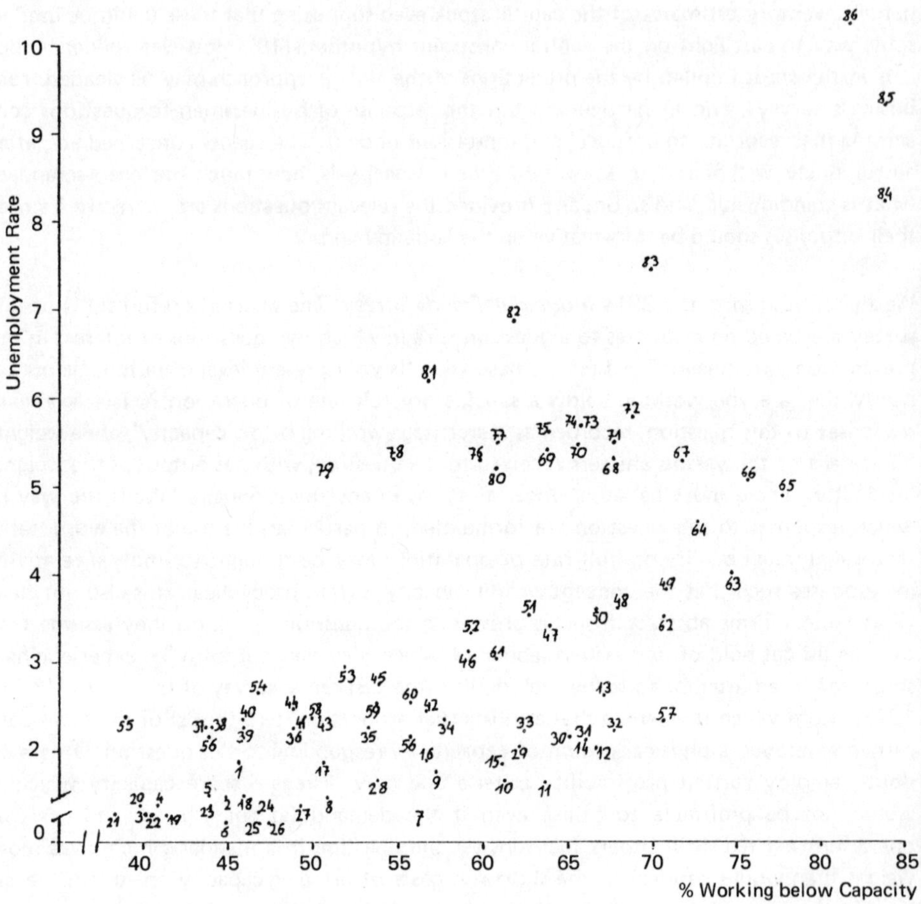

The second question of interest in the CBI survey asks: 'What factors are likely to limit your output over the next four months?', and invites respondents to indicate the *most important factor* or factors among the following: orders or sales; skilled labour; other labour; plant capacity; credit or finance; materials or components; other. Figure 6.3 shows a plot of the proportion of respondent firms indicating 'plant capacity' against those indicating 'orders or sales'. Whilst the raw figures are themselves of some interest, indicating as they do the dominance of the 'Keynesian' 'sales' variable, and there is – as might be expected – evidence of an inverse relationship between the two constraint variables, there is also a suggestion in the data that the proportion of firms citing capacity

Figure 6.3

Orders – plant capacity relationship
C.B.I. survey 1960–1981

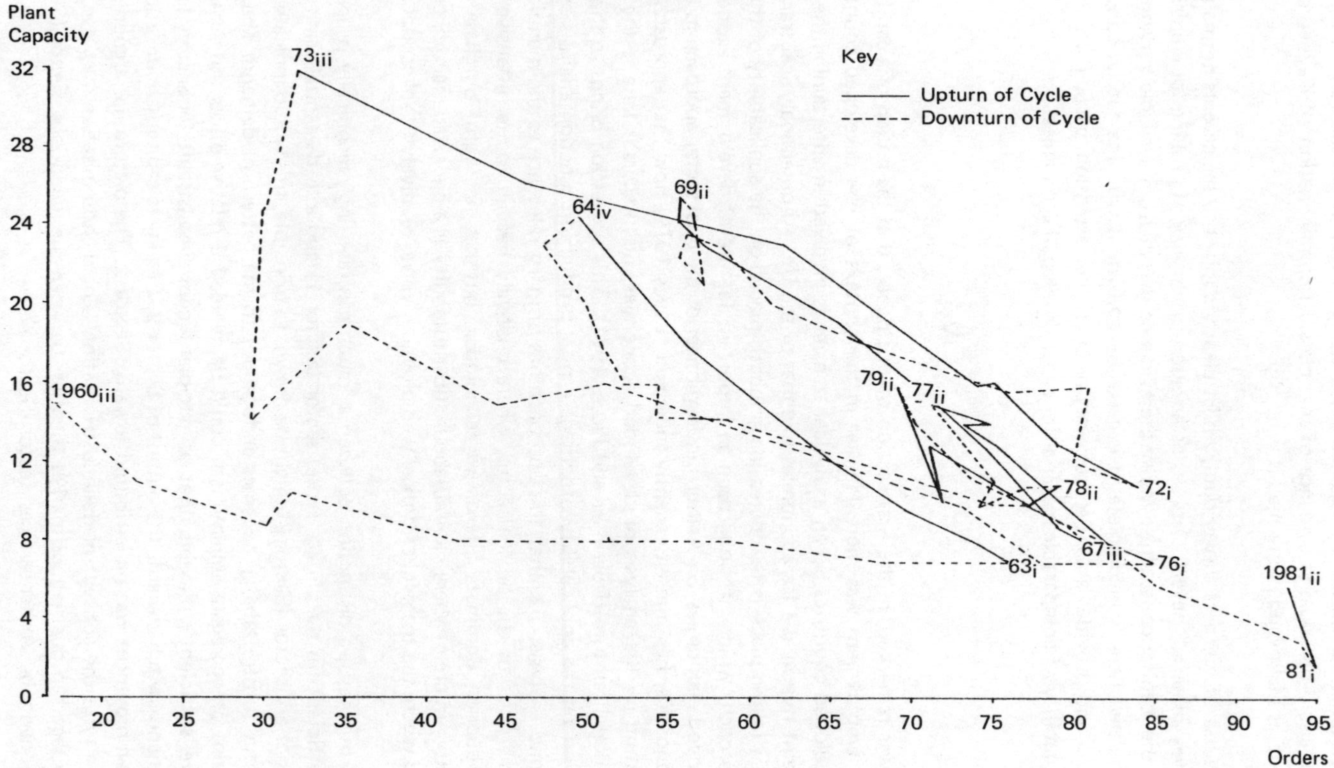

limitations has moved up against those citing orders in the successive cycles(13). This, too, could be taken as evidence of the 'classical contamination' of Keynesian unemployment, as Malinvaud has termed it.

The use of business survey data, whilst clearly subject to the caveats normally applied to survey material, nevertheless seems an appropriate way of probing for empirical evidence on the 'capital constraint'; whilst the evidence drawn from available survey material and presented here is incomplete, it is certainly consistent with the capital constraint hypothesis and provides a data source worthy of further attention, particularly in view of the availability of comparable material for other developed economies.

IV

It was remarked, in the first section of this paper, that the notion of a capital constraint on employment was more familiar in the context of less developed countries than in developed countries, so an analytical transfer is involved in entertaining the capital constraint hypothesis for economies like that of the UK. Another analytical transfer that has been taking place is the increasing emphasis placed on the applicability of the dual sector approach, which has long been an important feature of development economics, to developed economies. Sir Arthur Lewis, pioneer of the dual sector approach in development economics, has himself recently indicated (Lewis 1979) how that approach may have a bearing on the analysis of developed economies; his precursor here is the dual labour market literature (Doeringer and Piore, 1971). This suggestion brings to the fore a limitation on the applicability of vintage capital production function analysis as macro-economic analysis, viz. that this approach has primary relevance to the manufacturing and some parts of the service sector, where relatively heavily capital intensive methods of production dominate alternative techniques, but has no useful purchase outside this sector, in areas where capital/labour substitutability is a preferred maintained hypothesis and where the techniques typically employed involve 'relatively little' capital.

On this basis, a distinction between a 'much capital-using', technically progressive fixed-coefficient (in the vintage sense) sector (Sector 1) and a 'little-capital-using', technically stationary sector (Sector 2) might be drawn. In principle, this would indicate that capital-labour substitutability becomes endogenous to the pattern of demand. The capital constraint on aggregate employment could be avoided if relative prices and demand patterns were sufficiently flexible that an incipient capital-constraint in Sector 1 produced a demand switch towards the output of Sector 2. Aggregate capital/labour ratios would fall as employment was redistributed towards Sector 2. The picture has a good deal in common with the concept of de-industrialisation. The dichotomisation may also parallel that envisaged in dual labour market theories, between the 'good jobs' sector (Sector 1) and the 'bad jobs', 'other services' sector (Sector 2).

The question arises whether such transfers are (a) feasible and (b) whether, if so, they represent the passive output of a beneficent process or the outcome of a vicious or, at least, less beneficent process.

Thus, if the demand for 'other services' is sufficiently income elastic, the rising productivity available through embodied technical progress in the advanced sector (Sector 1) will imply a process of deindustrialisation. With beneficence, this allows an employment transfer to the 'little-capital-using' sector, and represents a passive adjustment to an endogenous 'taste change'. If real wages in the little-capital-using sector are in equilibrium with those in the advanced sector, the income effect must work against a relative price effect as the opportunity cost of service output rises with increasing Sector 1 productivity.

The process may not be so benign, however. Dual labour market theory suggests that Smith's law of the equalisation of net advantages is not perfectly observed. In the advanced sector, labour unions may be sufficiently well entrenched to command, or seek to command, a share of the quasi-rents accruing to new vintages of capital equipment. The consequences of a real wage push of this kind may involve all of the following: accelerated scrapping; decline in net investment; increase in (more capital-intensive) replacement investment. It is not clear that the employment released from Sector 1 by this process can be absorbed in Sector 2, even though the relative price effect favouring industrial goods demand is attenuated. State intervention to subsidise services carries with it implications suggested by Bacon and Eltis (1978); failure to intervene implies a growing reserve army of the unemployed and/or a widening of the gap between the good jobs sector and the bad jobs sector. This way of picturing a 'vicious' process may have a different initiating force; it need not be that the 'cause' of the problem is an access of aggression by the 'aristocracy of labour'. All that is required is that labour aspirations and power in the advanced sector are sufficiently well entrenched as to allow real wage bargaining to become detached from the economy's potential to deliver the real wage bargained for in such a way that any deterioration in that potential results in the sequence of accelerated scrapping and unemployment described earlier. The location of the deterioration may have to do with oil price shocks; technology transfer to NICs; decreasing returns from R and D, or any of a number of causes. The notions of the dual labour market contrasting a well-organised, relatively highly paid advanced sector with a less organised, less advanced and less highly paid sector serve to suggest that such shocks are not easily absorbed by the economy and result via 'inappropriate' real wages in a period of unemployment, and the appearance of de-industrialisation and the capital constraint.

To give licence to the unbridled liberties of the imagination is hardly the best way of concluding a paper. To set matters in the perspective of the main theme explored here, though, it seems important to stress that important as demand deficiency undoubtedly is – in a global context – in explaining, proximately, probably the greater part of our present unemployment, there is undoubtedly more to it than that. The full employment of the period from the mid-1940s to the mid-1960s is not the historical norm, but rather the exception. It seems doubtful that it had much to do with the learning of Keynesian economics: there is indeed an element of tragic irony in the fact that it is only when the world has come face to face with its major post-war recession and needs the application of Keynesian remedies, that the political will to enforce them has been found wanting. But, even if it were present, the problems represented by the capital constraint hypothesis (weak or strong forms) would have to be faced. There does seem to be some evidence in favour of it; about its ultimate causes we are much less clear.

Footnotes

(1) See also Sautter (1978).

(2) The fact that observed unemployment includes 'benefit-induced' unemployment indicates that L_S^* in the above argument should be appropriately defined so as to allow for this. Otherwise, there is also an unemployment benefit constraint on the realisation of L_S^*.

(3) Of course the classical case can be reinstated if, instead of assuming that equipment is scrapped, it is assumed only that it is scheduled out of production for the time being and is again available for use so soon as the real wage excess is removed. This decision whether to 'mothball' equipment or to scrap it is clearly a complex one dependent (*inter alia*) on expectations of the future course of real wages and other production costs and of technical progress, anticipations of demand, and the opportunity cost of retaining idle (or diverting to an alternative use) currently unprofitable equipment.

(4) *Per contra,* in Solow *et. al.* (1966) it is assumed for the bulk of analysis 'that at each moment of time the surviving stock of capital is adequate to employ the whole labour force' and that the alternative regime in which 'output is limited by a shortage of capital while labour is redundant, has no application to an advanced industrial economy' (*ibid.* p. 110). This is a matter of *a prioristic* definition, however.

(5) Whilst the literature tends to concentrate upon labour as the only variable factor of production, and thus emphasises the wage cost element of production costs, recent events may be read as indicating that the sharp rise in energy, especially oil, prices may have reduced the viability of energy-intensive production processes. Thus Artus (1977) has argued that the potential output of Western economies should be regarded as having been cut by the rise in energy prices (although his neo-classical production function approach seems less obviously sympathetic to such an argument than the vintage approach).

(6) There must be some arbitrary rationing of capacity in these circumstances. In a vintage model, the scrapping condition also provides a hierarchical ordering for the withdrawal of capacity from productive use, so that if Malinvaud's constraint was thought of as the weighted average capital-labour ratio of the set of vintages making up the fixed capital stock, less labour-productive equipment (earlier vintages if past technical progress have been labour-augmenting) would be scheduled out of current production first. That it would not be scrapped seems to require that entrepreneurs do not anticipate the perpetuation of Keynesian unemployment. (On the importance of regime-anticipation in rationing models, see Portes and Muellbauer (1978)).

(7) In both situations a downward adjustment of real wages is thought likely, but whereas this reduces the probability of remaining in the Marxian regime, it increases that of remaining in the Keynesian one.

(8) This is not only because it is the expected path of real wages which (presumably) enters the investment decision and perfect foresight cannot be assumed, but also because – as the previous section of this paper emphasised – variations in the real wage could have implied a different set of macroeconomic regimes.

(9) Of course, something can be done to test the conditionality of the predictions by carrying out sensitivity tests for the response of the predictions to change in the assumptions.

(10) Such data can of course be used in a production function approach but as this is generally implemented on the assumption of substitutable labour and capital, the use of capital stock series in this context will not yield a capital constraint, although they may yield predictions of a decline in productive capacity in recent years (cf. Artus, 1977).

(11) Up to 1971, the surveys were completed every four months, being put on a quarterly basis thereafter. The data scatter shown in Figure 6.2 is based on quarterly interpolations of the four-month data for the earlier period.

(12) It is also consistent with hypotheses that maintain that the increase in unemployment is 'benefit-induced'.

(13) In an endeavour to test this hypothesis rigorously, a regression was run with the proportion citing capacity (P) as the dependent variable, and with orders (O) and 'the cycle' (C), of which four were distinguished, as regressors. Orders were entered separately according as to whether this variable was rising or falling. The regression yielded the following results (t-statistics in parentheses):

$$P = \underset{(2.00)}{25.31} - \underset{(7.41)}{0{,}253(0^{+})} - \underset{(5.45)}{0{,}193(0^{-})} + \underset{(2.42)}{1.25C.}$$

However, the overall fit ($\bar{R}^2$ = 0.44) was not impressive; not surprisingly, the DW statistic was quite low, at 0.44. The cyclical characterisation of the data towards the end of the period is not strong (cf. Figure 6.3) and alternative experiments were carried out specifying more cycles, but with broadly comparable results.

References

Artus, J. R. (1977) 'Measures of potential output in manufacturing for eight industrial countries', *IMF Statistical Papers,* March, pp. 1–35.

Bacon, R. and Eltis, W. (1978) *Britain's Economic Problem: too few producers* 2nd edition (London: Macmillan).

Doeringer, P. B. and Piore, M. J. (1971) *Internal Labour Markets and Manpower Analysis* (London: Heath and Co).

Dreihuis, W. (1977) Capital-labour substitution and other potential determinants of structural employment and unemployment, *University of Amsterdam Research Memorandum,* no. 7708.

den Hartog, H. and Tjan, H. S. (1976) 'Investments, wages, prices and demand for labour (a clay-clay vintage model for the Netherlands)', *De Economist*, vol. 124, no. 112, pp. 32–55.

de Klerk, R. A., van der Laan, H. B. M. and Thio, K. B. T. (1977) 'Unemployment in the Netherlands: a criticism of the Den Hartog-Tjan vintage model', *Cambridge Journal of Economics,* September.

Lewis, Sir Arthur (1979) 'The dual economy revisited', *Manchester School,* September, pp. 211–229.

Malcolmson, J. M. (1975) 'Replacement and the rental value of capital equipment subject to obsolescence', *Journal of Economic Theory,* vol. 10, pp. 24–41.

Malinvaud, E. (1977) *The Theory of Unemployment Reconsidered* (Oxford: Blackwells).

Malinvaud, E. (1978) 'Nouveaux développements de la théorie macroéconomique du chômage', *Revue Economique,* January, pp. 9–25.

Malinvaud, E. (1980a) *Profitability and Unemployment* (Cambridge: Cambridge University Press).

Malinvaud, E. (1980b) 'Macroeconomic rationing of unemployment' in Malinvaud, E. and Fitoussi, J. P. (eds.) *Unemployment in Western Societies,* (London: Macmillan).

McCracken Report (1977) *Towards Full Employment and Price Stability* (Paris: OECD).

Portes, R. and Muellbauer, J. (1978) 'Macroeconomic models with quantity rationing', *Economic Journal,* December, pp. 788-821.

Price, R. H. (1977) 'The CBI Industrial Trends Survey – an insight into answering practices', *CBI Review.*

Salter, W. E. G. (1960) *Productivity and Technical Change* (Cambridge: Cambridge University Press).

Sargent, J. R. (1968) 'Recent growth experience in the economy of the United Kingdom', *Economic Journal,* March, pp. 19–42.

Sautter, M. (1977) 'Investissement et emploi dans une hypothèse de croissance ralentie', *Economie et Statistique,* October.

Solow, R. M., Tobin, J., von Weizsäcker, C.C. and Yaari, M. (1966) 'Neoclassical growth with fixed factor proportions', *Review of Economic Studies,* vol.42, pp. 79–115.

Stamler, H. V., Hutton, J. P. and Stern, J. (1978) 'Employment in manufacturing industry in a vintage capital model', *Government Economic Service Occasional Papers (UK).*

DATA APPENDIX

The data used in constructing Figures 6.2 and 6.3 are set out below.

Unemployment in the UK 1960–1981 *ad Figure 6.2*

		% working below capacity	Unemployment rate
1960	1	45.75	1.9
	2	42.50	1.5
	3	40.25	1.3
	4	41.00	1.4
1961	1	44.0	1.5
	2	45.00	1.2
	3	56.50	1.2
	4	51.00	1.5
1962	1	57.75	1.8
	2	61.50	1.7
	3	64.0	1.7
	4	67.0	2.1
1963	1	67.75	2.7
	2	66.50	2.2
	3	63.0	1.9
	4	57.0	1.9
1964	1	51.75	1.9
	2	46.0	1.5
	3	41.50	1.3
	4	40.0	1.4
1965	1	38.5	1.3
	2	40.5	1.3
	3	44.0	1.4
	4	47.0	1.3
1966	1	47.0	1.2
	2	47.5	1.2
	3	49.5	1.4
	4	54.0	1.7
1967	1	62.25	2.1
	2	65.50	2.2
	3	66.50	2.2
	4	68.0	2.3
1968	1	62.75	2.3
	2	58.00	2.4
	3	53.50	2.3
	4	49.0	2.3
1969	1	43.75	2.3
	2	44.0	2.3
	3	46.0	2.3
	4	46.0	2.4
1970	1	49.75	2.4
	2	57.00	2.5
	3	50.50	2.5
	4	49.0	2.5
1971	1	54.25	2.8
	2	59.50	3.2
	3	64.33	3.5
	4	68.33	3.7
1972	1	71.0	3.9
	2	67.0	3.7
	3	63.0	3.6
	4	59.0	3.4
1973	1	52.0	3.0
	2	47.0	2.7
	3	39.0	2.4
	4	44.0	2.2
1974	1	71.0	2.4
	2	50.0	2.4
	3	54.0	2.6
	4	56.0	–
1975	1	61.0	3.1
	2	71.0	3.6
	3	75.0	4.1
	4	73.0	4.7
1976	1	78.0	5.0
	2	76.0	5.2
	3	72.0	5.4
	4	68.0	–
1977	1	64.0	5.5
	2	66.0	5.6
	3	66.0	5.8
	4	69.0	5.9
1978	1	66.0	5.8
	2	66.0	5.8
	3	64.0	5.7
	4	60.0	5.4
1979	1	61.0	5.6
	2	55.0	5.4
	3	51.0	5.2
	4	61.0	5.3
1980	1	63.0	5.7
	2	70.0	6.2
	3	76.0	7.0
	4	84.0	8.4
1981	1	84.0	9.5
	2	82.0	10.4

Orders – Plant Capacity Relationship *ad Figure 6.3*

		Order	Plant capacity			Order	Plant capacity			Order	Plant capacity
1960	1			1968	1	75.25	12.00	1976	1	85.0	7.0
	2				2	71.00	15.50		2	82.0	8.0
	3	16.75	14.75		3	65.25	19.25		3	75.0	13.0
	4	22.00	11.00		4	57.00	23.00		4	73.0	14.0
1961	1	30.25	8.75	1969	1	55.50	24.50	1977	1	75.0	14.0
	2	30.50	9.50		2	55.50	25.50		2	71.0	15.0
	3	31.50	10.25		3	56.25	24.75		3	75.0	11.0
	4	47.00	8.00		4	57.00	21.00		4	74.0	10.0
1962	1	57.75	8.00	1970	1	55.50	22.50	1978	1	22.0	11.0
	2	65.00	7.50		2	56.00	23.50		2	29.0	11.0
	3	68.50	1.00		3	58.00	23.00		3	77.0	10.0
	4	73.00	1.00		4	61.00	20.00		4	71.0	13.0
1963	1	76.00	7.00	1971	1	68.50	17.75	1979	1	72.0	19.0
	2	74.00	8.00		2	76.00	15.50		2	69.0	16.0
	3	69.50	9.50		3	80.75	15.83		3	70.0	15.0
	4	65.00	70.00		4	80.00	12.37		4	74.0	11.0
1964	1	56.00	17.25	1972	1	84.0	11.0	1980	1	82.0	8.0
	2	51.50	22.00		2	74.0	13.0		2	85.0	7.0
	3	49.25	24.50		3	75.0	16.0		3	91.0	4.0
	4	47.00	23.00		4	74.0	16.0		4	94.0	3.0
1965	1	47.00	23.00	1973	1	62.0	23.0	1981	1	95.0	2.0
	2	49.50	20.50		2	46.0	26.0		2	93.0	6.0
	3	52.00	17.50		3	32.0	32.0				
	4	52.00	16.00		4	25.0	30.0				
1966	1	54.25	16.00	1974	1	29.0	14.0				
	2	54.00	14.50		2	35.0	19.0				
	3	58.50	14.25		3	44.0	15.0				
	4	75.00	9.00		4	51.0	14.0				
1967	1	77.25	9.75	1975	1	73.0	10.0				
	2	79.50	9.00		2	78.0	7.0				
	3	80.50	8.25		3	82.0	7.0				
	4	79.00	9.00		4	83.0	7.0				

Chapter 7

INFLATION IN THE USSR AND EASTERN EUROPE (1)

Nita Watts

It has for long been generally accepted that excess demand, or the existence of a sellers' market, is an essential element in the chosen 'command' economic systems of the USSR and the countries of Eastern Europe (2). Given the stress on full utilisation of productive capacities and rapid economic growth as policy objectives, this can hardly be contested so far as the inter-enterprise 'market' in fuels, raw materials and intermediate products is concerned. Whether the functioning of the system necessarily depends also upon a sellers' market for all final output – capital goods and consumer goods – is perhaps worth considering as a question, despite the considerable volume of literature accepting that it does. A second question is whether significat 'cost-push' forces can be expected to exist in these economies. Finally, is it conceivable that they were in fact managed for some twenty years up to the mid-1970s, and in several countries virtually up to the end of the decade, so as to hold the average annual rates of increase of prices in the market for consumers' goods to two per cent or less? This is the maximum rate of increase indicated by any of the official consumer price indices, which show a rise of about 45 per cent over the twenty years to 1975 in Poland and, at the other extreme, about a 10 per cent fall in the German Democratic Republic (GDR). The Soviet index for 1975 is almost precisely the same as that for 1955 (and significantly lower than in some earlier years) and only in Poland (in 1957 – 58) have the official price indices risen by more than about two per cent in any single year up to 1973.

In all these countries, of course, prices throughout the system are not, in principle, market determined. Either they are fixed by a central price authority or if price fixing powers are devolved to lower authorities – as they always have been in a very minor degree in all countries and were on a major scale in the GDR after 1967 – the principles on which prices are determined are laid down by central authority and, in general, 'market-clearing' is not included among them. To the extent that market clearing prices are the aim in the consumer-goods markets, the turnover tax is, in principle, the instrument for equating consumer demand to plan-determined supply.

The factors ensuring that the inter-enterprise market in fuels, materials and intermediate products is a sellers' market hardly need yet another reiteration. Long experience of receiving almost (or quite) impossibly demanding output plans and inadequate, or at least irregular, material supplies has induced the enterprise director habitually to understate his production capability and to overstate his need for material and labour inputs when providing his superior authorities with the information on which his plan targets should be based. It has induced in him an insatiable appetite for fuels, materials and components – to put into stock against future needs even if they are not required for current production. His immediately superior authority (industrial association, trust or industrial ministry) will be only in part his ally – out of sympathy with the hoarding of material inputs at the enterprise if this prevents the relief of supply shortages in other enterprises under its control, but equally interested with him in securing easy output plans and lavish input allocations for the ministry or trust as a whole. The central planners, aware of the strong incentives to understate production possibilities and to overstate input needs, set output (or delivery or sales) targets exceeding the possibilities reported to them from below and issue allocations of materials, etc., (or approve plans for their use) exceeding the likely availabilities reported to them; and so the circle is completed (3).

The investment-goods market

But does a belief in 'taut planning' to mobilise 'reserves' of productive capacity that would otherwise remain hidden imply that the planners must also logically approve plans for fixed investment that exceed the likely availability of construction capacity, machinery, etc.? The short-term argument for mobilising reserves can, of course, be applied to every stage of production and distribution preceding delivery to the final user or consumer. But given (a) that the purpose of long-term and medium-term (5 years) investment plans is not merely to expand total productive capacity but also to bring about changes in the economic structure and technological advance, and (b) the fact that it is impossible for the central planners to prescribe in minute detail the outputs to be produced each year to meet the needs, which they cannot know in every detail, of investors in that year, it might be argued that investment plan priorities are more likely to be achieved if authorisations for expenditure are limited to a level which obliges the producers of equipment to look for customers in order to fulfil their annual output (or sales or delivery) plans. Even if output of goods for stock is allowed to count towards plan fulfilment, rising stocks of the least wanted investment goods could still – if final investment demand was sufficiently limited – signal the need for changes in producers' output or 'assortment' plans or for the re-equipment of the investment goods industries.

However, while it is certainly not unkown for some types of, usually rather simple, machinery to appear as surpluses of 'soft' goods readily available for export, over-ambitious investment plans and excess demand for investment goods in general have been a normal characteristic of these economies. The symptoms of overstrain in this sector – an excessive number of projects started at the beginning of each five-year plan period, with subsequent delays in completions and increases in construction costs and the tying up of resources unproductively in an enormous 'stock' of uncompleted investment projects – have been a cause of almost continuous official lament and criticism in every country; and strain on supplies of investment goods leads to other increases in costs also. 'A construction firm which cannot find steel beams of the size and shape required uses the larger size; and this is true for cement, paint and the like. All this leads to increases in unit costs' (Rychlewski 1972). And the firm might, alternatively, 'economise' in the use of scarce materials, with a subsequent early need for repairs or even reconstruction.

Of course, delayed completions could reflect the inevitable failure to match precisely the *details* of planners' orders for output with the needs of those authorised to undertake investment expenditures even if, in total, output capacities and authorised expenditures were equal. But if this were the sole cause we would expect to see surpluses of some types of investment-goods capacity arising more often than they seem in fact to have appeared.

While not only the final plans but also the preliminary 'plan directives' have usually shown governments to be aiming at extremely high rates of investment, the almost continuous tension in the investment goods market also stems in part from a virtually insatiable demand from most investors themselves, at least for extensions of capacity (modernisation may be another matter, see below). To the industrial investor capital is cheap, and used to be cheaper. If investment is financed from a non-repayable grant from the budget, or out of retained profit which can be used for no other purpose and is likely to be skimmed off by higher authority if not immediately spent, it is virtually costless. Admittedly fixed assets have, for many years past, incurred an annual capital charge (around 5 per cent of their gross value in most countries) and depreciation charges must be set aside out of the enterprise's revenues on the basis of a centrally determined 'life' for the type of equipment or building; but, in general, product prices have been fixed on a basis which incorporates such charges, as costs to be covered with a margin of profit. The more recent changes, to the financing of enterprise investment through interest-bearing, repayable bank credit rather than budget grants, have for similar reasons made little difference to the enterprise director's view of the cost of investment.

But even if the incurring of extra capital taxes and depreciation charges, or of obligations to pay interest on bank credits, does carry a risk of reduced total profit or profitability (return on fixed assets), this may well be of little concern to the enterprise director. His 'success' in the eyes of his superiors, and the achievements that assure him bonus additions to his salary and good prospect of promotion, do not depend *primarily* upon increasing his enterprise's profits. Neither do increased profits generally make a great deal of difference to the size of the funds left at the disposal of the enterprise director for use on his own responsibility, for payment of bonuses, the undertaking of small investments, etc.; and it matters little to him whether he hands on the surplus of his gross revenues over his material and labour costs – to the state budget, to his superior trust, or to the bank – in the form of taxes and charges or in the form of profit.

Interest in increasing productive capacity is felt at least as strongly by the industrial enterprises' superior authorities — the trusts and/or industrial ministries — and they may have good reason to add additional demands themselves. Generally speaking, enterprises are not nearly as interested in innovation as they are in expanding existing activities. Introduction of genuinely new products or processes may involve argument *ab initio* with superior authority about input 'norms' and output plans, rather than continuing from established precendent; re-equipment with more modern machinery, even to produce the same output as before, may mean a temporary check to the steady year-by-year expansion of production and difficult argument, both to get plan targets modified while the process is going on and also to avoid increases in subsequent output plans of such an extent that modernisation of his capacity makes the director's plan-fulfilment task more difficult rather than easier. Thus ministries may add their own demands for new, innovating, capacities.

Departments of government concerned with agriculture or with social and economic infrastructure investment, and the regional authorities, will be no more inhibited in pressing their claims than the industrial ministries, and the central planners — or their political masters — may themselves see a need for major structural changes involving heavy investment demands (e.g. Khrushchev's drive to expand the Soviet chemicals industry). The central planners thus normally find themselves facing at the start of the preparation of each five-year plan, demands for investment allocations totalling more than the economy can possibly support. The demands are always pruned, but not enough to avoid extreme tension in this sector.

A number of economists with direct experience of the working of the eastern European economies have examined the investment cycles, characteristic of their economies, resulting from over-ambitious investment plans (4). An investment boom — and particularly a boom in new starts at the beginning of a five-year plan period — leads often to a faster rate of investment expenditure than the average intended for the plan period, and sometimes to formal upward revision of the plan target. Eventually, however, this is likely to produce intolerable strains on either the balance of payments or consumers' real incomes (as consumer goods industries are starved of materials diverted either directly to the investment goods sector or to exports) and/or to lead to intolerable accumulations of uncompleted projects, increases in costs, and declining productivity of investment. Cut-backs in investment authorisations, and particularly in new starts, then follow; but as soon as the most obviously excessive tension has been eliminated, over-authorisation starts again.

The generally accepted explanation of the over-ambitious investment plans of the 1950s has been 'an impatient forcing of fast economic growth' (Soós 1975, and Kornai 1971, p. 321) — insistence by the planners and their political masters on optimistic assessments of production, and/or export and import, possibilities and on allocating to consumption the minimum required to avoid popular unrest or 'concealed strikes' by disgruntled workers. In more recent years, in some countries at least, the central authorities' insistence on maximum growth rates has given place to a much greater concern with the pattern of growth and the quality of output and has also accorded a higher priority to consumers' satisfaction; but, it is asserted by some observers, the pressure of investors' demands has been more than the planners could effectively resist. In Hungary, it has been argued, demands from enterprises and industrial ministries before the 1968 reforms, all 'motivated by good intentions: they indeed believed that it was the implementation of their investments that served the economic development of the country' (Soós 1975), could never be sufficiently resisted. Lack of detailed knowledge of needs and possibilities on the part of the central planners is one suggested reason; another is the tendency for the costs of projects proposed to the planners to be deliberately understated (and, by implication, their 'efficiency' or likely rates of return to be overstated) in the effort to 'get into the plan'. Once projects were approved and work started, the investor had a strong claim to allocations of extra resources, above the needs originally estimated, to avoid the obvious waste of leaving a project unfinished; and all investors would have an incentive to prefer 'starts' to 'completions' given the reasonable expectation of later cut-backs of planned starts as total commitments proved to be excessive.

However, the argument that the central planners *must* inevitably succumb to pressure to undertake too large investment commitments has been contested. Janusz Zielinski has argued that the Polish Central Planning Board has to slash the requirements notified to it in any case, and could well reduce them further, that the effectiveness of its action when it does decide upon a firm restraint of investment activity has demonstrated its power and that 'it is known that planned investment costs are on average twenty-five to thirty per cent lower than actual investment costs', yet no adequate allowance is made for this. Despite earlier experience of crises of over-investment and the need for drastic cut-backs during the plan period, virtually every new plan is again too taut. His explanation is that 'the CPB treats personal consumption as a *cost* of growth rather than the ultimate goal of growth' and will effectively restrain investment only when the physical (technical and organisational) limit on the economy's capacity to invest has been reached – and excess demand pressure results in rising construction costs, lengthening completion periods and rising stocks of unfinished projects – or when political pressures 'from below' impose a higher priority for consumption (Zielinski 1973).

But if both investors' demands and planners' (and political authorities') preferences tend to produce over-ambitious investment plans, there could also be a further reason for the latter to prefer 'excess' demand to 'inadequate' demand in the investment goods sector. It may be wasteful to use unnecessarily large steel beams on a particular construction site (see above) but will it not also appear wasteful if stocks of good steel beams build up with nobody wanting to use them? If output plans cannot quickly be adjusted to users' preferences, then does it not appear sensible to ensure sufficient demand in the short run to guarantee that anything usable – even if not ideal for its purpose – will be used? It is not a view that the writer, or all Eastern European economists, would readily accept; but it cannot be dismissed as being obviously without influence on the authorities concerned.

So far we have been considering whether there is normally a 'planned' tension in the investment sector. But one must also ask whether unplanned increases in demand for investment goods are possible. When the only sources of finance were budget allocations or specifically approved retentions of profit or of depreciation funds these were completely subject to planners' authorisation and the banking system's control; and when bank credit later assumed a role in investment financing this did not greatly weaken the central planner's ability to limit the maximum investment finance available in any period (5). The more recent moves towards some self-financing on the basis of authorised retentions of a percentage of profits earned by the enterprise has, however, weakened central control of investment to some small extent. The level of profits in a given period can only be forecast, not precisely determined, by the central planners. But the degree of uncertainty about the total availability of investment finance has in some cases been limited by permitting independent enterprise use of only a small proportion of the funds arising from above-plan profit and, in general, the extent to which available funds can automatically vary with changes in profits has been small. Moreover, it is always possible for enterprise development funds to be frozen by the bank or skimmed off by higher authority if their total exceeds the planners' expectations (6); though if this is a frequent occurrence the incentives to seek profit and to plough back profits only into 'efficient' investment projects will, of course, be weakened.

The fact of prevailing 'tension' in the investment sector remains, most probably at least preferred by the authorities to any obvious slack but also, from time to time, exceeding their desires. Whether this condition should be termed either 'inflationary pressure' or 'suppressed inflation' is perhaps not a very interesting question. It tends to make investment costs higher than they would otherwise be (even though the prices of individual capital goods do not automatically rise because of excess demand for them) but this has no automatic impact on prices in other sectors. However, the balance of consumers' incomes and supplies of consumers' goods may be affected to the extent that resources are diverted away from planned production of consumers' goods, including housing, or that above-plan employment and wage payments occur in the investment goods industries. Either development will tend to intensify pressure on consumer prices or 'suppressed inflation' in the consumer-goods market.

The consumer-goods market

In a system in which 'factory-gate' prices for all goods and services are fixed so as to cover the costs of labour and material inputs, depreciation, capital charges and interest *plus* a pre-determined profit margin, a balance of total consumers' expenditure with the value of goods and services available for consumption in any period requires that profit margins and taxes on marketed consumers' goods and services must be so adjusted as to ensure that the total non-wage content of their marketed value equals the total of labour income generated outside consumer-goods production *plus* transfer incomes (pensions, etc.) *minus* taxes on incomes and any willing saving (net) by consumers. And, so long as profits are skimmed off to the state budget or retained only for planned investment expenditures, it does not matter whether profit margins or turnover taxes play the major role in securing the desired balance.

Leaving for later comment the rather ambiguous concept of 'willing saving' in a Soviet-type economy, let us suppose that the central planners do indeed aim for such a balance in the consumer-goods market. What can then happen to disturb the planned balance?

Until the mid-1960s, at least, plan targets for all employing institutions, other than collective farms, in all countries normally included an upper limit to the annual wage bill. However, these limits were often renegotiated upwards during the year if the enterprise could persuade its superior authority that fulfilment of its output plan was impossible with the employment and/or average wage target originally set. Moreover, it was generally permissible for an enterprise to exceed its planned wagebill if the gross output or sales plan was also overfulfilled, the permitted percentage excess being linked by some co-efficient (less than 1) to the percentage overfulfilment of the output plan. In addition, it was frequently, though not invariably, the case that the rewards or penalties attached to success or failure in meeting output targets outweighed those attached to employment or wage bill targets, so that if it was impossible to satisfy both demands, the enterprise director was likely to put achieving his target output before respect for his wage-fund limit (7).

In the 1970s, practice changed in some degree in most countries. In Poland it became the practice, over an increasing range of industrial enterprises, to link the permitted percentage increase in the wage bill over the previous year's level to the percentage increase in value added (value of sales at factory-gate prices *plus* any subsidy paid to the enterprise *minus* expenditure on material inputs and any turnover tax paid). In the GDR there was a similar linking of the annual increase in the wage bill to the increase of labour productivity. In most countries, a link was introduced between profits (or profitability) realised by the enterprise or trust and the bonus fund added to the wage bill (Adam 1976).

Thus there has always been a fairly strong tendency in all countries for actual wage bills to exceed the levels implied by the initial plans handed down to enterprises. If the central planners attempted to allow for this tendency for 'wage bill drift' in setting the initial plans, as would seem to be a natural reaction after some years' experience(8), this still implies that the overall plan for consumers' incomes and supplies normally contains a significant element of 'forecast' on the income side – an element that must, on the whole, have been increased by the more recent changes in wage and bonus systems. On the other hand, the tendency for employment to exceed planned levels has become less as reserves of under-employed labour in agriculture are absorbed and activity rates approach their maxima.

If total personal incomes in fact rise faster than the planners anticipate and this is matched by above-plan output of consumers' goods, the planned balance in the market need not be disturbed. But if 'taut planning' means that enterprises producing consumers' goods have greater difficulty in acquiring material inputs than do those in the 'priority' producer-goods sectors, there is obvious danger of unplanned tension in the consumer-goods market.

Another significant source of consumers' incomes, other than wage payments and transfer incomes, is the collective farm sector; and this is also a very significant source of supplies to the consumer-goods market – supplies varying not mainly with the authorities' output plans but with the weather. The traditional collective farm system made personal income per hour's or day's work on the collective a residual, dependent on the farm's gross earnings *minus* other necessary or obligatory expenditures. This tended to ease the problem of managing demand in the urban consumers' market, by forcing the farm population to bear a disproportionate share of the variations in per capita real income resulting from harvest fluctuations; and the state procurement agencies' practice of paying higher prices for deliveries above the 'obligatory' or contractual minimum, while marketing all supplies at a fixed retail price, even reinforced this tendency. But it was mitigated to some extent by rising prices on the free, collective-farm markets (on which some collective-farm produce as well as the products of the household plots are sold) in a bad year. However, the pricing practice of the state agencies would tend to open a gap between the planned total of all consumers' incomes and the planned value of total supplies of marketed goods in a year of good harvest.

The spread of fixed (minimum) hourly wage systems to the collective farms in recent years has tended to stabilise individual income from work in the collective, as compared with the earlier practice, with wage reserves being built up in the farm's account in good years and drawn upon, possibly together with bank credit, in bad years.

Clearly planners' short-term control of the consumer-goods market is less than cast iron; and there may also sometimes be factors making it difficult even to plan for overall balance at stable prices. Quite apart from the hazards of harvest fluctuations, the steady growth of real per capita consumption may be threatened by the emergence of pressing new investment or defence priorities and/or by balance of payments constraints. The latter are unlikely to be very important – at least as short-run constraints – for a country as large as the Soviet Union; but they can be, and have been, significant for the more trade-dependent countries. But the pressures tending to bring about continuous increases in money wages are in fact quite strong.

Wage tariffs for different industries, occupations, grades of skill and (possibly) regions are normally fixed by central authority and adjusted at intervals. If at any time they do not prove effective in attracting the quantity and quality of labour that enterprises need, there will tend to be unofficial adjustment – for example by enterprises offering the workers they wish to recruit a higher skill grading than is strictly appropriate or relaxing work 'norms' so that bonuses, or higher piecerate earnings, are more easily achieved. General discontent on the part of workers in a particular enterprise or area, or more generally, can also manifest itself in various ways, including lower productivity, even though trade unions are not independant of the Party and Government and overt shop floor pressure, or open protest in the streets, are rather rare phenomena.

Hungarian and Polish economists have estimated that in both of these countries about a four per cent minimum annual increase in per capita money wages is required, if cuts in particular wage rates are to be avoided, to provide for necessary adjustment of differentials and for the tendency for the proportion of workers in the higher grades of skill to increase (Gadó 1976, pp. 69 - 70). It might well seem desirable to the planners to concede more than this minimum rate of increase, even if real resources for consumption were constrained, if it were felt that some degree of money illusion contributed to satisfaction from rising money income even though the real increase was much less than the nominal rise.

However, the average annual rates of increase of wages paid in the state sector in the twenty years up to 1975 seem, in most countries, to have been held very close to the minimum suggested above (see *Table 7.1*).

Per capita money incomes from all sources increased much faster in most countries, largely as a result of rising activity rates, shifts in the pattern of employment from agriculture towards industry, extending social security coverage and more rapid increases in non-industrial incomes in the later years. Increasing monetisation of the rural economy also undoubtedly accounts for some part of the rise of per capita money income, and this is likely to have been particularly important in Bulgaria and the USSR, among the countries for which figures are available.

There have, not surprisingly, been large variations in the year-to-year rates of change in both per capita wages and per capita income from all sources. In some years particularly large wage increases in some countries have obviously reflected political pressures (e.g. increases in per capita wages of twenty per cent in Hungary and fourteen per cent in Poland in 1957) and in others per capita income in the whole economy has risen sharply as a result of a deliberate change in income distribution policy. Such a change was

Table 7.1

Annual percentage trend rates of growth 1955 – 75

	Consumer price index	Money wages in the state sector	Per capita money incomes
Bulgaria	0.44	4.5	8.5
Czechoslovakia	0.41	3.4	5.1
GDR	– 0.41	3.5	4.3
Hungary	0.97	4.1	6.8
Poland	1.55	4.8	7.8
Romania	0.20	5.5	..
USSR	0.02	3.7	5.8

Notes: Bulgaria: retail prices of goods in state and cooperative retail trade; gross money wages; gross money income from all sources.
Czechoslovakia: prices of goods and services (index for wage and salary earners); wages as above; disposable money income from the socialised sector.
GDR: consumer price index for goods and services; wages as above; disposable money income from all sources.
Hungary: prices as Czechoslovakia; net money wages; money incomes as Bulgaria.
Poland: prices as GDR; net money wages; money income as Czechoslovakia.
Romania: prices and wages as Bulgaria.
USSR: prices and wages as Bulgaria; disposable money incomes from the socialised sector plus income from private sales of foodstuffs to the private sector.

Source: Portes (1977).

indicated, for example, by the large increases in procurement prices for farm products in Hungary in 1966 and 1967, producing an increase in per capita income from work in the whole economy of thirteen per cent from 1966 to 1968 while per capita wages rose by only half as much.

Years of particularly large increases in money incomes have usually been years of above average increases also in real incomes in these countries, supported by extra imports of industrial consumer goods or allocations of materials to the consumer goods industries, by good harvests or by reduction in exports or increases in imports of food. But even if it should be impossible in a particular year to keep consumers' supplies increasing in line with the desired or enforced rise of consumers' money incomes, the planners may still see good reasons to prefer temporarily increased market tension to the increases in turnover tax and in official prices which would mop up the excess purchasing power.

It has in fact been the normal practice to avoid substantial revisions even of the structure of consumer-goods prices except at long intervals. One reason is that control of the price structure is one of the instruments regulating the distribution of real income; and income distribution considerations have, for example, contributed to decisions to subsidise food prices even in conditions of extreme and persistent excess demand for many high-quality foods. Short-term income elasticity of demand for such foods (e.g. good quality meat) is everywhere high; but it would be difficult to adjust prices accordingly in times of intensified scarcity without disturbing the distribution of real income. It may be felt that rationing by ability to queue or to search for a shop with the goods the buyer wants is in some way 'fairer' than rationing by the purse. Secondly, price increases tend to be extremely unpopular and to call attention to the 'unreality' of money income increases more forcefully than do somewhat intensified shortages. Thirdly, it may actually be easier to exercise a continuous control of both money wages and real consumption levels and patterns if the general price level remains stable and the price structure changes only slowly or infrequently. Income earners can feel confident that money incomes and accumulated savings and pension rights are not likely to depreciate sharply in real value; and people with confidence in the stable purchasing power of their savings may be somewhat more willing to put up with shortages. The consumer unable to buy the refrigerator he wants will be more willing to wait if he knows that the money he sets aside will still pay for it if he finds it in the shop a year later; and he can pay a deposit to secure a place in the queue for some particularly scarce good knowing that when he eventually reaches the head of the queue the real value of his deposit will not have fallen significantly(9). Finally, the revision of consumer-goods prices is an enormous administrative exercise, and not one that any administration would wish to undertake often or at short notice.

It may be appropriate at this point to digress to take up the question of cost-push pressure on prices in a centrally-planned economy. So far as wage costs are concerned, it has already been suggested that increases in wages exceeding the central authorities' intentions are more likely to be a result of strong demand in some parts of the labour market than of workers' pressure. Should such wage increases occur, for whatever reason, and should the increases exceed the growth of labour productivity so that wage costs per unit of output rise, there is no automatic transmission of increases in unit costs to prices. Increases in unit wage-costs in one year may be offset in another and, if they are, longer-term price stability need not be disturbed even though long-term policy is to relate prices to production costs. Wholesale prices, as represented by official index numbers, have in fact risen moderately over the years in all countries, reflecting both price reforms which have tended to increase profit margins and rising wage costs in some sectors. Nevertheless, spasmodic wage-cost inflation tends to produce problems of short-term demand management, as discussed above, rather than direct cost-pressure on prices.

The same is true of rising costs of imported goods. These are sold on the domestic market at the prices fixed by the national price office irrespective of any variations in the foreign exchange prices paid for them. However, worsening terms of trade, requiring an increased volume of exports to finance a given volume of imports, can complicate the problems of demand management in a trade-dependent economy.

The one case in which cost-push pressures are not transformed by the mechanisms of these economies into intensified problems of demand management is when the success indicators and incentive systems encourage enterprise directors to reduce the quality of products or to substitute higher priced for lower priced goods in their outputs. By introducing 'new' products, enterprise directors may be able to get approval for 'padded' cost estimates which make it easier to reach gross output or sales targets and/or to achieve premium-earning profits; and complaints about the introduction of spurious 'new' or 'better quality' products have been widespread, as have been complaints about worsening quality of some others [Nove (1977) pp. 248-9, Haffner (1975), Bornstein (1976) and Fallenbuchl (1977)].

So far, we have been considering the factors which may contribute to the development in any period of a lack of balance between consumers' incomes and supplies which differs from the planners' intentions. There remains the question whether the authorities are likely to *plan* for some degree of 'excess demand' in the consumer-goods market.

Stalin's expressed preference is well known: 'Here in the Soviet Union consumption (purchasing power) of the masses grows continuously, advancing ahead of the rise in production ... the growth of the domestic market will advance beyond the growth of industry, serving as a spur to industry continually to expand production' (10): And the central planners may well prefer to aim at some overall excess consumer demand, rather than risk deficient demand, for reasons similar to some of those suggested above in the case of investment planning.

They have only imperfect knowledge of either consumers' preferences or production possibilities, and it is in any case impossible for them to prescribe in minute detail the types, qualities and quantities of consumer-goods to be produced by each enterprise. But the directives and incentives given to enterprise managements are not such as to call forth precisely that assortment of goods that matches consumers' preferences at the going (centrally fixed) prices. Whether the major 'success indicator' is value of output (or sales) or whether it is profit, the enterprise director is not concerned to know whether there are customers for the goods he produces unless final demand is so slack that the trade network simply refuses to take certain goods off his hands. But in such conditions, there will be demonstrated an obvious waste of resources, in the form of a piling up of stocks of unsaleable goods. This may be a demonstration that the planners prefer to avoid so far as possible and, up to a point, consumers who cannot get what they want can be induced – with money to spare – to take what they can get(11).

Finally, the planners can reflect that there is little danger of any chain reaction through the economy from excess consumer demand; imports will not automatically be sucked in or potential exports diverted to the home market; labour and materials will not be switched from investment goods to consumer-durables production simply because demand for the latter is strong, though high profit margins on them may have this effect — but profit margins do not necessarily reflect demand.

It is in fact extremely difficult to judge whether 'suppressed inflation' in some clearly definable sense is a normal condition of the consumer-goods market in these economies. Certainly there have been shortages of some goods at virtually all times, and certain goods are perennially scarce: 'the consumer may wait for months or even years for a flat, telephone, car ... young people born during or following the war who have not travelled abroad consider it natural that in Hungary ... veal is never obtainable in the shops' (Kornai 1976). Evidence of specific shortages is to be found in the literature of all countries of the area, as well as being observed by any foreign visitor, while there are black markets in the foreign currency that gives access to goods in the foreign exchange shops. People are clearly being obliged at most times to accept a pattern of consumption different from what they would choose if infinite supplies of all goods were available with the going structure of prices. But would their total expenditure on consumption be higher in those conditions but with unchanged money incomes? Is there normally involuntary saving by consumers?

Many western observers and some economists in the eastern European countries would argue that there is a considerable element of involuntary saving in the rise of personal savings deposits which has everywhere occurred; and in the Soviet Union there have been expressions of anxiety at the build up of 'postponed demand'. It is argued that the piling up of stocks of unsaleable goods, frequently reported over many years, does not mean that consumer saving would be unchanged if the assortment of goods and services available were different: living standards are now high enough that people will save in the hope of finding what they want eventually rather than mop up all that is available(12). Moreover, larger liquid money balances are held than would otherwise be desired, in order that no opportunity may be missed to buy any of the more scarce goods when they appear.

Others argue that rising consumers' savings appear to reflect quite unsurprising or even rather low savings propensities, given the increase of real incomes, expectations of increasing availability of consumer durables, and the fact that to secure many of these — including new housing — large pre-payments may be required.

The ECE secretariat concluded in 1974 that 'The accumulation of savings is as a rule determined less and less by the negative inducement of the unavailability of some consumer goods in the required quantity or quality and is now increasingly determined by long-term motivations of safety and future spending.' They noted the significance of advance saving in the finance of new housing and purchases of consumer durables, which a Hungarian survey suggested accounted for over 60 per cent of the savings of families questioned (13). Statistical work so far done in this field has produced estimates of long-term personal savings ratios in the USSR and Eastern European countries in the range of 2 - 5 per cent. Nobody would deny that involuntary saving has occurred at certain times of particularly rapid rise of consumers' incomes and/or exceptional constriction of supplies: but the question whether suppressed inflation and involuntary saving are the norm in these countries remains in dispute [see UN Economic Commission for Europe (1967) part I, pp. 116-7, Pickersgill (1976), Bornstein (1976), Schroeder and Severin (1976), Lacko (1975) and Portes and Winter (1978)].

It is in fact difficult to judge what is 'normal' saving behaviour in economies characterised by full employment, collectivised agriculture, pensions schemes always fairly comprehensive and becoming more so over the years (though still generally providing only relatively low living standards), relatively narrow dispersion of personal income (in some of them, at least) and a restricted range of, generally low-yielding, assets in which savings can be held. Moreover, while wealth and privilege may be found together, it is not wealth alone that buys privilege, in the form of access to superior housing, holiday or hospital accommodation and education for children, or the right to foreign travel, etc. (14). On the other hand, the fact that consumer credit is relatively limited and that for the goods most in demand large advance payments are required, would tend to encourage saving as hopes rise of increasing supplies of such goods.

Finally, the question remains whether the official consumer price indices do represent the actual rates of price inflation in these countries, maintained certainly with 'micro' imbalances — shortages of some goods, surpluses of others in process of only gradual correction by price and/or output adjustment — and, from time to time (possibly persistently) involuntary saving. The official indices are fairly generally mistrusted, certainly within the countries concerned and by most foreign observers.

The problem of reflecting changing quality in price indices is one that has nowhere been solved. In a perfectly competitive economy the replacement of one variant of a good by a higher-priced variant would occur only if consumers derived extra satisfaction from the higher-priced good. In an imperfectly competitive western economy, we cannot assume that this must be so; still less can we assume it in the economies under discussion, for reasons already indicated. The practice in the Soviet Union is to calculate a price index using current expenditure weights applied to index numbers of official prices of 'typical' products in each expenditure group (15). These typical products can include variants no longer available, though still in the official price lists, because they have been replaced by higher-priced substitutes. Moreover, the introduction of genuinely new products at specially high temporary, 'incentive' prices will of course be reflected in consumers' expenditures but not in the 'typical' price indices; these incorporate new products only when they are in large-scale production at lower normal prices. Some other countries use somewhat different methods (e.g. a fixed basket of goods, revised at intervals, as the basis for the index) but in varying degree they are subject to similar criticisms, even when the indices cover, in principle, both official and free market prices.

The writer has been impressed by the unanimity with which Polish economists, discussing the rise in real wages in that country during the first half of the 1970s have spoken of 'increases in real incomes, not of course as great as official figures suggest, but still large'. The President of the Hungarian Price Office has stated that in conditions of market tension 'concealed price increases practically equal an annual 2 per cent increase of .... consumer prices' (Csikós-Nagy, 1972 p. 829). In the Soviet Union, a widening gap between food prices in state shops and on collective farm markets from the mid-1960s to the mid-1970s casts further doubt on the official picture of price stability (16); and in Poland food prices on the free market certainly rose more than twice as fast as those in state shops over the twenty years to 1975 (17). Black markets, bribery, conditional sales and the hiring of queuers for scarce goods have all been reported in various countries.

Attempts to recalculate the growth of real per capita consumption in the USSR (1955 to 1975), Hungary and Poland (both 1955 - 1967), however, suggest that if we accept that official statistics do not overstate the growth of money incomes — and there seems to be no reason why they should — the underestimate of the increases in consumers' price levels over the same years cannot be more than about one to one and a half per cent a year in the first two countries and rather more in Poland (18), bringing these three countries up to rates ranging from some one and a quarter per cent to three per cent a year.

Hungary is the one eastern European country covered in a recent attempt to compare absolute consumption levels, on the basis of national data revalued at 'international' prices (19). This shows Hungary with a per capita consumption level in 1970 some sixty-six per cent of that of the United Kingdom, and the two countries' national statistics indicate that in 1955 per capita consumption levels (with approximately the same coverage) were about 50 per cent and 75 per cent, respectively, of those reached in 1970. Acceptance of national price and expenditure indices at their face value implies that the people of Hungary enjoyed, or endured, in 1955 a standard of living only some 43 per cent of that of the UK population at the same time, or not quite one-third of the level reached in the UK by 1970. If we accept an alternative estimate of the growth of Hungarian consumption levels which implies adding another one and a half per cent a year to the official price index, Hungarian standards in 1955 were rather more than half those in the UK at the same date or some 40 per cent of the UK's 1970 level.

Particularly large excesses of British over Hungarian standards (valued at 'international' prices) in 1970 appear in private motoring and air travel, housing and consumption of the newer consumer durables (other than radios and television sets). If we assume that per capita consumption of all of these except housing was negligible in Hungary in 1955, and if we allow for housing standards being still lower in 1955 than in 1970, the gaps between Hungarian and UK consumption levels implied by an assumed one and a half per cent understatement of the annual rate of price increase in Hungary certainly do not seem unbelievably wide.

Richard Portes has stated more directly that 'it would be difficult to argue that living standards have not at least doubled over the past two decades' (i.e. up to 1975) in the USSR and Eastern Europe (Portes 1977); and perhaps it is. If so, we again come back to estimated annual rates of price inflation in the one and a quarter to three per cent range in most countries (20).

It must be concluded that, even if official price indices understate the real rise of prices by some one to two per cent a year, consumer price inflation was kept to a relatively slow rate in most eastern European countries from the mid-1950s to the mid-1970s. It is difficult to judge the degree of suppressed demand underlying this relative price stability; but it probably diminished over the years in most countries even though the patterns of demand and of supplies obviously still do not match at all well in most countries even today. The planners may well see good reason to err in the direction of planning for some excess, rather than deficiency, of overall demand for consumer goods. The avoidance of more than the planned excess, if any, of demand in the consumer goods market depends essentially on the control of wage bills and farm-gate prices. Wage-bill control has never been absolutely effective, in the sense that enterprises have adhered precisely to the wage bill or employment and average wage targets handed down to them; but it is reasonable to suppose that planners' ability to forecast, and to allow for, 'wage-bill drift' has grown with experience. Consumer credit can be tightly controlled in total and limited only to goods for which an increase in demand is desired, and requirements for advance payment for particularly scarce goods can be used both to encourage and to immobilise consumers' savings, at least in the short term. Finally, the fact that unit cost increases, whether reflecting increased wage costs or import prices, are not automatically, and need not be immediately, passed on to domestic market prices removes much of the danger of a cost-price spiral.

Nothing has been said here, except by implication, about the costs of operating an economy on the basis of sellers' markets combined with relative overall price stability and inflexible price structures. It is too large a topic to explore here even had it not already been explored in depth by others. The costs can be stated in summary terms as the blurring of the signals to the planners that should indicate relative scarcities, misallocation of resources as a result of irrational investment decisions and neglect to exploit fully the cost-minimising opportunities offered by foreign trade, discouragement of technological advance and some sacrifice of potential consumers' satisfaction from the real resources the authorities choose to allocate to consumption. There is reason to assume that these costs become more significant as the economies themselves and the objectives of economic policy become more complicated and as labour reserves are exhausted. They are, of course, the costs of these countries' chosen economic systems as a whole, not simply the costs of relative price stability, fairly effective control of income distribution and full employment.

The impact of the 'western world's' price inflation and recession in the 1970s

So far, this discussion has concentrated on developments in the Soviet and eastern European economies up to 1975; but by the end of the 1970s the picture of general relative price stability was changing in several countries, and most drastically in Poland and Hungary.

Accelerated price inflation in the western world in the early 1970s and the onset of recession in the industrialised western countries about 1974/75 both worsened the terms of trade of the CMEA countries in their relations with the West and resulted in slack demand in western markets, more intense competition and sometimes increased difficulty of access for their exports. Prices in intra-CMEA trade did not immediately reflect price changes in the western world. In the first half of the 1970s intra-CMEA trade prices were, in principle, based on the average world-market prices of 1965 - 69; but in 1975 the decision was taken to change to a five-year moving average of world-market prices. The result was greatly to improve the terms of trade of the USSR, probably to leave those of Poland little affected and certainly to worsen the terms of trade of Hungary, Czechoslovakia and the GDR.

Thus increasing difficulties in exporting to western markets and/or worsening terms of trade tended to hamper economic growth in most of the eastern European countries in the later 1970s, and particularly in the most industrialised and/or most trade-dependent of them. But the actual adverse effects were reduced – or at least postponed – by the ease with which they found themselves able to raise credit in the West to finance part of their import bills.

With slackening growth of total output from the first to the second half of the 1970s – certainly *not* attributable in most countries mainly to the impact of changes in external conditions, but accentuated in many of them by difficulties linked with such changes – rates of increase of real wages (and of average real incomes of all kinds) also fell, in varying degree from one country to another (see *Table 7.2*). In most countries this was brought about by effective control of the growth of money incomes and with a continuing relatively stable consumer price level, at least up to 1979. In the Soviet

Table 7.2

Annual percentage increases of NMP, real wages, per capita real incomes and retail prices 1971 – 75 and 1976 – 80

	NMP		Real wages		Per capita real incomes		Retail prices	
	1971-75	1976-80	1971-75	1976-80	1971-75	1976-80	1971-75	1976-80
Bulgaria	7.8	6.2	2.8	0.8(a)	5.8	2.4	0.2	1.7(a)
Czechoslovakia	5.7	3.7	3.4	1.3(a)	4.5	1.9	0.1	1.9(a)
GDR	5.4	4.1	3.7	3.1(a)	5.5	4.3	−0.1	—(a)
Hungary	6.2	3.2	3.4	0.6	4.6	1.7	2.8	6.3
Poland	9.8	1.6	7.2	1.6	9.6	2.8	2.5	6.9
Romania	11.3	7.1	3.8	(4.9)(b)	8.0	5.0	0.5	1.8
Soviet Union	5.7	4.4	3.7	2.9	4.4	3.3	−0.1	0.6

(a) 1976-79 (b) Real wage fund

Sources: UN, ECE, *Economic Survey of Europe in 1980* and *Survey* for 1976, Part II.

Union and the GDR the consumer price indices remained virtually stable throughout the period, with mounting subsidy bills offsetting increases in producers' prices. But by the end of the decade other countries were generally raising consumer prices rather faster than before, though still generally moderately. The stated aim was to limit the rise of subsidies; relief of market tensions – or limitation of them where money wage increases threatened to outstrip growth of supplies – may also have been a motive in some cases.

Hungary (discussed in the next section) and Poland are obviously exceptions to this general picture of continuing price stability. In Poland large real-wage increases were conceded during the first half of the 1970s to reduce popular discontent and in the hope of stimulating labour productivity and, with a concurrent investment drive intended particularly to develop capacity for exports to the West, necessitated large foreign borrowing. Failure of the desired exports to materialise, attempts to limit the growth of external debt, increasing disintegration of the national planning and management system and a resurgence of popular discontent had all reduced the Polish economy to a state of crisis by the end of the decade; external debt amounted to some $ 20 billion and debt service threatened to pre-empt the greater part of Poland's annual earnings of convertible currency; output actually fell in 1979 and in 1980; real wages fell in 1978 and did not significantly exceed the previous year's level by 1980. The consumer price index has risen partly as a result of deliberate attempts by the authorities to limit subsidies and establish a more rational price structure, partly because it was virtually impossible to limit money wage increases to match the possible growth of real consumption levels; and also underlying the rise of consumer prices have been both 'incentive' increases in farm-gate prices and also increases in factory-gate prices resulting in part from the weakened central control and the profit incentives linked with an earlier half-hearted 'reform' of the planning and management system. Even with the increases in consumer prices, shop-shortages and other signs of 'suppressed inflation' have intensified during the later part of the decade.

Hungary since 1968

The 'new economic mechanism' introduced in Hungary in 1968 was intended to establish a managed market economy. The main objective of the comprehensive changes in the system was greater economic efficiency; objectives – or constraints – carried over from the past were full employment, the preservation of an acceptable distribution of income and stability of the price level.

The intention was progressively to free prices for determination by the market, with a unitary exchange rate relating domestic and foreign prices and allowing world prices to influence the domestic price and production structures. Enterprises motivated to seek profit would trade freely with each other, with the final consumer and with foreign buyers and sellers. Materials allocations (with a very few exceptions) and production targets would cease to exist (though enterprises might be required to accept contracts for exports to other CMEA countries). Enterprise managements would bid freely for labour and workers would share in the profits of their enterprises. Enterprise directors would take their own investment decisions, financing investment from retained profits and bank credit.

The commitment to full employment has so far proved to mean no visible unemployment. Dismissal except for misconduct has been virtually impossible and an 'incomes policy' based on regulation of the increase in the average per capita wage in each enterprise has tended to encourage recruitment of unskilled workers, while there has continued to be a fairly strong pressure of demand overall. Price stability was at first defined as an upper limit of two per cent on the annual rise of the consumers' price level. These constraints obviously asked a great deal of the managers of an economy heavily dependent on foreign trade and in which – despite a prior price reform in what generally proved to be the right directions – price and output structures were expected to require considerable adjustment.

The chosen instruments for control of aggregate demand were initially (a) a form of average-wage control combined with regulation and progressive taxation of that part of enterprise profits available to pay bonuses (the sharing fund), and (b) taxation of profit retained in the development fund on a scale intended to keep most enterprises fairly heavily dependent on bank credit for investment finance, the availability and price of credit being centrally controlled (21). An effective devaluation of the forint, the customs tariff, a 'quota' for imports of consumer-goods and some indirect control measures and special temporary taxes were relied upon to prevent an excessive leakage of demand to imports (22). Temporary export subsidies were introduced to maintain the necessary level of exports until production patterns could be adjusted to take up newly profitable export opportunities. The subsidies proved to be less temporary than had at first been hoped but were increasingly transformed, in the first five years, from specific subsidies into supplements to an enterprise's export earnings – encouraging choice of the most profitable product-mix – and more recently have taken the form of similar supplements at the same rate for a whole branch of industry. The freeing of prices for determination by market forces initially affected producers' goods more than consumer goods (in 1969 only about twenty-five per cent of retail trade turnover represented sales at free prices). It was hoped that centrally-determined fixed prices and price limits would be progressively eliminated, but a continuing need was envisaged for a less precise and direct control through supervision of enterprises' pricing practices by the state Price Office. The extreme concentration of Hungarian industry implies widespread monopoly power, particularly so long as balance-of-payments constraints make complete freedom to import impracticable; and unholy alliances of managements and workers to exploit such power are an obvious danger. On the other hand, industrial concentration makes effective Price Office policing much easier than it would otherwise be.

The first five years of operation of the new economic mechanism revealed a number of strains. An unforeseen investment boom in 1970 - 71 was brought under control by credit restriction, freezing of enterprises' development funds in various ways, bans on new starts and cut-backs in centrally-financed expenditures. But more of a threat to the reformed system was the conflict that emerged between, on the one hand, the close links between individual earnings in industry and enterprise performance and, on the other, a pattern of income distribution acceptable both to the authorities and to major groups of income earners.

The system of industrial income regulation at the beginning of the 1970s, after some amendment of its original form, can be summarised as follows: Profits in any year (after payment of capital charges and wage-bill tax) were first subject to a local tax and a compulsory percentage set to reserve; the residue ('profit' in the Hungarian terminology and in the formulae referred to below) was then divided according to a prescribed formula (dependent on the ratio of wage bill to capital employed) between the enterprise's development and sharing funds, the former being subject to a flat rate tax of sixty per cent and the latter to a progressive tax depending on the relation of its value to the wage bill; any increase in the per capita wage bill over the previous year's level attracted additional tax to be paid from the sharing fund, the rate of tax (progressive) depending on the actual percentage increase of the average wage in relation to the percentage increase in a 'wage increment indicator' of the form $\frac{\text{wage bill and profit}}{\text{number employed}}$. The residue of the sharing fund was then available to pay wage and salary bonuses.

The system sufficed to keep the growth of per capita money wages under fairly tight control (an average annual percentage increase of five per cent from 1968 to 1972, while all 'income from work' per capita rose by six per cent annually but wages in state industry by only four per cent); but it did not prevent discontent among urban workers and, in the eyes of the authorities, a deteriorating pattern of income distribution. Discontent among industrial workers reflected (a) a redistribution of income towards the peasants, started quite deliberately before 1968 and later reinforced by the effects of the setting up of industrial and other enterprises by the collective farms as the reforms gave them more independence to determine their activities; (b) some quite startlingly large earnings from moonlighting and other private artisan and trading activity as official restrictions on the latter were relaxed and access to materials eased; (c) inter-enterprise differences in wages and profit shares reflecting not only — or even mainly — differences in workers' effort and managerial efficiency but also past investment decisions, for which neither had been responsible, and the varying incidence of price controls and special taxes and subsidies (23).

Another source of resentment — a higher limit on profit shares (as a percentage of wages) for managerial staff than for manual workers — was corrected as early as 1969.

In 1971 new regulations attempted to restrict moonlighting, and taxation on private trading and artisan earnings became more progressive. But during 1971 - 72 there was increasing evidence, and complaint, that workers in the larger state enterprises were losing ground in relation to those in other sectors; and in March 1973 a break in the linking of wages to enterprise performance came with the conceding to all manual workers in state industry of wage increases up to 8 per cent, without additional taxation falling on the sharing fund and with tax remissions and subsidies being provided if an enterprise's earnings were otherwise inadequate to pay at least sixty per cent of the increase. In the same year provision for, in effect, confiscation of profit resulting from 'unjustified' price increases tended to limit particularly high enterprise earnings.

It might well have been doubted from the beginning whether the necessary transformation of the production structure could be brought about without significant unemployment, simply by enterprise managements adapting their output patterns (though here the intense industrial concentration should have been a helpful factor) and workers moving from low-profit-low-wage enterprises to the more profitable. The payment of subsidies to finance 'adequate' wage increases everywhere tended to slow the process of change still more, though some restructuring was certainly achieved. However, by 1973 it had been decided that six large enterprises would have to be taken under ministerial control again, for major reconversion to be financed from central funds and staged so as to avoid significant unemployment.

Up to 1974, wage regulation and other means of demand management *plus* subisidies and direct price controls had sufficed to hold the rate of increase of the consumers' price index to an average of two per cent a year. Both centrally-fixed and free prices had changed to some extent in response to differing cost and demand pressures (with the latter rising, on average, about two and a half times as fast as the former), and the assortment of goods and services had become more varied and better adapted to demand patterns.

With the world price inflation of 1973 - 75, the Hungarian economy came under increased strain. The terms of trade with 'rouble-account' countries worsened by about eight per cent and with convertible currency countries by about twenty per cent, implying a loss estimated at the equivalent of a full year's 'normal' increment of GDP. Large-scale borrowing abroad lessened the immediate impact on the growth of resources available for domestic use, but there was no increase in real wages in 1976, though rises of three to four per cent followed in each of the next two years.

The forint was at first revalued in terms of the dollar simply to keep its exchange value stable in terms of other western currencies, though further revaluation followed after 1976. It has been persuasively argued by Richard Portes (24) that revaluation of the forint should have played a larger, and earlier, role in controlling domestic price inflation: since price elasticity of demand for most hard-currency imports is likely to be low and Hungarian exports to western markets are probably limited less by price than by availability, inadequate marketing techniques and limited access to markets, revaluation would have done little harm to the balance of payments with the West and would have had less incentive-distorting effects than the measures actually adopted to cushion the impact of the world price inflation on the Hungarian economy. These took the form of an extension of central price controls and a tremendous proliferation of (often enterprise-specific) special import subsidies and export taxes – the latter largley motivated by income-distribution considerations.

Together with continuing regulation of the rise of money wages these measures kept the rate of increase of the consumer price level to a relatively moderate four to five per cent in each of the years 1976–78 – though direct subsidies to consumer prices reached a value equivalent to fourteen per cent of total retail trade turnover by 1979 – and there seems to have been little significant increase in market tension. But continuing or reinforced price controls, some small amount of materials allocation and the proliferation of special taxes and subsidies must have made it increasingly difficult for enterprise directors to make rational investment decisions. Indeed, as early as 1974, the Minister of Finance was saying that the effects of special subsidies to enterprises were such that 'all profitability calculations on investment projects are distorted', and the situation must have worsened thereafter.

In such conditions it might well seem reasonable to take steps to reinforce central control of investment – the central authorities at least being in a better position than the individual enterprise director to assess the current distortions in the economy and their likely duration. In fact changes in the overall balance of price controls and fiscal measures after 1976, and in regulations affecting the enterprises' development fund and investment activity, all tended to make enterprises' investments more dependent on external finance and/or superior authoritys' approval. The effect, however, seems to have been greatly to increase the influence of the industrial ministries, which few Hungarian economists seem to think was conducive to economic rationality (25).

It may be noted, however, that the restriction of enterprise autonomy in this field may also have been intended to deal with the old problem of excessive new starts and long delays in completing projects. In this respect, the working of the NEM had not proved noticeably superior to the old system, perhaps partly because, until modification in 1976, it involved the automatic accumulation of investment funds by any enterprise making any profit, with the use of these funds virtually restricted to ploughing back in its own line of business or leaving on deposit at a relatively low rate of interest, and always with the risk that such deposits might be blocked or appropriated by higher authority (26).

By 1976 the original wage determination system was being modified to a shape that persists, with slight further modifications, today. There are, broadly, three systems in operation: (a) centrally-determined maximum rise in either wage-bill or average wage (not necessarily the same for every sector) permitted without 'penal' taxation of the sharing fund; a guaranteed minimum increase to be financed by subsidy or tax remission if necessary; progressive 'penal' taxation of the sharing fund for enterprises paying more than the maximum wage or wage bill; (b) average wage increase payable without penal taxation of the sharing fund fixed in relation to the 'wage increment indicator' mentioned above, the co-efficient and subsequent progressive tax rates centrally determined; also a guaranteed minimum wage increase; (c) total wage-bill increase regulated in relation to increase of 'value added' (profit as defined above plus wages); progressive taxation of the sharing fund as wage bill rises above the level indicated by a centrally-fixed co-efficient; a supplementary 'average-wage brake' and a guaranteed minimum.

Over the years, wage-bill control (with or without a supplementary 'brake' limiting the possible rise of the average wage) has increasingly superseded the earlier average-wage control, the changes in the system representing a continuing effort to reconcile the maintenance of a 'satisfactory' distribution of personal income with encouragement of individual effort and of labour-saving by management in an economy with a static, and fully-employed, working-age population. The latest stage in this process, in 1980, involves the abandonment of progressive 'penal' taxation of the sharing fund in favour of a flat rate tax once a stated percentage increase in the wage bill is exceeded, with tax concessions for enterprises reducing their labour force.

The wage-bill increase permitted without penalty in 1980 was nine per cent and this relatively high figure reflects a major new step in Hungarian economic policy in the previous year. It was then decided that an effort must be made to rationalise the now appallingly distorted structures of prices, taxes, subsidies, incentives and consequently output. Producers' prices would be aligned, over a relatively short period, to the world-market price structure and the consumer price structure correspondingly reformed. There was a nine per cent rise in the retail price index, as part of this process, in 1979 and again in 1980 and a further rise of four to five per cent is forseen in 1981. The area of centrally fixed prices has been somewhat reduced and more decontrol appears to be in prospect.

Constraints imposed by attempts both to improve the balance of payments with the western world and to bring about, partly related, changes in the production pattern have drastically slowed the recent growth of output, to a negligible increase in the two years 1979 – 80; real personal income has been virtually frozen at the 1978 level and little increase, if any, is expected in 1981. In these conditions, tight control of money wage increases is bound to continue, though in other respects it seems that some progress towards realisation of the original intentions of the New Economic Mechanism is being resumed. It is arguable that the general rise in the price level, already recorded and in prospect, might have been less if the Hungarian authorities had revalued the forint earlier, rather than engulfing the economy in a morass of special subsidies, taxes and controls which tended to suppress – or produce distorted – incentives for structural change, and from which it is difficult to extricate the economy without allowing the general price level to rise significantly. However, the process still appears to be one of controlled – not of 'run-away' – price inflation.

Footnotes

(1) I am most grateful for helpful comments on a much earlier first draft of this paper from Dr. W. Brus, Mr. E.F. Jackson and Professor Richard Portes. I am, of course, responsible for the mistakes and infelicities that remain.

(2) This paper is concerned with the economies of the USSR and Eastern Europe, excluding Yugoslavia; and the discussion up to p. 145 should be seen as applying to the Hungarian economy only up to the introduction of the 'New Economic Mechanism' in 1968. The period covered is the years of apparent relative price stability since the extreme inflations of the early post-war years were brought to an end at some time in the first half of the 1950s in all countries.

(3) There have been brief periods in several countries when the pressure of 'taut' plans has been relaxed; but periods of relative relaxation have seldom been so 'slack', or so prolonged, as to change the customary behaviour of enterprise directors.

(4) See for example Goldman (1964), Soós (1975) and Zielinski (1973) pp. 36 - 44.

(5) However, even though the central planners could co-ordinate budget grants, authorised retentions of profit and depreciation funds and the investment-credit plan of the banking system, there could at all times be some 'leak' of extra funds into finance of fixed investment via the never entirely effective control of working capital funds and short-term credit. These could not, in principle, be used to finance fixed investment; but it would require considerable courage for a local bank official to refuse credit to keep work going on an investment project backed by the director of an important enterprise and the local Party authorities.

(6) See Seidenstecher (1975), Granick (1975) pp. 75, 153 and 202 and Zielinski (1973) p. 256.

(7) In principle, such over-spending should have been prevented by the banking system's control of payments by enterprises. Not only must all inter-enterprise payments be made through bank accounts, with inter-enterprise credit forbidden – though delays in meeting bills may in fact produce an involuntary granting of credit from one enterprise to another – but the bank has the duty to ensure that cash withdrawals to pay wages (and all are paid in cash) do not exceed the enterprise's planned wage bill *plus* any duly justified above-plan or bonus payments. Like other financial controls, this has not always worked perfectly; but it could be used effectively to enforce any real determination (only rarely apparent in the earlier years) to make control of wage payments an overriding priority.
The control function of the banking system is reinforced by the 'cash plan', which covers the expected cash receipts and permitted out-payments by the banking system (about 80 per cent of outpayments are wages) broken down for short periods (e.g. quarters) and by region and district. But the problems of co-ordinating in time the local banking offices' cash plans with the wage bill plans of enterprises in their locality have proved virtually insuperable – see Garvey (1976) and UN Economic Commission for Europe (1967) ch. 8, pp. 4 - 5.

(8) According to the ECE secretariat, the practice in Poland has indeed been 'to provide [in the planned balance of consumers' demand and supplies] for a wage-fund increase larger than is implied by the plan for the growth of employment and average wage' (UN Economic Commission for Europe (1967) ch. 10, p. 11).

(9) The waiting time in the queue can be long. In Hungary in the two years 1967 and 1968 'valid orders' (on which deposits had been paid) for cars were more than double the number of deliveries to customers in the two years, with the excess of orders over deliveries for three out of four makes of car increasing sharply from one year to the next. For the two scarcest makes of car 'valid orders' in 1968 were four times the year's deliveries (Kornai, 1971 p. 241).

(10) Report to the 16th Party Congress, 1949.

(11) The relatively ineffective control of short-term credit, already mentioned, itself adds to the danger that unsaleable stocks will pile up. Trading organisations can claim bank credit to finance the holding of stocks and only the central authorities, if they become concerned about the volume of outstanding credit or other evidence of stock accumulation in the trade network, can take action to change the price structure or to tighten control of producers' 'assortment' plans. However, cut-price sales for surplus goods have become increasingly common in recent years.

(12) But stocks of unsaleable goods can reach large volumes. In the Soviet Union in 1972 'obsolete and unmarketable' goods were said to account for 12 per cent of total non-food stocks in retail trade (Schroeder, 1975).

(13) UN, ECE, *Economic Survey of Europe in 1974,* Part I, pp. 116 – 7.

(14) Though this has become less true of housing in several countries as individual or cooperative purchase increasingly replaces renting from public authorities.

(15) I. e. $\dfrac{\Sigma p_1 q_1}{\Sigma \frac{p'_0}{p'_1} p_1 q_1}$ when $\dfrac{p'_0}{p'_1}$ is the index of 'typical' prices for the expenditure group: see UN Economic Commission for Europe (1967) ch. 7, p. 60.

(16) Nove (1977) p. 24 shows ratios of free market to official prices as follows (official prices in each year = 100), 1965, 137; 1970, 145.5; 1973, 164.5. But differences in quality may justify some part, at least, of the discrepancies.

(17) But this has not been a continuing tendency throughout the period. Free market prices have shown greater year-to-year fluctuations, at times falling for a year or two, while state retail prices have drifted upward more steadily.

(18) Howard (1976), Schroeder and Severin (1976) and Portes (177). The first study, and the others noted by Portes, all estimate the rates of increase of real per capita consumption at about four per cent a year.

(19) Kravis and others (1978). The comparisons cover consumption including some state-provided services, such as health and education.

(20) Bulgaria is obviously out of line, in terms either of the increase in per capita income shown in the table or of 'concealed' price inflation; but the rise in per capita money income in that country undoubtedly overstates the rise in total per capita income in cash and in kind.

(21) In fact the interest rate on credit for fixed investment was set at only five per cent; but working capital (no longer even formally rationed to the enterprise) could be made extremely expensive and, on occasion, has been.

(22) The bank's scrutiny of applications for investment credit, for example, took into account the foreign exchange costs, as well as prospective yields of projects, and at times large advance deposits for imports of equipment have been required. Moreover, licenses for all imports are required and have on occasion been refused on the grounds that domestically produced substitutes were available – see Granick (1975) pp. 273 - 4.

(23) Special subsidies and/or tax concessions had not been confined to those necessary to ensure a sufficient volume of exports; and making a case for a subsidy came – according to some observers – to be as important a part of an enterprise director's activities as negotiating for an 'easy' plan had been in the past.

(24) Portes (1977) and a paper presented to a conference in Budapest in November 1978.

(25) It is also of interest that an amendment of the system of bonus payments to enterprise managements made these somewhat less dependent on enterprise profit (a bonus of no more than thirty per cent of basic salary can now be received under this head) but also dependent on superior authority's assessment of their performance (which can give up to an extra twenty per cent of basic salary).

(26) The obligation to allocate part of profit to the development fund according to formula has now been abolished and the tax rate on the fund has risen somewhat. The requirement for contributions from enterprise funds as a condition for bank credit also limits the free use of own funds.

References

[1] ADAM J. (1976) 'Systems of Wage Regulation in the Soviet Bloc', *Soviet Studies,* vol. 28, no. 1.

[2] BORNSTEIN M. (1976) 'Soviet Price Policy in the 1970s' in Joint Committee of the Congress of the United States *The Soviet Economy in a New Perspective* (Washington).

[3] CSIKÓS-NAGY B. (1972) 'Profit in Socialist Economy', *Economie Appliquée,* vol. 25, no. 4.

[4] FALLENBUCHL A.M. (1977) 'The Polish Economy in the 1970s' in Joint Committee of the Congress of the United States *East European Economies Post-Helsinki* (Washington D.C.).

[5] GADÓ O. (1976) *The Economic Mechanism in Hungary – How it Works in 1976* (Budapest: Akadémiai Kiadó) pp. 69–70.

[6] GARVEY G. (1976) *Money, Banking and Credit in Eastern Europe* (New York).

[7] GOLDMAN J. (1964) 'Fluctuations and Trend in the Rate of Economic Growth in some Socialist Countries', *Economics of Planning,* vol. 4, no. 2.

[8] GRANICK D. (1975) *Enterprise Guidance in Eastern Europe* (Princeton), pp. 75, 153 and 202.

[9] HAFFNER F. (1975) 'Pricing' in Hohmann H., Kaser K. and Thalheim K. *The New Economic System of Eastern Europe* (London).

[10] HOWARD D. (1976) 'A Note on Hidden Inflation in the Soviet Union', *Soviet Studies,* vol. 28, no. 4.

[11] KORNAI J. (1971) *Anti-equilibrium* (North Holland)

[12] KORNAI J. (1976) 'Pressure and Suction on the Market', in Thornton J.: *Economic Analysis of the Soviet-type System.* (Cambridge: Cambridge University Press).

[13] KRAVIS I.B. and others (1978) *International Comparisons of Gross Product and Purchasing Power* (Baltimore: John Hopkins University Press).

[14] LACKO M. (1975) 'Savings and the Supply Situation', *Acta Oeconomica,* vol. 5, nos. 3–4.

[15] NOVE A. (1977) *The Soviet Economic System* (London).

[16] PICKERSGILL J. (1976) 'Soviet Household Saving Behaviour', *Review of Economics and Statistics,* vol. LVIII, no. 2.

[17] PORTES R. (1977a) 'The Control of Inflation: Lessons from East European Experience', *Economica,* May.

[18] PORTES R. (1977b) 'Hungary: Economic Performance, Policy and Prospects', in Joint Committee of the US Congress *East European Economies Post-Helsinki* (Washington, D.C.).

[19] PORTES R. and WINTER D. (1978) 'The Demand for Money and for Consumption Goods in Centrally Planned Economies', *Review of Economics and Statistics,* vol. LX, no. 1.

[20] RYCHLEWSKI E. (1972) 'The Investment System of a Socialist Economy', *Economista,* no. 4 (English translation in *Eastern European Economics,* vol XII, no. 1, 1973).

[21] SCHROEDER G. (1975) 'Consumer Goods Availability and Repressed Inflation in the Soviet Union', in NATO, *Economic Aspects of Life in the USSR* (Brussels).

[22] SCHROEDER G. and SEVERIN B. (1976) 'Soviet Consumption and Incomes Policies in Perspective', in *The Soviet Economy in a New Perspective* (Washington D.C.).

[23] SEIDENSTECHER G. (1975) 'Capital Finance' in Hohmann, Kaser and Thalheim (eds.) *The New Economic Systems of Eastern Europe*, (London).

[24] SOÓS K.A. (1975) 'Causes of Investment Fluctuations in the Hungarian Economy', Közgazdasági Szemle, no. 1, reproduced in *Eastern European Economies,* 1975-76.

[25] UN ECONOMIC COMMISSION FOR EUROPE (1967) *Incomes in Post-War Europe (Geneva), ch. 8, pp. 4–5.*

[26] ZIELINSKI J. (1973) *Economic Reforms in East European Industry – Poland* (London), pp. 36–44.

Chapter 8

POLISH ECONOMIC MANAGEMENT 1970–81*

G. Blazyca

It should be admitted at the outset that well-considered and ably executed management of economic processes in Poland has, over recent years, been remarkably difficult to detect. In fact, many people believe that the Polish economy has been drifting aimlessly ever since the fateful moment in late 1972 when the now discredited leadership of the day took the decision to launch a consumption and investment boom of gigantic proportions. Thus this supposedly centrally-planned economy has been accused of having been subject to little effective overall guidance or direction for almost ten years.

Many intriguing questions are raised by this exhibition of spectacular but uncontrolled economic forces, in what was supposed to be an economy organised in such a way as to permit, at least in principle, detailed management through economic command. If anything, centrally-planned economies are surely meant to be under control. The anarchy of the market is, after all, meant to be absent. There is, however, another kind of anarchy which, as Polish experience dramatically shows, can emerge when individual powerful institutions of the command economy each set about vigorously promoting their own narrow interests, undisciplined by any overall authority *or* by the will of the people. But how can the 'steering centre' lose the ability to direct economic events? What becomes of the economic plan? What, in particular, happened to economic management in Poland between 1970 and the August strikes of 1980?

These and many other issues were keenly discussed in Poland during the seventeen months to December 1981 when economic debate openly raged once again. In the 1970s real economic dispute was a clandestine affair, one that could have no impact on the officially held perception that, despite difficulties, economic performance was broadly successful. With the Baltic strikes and the enormous victory of the workers it seemed as if the style of the past thirty years of government in Poland had been firmly rejected. Little did the participants in that drama know that in just over a year's time a regime would be imposed the likes of which had not been seen since the 1920s and 1930s when Pilsudski and his colonels ruled the Polish eagle's roost.

While there are of course a multitude of differences between the two periods, one thing they both have in common is that rule was erected on the shaky foundations of brute

* My thanks are due to Christopher Saunders for taking on the burdensome task in 1974 of directing my research on the Polish economy. Without his help and encouragement it would never have matured so quickly into a D.Phil. thesis. He is, of course, in no way responsible for errors of judgement in the present paper.

force. What the Polish military rulers believe can be achieved by this in the early 1980s is unclear. Indeed what many people find deeply puzzling is precisely how, after declaring its 'state of war' on Poland, the Army intends to extricate itself from the position it has so forcibly been occupying. Most people find it inconceivable that a reign of terror can be effective in economic terms even if it could be sustained – which itself is most unlikely.

Poland's economic problems are deep-rooted. The imposition of martial law disproved the claims of General Jaruzelski that he intended to adopt the robe of the reformer. Although clad in that fashion, despite the General's uniform when he spoke on television on 13 December 1981, it is clear that it was for the sake of appearances only. What sort of economic reform can be based on the shootings, beatings and internment of workers' leaders? Can incentive mechanisms, independent and self-financing enterprises really work in that sort of environment? The key to economic success is surely to liberate in people a voluntary desire to work with enthusiasm. Shooting coal miners in a country as heavily dependent on its coal industry as Poland is hardly likely to achieve this.

Ever since the signing of the Gdansk Agreement, now consigned to the dustbin of history, a vacuum in Polish political and social life has been clearly apparent. This political emptiness was simply a continuation of the absence of economic control in the 1970s. In the eyes of society the Party did not have the authority to act and Solidarity was unsure of its role on the political stage. Despite this fundamental problem there was at least discussion, not least a lively and heated economic discussion, which went on right to the day the material law decree was announced. So long as talks were taking place there was hope that a social consensus or an historic compromise could have been reached through which the people would have found a willingness to apply themselves to overcoming the country's deep economic crisis. That discussion has ceased and with it any real route to a solution. Because of the inability of an Army indefinitely to run a modern economy successfully and because of the growing ineffectiveness of traditional central planning, this discussion will at some time have to be resumed. It is because the economic debate of those seventeen months will have more than an historic interest that we summarise its main features in this paper.

Polish economic performance in the 1970s has been analysed elsewhere(1). It is unnecessary to go over that ground again here. Instead we concentrate on four particular themes which have not yet commanded much attention, but which may be of some help in understanding the trend of the Polish economy. First we consider some of the features of Polish economic administration between 1970 and 1980 which have contributed considerably to the growing economic paralysis. This leads to the second issue, a brief review of the main currents of discussions concerning Polish economic reforms liberated by the Gdansk and Szczecin events but then stamped out by Jaruzelski. The third issue concerns the question how likely it is that Polish economic problems will soon appear in other centrally planned economies. And lastly we turn to one of the most basic problems, how to achieve structural economic changes by means of socially acceptable economic policies; although this is a problem faced by all modern industrial countries, it emerges particularly severely in the East European bloc due to central planning 'rigidities'. It is worth reminding ourselves that many Western industrialised countries – not least the United Kingdom – are badly in need of new ideas for achieving smoothly, and without too much social upset, the structural changes required to cope successfully with both the internal and external economic problems which have emerged since the early 1970s.

Polish economic planning 1970–80

As is well known Gierek came to power as a result of the social upheaval of December 1970. He promised a renewal of social and economic life. The economic package to achieve this consisted of an attempt to thoroughly modernise the Polish industrial structure through imports of investment goods mainly from the West and financed by loans. An extremely rapid modernisation (with correspondingly large borrowing) was aimed at in the hope that during the second half of the 1970s increased production set in motion by means of foreign licences would ensure the repayment of external loans. Meanwhile an economic reform was initiated in 1973 based on the principle of strengthening central planning while simultaneously liberating enterprise initiatives. The key subject of reform was therefore the enterprise, understood as a 'Giant Economic Organisation' based on the association level of economic management (midway between ministry and individual productive units). Fairly quickly signs began to appear that in the economic sphere all was not as it should have been. The Five-Year Plan for the 1971–75 period was overfulfilled on critical indicators to an extent that should have aroused the suspicion that something peculiar had happened to the idea of planning. Wages which should have grown by 17 per cent had in fact risen by over 40 per cent. The figures for investment tell the same story of uncontrolled expansion; with a target for investment growth of 7.7 per cent p.a., investment actually grew on average by 18.4 per cent per annum. Output growth rates were also high, but it soon became clear that much of this consisted simply of additions to stocks(2). Price manipulations by large firms also helped to inflate output growth figures. Inflationary pressure mounted in the economy. The authorities decided to take action to steer the economy back to controlled economic development. An economic 'maneouvre' was devised with a threefold aim: (i) to cut and restructure investment spending, (ii) to speed up production for the home market, and (iii) to liquidate the trade deficit on the convertible currency account. Central control was reasserted (or so it was thought at the time), directives to enterprises multiplied as did the restrictions being imposed on the use of resources. Yet despite this, performance continued to be unsatisfactory. It became clear that the central planning authorities had in fact lost all control over the direction of economic activity. It did not take long for this economic disorganisation to spill over into social rupture and political crisis. Various attempts during the 1970s by the authorities to disguise the real loss of authority that had taken place in the economic sphere simply served to exacerbate social problems by increasing the sense of demoralisation being felt throughout society and in the economic management hierarchy. Not only was an increasing proportion of resources distributed as the result of purely political pressure, but the resulting pattern of allocation was devoid of any economic rationale. In fact, final output began more and more to be shared out through the vagaries of the queuing device. For some, however, privilege provided ready access to goods and services, heightening social tensions.

As plans for wages and investment growth were monstrously overfulfilled, it became fashionable to speak of 'open-planning'. However, what was really happening had more in common with, as Brus has said, 'planning chaos'. More generously a senior journalist (Chelstowski) on the staff of the weekly *Zycie Gospodarcze* has put the current crisis down to 'errors in economic policy and the real *atrophy* of central-planning'. Even the reform document prepared in November 1980 stated, 'the idea of 'open-planning' justified economic arbitrariness'. It went on, 'economic decisions were taken as the resultant of an interaction of forces expressing group interests, to the detriment of general economic balance and effective economic development'. The increased use of directives by the centre, the ever more detailed interference in production decisions served only to diminish the authority of economic management by command. The expansion of priority tasks was of course contradictory, as Nuti has pointed out, as well as being counterproductive since, given a large number of 'priorities', enterprises were forced to choose which of them actually to accord priority. As many economists would have predicted (and many did although denied a public platform), performance deteriorated as a consequence of this proliferation of directive tasks. With the lack of systematic criteria to guide decision-making, choices came, more frequently and at more levels of the management hierarchy, to be made in a haphazard manner.

Due to the pattern of industrialisation traditionally favoured in Soviet-type planned economic development, strong branch interests have been erected which play a key role in the resource allocation process. This branch particularism has been noted by many Polish economists. Jerzy Kleer in a typical manner explains that 'it is well known that every ministry, every association and every enterprise is in a good position to present weighty arguments justifying extra resources'. Some, however, would seem to be stronger than others and more consistently successful in winning resources. Hence the frequent complaints made by Polish economists of the 'petrification' of industrial structure and of the tendency to self-reproduction of an extensive type of economic growth(3). Perhaps some indication of this parochialism is evident in a consideration of the variability of growth rates of fixed assets across sectors of industry (see *Table 8.1*). One might expect strong 'particularism' to lead to relatively little variability once the basic pattern of industrialisation has been achieved.

A great degree of variability is to be expected in the early days of industrialisation when particular sectors are singled out for special attention and privilege. Such intense selecti-

Table 8.1

Variability of annual average growth rates of fixed assets over time

	Coefficients of variation (%)			
	1951–55	1956–60	1961–65	1966–70
Bulgaria	75.6	48.7	47.9	30.9
Czechoslovakia	58.7	44.0	45.9	39.1
GDR	n.a.	50.0	33.8	35.3
Hungary	64.5	29.5	41.2	47.2
Poland	62.7	55.1	26.2	27.8
USSR	28.3	43.5	29.7	25.6

Note: Data for this group of countries were readily available in *Structure and Change in European Manufacturing,* UN/ECE, 1977, pp. 254–55. Average annual growth rates are given for each of the fourteen industrial sectors for each country, except the USSR, where only eleven sectors are detailed due to the fact that light industry is not disaggregated.

vity could not possibly be maintained without disastrous consequences for the balance of industry structure. Thus, over time, sectors tend to benefit more equally in terms of the growth rates of fixed assets. It may be the case, however, that that kind of 'evenness' may go too far, thereby inhibiting, because of entrenched interests, selective development at a later stage. Certainly, the extremely modest variation in growth rates of fixed assets among Polish industrial branches in the 1960s is striking. Is there perhaps some indication in these figures that particularism has been more severe in Poland than elsewhere in the region? Is it possible that the Polish authorities have, for some reason, found it more difficult than others to resist the investment demands of each branch? (It is interesting that the figures point to the Soviet Union sharing the same problem.) Lack of knowledge of the detailed situation in other planned economies prevents us from making any strong judgement on this point but one is impressed with the frequency with which the 'petrification' of the Polish industrial structure comes in for criticism in the Polish literature.

The problem seems to have been considered as severe in the 1960s, leading the authorities to attempt a specific policy of selective development in 1969. The idea behind the new policy was 'to ensure priority for the development of those branches which are carriers of technical progress and those able to expand exports' (Zielinski). To aid the process of selective development products, enterprises and industrial branches were to be categorised according to whether they were singled out for speedy development (Category I), modest development (Category II) or stagnation (Category III). Over 1971–75 Category I should have had allocated to it 63 per cent of new fixed capital, Category II should have received 25 per cent and Category III only 12 per cent. One observer (Zielinski) believed, however, that one could 'hardly speak of "selective development" if almost two-thirds of enterprises are singled out for speedy development and only 12 per cent as the ones for which expansion is not envisaged'. According to another author, firms maneouvred to block the selective development plan. Staniszkis has commented that selective development was supposed to be about investing 'only in selected fields and plants whose production conforms to quite rigorous standards of modernity', yet 'as many as 80 per cent of firms reported that their production met these standards'.

It would be interesting to enquire whether selectivity had met with more success in the 1970s. Unfortunately data on fixed assets growth rates in the same format as that already given is not yet available. One might suggest, however, that the second half of the decade may have been a more propitious time for selectivity than the period 1971–75. The standard deviation of annual average investment growth rates over 1971–75 equalled 9.6 percentage points (across industry divided into 21 sectors), while the mean growth rate for the period came to 21.9 per cent per annum. For 1976–77, on the other hand, the standard deviation equalled 14.1 points, while the average growth rate of investment was zero(4) over those years. There is at least the suggestion of greater selectivity (more variability) in more recent years. On the other hand, the greater selectivity of more recent years may be due to traditionally favoured industrial sectors winning ever *greater* shares of investment resources. For example, one of the most noticeable changes in investment share between 1971–75 and 1976–79 occurred in ferrous metallurgy which took in the earlier period 8.7 per cent of all industrial investment and 11.7 per cent in the later period(5).

There can be little doubt that the branch interests that exist in Polish industry have wielded a negative influence on economic development. In the absence of a strong central authority with its own clear view of preferred lines of development that branch structure may have been particularly damaging in Poland as compared with other East European economies where planners have not resigned their planning responsibility.

It seems to be generally understood and accepted that the present branch structure of industry is often a barrier to effective economic development. The reform document prepared in 1981 went so far as to say 'the present dominant branch principle has no justification' and 'there should be a departure from the principle of "branch purity". There should be no obstacle to enterprises of one branch starting to produce the output commonly associated with another branch.'

It would seem that the combination of strong branch interests and lack of central authority has been particularly harmful for the Polish economy over the 1970s. To arrive in 1980 with huge foreign debts, a large balance of payments deficit, negative growth, enormous inflationary pressure and an unstable political situation hardly smacks of a well considered planned economic development since 1970. The question is, can the Polish economy be cured of the malady which leads it to stumble from one crisis to another? Many believe that it can be so cured and the recently cut short reform debate gives some indication of the remedies considered necessary.

Polish economic debate August 1980 to December 1981

'To increase enterprise independence and strengthen central-planning' is an old if somewhat confusing slogan. Under its banner the ill-fated reform of 1973 was constructed, partially implemented, then dismantled. It is now clear that this experiment aimed to strengthen central planning rather than liberate a greater enterprise initiative. As it turned out it actually failed to build a stronger, more effective central planning system, and any effect on the greater independence of enterprises was more in the nature of pure accident. This unsatisfactory result no doubt contributed to the economic chaos characterising most of the last decade in Poland. Some may be surprised that the 1973 banner of the reformers was refurbished and taken out of retirement to express the intention behind the most recently proposed reform. However, reform intentions in 1980 seemed in important ways substantially different from those of 1972.

The tenor of Polish economic discussion from August 1980 to December 1981 was in favour of the enterprise (and not necessarily giant economic organisations of the association or 'zjednoczenia' type). The enterprise was at the centre of debate and the reform aimed to create an economic environment where the largely self-financing enterprise would choose its own production profile and future course of development. The central plan as it has been known, (that is, as a directive task, and resource allocating device) was to disappear. Planning should concentrate on strategic issues of long-term development and major structural change. It was hoped that enterprise decisions would be satisfactorily influenced through the use of a range of financial and fiscal instruments. The role of the bank and functional ministries would be enhanced, that of the branch ministries would be diminished if not entirely eliminated. Branch sanctity would be overthrown in favour of enlarged possibilities for enterprise product diversification and horizontal enterprise to enterprise communication. Thus it seems broadly that a reform of the Hungarian 'New Economic Mechanism' type was aimed at, though with some critical differences. Given Polish experience and history this was always the favourite direction for reform. In Poland a wide range of merely *technical* devices for potentially improving performance have been tried and been seen to fail. The 1960s was a favourite time for reform of this type. The 1973 reform groped towards an 'administrative decentralisation' in favour of the giant economic organisations mentioned earlier and known in Poland as 'WOG'. That reform was, as it turned out, counter-productive. In Poland reform substitutes have also been played with in such policies as modernisation through technology imports and have also failed. The only thing that has not systematically been tried in Polish conditions is reform of the type of 'economic decentralisation' and it was this policy that was proposed for 1982.

Of the other considerations relating to reform (and here there is a significant departure from the NEM model), none could be as critical as the role of workers' organisations in the planning and economic management framework. At one level some saw the guarantee that genuine reform would take place as being embodied in the very existence of the new trade union movement. It may have been possible and easy for the authorities to go back on previous reform commitments but surely the presence of independent trade unions on the scene in the early 1980s would prevent a similar occurrence? This at least was the hope of many participants in the reform discussions.

On a more detailed level, the nature of the planned participation of workers in economic management was of great interest. This key issue was, however, never resolved despite the fact that it was often at the centre of the many tumultuous events of 1981. Nonetheless we can say that it was absolutely clear that workers' participation was seen by almost everyone as being essential to reform. On the issue of the people claiming the right to an economic voice, the new trade unions had set the ball rolling by winning the right to take part in discussion on the future distribution of the social product as between consumption and investment. That much was built into the Gdansk-Szczecin Agreement. Also of great importance from August 1980 onwards was the widespread demand for democracy at all levels of society, from the Sejm to local government, from the trade unions to the inner life of the Party. Other channels to Solidarity existed, and could have been extended, through which the people would influence economic events, as the process of social, political and economic renewal gathered force. Solidarity representatives were actively participating, despite healthy and well founded suspicions, in the official government reform committees. While its own view of the most desirable reform may not have been well developed, it would be mistaken to underestimate the importance of Solidarity's involvement in the general discussion. It is also worthy of note that such emphasis being given to workers' self-management was in itself in very sharp contrast to the 1972 reform, which had an overwhelmingly 'managerial' and technocratic style.

The 1980–81 focus on self-management should not be confused with the previously existing formal organs of workers' participation, the so-called "Conference of workers' self-management", which was purely window dressing and, in most cases, had nothing to do with enterprise management. A widespread feeling was that workers' councils should be re-established in plants as they had existed in a spontaneous post-1956 movement, a movement that had been, in the view of many, 'needlessly and illegally liquidated'(6). The enterprise plan should be set up jointly by managers and workers in a kind of 'social contract'. Indeed, rather than workers' self-management, some preferred the all embracing slogan 'self-management by the enterprise crew'.

All-in-all it seemed that reform was quite properly considered as a social activity in 1981 where in the past it seemed to be viewed as a simple technical problem. Perhaps one of the most significant consequences of the recent and continuing Polish turmoil was the emerging realisation that economic problems are unavoidably also political in nature. Unfortunately, the lesson has not yet been learned by the Polish military government that the construction of an artificial political life devoid of a real impact on economic decision-making is likely eventually to do more harm than good. The Polish situation in late 1980 was well described by Chelstowski who summed up a discussion on workers' self-management as follows(7):

> 'We are faced with the huge problem of socialising the process of economic management, giving the process an authentic social character, surmounting any technocratic difficulties which would stand in the way of management by the people. Workers' self-management will be a huge step forward in this respect. It appeared that nationalisation of the means of production was synonymous with their socialisation and so the whole problem was firmly in hand. It is clear now that the problem was absolutely *not* in hand. In my view one of the fundamental sources of conflict in the summer of 1980 was that the process of socialising the means of production was frozen. A bureaucratised, purely formal workers' self-management could not give rise to authentic control. Creating a role for workers in economic management permits – despite the damaging economic situation – the possibility of solving the most difficult problems of the economy and so too of laying the basis from which accrued social problems can be tackled. We must quickly grasp this opportunity.'

It seems that in December 1981 this opportunity was firmly and deliberately rejected.

Can Polish problems be expected shortly to appear in other centrally planned economies?

Since almost all East European economies are centrally planned, it might be expected that the problems of one will, at some time or another, become the difficulties of all members of the club. There has been some justification for accepting this view but, as we will argue below, it is not inevitable that an economic crisis of the Polish type will reappear elsewhere in time to come. On closer examination enough specific factors can be seen to have been operating in Poland.

Of course, the East European economies do share the same model of economic organisation – central planning organised in a hierarchical fashion and resting critically on branch ministries for its implementation. The one exception to this is Hungary where greater legitimate possibility exists for independent enterprise decision-making, but, until 1968 Hungary also utilised a traditional Soviet-type central planning model. The use of central planning may be commended as a device ensuring rapid industrialisation of predominantly agricultural economies. At least, central planners could generally justifiably claim some success in achieving that aim. In Poland this is particularly true as the data in *Table 8.2* on the sectoral composition of national income and employment indicate.

Table 8.2

The structure of the Polish economy
(percentages)

	National income 1950	National income 1970	National income 1978	Employment 1950	Employment 1970	Employment 1979
Agriculture	52	23	14	53	34	31
Industry	26	47	53	26	36	38
Construction	7	11	12			
Others	15	19	21	21	29	31

Source: Secomski, K., 'Przemian strukturalne w okresie trzydziestopieciolecia PRL', *Gospodarka Planowa,* no. 6, 1979.

Throughout the 1960s it became clear, however, that high rates of growth were increasingly difficult to maintain both in Poland and elsewhere in the region. To sustain high growth rates became more expensive in terms of the resource cost of each unit of output. Again, for Poland *Table 8.3* indicates the need in the late 1960s to devote greater and greater quantities of investment resources to production in order to prevent the growth rate from slipping down.

Table 8.3

Average annual growth rates of output and inputs

	1951–55	1956–60	1961–65	1966–70
	(percentages)			
National income	8.6	6.8	6.4	5.8
Employment	1.6	0.9	1.4	1.9
Productive fixed capital	3.4	4.1	4.6	6.2

Source: Nasiłowski, M., *'Analiza czynników rozwoju gospodarezego PRL',* 1974.

The planners in Poland responded by finding more investment resources to contribute to production, thus making use of the input marshalling quality of traditional central planning. The squeeze on consumption this entailed led, through extremely low real wages growth (1.8 per cent p.a.) during the 1960s, to the dissatisfaction and frustrations violently expressed in December 1970. It is a feature of central planning that the authorities at the summit of the economic hierarchy often believe that they alone can solve pressing economic problems and that they can do this simply by the issue of further commands. There is therefore a danger that the planners, when faced with a difficulty like a potential growth rate slow-down, will take direct action against consumption to 'solve' the problem. If consumption growth should be compressed too far, the possibility of social unrest becomes more likely. It is clearly of immense value to know when the politically sensitive minimal rate of growth of consumption is being approached. In Poland the authorities in the late 1960s seemed unaware of the imminence of that consumption threshold. In other centrally planned economies social unrest stemming from the same planning errors seem to have been avoided, at least since the 1950s. Perhaps the main difference between the Polish authorities compared with others is simply that in Poland the process of political communication has been particularly deformed and so there has been less awareness of popular feeling than has been the case in other planned economies.

If there is room for argument as to which have been the most 'sensitive' leaderships, there has been general acceptance of the thesis that central planning has operated with diminishing effectiveness with the passage of time. This has led throughout the region to an analysis of this problem using the framework based on the extensive/intensive growth distinction. When factors of production are relatively abundant or easily found there is some sense in aiming for growth simply through 'widening' production, building more factories, providing more jobs, or so-called extensive growth. As labour and capital become harder to find, growth has to come about through productivity improvements, through greater efficiency, that is, growth has to be of the intensive type. But while the growth slow-down problem is common to all centrally planned economies (CPEs) and has been analysed in the same way from Prague to Bucharest, it seems to have been only in Poland (over the last two decades) that the planners' reaction to the problem has forced people to take to the streets in protest.

Perhaps another insight into the problem is given by a consideration of what could be termed foreseen and unforeseen consequences of central planning. Rapid industrialisation was clearly anticipated as the major benefit to be derived in Poland from application of the Soviet model of development. This brought with it the problem (unforeseen) of diminishing efficiency in resource use (partly explained by the fact of the economy becoming more complex and therefore more difficult to manage in the traditional manner). Another unanticipated difficulty stems from the particularism of branch interests, interests which are built into the original structure of centrally planned economic organisation. This is a growing problem in all CPEs, partly simply because of the very existence of branches regardless of the particular sector in question, and partly because of the dominance in the economic management apparatus of traditionally favoured sectors of industry. The latter are guaranteed a continuing influence on economic development. In Poland this has been large enough to thwart modernisation programmes like that of the 1970s. One consequence of this – a lack of industrial adaptability – is an extremely serious problem for all centrally planned economies. It may be, however, that Poland has suffered more than most CPEs due to sectoral parochialism resulting from the weakness since 1970 of the steering centre. The loss of economic control on the part of the highest authorities is so far the peculiarly Polish phenomenon which would seem to have been the key ingredient to the mix of factors (as outlined above: diminishing effectiveness of central planning; branch particularism; and lack of effective channels for communication of popular feeling) leading to the 1980 crisis.

Our argument is simply that an economic crisis as severe as the Polish crisis is exceptional and avoidable, provided the deformations in Polish political and social life which have been evident in the 1970s are also avoided. The key to success in this respect is surely a strong leadership well able to mediate competing (possibly branch) interests and in touch with popular feeling. But while this may be enough to avoid crisis on the Polish scale, it may not be enough, given the long-term tendency of the decreasing effectiveness of central planning, to avoid a slower deterioration in economic and social life. The key problem facing all CPEs is surely how to modernise their economies, how to secure the structural changes needed to provide an industrial sector which is able to satisfy the demands of sophisticated consumers at home and internationally. While central planning proved immensely useful in securing broad changes in the economic structure, from agriculture to industry, it does not seem so useful in achieving the fine structural adjustments now needed within manufacturing industry alone.

Can the economic structure of CPEs be made more flexible and readily adaptable to shifts in demand?

While the problems posed by the current structure of industry in Poland may be more severe than for other CPEs, all share the basic characteristic of unadaptability. Mechanisms permitting changes in product structure are bureaucratised and therefore clumsy and slow to operate. Product innovation occurs relatively rarely compared with the situation in market economies. When product quality changes it is as likely to be deterioration as improvement. Most CPEs have difficulty in selling manufactured goods on world markets or at least on those markets where there is a strong Western participation. Polish exports to the West consist mainly of coal and foodstuffs and some groups of low unit value consumer goods such as footwear. The story is a similar one for other planned economies. It is easy to see that the problem is how to get into the manufacture of goods for which the income elasticity of demand is high. Indeed, many weaker Western economies could also benefit from advice on this problem. The difficulty though is somewhat exacerbated for the centrally planned economies because adaptability involves resource reallocation and any resource transfer is made difficult by vested branch interests and the danger of temporary unemployment.

The key problem for central planners is how to achieve a much more rapid rate of innovation and diffusion of new goods and a more rapid rate of withdrawal of the obsolete. It is surely unlikely that means can be devised to ensure success with the former without at the same time dealing with the second problem. As has been said, the difficulty is not unique to Poland. Ever since the adventurous Hungarian economic reform of 1968 the problem of a fine structure of industrial output has remained. According to Kornai, during the first ten years of the reform practically no bankruptcies occurred. Other well known Hungarian economists [e.g. Faluvégi (1975) and Friss (1973)] have also criticised the powerful tendencies towards continued production of old and obsolete output. The mechanism of a fine structural change has been exceedingly top-heavy, involving the setting up of Ministerial Commissions to survey sectors of industry for obsolete production. It is interesting to note that where suitable structural changes did take place it seems to have been largely due to central decisions within 'complex programmes' which began to overcome branch barriers to industrial progress, such as the vehicle production or computer technology programmes (Friss 1973). Such complex programmes may prove to be the only effective mechanisms for structural change if the full implications of reform of the NEM-type are rejected.

Plant closure is a difficult issue for socialist planners. Some reports indicated that the Czech authorities were seriously concerned with this problem in the 1960s when labour shortages seemed severe. Another report had it that during 1970–74, 219 obsolete Czechoslovak plants were shut down, 'liberating', however, only 3000 or so of the skilled workers for relocation to other parts of industry where manpower shortages were critical(8). The basis of the legitimacy of the East European authorities, or, what Kornai (1980) calls 'the ethical principles of a socialist economy' makes for obvious difficulties when industrial restructuring is discussed. But the result of these pressures on economic performance is easy to see. In the case of Czechoslovakia one commentator noted that prior to the Dubcek reform attempt, 'the whole republic had been turned into a "social institution", wages had become a guaranteed "pension" and mediocrity a national "affliction" ' (Pravda). The same can be said of many, if not all, East European economies in the early 1980s.

How then did Polish reformers see the solution to this problem? They certainly placed the (largely) self-financing enterprise at the centre of the reform stage. For the enterprise to operate in this way (making its own output and investment decisions), genuine independence in decision-making is essential. But, as Fedorowicz (1980) has recently put it, 'the postulate of maximal freedom and independence for enterprise decisions implies their full responsibility for economic results'. Another Polish economist (Knapik, 1980) goes on, 'rewards will clearly depend on good results, but full responsibility must also imply the acceptance of the consequences of bad management. These are brutal economic truths but this is the only way to escape from the present economic impasse'.

What form should these 'consequences' take? A liberal dose of hesitation in discussing this issue could be detected and it is true that little explicit debate of 'appropriate' measures has taken place. Perhaps Pajestka has gone further than most in stating his view (reminiscent of our own Keith Joseph) that,

'We must support the thesis of the self-financing of development expenditures. Those enterprises that are healthy and effective on the home and foreign markets should be given further encouragement. Others should be given three to four years of hospitalisation. Either they recover good health or they should be liquidated(9).'

The official reform document summing up the state of thinking on this issue stated that 'some procedure should be made clear for the enforced reorganisation or liquidation of loss-making enterprises.' The need for bankruptcy has been tentatively approached by one or two participants in recent Polish economic debate. Pajestka believes that a central issue for reform is to provide some mechanism which will generate an 'economic compulsion' favouring efficient economic decision-making. During the 1972–73 reform discussions, some participants spoke of the need for 'forced incentives' alongside those other incentives of an orthodox type. The problem was that while that reform did provide new incentive mechanisms, there was still a lack of any systematic pressure *compelling* enterprises to take the sort of decisions desired by the centre. Thus in 1973 firms could increase their wage fund through raising the net output success indicator and they could do this by increasing sales or reducing costs. But because of lack of any compulsion to reduce costs enterprises chose to promote sales, this being by far the easiest thing to do in a sellers' market to get better results. In fact, the simplest thing to do was to raise output prices and manipulate the assortment being produced in favour of supposedly higher quality and higher priced goods. Some mechanism which actually compels 'good' behaviour is undoubtedly essential in a modern socialist economy. Recent experience in Poland shows that simple directives are not satisfactory here. The problem, of course, is that many people are concerned at the prospect of unemployment resulting from the operation of any purely economic compulsion.

The economic experts of Solidarity were particularly anxious to avoid identification with any economic reform which might have produced some unemployment. A satisfactory solution to the problem of managing structural change was not found, which is hardly surprising given the gigantic nature of the problem; but the important point was surely that until the military takeover, serious social discussion continued. The significance of this discussion should not be underestimated. After all, market-guided processes leading to structural change create severe social tensions in Western economies where we might usefully begin our own debate on how to improve the management of economic development and change.

For many in Poland there was real hope that out of the involvement of all members of society in shaping the economic future, there would have come a lasting commitment and enthusiasm, and this would have provided the device to secure a successful transition from extensive to intensive economic growth. At last it seemed that workers were being treated as 'partners rather than adversaries' in economic matters. In 1980–81 the 'renewal' of Polish social and political life opened up many channels through which people would have been able to shape their own ideas of future economic development. If General Jaruzelski had not made yet another attempt to distort that democratic process it might have been possible that some socially acceptable solution to the structural problems of industry could have been found. An economy operating under martial law is unlikely to have the capacity to solve these problems.

In 1980 it seemed that what was about to go on trial in Poland was the thesis that democracy can be an important factor favouring productivity growth. Sadly, the Polish army, by its violent action in December 1981, ensured another postponement of that historic experiment.

Footnotes

(1) See Blazyca (1980) and (1982), and Nuti (1981).

(2) Throughout the 1970s the economics press has been used to direct attention to the growth of 'ineffective' stocks, especially in industry. The problem has been continuing, perhaps even worsening with the passage of time. Thus a recent author has pointed to the eight per cent growth in stocks held by industry in 1979 and commented that this represents a rate of growth nearly three times that of industrial output (see Wojciechowski, 1980).

(3) For an explanation of this term see p. 167.

(4) This data is from *Rocznik Statystyczny 1978*, p. 137.

(5) This data is from Gwiazdzinski (1980) who also indicates the 'deformation' of the investment process in Poland in recent years:

Table 8.4

Share of total industrial investment taken by ferrous metallurgy (%)

	1966–70	1971–75	1976–79
Poland	6.7	8.7	11.7
Bulgaria	8.1	5.9	4.3
Czechoslovakia	9.0	6.9	8.8
GDR	5.5	5.0	8.0
Hungary	6.7	5.8	6.5
USSR	7.7	7.4	6.5

(6) Drawn from a discussion on workers' self-management organised by Życie Gospodarcze. See 'Samorząd robotniczy: zawierzyć zalogom', *ZG*, no. 48, 1980.

(7) Ibid.

(8) Data is from *ABSEES*, vol. IV, no. 2, 1973, p. 154.

(9) See the discussion on this organised by Życie Gospodarcze, 'Czy reforma jest dobra na wszystko?', *ZG*, no, 47. 1980.

References

Blazyca, G. (1980) 'An Assessment of Polish Economic Development in the 1970s', *European Economic Review*, no. 14, pp. 101–116.

Blazyca, G. (1982) 'The Degeneration of Central Planning in Poland' in Woodall J. (ed.) *Policy and Politics in Contemporary Poland* (London: Frances Pinter).

Brus, W. (1977) 'The Polish October Twenty Years After', *The Socialist Register 1977* (Merlin).

Faluvegi, L. (1975) 'Economic Development: Economic Structure, New Phenomena in the World Economy', *Acta Oeconomica*, vol. 14, nos. 2–3.

Fedorowicz, Z. (1980) 'Zasady funkcjonowania przedsiębiorstw', *Życie Gospodarcze*, no. 44.

Friss, I. (1973) 'Practical Experiences of the Economic Reform in Hungary', *Eastern European Economics*, Spring.

Gwiazdziński, J. (1980) 'Za duzo stali', *Życie Gospoarcze*.

Kleer, J. (1976) 'Partykularyzm', *Polityka*, no. 47.

Knapik, J. (1980) 'Propozycje na dzis', *Życie Gospodarcze*, no. 46.

Kornai, J. (1980) 'The Dilemmas of a Socialist Economy: The Hungarian Experience', *Cambridge Journal of Economics*, vol. 4, June.

Macieja, J. (1978) 'Obnizenie materialochlonności i energochłonności produkcji strategicznym gospodarki w latach osiemdziesiatych', *Godpodarka Planowa*.

Nasilowski, M. (1974) *Analiza czynników rozwoju gospodarczego PRL*, (Warsaw: PWE).

Nasilowski, M. (1980) 'Reorientacja myslenia i działania', *Życie Gospodarcze*, no. 45.

Nuti, D.M. (1980) 'Industrial Enterprises in Poland 1973–1980; Economic Policies and Reforms', *CREES Discussion Paper*, University of Birmingham.

Nuti, D.M. (1980) 'The Polish Crisis: Economic Factors and Constraints' in Miliband, R., Saville, J. (eds.) *The Socialist Register 1981* (Merlin).

Pravda, A. (1973) 'Some Aspects of the Czechoslovak Economic Reform and the Working Class in 1968', *Soviet Studies.*

Secomski, K. (1979) 'Przemian strukturalne w okresie trzydziestopiecolecia PRL', *Gospodarka Planowa*, no. 6.

Staniszkis, J. (1978) 'Adaptional Superstructure – The Problem of Negative Self-Regulation' in Wiatr J. (ed.) *Essays in the Methodology of Polish Social Sciences* (Amsterdam: North-Holland).

Staniszkis, J. (1979) 'On Some Contradictions of Socialist Society: The Case of Poland', *Soviet Studies,* April.

Wojciechowski, T. (1980) 'System zaopatrzenia – barier i rezerwy', *Życie Gospodarcze,* no. 15.

Zielinski, J.G. (1973) *Economic Reforms in Polish Industry* (Oxford: Oxford University Press).

For the initial statement of economic reform intentions see 'Wstępne założenia reformy gospodarczej', *Życie Gospodarcze,* no. 47, 1980.

PART III

DISTRIBUTION OF EARNINGS

Chapter 9

THE STRUCTURE OF INDUSTRIAL EARNINGS IN SEVEN WEST EUROPEAN COUNTRIES

L. Needleman

1. Introduction and summary

This paper examines some aspects of the structure of the earnings of full-time industrial employees in France, the Federal Republic of Germany, Italy, the Netherlands, Belgium, Luxembourg and the United Kingdom. The information relating to the first six countries, the original member countries of the European Economic Community, is largely derived from a great survey of industrial earnings in October 1972 conducted by the Statistical Office of the European Communities (Eurostat) and published by that organisation in 13 large volumes during 1975 to 1977. The data were collected using a standardised procedure in all the countries, so that comparisons between countries can be made with much more confidence that like is being compared with like than is usually the case in international comparisons.

Though the UK was not included in the Eurostat survey, for many of the topics covered, comparable information was collected in Britain in April 1972 and published in the Department of Employment's *New Earnings Survey 1972.* The categories in the two studies do not correspond exactly; thus the Eurostat study includes employees of all ages while almost all the detailed information in the British survey relates to adults, defined as women of 18 years and over and men of 21 years and over, but for many aspects of earnings structure, reasonably reliable comparisons can be made between the British situation and that of the six countries of the European mainland.

Only a few features of the structure of earnings can be examined in the space available*. Differences in sex and occupation are often considered to be the two most important explanations of differences in earnings between individuals and the effects of these two factors are explored in Section 2 of this chapter. The broad occupational structure of persons appears to be much the same in all seven countries and the concentration of roughly four-fifths of women in industrial employment in the three worst-paid occupational groups also appears to be a common feature. The largest occupational earnings differentials between males were found in France and Italy, the countries with the lowest average earnings for men, using purchasing power parity exchange rates to compare earnings in the different countries. But while France and Italy had the highest occupational differentials for men, they had the lowest earnings differentials between the sexes of all the countries in the sample, the country with the greatest differences in earnings between the sexes being the UK.

The distribution of employees and earnings by size of establishment in the six mainland countries is examined in Section 3. In all the countries average earnings appeared to increase with the size of establishment, though the effect of size of establishment on average earnings was much less in Germany and the Netherlands than in the other countries. Moreover, a higher proportion of men worked in the largest establishments than did women, so that part of the observed difference in average earnings of men and women may be explained by the lower proportion of women in large establishments. However, this structural effect will be moderated by the tendency of the ratio of female to male earnings to be greater in large than in small establishments.

In Section 4 inequality of earnings is explored. Information is presented for each country from which Lorenz curves of earnings can be constructed. The precise inequality ranking of the earnings distributions of the seven countries depends on which index of inequality is employed, but most of those in common use would classify France as having had the most unequal distribution of industrial earnings, followed by Italy and the UK at roughly the same level, then the Netherlands, followed by Belgium and then the Federal Republic of Germany, with Luxembourg having had the least unequal distribution of all. On partitioning the variance of earnings in each country, we find that in six of the countries, other than West Germany, over 70 per cent of the total variation occurred within and between male occupational groups and that a substantial proportion occurred within the male, non-manual group. Differences within and between female groups, and, within and between men and women in the same occupational groups, would appear to have been relatively unimportant in explaining the overall variation in earnings.

* Another analysis of these data has been made by Saunders and Marsden (1979) and (1981) – Ed.

2. Earnings by occupational group and sex

The distributions of full-time industrial employees of both sexes by country and occupational group are given in Table 9.1.

The broad occupational pattern of industrial employment was similar in all seven countries. In each of the countries, male manual workers accounted for over 55 per cent of all industrial employees and manual workers of both sexes accounted for 70 per cent or more.

At the more detailed level within individual countries — between 28 per cent (in Italy) and 36 per cent (in the UK) of all industrial employees were skilled manual workers, between 22 per cent (in the UK) and 31 per cent (in Italy) were semi-skilled and, between 11 per cent (in the Netherlands) and 25 per cent (in Luxembourg) were unskilled.

The distribution of employees across the non-manual occupational groups was not available for the UK, but for the other six countries, in all cases, less than 1.5 per cent of

Table 9.1

Distribution of industrial employees by country and occupational group, 1972

Percentages

Occupational group	France	West Germany	Italy	Netherlands	Belgium	Luxembourg	UK
Manual workers							
Skilled	32.4	32.9	28.1	31.1	28.4	30.8	36(a)
Semi-skilled	25.6	24.8	31.2	29.3	29.1	29.5	22(a)
Unskilled	15.0	17.4	23.6	11.3	23.8	27.7	13(a)
Total	72.9	75.0	82.8	71.7	81.3	85.1	70.9(a)
Non-manual workers							
Higher management	1.1	1.1	0.8	1.0	1.4	0.8	n.a.
Other executives	4.5	5.1	3.3	3.8	2.6	1.5	n.a.
Assistants	5.8	10.0	5.8	6.0	5.6	5.9	n.a.
Clerical staff	11.0	6.0	5.3	13.8	6.7	4.6	n.a.
Foremen	4.6	2.8	2.0	3.7	2.4	2.0	n.a.
Total	27.1	25.0	17.2	28.3	18.7	14.9	29.1
Grand total	100.0	100.0	100.0	100.0	100.0	100.0	100.0

(a) Estimated

Sources: For all countries other than the UK, *Statistical Office of the European Communities, 1975–1977,* Vols. 2A, 3A, 4A, 5A, 6A and 7A, Tables II/A/4 and III/A/4. For the UK, Department of Employment, 1973, Tables 80 and 81, pp. 132–135.

employees were classified as engaged in higher management. The percentages of executives, other than those in higher management, varied by country from 1.5 per cent in the case of Luxembourg to just over five per cent in the case of West Germany. The category of 'Assistants', defined in terms of having 'an advanced level of secondary education or equivalent professional experience' accounted for roughly six per cent of industrial employees in all six countries other than West Germany, where they accounted for eleven per cent of the total. Clerical workers accounted for about four and a half to six and a half per cent in four of the countries, but for eleven per cent in France and almost fourteen per cent in the Netherlands. The observed proportions of assistants and clerical workers may entirely reflect genuine structural differences, but the pattern is slightly suspicious and there is the possibility that the classification of occupations may differ a little from country to country, so that a given group of employees might be classified as clerical workers in France, but as assistants in West Germany.

The ratio of the sexes in different occupational groups varied greatly from country to country, as indicated in Table 9.2.

Table 9.2

Numbers of female industrial employees (full-time) by country and occupational group as percentages of males in corresponding categories, 1972

Occupational group	France	West Germany	Italy	Netherlands	Belgium	Luxembourg	UK
Manual workers							
Skilled	7.5	3.1	16.0	3.1	8.2	0.6	9.5(a)
Semi-skilled	51.2	45.4	40.3	18.1	26.9	4.8	26.5(a)
Unskilled	70.5	120.0	56.9	31.9	53.0	9.0	30.9(a)
Total	30.7	32.0	34.8	12.8	25.6	4.4	18.9
Non-manual workers							
Higher management	5.8	2.7	2.6	0.8	7.3	—	n.a.
Other executives	9.6	8.0	9.0	1.5	9.1	—	n.a.
Assistants	11.5	47.2	24.4	5.9	25.6	9.4	n.a.
Clerical staff	166.4	286.6	126.4	45.4	73.1	42.1	n.a.
Foremen	7.0	1.2	9.5	2.4	6.7	9.1	n.a.
Total	43.6	47.9	36.1	20.4	31.1	15.8	41.7
Grand total	33.9	35.7	35.0	14.8	26.6	5.9	24.8

(a) Estimated

Sources: For all countries other than the UK, *Statistical Office of the European Communities, 1975–1977,* Vols. 2A, 3A, 4A, 5A, 6A and 7A, Tables II/A/4 and III/A/4. For the UK, Department of Employment, 1973, Tables 80 and 81, pp. 132–135.

Even if we disregarded the special situation in Luxembourg, where about sixty per cent of the labour force worked in the iron and steel industry, which traditionally employs very few women, the number of female industrial employees was less than fifteen per cent of the number of corresponding males in the Netherlands, but the proportion was over a third in France, Italy and West Germany.

In all the countries, women in industry were heavily concentrated in the three low-paid, low-status, occupational groups of semi-skilled and unskilled manual workers and clerical workers. In all of the six mainland countries, 79 per cent or more of female industrial employees were in these three occupational groups, with the percentage being 89 per cent in the case of the Netherlands. The occupational classification used in the UK in 1972 was slightly different from that used in the Eurostat survey, but the concentration of women in the low-paid occupational groups appeared to be broadly comparable with that found in the other countries in the sample.

Women in all countries accounted for a very small proportion of the jobs in the two most highly-paid groups, higher management and other executive posts, though the proportions were higher in Belgium, France and West Germany than in the other countries, with the Netherlands having a strikingly low proportion. Women in these two groups accounted for 1.8 per cent of all female industrial employment in France, for 1.5 per cent in both Belgium and West Germany, for 1.1 per cent in Italy, but for only 0.5 per cent in the Netherlands.

There was great variation between countries both in the proportion of all industrial employees that were clerical workers, and in the proportion of clerical workers that were women. Thus, there were almost three female clerical workers to each male clerk in West Germany, but more than two males to every female clerk in the Netherlands. Nevertheless, a third of all female industrial employees were clerical workers in the Netherlands, while the proportion was only half as great in West Germany. The explanation was that clerical workers accounted for a much higher proportion of the workforce in the Netherlands than in West Germany.

The ratio of females to males among foremen was low in all the countries, but particularly so in the Netherlands and West Germany. In West Germany, only one in 800 female industrial employees was a 'foreperson' or supervisor. In France, by contrast, the corresponding ratio was one in 80.

Turning now to earnings – Table 9.3 gives the average monthly earnings before tax for men by country and occupational group, expressed in terms of pounds sterling. The exchange rates used, purchasing power parity (PPP) exchange rates for consumers' expenditure, were designed to represent equivalent purchasing power by consumers within the seven countries, and hence are more appropriate to use in international comparisons of living standards than are the official exchange rates. Details of the sources and methods used in the construction of the PPP exchange rates are given in an appendix at the end of this chapter.

The monthly earnings figures in Table 9.3 exclude bonuses that were not paid monthly. There is no information on the average size of these bonuses in the UK, but in some of the other six countries they accounted for a substantial proportion of total annual

Table 9.3

Mean monthly gross earnings of full-time men in industry by country and occupational group, October 1972

Pounds, at purchasing power parity exchange rates for consumers' expenditure

Occupational group	France	West Germany	Italy	Netherlands	Belgium	Luxembourg	UK (a)
Manual workers							
Skilled	126.8	171.9	113.3	165.2	159.2	192.3	166(b)
Semi-Skilled	101.5	151.7	97.3	148.9	144.4	174.1	157(b)
Unskilled	94.6	138.8	84.8	135.5	129.3	159.8	138(b)
Total	114.1	161.2	100.6	154.9	146.8	177.0	160.0
Non-manual workers (c)							
Higher management	420.8	331.3	396.8	383.9	303.7	336.4	n.a.
Other executives	295.4	251.5	235.5	320.5	274.8	337.3	n.a.
Assistants	182.1	192.8	167.2	231.4	202.2	251.0	n.a.
Clerical staff	134.8	144.5	115.5	167.3	166.3	200.3	148(d)
Foremen	180.0	216.6	146.3	204.9	215.5	233.8	186(e)
Total	207.0	216.1	183.5	221.1	214.1	249.4	206.0
Grand total	137.4	173.6	114.7	172.7	158.7	186.6	171.8

(a) The original survey data for the UK relate to weekly earnings in April 1972. But between April and October 1972 average earnings in all industries increased by 8.3 per cent and it has been assumed that male industrial earnings in all occupational groups increased by that percentage over the same period. It has been assumed there was the equivalent of 4.33 weeks' earnings in monthly earnings.

(b) Estimated.

(c) In the six mainland countries, monthly earnings exceeding a certain ceiling figure were not recorded. The ceiling earnings, in terms of pounds at purchasing power parity exchange rates at October 1972 were: France £ 703.7, West Germany £ 455.5, Italy £ 666.2, the Netherlands £ 716.8, Belgium £ 552.2 and Luxembourg £ 548.5. The earnings figures for higher management in this table are the average earnings of those with earnings below the ceiling level.

(d) Office and communications workers, all industries and services.

(e) Supervisors and foremen, all industries and services.

Sources: For all countries other than the UK, *Statistical Office of the European Communities, 1975–1977,* Vols. 2A, 3A, 4A, 5A, 6A and 7A, Tables II/B/11 and III/B/4. For the UK, Department of Employment 1973, Table 74, pp. 123–124. See Appendix for details of the estimation of purchasing power parity exchange rates.

earnings. For manual workers of both sexes, such bonuses contributed from 3.6 per cent of total annual remuneration in France, to 13 per cent in Italy. In all six countries, bonuses accounted for a higher proportion of the annual earnings of non-manual employees than of the earnings of manual workers, and typically, for a higher proportion of the earnings of highly-paid employees in this category.

Ignoring the effects of such bonuses and of social security contributions paid by employees, men in industrial employment in four of the countries, Luxembourg, West Germany, the Netherlands and the UK, had broadly comparable average gross earnings in 1972 of between about £ 170 and £ 190 a month. Male earnings in Belgium were roughly 10 per cent or so lower, and in France, about 20 per cent lower, while in Italy, average male earnings were only about two-thirds the average earnings of men in the four countries with the highest average levels of pay.

In all seven countries, semi-skilled men in industry earned 80 per cent or more of the earnings of skilled men and unskilled men earned between 74 per cent and 83 per cent of skilled earnings. The ratios for both semi-skilled and unskilled men were substantially lower in France and Italy than in the other countries, and were marginally the highest in the UK.

Among non-manual employees, men in higher management were highly paid in France and Italy, both in comparison with the higher management of the other countries and with other occupational groups within their own countries. In both these countries, the average earnings of males in higher management were over three and one-third as great as the earnings of skilled workers, whereas in the other four mainland countries, the ratio was roughly two to one.

Male clerical workers were paid slightly more than skilled manual workers in five of the seven countries, but only 89 per cent as much in the UK and only 84 per cent as much in West Germany. Foremen earned between about 20 per cent and 35 per cent more than skilled manual workers in five of the countries, but 42 per cent more in France and only 12 per cent more in the UK.

While earnings differentials for skill were great in France and Italy and small in the UK, earnings differentials between the sexes were largest in the UK and least in Italy and France (see Table 9.4).

In 1972, the average female industrial employee earned only half the corresponding average male earnings in the UK. In the Netherlands the proportion was 58 per cent, while in the other five countries in the sample, the proportion was over 60 per cent, and over 70 per cent in France and Italy. In all seven countries, the ratio of female to male earnings was higher for manual workers on average than for non-manual workers. But

Table 9.4

Mean monthly gross earnings of full-time female industrial employees as percentages of the mean earnings of corresponding male groups, by country and occupational group, October 1972

Occupational group	France	West Germany	Italy	Netherlands	Belgium	Luxembourg	UK
Manual workers							
Skilled	76.4	66.4	67.7	64.2	62.1	65.0	n.a.
Semi-skilled	83.9	68.2	77.3	62.8	67.5	73.7	n.a.
Unskilled	89.8	72.0	91.8	66.4	75.7	54.1	n.a.
Total	75.9	63.4	76.1	60.6	66.7	58.9	51.9
Non-manual workers (a)							
Higher management	80.5	85.7	53.7	74.1	59.3	49.3	n.a.
Other executives	77.5	82.3	77.9	77.4	60.5	50.4	n.a.
Assistants	89.6	79.1	86.0	76.7	70.4	66.3	n.a.
Clerical staff	79.8	76.8	83.7	62.5	72.0	59.5	63.6(b)
Foremen	72.9	69.2	75.4	69.2	59.7	56.1	64.2(c)
Total	57.9	61.4	62.5	50.8	60.5	52.9	45.1
Grand Total	70.9	64.2	72.6	58.3	65.8	61.3	50.8

(a) See note (c) to Table 9.3.

(b) Office and communications workers, all industries and services.

(c) Supervisors and foremen, all industries and services.

Sources: See Table 9.3.

neither these ratios nor those relating to the eight occupational groups in Table 9.4 are particularly revealing, since like is seldom being compared with like. A finer classification of occupations than that in Table 9.4 would almost certainly show that in 1972, in the six mainland countries as well as in the UK, men and women were rarely doing the same jobs.

The 1971 Population Census for the UK distinguished 222 occupations. Calculating the ratio of women to men in each occupation, ranking occupations by their female-to-male ratio and then cumulating, the results shown in Table 9.5 are obtained.

In the UK, in 1971, some 40 per cent of women were employed in occupations which employed only two per cent of all male employees, and, 70 per cent of women worked in occupations employing only ten per cent of all male employees. If we calculate the 'Gini index of segregation' (Duncan and Duncan, 1955, p. 211), measured analogously to the Gini coefficient of concentration, so that the index would be one if no occupation contained both men and women, and zero if the proportions of men and women were the same in all occupations, then the index for the data in Table 9.5 is 0.77.

Table 9.5.

The segregation of employed males and females in occupations, Great Britain, 1971 (a)

Cumulative percentage of females in employment in occupations with the highest female-male ratios	Cumulative percentage of males in employment in occupations with the highest female-male ratios
%	%
10	0.07
20	0.37
30	0.98
40	2.04
50	3.70
60	6.72
70	10.23
80	14.22
90	25.20
100	100.00

(a) The figures relate to all occupations and include part-time as well as full-time employees.

Source: Office of Population Censuses and Surveys, 1975, Part II, Table 4, pp. 51–56.

3. Earnings by size of establishment and sex

The distribution of industrial employees by size of establishment in the six mainland countries is given in Table 9.6.Apart from Luxembourg, where the major employers were a few large iron and steel firms, the pattern was fairly similar in all the countries, with roughly one-third or less of employees in establishments employing less than 100 workers, another third of employees in establishments with between 100 and 500 workers and rather more than a third in establishments employing 500 or more persons. Among the five larger mainland countries, West Germany stood out as having the highest proportion of employees, almost one-third, in the largest size of establishment, and the lowest proportion of workers in the smallest establishments.

In all six countries, Table 9.7 shows that average earnings tended to increase with the size of establishment, the rate of increase being greatest in Luxembourg, Italy and Belgium, and least in West Germany and the Netherlands. It is clear, however, that keeping other

Table 9.6

Distribution of industrial employees by size of establishment, six countries, 1972

Percentages

Size of establishment, number of employees	France	West Germany	Italy	Netherlands	Belgium	Luxembourg
10– 49	17.9	15.3	20.1	19.2	17.7	8.6
50– 99	12.1	10.9	13.4	14.3	10.8	9.1
100–199	13.7	12.6	14.3	14.1	15.4	7.9
200–499	19.0	17.3	17.7	17.3	17.6	9.5
500–999	13.9	11.7	10.7	11.9	13.1	5.7
1000 and over	23.4	32.2	23.9	23.2	25.3	59.1
Total	100.0	100.0	100.0	100.0	100.0	100.0

Source: Statistical Office of the European Communities, 1975–1977, Vols. 2A, 3A, 4A, 5A, 6A and 7A, Tables I/C and V/C.

Table 9.7.

Indices of mean monthly gross earnings of full-time industrial employees by size of establishment, six countries, 1972

Size of establishment, number of employees	France	West Germany	Italy	Netherlands	Belgium	Luxembourg
10– 49	94.2	98.1	84.0	95.5	88.3	78.0
50– 99	93.9	98.3	89.5	95.2	89.4	78.6
100–199	94.6	96.8	94.4	97.5	94.0	82.0
200–499	97.0	97.7	101.4	101.4	97.1	86.4
500–999	103.0	98.7	108.9	104.6	105.5	90.0
1000 and over	111.5	104.4	117.7	106.4	118.6	112.1
All establishements	100.0	100.0	100.0	100.0	100.0	100.0

Source: See Table 9.6.

factors constant, size of establishment explains a much smaller proportion of the variation in earnings within countries than do, say, occupational differences.

Table 9.8 shows female earnings as a percentage of male earnings by size of establishment for manual and non-manual workers separately in the six mainland countries. In all the countries, for both manual and non-manual workers, the ratio of average female earnings to average male earnings was higher in establishments employing 1000 or more persons than in establishments with less than 1000 workers. There was a tendency for the ratio

Table 9.8

Mean gross earnings of full-time female industrial employees as percentages of the mean earnings of corresponding male groups, by country, manual/non-manual category and size of establishment, October 1972

Female earnings as a percentage of male earnings

Size of establishment, number of employees	France	West Germany	Italy	Netherlands	Belgium	Luxembourg
Manual workers (a)						
10–49	77.0	63.1	77.6	62.3	69.4	59.1
50–99	76.8	64.5	76.7	63.6	70.0	63.2
100–199	77.4	67.0	77.3	63.6	68.6	66.6
200–499	78.0	70.3	78.1	68.7	71.6	84.4
500–999	77.7	71.4	79.2	66.7	72.9	70.8
1000 and over	79.2	73.0	82.9	70.0	71.6	83.1
Non-manual workers (b)						
10–49	55.5	62.5	68.4	48.3	61.1	50.1
50–99	56.9	63.1	66.9	50.6	60.4	52.1
100–199	57.3	61.8	65.4	51.4	60.6	52.1
200–499	57.7	61.9	62.0	51.4	61.3	52.6
500–999	59.3	61.5	62.2	52.7	61.3	53.9
1000 and over	61.1	61.9	62.9	54.2	65.0	62.1

(a) Hourly earnings.
(b) Monthly earnings.

Sources: See Table 9.6.

of manual workers to increase with the size of establishment in all countries, apart from Belgium, but the pattern for non-manual workers was less distinct. There appears to be very little information on either the number or the average earnings of female workers by size of establishment in the UK.

There have been suggestions in several studies (see, Chiplin and Sloane, 1976, pp.46–47) that part of the observed difference in the average earnings of men and women may be explained by women being relatively concentrated in small establishments or firms, which typically tend to pay both men and women poorly compared with larger firms.

In the six countries in this study, other than the U.K., it was indeed the case in 1972 that a much higher proportion of men than of women were employed in establishments with 1000 or more workers, and that the larger establishments paid higher wages on average than did the smaller ones. But the differences in pay by size of establishment were not great enough to explain more than a relatively small part of the difference in the average pay of men and women, and, as Table 9.8 shows, the ratio of female to male earnings was greatest in the largest establishments.

4. Inequality of earnings

The Eurostat study, *Structure of Earnings in Industry,* gives the distribution of gross earnings using 27 earnings intervals, while some 16 earnings intervals are distinguished in the corresponding survey for the UK, the Department of Employment's *New Earnings Survey 1972.* Estimating the means of earnings intervals, using the method given in Needleman (1978) Section IV, the total earnings received by persons in each income interval can be calculated and hence the Lorenz curves can be constructed.

Table 9.9 shows interpolated points on the Lorenz curves relating to the earnings of all full-time industrial employees in seven countries. There are many summary measures of the degree of inequality of an earnings or income distribution, and as is well known, the ranking of distributions using one measure may often be quite different from the ranking obtained using another measure [Yntema (1933) pp. 429–431; Ranadive (1965), p. 122 and Champernowne (1974) pp. 794–799].

However, where the Lorenz curve for one distribution, say, y, lies entirely above the Lorenz curve of another distribution, x, then it would generally be accepted that distribu-

Table 9.9

The size distribution of gross monthly earnings of full-time industrial employees in seven countries in 1972

Cumulative percentage of gross earnings

Cumulative percentage of persons	France	UK	Italy	Netherlands	Belgium	West Germany	Luxembourg
5	2.09	1.92	2.05	1.72	2.27	2.33	2.23
10	4.72	4.36	4.82	4.22	5.39	5.24	5.52
20	10.80	10.27	11.14	10.94	12.02	11.80	13.15
30	17.20	17.38	18.27	18.91	19.70	19.42	21.62
40	24.49	25.50	26.08	27.45	28.12	27.81	30.46
50	32.52	34.46	34.56	36.64	37.12	36.92	39.95
60	41.26	44.34	43.79	46.50	46.68	46.74	50.01
70	50.87	55.16	53.95	56.80	56.95	57.37	60.48
80	61.76	67.11	65.29	68.30	68.21	69.03	71.37
90	74.84	80.75	78.49	81.08	81.01	82.24	83.15
95	83.30	88.65	86.71	88.73	88.62	89.90	89.96

Sources: For all countries other than the UK, *Statistical Office of the European Communities, 1975–1977,* vols. 2A, 3A, 4A, 5A, 6A and 7A, Tables II/C/2 and III/C/2. For the UK, *Department of Employment, 1973,* Tables 30–33, pp. 64–68 and Tables 42–45, pp. 79–84. Average earnings within earnings intervals were estimated using the procedure in Needleman (1978) Section IV. Average earnings above ceiling levels were estimated by assuming that the frequency distribution of the highest earnings could be adequately approximated by the Pareto distribution. The method of interpolation used throughout was Lagrangian polynomial interpolation – usually quartic, but sometimes cubic.

tion y was less unequal than distribution x (Sen, 1973, Ch. 3) and most of the commonly-used measures of inequality would rank the two distributions in this order. In cases where the Lorenz curves of two distributions cross, the inequality ranking may vary according to the particular measure used, though if curve y lay above curve x at all deciles of earnings save one, or possibly two, where it lay very slightly below, most measures would rank distribution y as less unequal than distribution x.

Applying these, admittedly, crude ranking guides to the distributions of Table 9.9, we find that Luxembourg had the least unequal distribution in 1972, followed by West Germany, and closely followed by Belgium. There was then something of a gap before the next distribution, that of the Netherlands. Then there was another gap before the next two distributions, those of the UK and Italy, which appear to have been broadly comparable. Finally, the French earnings distribution is fairly strongly suggested as having been the most unequal of the seven distributions.

The data given in the Eurostat study make it comparatively easy to calculate the variances of the earnings distributions, and hence to derive for each distribution a commonly-used measure of inequality, the coefficient of variation.

Table 9.10 shows the coefficient of variation relating to the earnings distributions of the seven countries in our study. The rankings, and indeed the cardinal measures, of inequality indicated in Table 9.10 agree reasonably well with the rather impressionistic summary of the Lorenz curve comparisons of Table 9.9.

Table 9.10

Coefficient of variation of gross industrial earnings in seven countries in 1972

Percentages

Country	Coefficient of variation
France	52.8
Italy	47.6
United Kingdom	45.0
Netherlands	40.0
Belgium	37.1
West Germany	34.4
Luxembourg	31.4

Sources: For all countries other than the U.K., *Statistical Office of the European Communities, 1975–77,* vols. 2A, 3A, 4A, 5A, 6A, and 7A, Tables I/C and V/C. For the U.K. the source was *Department of Employment, 1973,* Tables 80 and 81, pages 132–135.

Differences in earnings between individuals can be explained in terms of differences in sex, age, occupation and many other factors. So, if an inequality index is to have analytical value, it must be capable of being disaggregated to show the importance of the particular determinants of differences in earnings. A number of inequality measures, including Theil's entropy measure (Theil, 1967, pp. 94–95) can be partitioned into within-group and between-group contributions to inequality, but often the contributions of differences between particular pairs of groups cannot be measured. If, however, we use as an index of inequality a measure closely related to the coefficient of variation, the variance, then the contributions to total inequality of differences between pairs of groups can readily be calculated.

Writing V as the variance of the whole group, V_i as the variance of the ith sub-group, W_i as the proportion of individuals in the group who are members of the ith sub-group and $\overline{X}_i$ as the mean earnings of the ith sub-group, then if there are N sub-groups in the group, we have

$$V \equiv \sum_{i=1}^{N} W_i V_i + \sum_{j=i+1}^{N} \sum_{i=1}^{N-1} W_i W_j (\overline{X}_i - \overline{X}_j)^2$$

where the first term on the right-hand side of the identity is the sum of the within-group contributions and the second term is the sum of the between-pairs-of-groups contributions.*

Using this partition formula, the variances of industrial earnings in the seven countries of the sample have been disaggregated in Table 9.11 to show the importance of differences within and between manual and non-manual workers, and, males and females.

In all seven countries, the variation within and between male groups accounted for over half the total variation in earnings, and in six of the countries, it accounted for over 70 per cent of the total. Variation within and between female groups accounted for less than ten per cent of the total variation in six of the countries and for only 12 per cent in the seventh, West Germany.

Differences in earnings between the sexes explained less than 20 per cent of the total variation in four countries, but between 20 and 25 per cent in Belgium and the UK, and over 30 per cent in West Germany. However, in most cases, less than half of the between-sexes contribution was accounted for by differences in earnings between sexes, within manual or non-manual groups. Table 9.11 distinguishes only two occupational groups. A finer classification of occupations would reduce the contribution of the between-sexes,

* The technique used is a generalised approach of a method to deal with N sub-groups employed by P.E. Hart and S.J. Prais (1956) p. 165, when partitioning a variance between two sub-groups.

Table 9.11

The partition of the variation of industrial earnings in seven countries in 1972

	Males	Females	Between sexes	Total
France				
Manual workers	15.4	2.0	1.6	19.0
Non-manual workers	42.7	4.9	2.6	50.2
Total within groups	58.2	6.9	4.2	69.3
Between groups	20.0	0.4	10.4	30.7
Total	78.2	7.3	14.5	100.0
Italy				
Manual workers	18.3	3.3	2.9	24.5
Non-manual workers	37.5	3.6	1.0	42.1
Total within groups	55.7	6.9	4.0	66.6
Between groups	20.7	0.6	12.2	33.4
Total	76.4	7.4	16.2	100.0
Belgium				
Manual workers	27.0	5.7	8.6	41.3
Non-manual workers	29.5	2.8	1.5	33.8
Total within groups	56.5	8.5	10.1	75.1
Between groups	13.8	0.2	10.8	24.9
Total	70.3	8.7	21.0	100.0
United Kingdom				
Manual workers	29.0	1.3	8.2	38.6
Non-manual workers	37.8	1.7	4.6	44.1
Total within groups	66.8	3.1	12.8	82.7
Between groups	5.3	—	11.9	17.3
Total	72.1	3.1	24.8	100.0
West Germany				
Manual workers	24.9	7.4	12.4	44.6
Non-manual workers	22.7	4.5	3.2	30.4
Total within groups	47.5	11.9	15.6	75.0
Between groups	9.8	0.5	14.8	25.0
Total	57.3	12.4	30.3	100.0
Netherlands				
Manual workers	20.4	1.9	4.5	26.8
Non-manual workers	43.6	2.6	3.1	49.3
Total within groups	64.0	4.5	7.6	76.1
Between groups	15.3	—	8.5	23.9
Total	79.3	4.5	16.2	100.0
Luxembourg				
Manual workers	46.8	3.0	4.7	54.5
Non-manual workers	22.6	1.5	1.1	25.1
Total within groups	69.4	4.5	5.8	79.7
Between groups	16.4	—	3.9	20.3
Total	85.8	4.5	9.7	100.0

Sources: See Table 9.10.

within-occupations inequality, considerably. This suggests that paying men and women equally for equal work, whatever else it might achieve, would have little effect on the total inequality of earnings. The major sources of inequality lie elsewhere. One such source, revealed in Table 9.11, is within the male non-manual groups. In each of the four countries with the most unequal distribution of earnings, France, Italy, the UK and the Netherlands, over 37 per cent of the total variation in earnings occur within the male, non-manual group. By contrast, in all the countries, other than Luxembourg and West Germany, the variation in earnings within the larger, male manual group was much less important.

Table 9.12

Purchasing power parity exchange rates for consumers' expenditure, October 1972

Country	Currency unit	Purchasing power parity exchange rate, national currency units per pound
France	Franc	14.21
West Germany	Deutsche Mark	9.88
Italy	Lira	1501.00
Netherlands	Guilder	8.37
Belgium	Belgian Franc	117.71
Luxembourg	Luxembourg Franc	118.50
United Kingdom	Pound	1

Sources: See text of the Appendix.

Appendix

Table 9.12 shows estimates of the purchasing power parity (PPP) exchange rates for consumers' expenditure in seven countries at October 1972. The exchange rates in the table were derived from two sets of PPP exchange rates relating to 1970 that were combined and then used as the basis for projections to October 1972.

Estimates of PPP exchange rates for consumers' expenditure in 1970 are given for France, West Germany, Italy and the UK in Kravis *et al.* (1975, Table 14.3, p. 233). Similar estimates relating to the original six member countries of the European Economic Community can be derived from Mayer (1974, Table 1–5, p. 725 and p. 674n). The two sources give slightly different estimates of the PPP exchange rates for the three countries,

France, West Germany and Italy, that were included in both studies. Compromise estimates were obtained for each of these three countries by taking the geometric mean of the two estimates for each country. Then, following Jones (1976, p. 84), the corresponding exchange rates for the remaining four countries were obtained by taking the geometric mean of the three exchange rates given when the compromise estimates for France, West Germany and Italy were in turn used as links.

Having obtained estimates for all seven countries for 1970, these were projected to October 1972 using the general index of consumer prices for the six original members of the EEC (*Statistical Office of the European Communities,* 1972, Table 7, p. 71 and *ibid.,* 1973, Table 6, p. 61) and for the United Kingdom the index of retail prices (Central Statistical Office, 1973a, table 403, p. 383 and *ibid.,* 1973b, table 172, p. 149).

References

Central Statistical Office (1973a) *Annual Abstract of Statistics,* no. 110 (London: HMSO).

Central Statistical Office (1973b) *Monthly Digest of Statistics,* no. 326 (London: HMSO).

Champernowne, D.G. (1974) 'A Comparison of Measures of Inequality of Income Distribution', *Economic Journal,* vol. 84, no. 336, pp. 787–816.

Chiplin, B. and Sloane, P.J. (1976) *Sex Discrimination in the Labour Market* (London: Macmillan).

Department of Employment (1973) *New Earnings Survey 1972* (London: HMSO).

Duncan, O.D. and Duncan, B. (1955) 'A Methodological Analysis of Segregation Indexes', *American Sociological Review,* vol. 20, no. 2, pp. 210–217.

Hart, P.E. and Prais, S.J. (1956) 'The Analysis of Business Concentration: A Statistical Approach', *Journal of the Royal Statistical Society,* Series A (General), vol. 119, part II, pp. 150–191.

Jones, D.T. (1976) 'Output, Employment and Labour Productivity in Europe Since 1955', *National Institute Economic Review,* no. 77, pp. 72–85.

Kravis, I.B., Kenessey, Z., Heston, A. and Summers, R. (1975) *A System of International Comparisons of Gross Product and Purchasing Power* (Baltimore: World Bank and John Hopkins University Press).

Mayer, J. (1974) 'Comparison Réelle du Produit Intérieur Brut des Pays de la Communauté Européenne, *Analyse et Prévision,* vol. 17, no. 6, pp. 643–781.

Needleman, L. (1978) 'On the Approximation of the Gini Coefficient of Concentration', *Manchester School of Economic and Social Studies,* vol. XLVI, no. 2, June, pp. 105–122.

Office of Population Censuses and Surveys (1975) *1971 Population Census, Great Britain, Economic Activity (10 Per Cent Sample),* Part II, (London: HMSO).

Ranadive, K. R. (1965) 'The Equality of Incomes in India', *Bulletin of the Oxford University Institute of Economics and Statistics,* vol. 27, no. 2, pp. 119–134.

Saunders, C.T. and Marsden, D.W. (1979) *A Six-country Comparison of the Distribution of Industrial Earnings in the 1970s,* Background Paper no. 8, Royal Commission on the Distribution of Income and Wealth (London: HMSO).

Saunders, C.T. and Marsden, D. (1981) *Pay Inequalities in the Community* (London: Butterworths).

Sen, A.K. (1973) *On Economic Inequality* (Oxford: Clarendon Press).

Statistical Office of the European Communities, *Monthly Bulletin of General Statistics,* Luxembourg.

Statistical Office of the European Communities (1975–1977) *Structure of Earnings in Industry,* 13 vols., Luxembourg, [undated, but published during 1975 to 1977].

Theil, H. (1967) *Economics and Information Theory* (North-Holland, Chicago).

Yntema, D.B. (1933) 'Measures of the Inequality in the Personal Distribution of Wealth or Income', *Journal of the American Statistical Association,* vol. 28, no. 184, pp. 423–433.

Chapter 10

THE DISPERSION OF WAGES IN THE CMEA COUNTRIES (INCLUDING A COMPARISON WITH AUSTRIA)

B. Askanas and F. Levcik*

1. It is evident that the differentiation of wages and salaries is not the only source of incomes inequality. Nevertheless, with increasing availability of goods and services in the centrally planned economies of Eastern Europe, differences in the living conditions of various income groups can best be characterised through money earnings.

This paper deals with the differentiation of wages and salaries in most of the CMEA countries in the 1960s and 1970s. Other factors influencing total incomes of wage and salary earners, such as the number of employed persons in households, transfer incomes and the use of free public services in kind, are not being considered. Also earnings from secondary employment or jobs remain outside the scope of this investigation, likewise state subsidies on some commodities and services which also contribute to a certain redistribution of incomes.

Obviously the inclusion of some or all the components mentioned could affect the distribution of overall incomes, which therefore may differ from the distribution of wages and salaries alone. However, it is not clear which of the income groups would in the end be favoured. While free public services and subsidised commodities and services will tend to favour the lower income groups, secondary sources of earnings – such as fees for professional services, authors' fees and similar earnings – are more likely the prerogative of higher income groups.

The number of income earners in households varies not only according to necessity (which is higher in lower income groups), but also according to the qualifications of wives (qualified women tend more often to keep their jobs even after marriage or child bearing than do unskilled female workers).

In an international comparison the question also arises as to how far the wage differentiation may be representative of the distribution of all incomes of the population, i.e. including the incomes of self-employed persons. Obviously in a market economy the share of incomes of self-employed persons in total personal income will be higher than in a

* The authors wish to thank Mrs. H. Askanas for the statistical work in this paper, and F. Prager for improving its English rendering.

centrally planned economy. But even between the CMEA countries the share of self-employed persons differs considerably from country to country. In Poland, for instance, where about 30 per cent of the active population work in private peasant holdings, the share of wages and salaries in total income of the population is smaller than in any other CMEA country.

The following analysis of the size distribution of wages and salaries is based on official statistics in Bulgaria, Czechoslovakia, Hungary, Poland and Romania. For the USSR, secondary sources based on papers published by Soviet authors had to be used, because official statistics are not available. The German Democratic Republic (GDR) has been excluded from the comparative analysis for lack of statistics. The data show the distribution of fulltime wage and salary earners (men and women, including juveniles other than apprentices) by income brackets in a selected month. The earnings include not only the basic wage or salary but also all kinds of premiums, bonus payments, profit shares (where applicable, as in Hungary) which are granted at irregular time intervals. Transfer payments, on the other hand, are not included. The number of income brackets in official statistics differs not only from country to country but also within a country over time. It is obvious that this affects, to a degree, the accuracy of the comparisons between countries, or over time. A greater number of income brackets permits greater precision to be attained in estimates of wage dispersion by size groups.

A host of relevant literature exits concerning various ways of measuring income inequality and wage dispersion and on the advantages and disadvantages of different measures. In this analysis the measures were chosen according to the quality of the original statistics, the least detailed and least precise original source being decisive for choosing the yardstick. Seeing that the extreme brackets are open-ended in most countries and as the distribution statistics available do not contain sufficient other information to be used with a degree of reliability, single inequality indicators, such as the Gini coefficient, the coefficient of variation, or the log variant cannot be used.

To characterise the dispersion of wages in this analysis, the first and the ninth decile, the first and the third quartile and the median were used. In ranking the original values by rising from the lowest to the highest wages, the first decile (D_1) indicates the maximum earnings the lowest 10 per cent of recipients reach, while the highest decile (D_9) indicates the minimum earnings the top 10 per cent of income recipients receive; likewise, the first quartile indicates the point dividing the lowest quarter of income recipients from the remaining three quarters. Similarly, the third quartile marks the point separating the top quarter from the rest.

The median (Me) income indicates the maximum reached by the lower paid half of the recipients. From these values, ratios were computed as measures of dispersion.

The deciles, quartiles and medians were computed by linear interpolation from the original data, grouped according to income bracket. As stated before, the number of income groups differs from country to country. The computed values are, of course, more reliable where the original source shows more detailed income brackets.

In most of the countries compared, the published distribution statistics refer to pre-tax earnings (1). It is obvious that the comparability of the wage dispersion suffers when tax rates differ from country to country. Insofar as income taxes are usually progressive, in countries with higher tax rates the inequality of wage distribution is over-estimated at the upper end. Similarly also a comparison of wage dispersion of a single country over time may be affected if, with increasing pre-tax earnings, the discrepancy between top and bottom groups is influenced by progressively growing tax rates.

The various measures of wage dispersion were computed from nominal values so that the development of wage differentiation is expressed over time in current currency units and not in values deflated by price indices. However, as we are using ratios such as $\frac{D_9}{D_1}$ or $\frac{D_1}{M_e}$, real instead of nominal values would not affect the results. But the influence of the development of consumer prices on real wage dispersion is not entirely eliminated as the changes in the cost of living in the top and bottom income groups may differ because of the differing consumption patterns.

2. In the following account the dispersion of wages and salaries in six European CMEA countries and the development over time of the degree of dispersion in the 1960s and 1970s will be analysed. As wages and salaries increased in all countries throughout the time observed, an increase of dispersion occurred if higher wages and salaries increased faster than the lower ones; likewise, a levelling of wages occurred when low wages increased faster than the higher ones. Table 10.1 gives the following picture:

The ratios of the upper to the lower quartile $\frac{Q_3}{Q_1}$ in the middle of the 1970s, which illustrate the dispersion of the middle income categories in the CMEA countries, do not differ too much from each other. The degree of dispersion in the lower part, measured by $\frac{Q_1}{M_e}$, reaches from 0.72 (Poland) to 0.82 (Romania); in the upper part, measured by $\frac{Q_3}{M_e}$, it reaches between 1.25 (Czechoslovakia) and 1.38 (Poland). The ratios show the most marked inequality $\frac{Q_3}{Q_1}$ for Poland, having the value of 1.92, as against 1.70 in Hungary and the Soviet Union, and around 1.60 in Bulgaria, Czechoslovakia and Romania.

From the beginning of the 1960s to the middle of the 1970s the dispersion of wages in the middle field (between Q_3 and Q_1) remained almost unchanged in Bulgaria, Czechoslovakia and Hungary. The spread widened somewhat in Poland and more so in Romania.

Differentiation narrowed considerably in the USSR between 1956 and 1968, the last year for which information is available.

If we extend the analysis to the upper and the lower reaches of the distribution (D_9 and D_1), more pronounced changes can be found in the dispersion of incomes from employment during the period observed. While wages by size groups became more equal in Bulgaria and Czechoslovakia, tendencies towards increasing inequality made their appearance in Poland, Romania and Hungary. However, neither in the first group of countries nor in the second have these tendencies, both in the upper and in the lower reaches, been clear-cut.

Both in Bulgaria and Czechoslovakia the levelling has been more pronounced in the upper than in the lower range of income distribution. Wages at D_9 in both countries increased less than the median wage and also less than the wages at the bottom decile. However, the somewhat faster increase of wages at D_1 in relation to the median wage indicates that the levelling applied also to the lower incomes. The process of wage levelling was more pronounced in Bulgaria, where the ratio of the upper to the lower decile $\frac{D_9}{D_1}$ decreased from 2.79 to 2.50, while in Czechoslovakia the dispersion narrowed from 2.50 to 2.44 only during the period observed. In Bulgaria the process of levelling occurred mainly in the first half of the 1960s and to a lesser extent in the early 1970s. In Czechoslovakia, likewise, a marked narrowing of the income dispersion occurred in the early 1960s, but this was followed by a period of increased wage differentiation (associated with the economic reform) that lasted until 1970. After a further period of stability there followed a new process of levelling of wages.

The USSR, too, belongs to the group of countries where a continued process of wage levelling could be observed; but in the Soviet Union it was far more pronounced than in the other two countries. Unfortunately, the available statistics enable one to calculate dispersion measures up to 1968 only (2). The development was initiated by a far-reaching wage reform, starting in 1956. The aim of the reform was to reduce the wage differences between employment groups which at the time where considered to be excessive (Volkov, 1974).

The wage reform was carried out in two stages. Between 1956 and 1961 workers and employees in the producing sectors were affected by the reform, and afterwards, up to the second part of the 1960s, wage rates in the service sectors were changed. Among the main elements of the new wages policy were repeated increases of minimum wages, a narrowing of the relation between the highest and the lowest wage rates, and a near complete freeze of the highest groups' salaries for prolonged periods of time. As a consequence of this policy the dispersion of wages by size groups narrowed considerably. The ratio of the upper to the lower decile $\frac{D_9}{D_1}$ narrowed between 1956 and 1968 from a value of 4.97 to

2.85. All the other dispersion measures showed a similar picture so that one can speak of a general levelling of wages in all income brackets in the Soviet Union during this period. While average monthly incomes from employment increased annually by 3.6 per cent, wages at the lowest decile increased by 7.7 per cent, but wages at the highest decile increased by 2.8 per cent only (3). In consequence, wage growth rates diminish steadily as one moves from left to right on the wage scale.

The roughly equal absolute increment in rouble values at almost all income levels is typical for the development of wages in the Soviet Union. Within the 12 years between 1956 and 1968 wages increased at the D_1 level by 36.5 roubles, at Q_1 by 38.9 roubles, while the median wage rose by 38.3 and wages at Q_3 by 40.3 roubles. Only at the upper range, at D_9 did wages increase somewhat more, viz by 50.3 roubles. To leave the wage difference in absolute terms between the income groups mentioned practically unchanged throughout the period observed implies, of course, a considerable narrowing of the relative spread in wage distribution. As to the further development of wage dispersion in the Soviet Union in the 1970s, only guesses are possible. The only statistics one can lay hands on are data on the development of minimum and mean wages. The ratio of minimum wage to mean wage was used as a proxy for the dispersion of wages in the lower half (Table 10.2). It is obvious that the conclusiveness of such a measure is far inferior to quantile measures. Unlike the quantiles, neither the average wage nor the minimum wage relates to a statistically observed number of recipients. In addition, the ratio of minimum to mean wages gives no information on the development of wage dispersion in the upper half of the income distribution. Anyway, between the mid-1950s and the end of the 1960s the ratio of minimum wage to mean wage shows similar tendencies of levelling as those observed in a quantile analysis. The ratio increased throughout the period, from 0.28 to 0.50. The levelling tendency was most pronounced in the 1950s. It continued throughout the 1960s, but the growth difference between minimum wage and mean wage was less pronounced than in the 1950s. In the 1970s the levelling tendency was coming to an end. Moreover, between 1971 and 1975 the minimum wage increased slightly less than the mean wage, and correspondingly the ratio dropped somewhat: from 0.50 to 0.48. We know nothing about the dispersion in the upper part of the wage distribution during the 1970s. If we assume that the dispersion did not change significantly since the end of the 1960s, the coefficient of inequality in the USSR in the mid-1970s must have been similar to that in the other CMEA countries ($\frac{D_9}{D_1}$ = 2.85 to 3.2).

The comparison of the dispersion of wages in the six CMEA countries between the beginning of the 1960s and the middle of the 1970s shows the following picture:

The limits of the coefficient of inequality $\frac{D_9}{D_1}$ at the beginning of the 1960s were between 2.0 (Romania) and 4.4 (USSR) in the early 1960s and between 2.4 (Czechoslovakia and Romania) and 3.8 (Poland) in the mid-1970s. The ranking of countries for the two periods by decreasing wage dispersion is given in Table 10.3. The direction of the arrows for the early 1960s indicates a tendency to widening or narrowing dispersion in the following years.

The ranking of the individual countries according to wage dispersion has not changed much within the fifteen years observed. In both periods Czechoslovakia and Romania were the countries with the lowest wage dispersion. The Soviet Union was the country with the most unequal wages at the beginning of the 1960s, but the more pronounced process of wage levelling during subsequent years brought Soviet wage dispersion down to the level of Hungary, leaving Poland by the mid-1970s as the country with the most unequal wages.

3. The observed changes in wage dispersion are the result of various, sometimes conflicting, partial processes. Various wage movements occurred in particular between economic sectors and within these sectors (e.g. within industry by branches), and also between social and occupational groups and between the sexes. In some cases these wage developments over time went in one direction, in which case they strengthened the tendencies of levelling, or of increasing wage inequality, respectively; in other cases they may have gone in contrary directions, with counterbalancing effects. Of the six CMEA countries, three, namely the USSR, Bulgaria and Czechoslovakia, went through a process of wage levelling. Available statistical evidence of wage development by economic sectors and industrial branches, as well as of changes in wage differentials between social and occupational groups in industry, by and large confirms the results of dispersion by size groups (Tables 10.4–10.9).

The partial wage movements in agreement with the overall picture of the development of wage dispersion by size groups were most pronounced in the USSR. There the wage differentiation by economic sectors narrowed considerably during the 1960s as wages in individual sectors tended to move towards the overall mean of wages for the total economy. The standard deviation decreased between 1963 and 1970 from 19.7 to 17.2, while in the 1970s the sectoral wage differentiation widened somewhat with the standard deviation reaching 18.8 in 1977. Similarily, wage differentials by industrial branches narrowed considerably in the last 15 years. The standard deviation decreased from 25.0 to 16.8 between 1960 and 1970, with a slight widening to 17.3 in 1975.

Wage differentiation by occupational groups can be observed for industry only where the official statistics distinguish between mean wages of manual workers, engineers and technical staff, and employees. The second group embraces not only engineers and technicians but also most of the managerial staff. The group of 'employees' includes mainly clerks and office staff, but also some qualified economists and accountants. Here too the main tendency of wage policy points in the direction of wage levelling. While in 1950 Soviet engineers and technicians had salaries on average more than three quarters higher than the average wages of manual workers, the difference continuously narrowed during the following 25 years, so that the mean salaries of this group by 1976 were only slightly more than a fifth higher than the average wages of manual workers. The average salaries of employees were some 7 per cent below the level of average wages of manual workers even in 1950. By 1960 they had dropped to a level almost 20 per cent below, remaining in more or less the same relation to the wages of manual workers in the 1960s and 1970s.

In Bulgaria and Czechoslovakia the development of wage differentiation by economic sectors and between occupational groups points to the same tendencies of levelling which have been observed by the quantile analysis. In Bulgaria the standard deviation of wage differentials by economic sectors narrowed from 15.4 to 12.5 between 1960 and 1976, in Czechoslovakia it decreased from 14.8 to 13.4. In Czechoslovakia the wage differences by industrial branches also narrowed, the standard deviation decreasing from 16.8 to 15.2 during the same period. In Bulgaria, however, wage differentials by branches within industry somewhat widened. The differentiation by occupational groups shows strong levelling tendencies in that country; in Czechoslovakia these are somewhat weaker. It is remarkable that further processes of levelling occurred in the subsequent years in Czechoslovakia, where there was a relatively very small wage inequality already at the beginning of the 1960s. Very likely this phenomenon can be explained by the relatively abundant supply of qualified manpower, while the demand for unqualified labour for heavy and dirty work could not be met.

In the other three CMEA countries the process of increased dispersion of wages by size groups cannot be unequivocally verified by sectoral and occupational statistics. In Poland wage differentiation by economic sectors and industrial branches has increased somewhat between 1960 and 1976, in line with increased wage dispersion by size groups; but at the same time wage differentiation by occupational groups narrowed. Apparently other processes, like the differentiation of wages according to individual performance or by enterprise results, determined the tendency of widening wage dispersion by size group. In Romania, wage levelling between economic sectors and industrial branches occurred only in the 1960s, but not in the 1970s, nor did a certain process of wage levelling by occupational groups continue after 1970. In Hungary, conflicting tendencies of wage policy affected the development of wage differentiation since the economic reform was initiated in 1968. While differentiation of wages by occupational groups decreased markedly, it increased by sectors, and more so by industrial branches. The general tendency of a stronger dispersion of wages by size groups was influenced likewise by payments according to individual performance and by enterprise results. It would surely have been still more pronounced if the government had not started, since the beginning of the 1970s, to control premiums and bonus payments, especially to management, more closely.

4. An inter-country comparison, such as has been attempted between countries of the same economic and social order, is nevertheless fraught with danger, considering the dif-

fering quality of the original data from which the dispersion ratios were obtained. This danger multiplies when one tries to extend the scope of comparison to countries with differing social structures. Still, a student of social and economic development of centrally planned economies would be curious to learn how far income distribution in these countries compares with inequality in a market economy.

In this study we try to compare dispersion ratios between the CMEA countries and Austria, a mixed economy country, with a sizeable public sector and with a long record of social reforms. Austria is, nevertheless, essentially a market economy with a large group of self-employed persons. According to a special statistical investigation made in 1970, the uppermost 10 per cent of wage and salary recipients liable to a withholding tax earned 24.4 per cent, and the top 1 per cent of these recipients earned 4.9 per cent of the total gross wage and salary income. On the other hand, the highest 10 and 1 per cent respectively of those liable to *income* tax (mainly self-employed persons) received 46.7 per cent and 19.7 per cent respectively of total income-taxed earnings. The wage and salary distribution is therefore very likely less representative of the differentiation of all incomes of the Austrian population than is the wage and salary distribution in the CMEA countries.

But this is only a minor flaw. It is more important that the withholding tax returns are of little use for investigating the incomes distribution, because an important part of the earners of lower incomes are not liable to the withholding tax and therefore remain outside the compass of an investigation based on tax returns. We have therefore used data from wage brackets statistics published by the Central Association of the Austrian Social Security Institutions. Most wage and salary earners are liable to social insurance contributions. 14 per cent of all wage and salary earners (permanent civil servants) remain outside. A quantile analysis for those liable to social security contributions is therefore possible.

The comparability with the data from the CMEA countries is, however, seriously affected because the Austrian statistics include apprentices and part-time workers; both these categories are excluded from the CMEA statistics. In addition, the higher income receivers at the upper end of the distribution scale are not included on the basis of their actual earnings but only at the statutory maximum for social security assessment. All recipients earning more are included at this maximum sum only. 12 percent of all registered recipients earn more than the statutory limit, and one cannot, therefore, calculate the highest decile, D_9 (4). The fact that apprentices and part-time workers are included in the Austrian statistics introduces a bias towards overstating inequality in comparison with the CMEA countries' statistics, while the statutory income limit for social insurance contributions and benefits understates inequality at the higher income level in relation to the median wage. What can be definitely said is that the bias at the lower end of the distribution scale weighs more heavily than the one observed at the upper tail.

It is known that 13 per cent of all recipients were apprentices earning very low incomes (Chaloupek, 1978). Very likely part-time workers also have substantially lower incomes than average full-time wage and salary earners. There is no information on the percentage of part-time workers in the total number of earners, but it is known that the share of part-time working women in the female labour force was 18 per cent in 1976; this amounts to a share of 7 per cent of all wage and salary earners. If we assume that the two categories that are not included in the CMEA country statistics belong to the lowest income groups, then one ought to exclude the lowest 20 per cent of recipients to make the Austrian social insurance statistics more comparable to the CMEA statistics. From the remaining 80 per cent of the original population of wage and salary recipients one can now compute quantile ratios which are more nearly equivalent to those of the CMEA countries. Of course, the adjustment of the original figures has its disadvantages, too. The frequency of recipients in the upper open-ended class becomes higher, so that at best one can calculate the 85th percentile (mid-point between 8th and 9th decile).

As expected, the ratios of inequality of wage and salary earnings in Austria (see Table 10.10) are now considerably lower than the ones calculated from the original unadjusted data as given in Table 10.1.

Compared with Poland, a CMEA country with the highest inequality of earnings, the degree of dispersion in Austria is smaller, especially at wage levels below the median. In Czechoslovakia, however, a country with a long record of wage levelling, wage inequality is still somewhat less than in Austria, especially at wage levels above the median.

With all due caution in view of possible inaccuracies and errors when estimating a new population of recipients for Austria reasonably comparable to the CMEA statistics, one can conclude that inequality of earnings in Austria, a market-type economy, does not differ drastically from the pattern observed in the CMEA countries with their state-socialist systems. Remembering that pre-tax earnings are being compared, and taking into account that taxes are more progressive in Austria (as in most Western European countries) than in the CMEA countries, a comparison of the dispersion of post-tax earnings might show a smaller degree of inequality in Austria than in the CMEA countries.

It should be noted, that very likely a similar income distribution by size groups between the countries compared appears only if men and women, wage and salary earners, unskilled and highly qualified personnel are all lumped together in one group of wage and salary recipients. Income differentials between sexes, social and occupational groups in Austria may well be bigger than in the CMEA countries. A more detailed study than ours would be required to get at the true facts. Quite probably there would also be bigger differences in income inequality if self-employed persons and recipients of unearned income were also to be taken into account.

Footnotes

(1) Only in Poland are data after 1972 given as after-tax earnings. To make the Polish data comparable with the other countries, pre-tax earnings were estimated for the later years.

(2) Data for the grouping of wages by size were taken from A. McAuley (1977) p. 225. He used the following Soviet sources: Shvyrkov and Aidina (1968) and Rabkina and Rimashevskaya (1972).

(3) According to Wiles (1974), Table IV, page 25, the decile ratio widened again somewhat in 1970 ($\frac{D_9}{D_1}$ = 3.2), the last year registered in Wiles' computations.

(4) 40 per cent of male salary earners earn more than this statutory limit.

List of Tables

Table 10.1

Dispersion of wages and salaries in CMEA countries and in Austria

(D = decile, Q = quartile, Me = median)

Bulgaria

	D_1	Q_1	Me	Q_3	D_9	ϕ Gross monthly earnings
			In Leva			
1960	47	56	73	95	131	78
1965	56	69	88	112	142	92
1971	76	93	117	150	193	126
1974	88	106	134	174	220	142
			Average annual growth rates in %			
1961–1965	3.6	4.3	3.8	3.3	1.6	3.3
1966–1971	5,2	5.1	4.9	5.0	5.2	5.4
1972–1974	5.0	4.5	4.6	5.1	4.5	4.5
1961–1974	4.6	4.7	4.4	4.4	3.8	4.4

Dispersion measures

	$\frac{D_1}{Me}$	$\frac{Q_1}{Me}$	$\frac{Q_3}{Me}$	$\frac{D_9}{Me}$	$\frac{Q_3}{Q_1}$	$\frac{D_9}{D_1}$
1960	0.64	0.77	1.30	1.79	1.70	2.79
1965	0.64	0.78	1.27	1.61	1.62	2.54
1971	0.65	0.79	1.28	1.65	1.61	2.54
1974	0.66	0.79	1.30	1.64	1.64	2.50

(continued)

Table 10.1 (continued)

Czechoslovakia

	D_1	Q_1	Me	Q_3	D_9	ϕ Gross monthly earnings
			in Kcs			
1961	903	1125	1439	1798	2253	1391
1966	987	1206	1538	1917	2368	1534
1970	1203	1479	1902	2391	2954	1937
1973	1348	1671	2143	2699	3320	2161
1975	1435	1765	2259	2827	3479	2304
1977	1534	1887	2414	3028	3736	2447
			Average annual growth rates in %			
1962–1966	1.8	1.4	1.3	1.3	1.0	2.0
1967–1970	5.1	5.2	5.5	5.7	5.7	6.0
1971–1975	3.6	3.6	3.5	3.4	3.3	3.5
1962–1975	3.4	3.3	3.3	3.3	3.2	3.7
1962–1977	3.4	3.3	3.3	3.3	3.2	3.6

Dispersion measures

	$\frac{D_1}{Me}$	$\frac{Q_1}{Me}$	$\frac{Q_3}{Me}$	$\frac{D_9}{Me}$	$\frac{Q_3}{Q_1}$	$\frac{D_9}{D_1}$
1961	0.63	0.78	1.25	1.57	1.60	2.50
1966	0.64	0.78	1.25	1.54	1.59	2.40
1970	0.63	0.78	1.26	1.55	1.62	2.46
1973	0.63	0.78	1.26	1.55	1.62	2.46
1975	0.63	0.78	1.25	1.54	1.60	2.42
1977	0.64	0.78	1.25	1.55	1.60	2.44

(continued)

Table 10.1 (continued)

Hungary

	D_1	Q_1	Me	Q_3	D_9	ϕ Gross monthly earnings
	in Forints					
1960	906	1128	1466	1875	2349	1547
1966	1060	1324	1731	2199	2740	1817
1970	1144	1478	2041	2730	3473	2129
1972	1244	1696	2378	3029	3906	2326
1974	1418	2067	2710	3576	4538	2652
1976	1695	2326	3074	3951	4965	2977
	Average annual growth rates in %					
1961–1966	2.7	2.7	3.0	2.7	2.6	2.7
1967–1970	1.9	2.8	4.2	5.6	6.1	4.1
1971–1976	6.8	7.9	7.1	6.4	6.1	5.7
1961–1976	4.0	4.6	4.8	4.8	4.8	4.2

Dispersion measures

	$\frac{D_1}{Me}$	$\frac{Q_1}{Me}$	$\frac{Q_3}{Me}$	$\frac{D_9}{Me}$	$\frac{Q_3}{Q_1}$	$\frac{D_9}{D_1}$
1960	0.63	0.78	1.30	1.62	1.66	2.59
1966	0.61	0.76	1.27	1.58	1.67	2.58
1970	0.56	0.72	1.34	1.70	1.85	3.04
1972	0.52	0.71	1.27	1.64	1.79	3.14
1974	0.52	0.76	1.32	1.67	1.72	3.20
1976	0.55	0.76	1.29	1.62	1.70	2.93

(continued)

Table 10.1 (continued)

Poland(1)

	D_1	Q_1	Me	Q_3	D_9	ϕ Gross monthly earnings
	In Zlotys					
1960	861	1166	1589	2116	2789	1683
						(1562)
1965	1041	1396	1878	2518	3672	2013
1970	1243	1641	2249	3056	4458	2458
	(1222)	(1575)	(2097)	(2742)	(3632)	(2235)
1972	1326	1834	2601	3469	4930	2759
	(1304)	(1760)	(2425)	(3113)	(4017)	(2509)
1973	1627	2188	2908	4038	5790	3077
	(1600)	(2100)	(2712)	(3623)	(4717)	(2798)
1976	2126	2818	3914	5405	8111	4367
	(2090)	(2705)	(3650)	(4850)	(6608)	(3971)
	Average annual growth rates in %					
1961–1965	3.9	3.7	3.4	3.5	5.7	3.6
1966–1970	3.6	3.3	3.7	4.0	4.0	4.1
1971–1976	9.4	9.4	9.7	10.0	10.5	10.1
	(9.4)	(9.4)	(9.7)	(10.0)	(10.5)	(10.1)
1961–1976	5.8	5.7	5.8	6.0	6.9	6.0
	(5.8)	(5.7)	(5.8)	(6.0)	(6.9)	

Dispersion measures

	$\frac{D_1}{Me}$	$\frac{Q_1}{Me}$	$\frac{Q_3}{Me}$	$\frac{D_9}{Me}$	$\frac{Q_3}{Q_1}$	$\frac{D_9}{D_1}$
1960	0.54	0.73	1.33	1.76	1.81	3.24
1965	0.55	0.74	1.34	1.96	1.80	3.53
1970	0.55	0.73	1.36	1.98	1.86	3.59
	(0.58)	(0.75)	(1.31)	(1.73)	(1.74)	(2.97)
1972	0.51	0.71	1.33	1.90	1.89	3.72
	(0.54)	(073)	(1.28)	(1.66)	(1.77)	(3.08)
1973	0.56	0.75	1.39	1.99	1.85	3.56
	(0.59)	(0.77)	(1.34)	(1.74)	(1.73)	(2.95)
1976	0.54	0.72	1.38	2.07	1.92	3.82
	(0.57)	(0.74)	(1.33)	(1.81)	(1.79)	(3.16)

(continued)

Table 10.1 (continued)

Romania

	D_1	Q_1	Me	Q_3	D_9	ϕ Gross monthly earnings
	In Lei					
1960	646	715	829	1020	1293	854
1965	751	826	990	1273	1693	1115
1970	930	1077	1309	1740	2256	1434
1971	943	1106	1347	1781	2290	1471
1972	952	1120	1373	1813	2326	1498
	Average annual growth rates in %					
1961–1965	3.1	2.9	3.6	4.5	5.5	5.5
1966–1970	4.4	5.5	5.7	6.5	5.9	5.2
1971–1972	1.2	2.0	2.4	2.1	1.5	2.2
1961–1972	3.3	3.8	4.3	4.9	5.0	4.8

Dispersion measures

	$\frac{D_1}{Me}$	$\frac{Q_1}{Me}$	$\frac{Q_3}{Me}$	$\frac{D_9}{Me}$	$\frac{Q_3}{Q_1}$	$\frac{D_9}{D_1}$
1960	0.78	0.86	1.23	1.56	1.43	2.00
1965	0.76	0.83	1.29	1.71	1.54	2.25
1970	0.71	0.82	1.33	1.72	1.62	2.43
1971	0.70	0.82	1.32	1.70	1.61	2.43
1972	0.69	0.82	1.32	1.69	1.62	2.44

(continued)

USSR(2)

	D_1	Q_1	Me	Q_3	D_9	ϕ Gross monthly earnings
			In Roubles			
1956	25.3	39.1	62.2	93.7	125.7	73.6
1957	26.5	40.4	66.3	98.6	134.7	75.7
1959	33.5	40.1	70.4	104.0	139.0	79.0
1961	31.7	47.7	72.1	102.9	140.7	83.9
1964	44.1	61.3	84.6	114.9	147.6	90.8
1966	50.6	63.7	87.4	121.6	166.8	100.2
1968	61.8	78.0	101.5	134.0	176.0	112.7
			Average annual growth rates in %			
1957–1961	4.6	4.1	3.0	1.9	2.3	2.7
1962–1966	9.8	6.0	3.9	3.4	3.5	3.6
1967–1968	10.5	10.7	7.8	5.0	2.7	6.1
1957–1968	7.7	5.9	4.6	3.0	2.8	3.6

Dispersion measures

	$\frac{D_1}{Me}$	$\frac{Q_1}{Me}$	$\frac{Q_3}{Me}$	$\frac{D_9}{Me}$	$\frac{Q_3}{Q_1}$	$\frac{D_9}{D_1}$
1956	0.41	0.63	1.51	2.02	2.40	4.96
1957	0.40	0.61	1.49	2.03	2.44	5.08
1958	0.48	0.57	1.48	1.97	2.59	4.15
1961	0.44	0.66	1.43	1.95	2.18	4.44
1964	0.52	0.72	1.36	1.74	1.87	3.35
1966	0.58	0.73	1.39	1.91	1.91	3.30
1968	0.61	0.78	1.32	1.73	1.72	2.85

(continued)

Table 10.1 (continued)

Austria

	D_1	Q_1	Me	Q_3	D_9
	In Schillings				
1960	535	1151	1635	2261	3041
1965	836	1839	2625	3588	4750
1970	1386	2761	3855	5206	6939
1971	1560	3052	4308	5851	7795
1972	1728	3371	4788	6561	8635
1973	1935	3736	5345	7309	9396
1974	2025	4299	6163	8461	10 457
1975	2417	4727	6855	9431	11 624
1976	2686	5113	7433	10 240	13 041(3)

Average annual growth rates in %

1961–1965	9.3	9.8	9.9	9.7	9.3
1966–1970	10.6	8.5	8.0	7.7	7.9
1971–1976	11.7	10.8	11.6	11.9	11.1
1961–1976	10.6	9.8	9.9	9.9	9.5

Dispersion measures

	$\frac{D_1}{Me}$	$\frac{Q_1}{Me}$	$\frac{Q_3}{Me}$	$\frac{D_9}{Me}$	$\frac{Q_3}{Q_1}$	$\frac{D_9}{D_1}$
1960	0.33	0.70	1.38	1.86	1.96	5.68
1965	0.32	0.70	1.37	1.81	1.95	5.68
1970	0.36	0.72	1.35	1.80	1.89	5.01
1971	0.36	0.71	1.36	1.81	1.92	5.00
1972	0.36	0.70	1.37	1.80	1.95	5.00
1973	0.36	0.70	1.37	1.76	1.96	4.86
1974	0.33	0.70	1.37	1.70	1.97	5.16
1975	0.35	0.69	1.38	1.70	2.00	4.81
1976	0.36	0.69	1.38	1.75	2.00	4.86(4)

(continued)

Footnotes to Table 10.1:

(1) Figures in parentheses: net wages; gross wages for 1972, 1973 and 1976 were estimated.

(2) Source: own calculations based on Alastair McAuley, 'The distribution of earnings and incomes in the Soviet Union' in *Soviet Studies,* April 2, 1977.

(3) 88th percentile.

(4) $\frac{P_{88}}{D_1}$

Note: In CMEA countries gross wages and salaries of full-time employees, without apprentices; in Austria gross wages and salaries of all employees including part-time workers and apprentices, without salaries of permanent civil servants.

Table 10.2

Average and minimum earnings in the Soviet Union

Year	Average earnings	Minimum earnings	Minimum in % of average earnings
	in Roubles		
1955	71.8	20	28
1960	80.6	31	38
1965	96.5	42	43
1970	122.0	60	50
1975	145.8	70	48
	Average annual growth rates in %		
1951–1955	12.2		
1956–1960	12.3	55	
1961–1965	19.7	37	
1966–1970	26.4	41	
1971–1975	19.3	16.7	

Table 10.3

Dispersion of wages and salaries

Ranking of six European CMEA countries

Coefficient of inequality $\left(\frac{D_9}{D_1}\right)$

Early 1960s		**Mid-1970s**		
1. USSR	4.44 ↘	1. Poland	3.82	
2. Poland	3.24 ↗	2.–3. USSR	2.85	(3.20)
3. Bulgaria	2.79 ↘	2.–3. Hungary	2.93	
4. Hungary	2.59 ↗	4. Bulgaria	2.50	
5. CSSR	2.50 ↘	5.–6. CSSR	2.44	
6. Romania	2.00 ↗	5.–6. Romania	2.44	

Table 10.4a

Wages and salaries in main sectors of the economy

Average earnings in the total economy = 100

Bulgaria

	1960	1965	1970	1976
Industry	102.3	103.0	99.9	101.4
Construction	122.9	121.4	121.3	117.7
Agriculture	95.0	89.0	86.8	96.8
Forestry	63.9	66.6	72.8	77.7
Transport	114.3	111.7	112.5	113.8
Communications	79.4	83.0	89.4	89.3
Trade	85.2	87.9	91.3	88.7
Housing, communal services	83.5	83.7	87.8	86.3
Science	92.9	105.4	111.6	106.1
Education, art	89.8	89.7	93.5	93.4
Health service	87.5	83.8	86.4	86.4
Finance and credit	86.2	92.9	93.1	91.2
Administration	101.2	107.5	114.6	114.7
Standard deviation	15.4	14.9	14.4	12.5

Table 10.4b

Wages and salaries in industrial branches
Average earnings in industry = 100

Bulgaria

	1960	1965	1970	1976
Electricity	102.5	107.4	112.9	113.2
Fuel	132.5	127.4	133.9	135.8
Ferrous metallurgy incl. mining	117.2	119.9	119.4	116.5
Engineering, Metalwork	107.5	104.2	104.8	105.3
Chemicals	102.5	100.0	103.2	102.0
Construction materials	108.8	105.3	106.5	107.3
Wood and wood processing	107.5	103.2	102.4	103.3
Pulp and paper	95.0	92.6	95.2	91.4
Glass and china	101.3	101.1	95.2	98.7
Textiles	86.3	87.4	85.5	86.8
Clothing	81.3	85.3	79.8	76.8
Leather, footwear	97.5	93.7	87.9	88.1
Printing and publishing	95.0	88.4	98.4	93.4
Food processing	88.8	94.7	92.7	93.4
Other	92.5	87.4	87.9	86.1
Standard deviation	12.9	12.1	14.1	15.7

Table 10.4c

Wages and salaries in industry(1)

Bulgaria

	Average monthly earnings			Salaries of engineers and technical staff	Employees' salaries
	Workers	Engineers and technical staff	Employees		
		in Leva		in % of workers' wages	
1950	464.5	707.7	500.6	152.4	107.8
1955	67.2	102.9	63.9	153.1	95.1
1960	81.0	115.1	76.0	142.1	93.8
1965	95.1	137.9	95.3	145.0	100.2
1970	122.9	172.4	126.0	140.3	102.5
1971	127.4	167.5	122.0	131.5	95.8
1972	132.0	176.5	127.0	133.7	96.2
1973	140.8	186.0	134.5	132.1	95.2
1974	144.1	187.4	131.9	130.0	91.5
1975	151.3	194.0	132.9	128.2	87.8
1976	153.6	187.5	127.9	122.1	83.3

(1) State industry only.

Table 10.5a

Wages and salaries in main sectors of the economy
Average earnings in the total economy = 100

Czechoslovakia

	1960	1965	1970	1976
Industry	105.6	105.4	101.5	101.5
Construction	111.4	113.9	113.3	112.3
Agriculture	81.5	87.6	93.2	96.2
Forestry	92.7	96.7	97.6	101.8
Goods traffic	108.1	110.0	117.2	116.3
Communications	88.3	87.8	92.2	88.2
Trade	80.8	83.5	85.3	84.5
Passenger transport	105.4	106.4	113.2	112.7
Housing	56.6	61.5	65.4	69.6
Communal services	77.1	73.1	78.2	76.8
Science	113.2	118.1	116.0	113.5
Education, culture	94.7	91.3	94.6	93.4
Health service	86.7	82.3	91.7	95.4
Finance and credit	96.9	94.7	111.7	104.1
Administration	101.7	103.9	105.9	106.5
Standard deviation	14.8	15.2	14.5	13.4

Table 10.5b

Wages and salaries in industrial branches
Average earnings in industry = 100

Czechoslovakia

	1960	1965	1970	1976
Electricity	109.9	109.9	110.6	109.5
Fuel	138.9	136.5	136.7	133.0
Ferrous metallurgy	120.1	119.9	116.9	120.0
Engineering	103.4	102.5	101.1	101.2
Chemicals	98.9	100.2	100.7	100.0
Construction materials	103.6	103.1	105.0	103.9
Wood and wood processing	89.7	89.4	92.5	91.6
Glass and china	90.0	87.6	88.1	87.9
Textiles	78.0	77.7	80.3	80.9
Leather	83.1	85.7	90.3	88.9
Food processing	89.9	88.3	95.1	93.2
Other	83.6	87.6	87.0	85.9
Standard deviation	17.5	16.8	15.5	15.2

Table 10.5c

Wages and salaries in industry

Czechoslovakia

	Average monthly earnings			Salaries of engineers and technical staff	Employees' salaries
	Workers	Engineers and technical staff	Employees		
		in Kcs		in % of workers' wages	
1950	886				
1955	1272	1607	1081	126.3	85.0
1960	1406	1642	1083	116.8	77.0
1965	1529	1835	1202	120.0	78.6
1970	1902	2310	1586	121.5	83.4
1971	1974	2383	1637	120.7	82.9
1972	2048	2444	1696	119.3	82.8
1973	2107	2532	1747	120.2	82.9
1974	2183	2605	1816	119.3	83.2
1975	2270	2671	1854	117.7	81.7
1976	2338	2759	1883	118.0	80.5

Table 10.6a

Wages and salaries in main sectors of the economy

Average earnings in the total economy = 100

Hungary

	1960	1965	1970	1976
Industry	104.0	101.4	98.3	100.7
Construction	104.1	103.6	110.5	110.9
Agriculture, Forestry	87.7	87.3	98.1	96.0
Transport, communications	97.2	101.0	105.1	106.2
Trade	90.6	90.5	93.3	89.5
Administration, culture, health service etc.	99.6	98.6	96.2	97.0
Standard deviation	6.8	6.6	6.4	7.7

Table 10.6b

Wages and salaries in industrial branches
Average earnings in industry = 100

Hungary

	1960	1965	1970	1976
Electricity	102.5	102.4	102.9	100.3
Metallurgy	105.2	105.6	105.5	110.7
Mining	138.8	140.1	141.7	143.4
Engineering	99.3	99.9	98.4	97.1
Electrical industry	97.2	100.1	97.9	96.1
Metal work	93.5	94.7	92.8	90.5
Chemicals	94.7	97.3	91.9	99.2
Construction materials	93.4	94.5	95.3	96.2
Wood and wood processing	91.5	90.0	88.7	88.1
Pulp and paper	92.5	91.5	91.8	104.4
Textiles	84.1	83.1	83.4	88.2
Clothing	84.7	82.3	75.8	76.6
Leather, footwear	96.8	86.5	83.8	83.7
Printing and publishing	93.1	91.8	92.8	97.1
Food processing	87.7	87.7	87.3	94.0
Other	90.7	87.7	87.8	84.8
Standard deviation	12.6	13.6	14.6	15.0

Table 10.6c

Wages and salaries in industry(1)

Hungary

	Average monthly earnings			Salaries of engineers and technical staff	Employees' salaries
	Workers	Engineers and technical staff	Employees		
		in Forints		in % of workers' wages	
1957	1486	2360	1418	158.8	95.4
1960	1574	2458	1492	156.2	94.8
1965	1707	2648	1638	155.1	96.0
1970	2039	3072	1968	150.7	96.5
1971	2114	3169	2054	149.9	97.2
1972	2210	3282	2149	148.5	97.2
1973	2449	3487	2263	142.4	92.4
1974	2626	3712	2408	141.4	91.7
1975	2803	3914	2559	139.6	91.3

(1) State industry only.

Table 10.7a

Wages and salaries in main sectors of the economy
Average earnings in the total economy = 100

Poland

	1960	1965	1970	1977[1]
Industry	110.1	109.0	107.5	106.1
Construction	115.6	118.1	121.5	114.6
Agriculture	79.6	81.1	84.4	102.2
Forestry	69.9	73.1	70.7	84.5
Transport, communications	96.1	100.5	100.9	102.5
Trade	83.9	85.8	85.2	83.2
Housing, communal services	94.1	91.7	95.3	89.7[2] 99.6[3]
Science	119.9	129.8	123.8	119.9
Education	85.4	83.8	83.1	80.1
Culture, art	90.4	89.7	92.6	84.2
Health service	77.5	76.7	74.9	76.8
Finance and insurance	92.5	91.1	97.4	83.4
Administration, justice	92.5	97.6	98.6	106.0
Standard deviation	14.8	16.5	16.1	15.1

1) Net wages
2) Housing
3) Communal services.

Table 10.7b

Wages and salaries in industrial branches
Average earnings in industry = 100

Poland

	1960	1965	1970	1976[1)]
Fuel and power industry	146.2	142.9	149.6	151.1
Ferrous metallurgy	123.3	125.1	125.5	126.3
Nonferrous metallurgy	126.2	123.2	127.8	129.8
Engineering	106.5	107.1	100.5	105.2
Transport equipment	107.8	107.6	105.0	106.5
Electrical industry	96.9	98.0	94.0	91.0
Metal work	97.1	96.5	93.3	93.5
Chemicals	96.2	96.8	94.9	93.3
Construction materials	90.6	92.8	92.8	94.4
Wood and wood processing	82.7	83.8	82.9	87.9
Pulp and paper	84.2	81.9	80.6	83.7
Glass and china	88.2	86.6	84.3	87.2[2)] 85.5[3)]
Textiles	83.8	81.7	82.8	83.9
Clothing	70.4	73.0	76.3	76.6
Leather, footwear	79.6	79.9	82.3	81.2
Printing and publishing	98.3	89.1	92.1	84.8
Food processing	83.4	83.7	83.4	84.2
Other	85.3	83.8	85.8	85.1
Standard deviation	19.0	18.5	19.5	19.5

1) Net wages
2) Glass
3) China

Table 10.7c

Wages and salaries in industry(1)

Poland

	Average monthly earnings			Salaries of engineers and technical staff	Employees' salaries
	Workers	Engineers and technical staff	Employees		
	in Zlotys			in % of workers' wages	
1950(2)	567	1020	703	179.9	124.0
1955(2)	1156	1809	1142	156.5	98.8
1960	1643	2575	1727	156.7	105.1
1965	1914	3082	2067	161.0	108.0
1970	2279	3417	2342	149.9	102.8
1971	2408	3555	2455	147.6	102.0
1972	2528	3689	2553	145.9	101.0
1973	2765	3989	2768	144.3	100.1
1974	3172	4482	3086	141.3	97.3
1975	3626	4990	3416	137.6	94.2
1976(3)	4168	5459	3722	131.0	89.3

(1) Net wages

(2) Gross wages

(3) According to new classification of January 1, 1976 – therefore not comparable with previous years.

Table 10.8a

Wages and salaries in main sectors of the economy

Average earnings in the total economy = 100

Romania

	1960	1965	1970	1976
Industry	103,9	104,0	99.9	98.9
Construction	102.7	106.1	108.4	112.2
Agriculture	85.6	90.5	92.5	98.5
Forestry	72.3	75.5	79.8	88.8
Transport	110.8	98.7	107.7	106 4
Communications	92.7	92.6	86.4	88.4
Trade	84.8	86.5	89.1	88.3
Housing, communal services	91.1	90.9	86.7	89.5
Science	119.2	110.1	110.0	112.1
Education, culture	102.5	97.7	100.8	100.6
Health service	93.8	92.4	93.4	93.9
Standard deviation	13.2	9.8	10.3	9.1

Table 10.8b

Wages and salaries in industrial branches

Average earnings in industry = 100

Romania

	1962	1965	1970	1974
Ferrous metallurgy[1])	118.5	115.8	120.5	121.7
Nonferrous metallurgy[1])	116.3	115.4	127.7	123.7
Engineering, metal work	113.9	110.8	107.8	108.1
Chemicals	103.1	99.3	104.1	101.0
Construction materials	89.1	92.3	95.6	96.7
Wood and wood processing	91.3	97.9	95.1	95.3
Paper and cellulose	97.6	96.3	98.4	93.9
Glass and china	97.6	100.7	97.6	103.6
Textiles	86.9	86.3	83.9	87.5
Clothing	80.8	83.6	81.7	82.3
Leather, footwear	89.8	92.0	88.5	92.5
Printing and publishing	97.4	96.9	97.6	91.9
Food processing	90.1	88.9	89.9	87.0
Standard deviation	11.9	10.4	13.4	12.7

[1]) including mining

Table 10.8c

Wages and salaries in industry

Romania

	Average monthly earnings workers	Average monthly earnings employees	Employees: salaries (1) in % of workers' wages
	in Lei		
1950	336	500.5	149.0
1955	529	761.5	144.0
1960	854	1075.2	125.9
1965	1112	1454.8	130.8
1970	1354	1997.0	147.5
1971	1385	2026.8	146.3
1972	1409	2027.8	143.9
1973	1479	2209.8	149.4
1974	1592	2368.8	148.8
1975	1756	2520.1	143.5
1976	1871	2680.7	143.3

(1) including engineers and technical staff

Table 10.9a

Wages and salaries in main sectors of the economy
Average earnings in the total economy = 100

USSR

	1963	1968	1970	1977
Industry	111.6	108.2	109.3	111.3
Construction	115.2	116.4	122.9	120.0
Agriculture	76.1	81.7	82.8	89.8
Transport	112.6	112.0	112.0	119.7
Communications	82.2	78.0	79.3	87.8
Trade	73.1	80.4	78.0	75.0
Housing, communal services	71.0	78.2	77.5	74.6
Science	124.4	114.7	114.3	106.2
Education	85.4	91.2	88.8	83.7
Culture			69.5	61.5
Art	–	81.9	77.7	70.1
Health service	70.3	80.0	75.4	70.1
Finance and insurance	88.6	91.8	91.3	89.8
Administration	106.1	104.8	100.2	87.8
Standard deviation	19.7	15.2	17.2	18.8

Table 10.9b

Wages and salaries in industrial branches

Average earnings in industry = 100

USSR

	1960	1966	1970	1975
Ferrous metallurgy	127.2	121.8	114.9	116.0
Nonferrous metallurgy	–	97.4	102.9	101.4
Mining	158.7	156.5	147.5	147.6
Engineering	98.0	95.8	95.9	95.9
Chemicals	103.2	104.2	102.6	101.9
Wood and wood processing	85.4	88.4	94.8	97.2
Furniture	82.6	85.2	91.8	93.6
Pulp and paper	102.7	96.2	98.1	101.0
Glass	–	94.6	100.7	99.2
China	–	86.7	93.9	90.9
Textiles	77.2	79.2	81.3	80.3
Clothing	64.9	71.2	71.1	71.2
Leather	83.4	87.9	90.6	87.8
Footwear	71.9	80.5	83.1	81.6
Food processing	79.7	83.0	86.4	87.7
Beverages	73.9	78.2	81.2	78.8
Tobacco	81.7	85.8	89.8	86.9
Standard deviation	25.0	19.9	16.8	17.3

Table 10.9c

Wages and salaries in industry(1)

USSR

	Average monthly earnings			Salaries of engineers and technical staff	Employees' salaries
	Workers	Engineers and technical staff	Employees		
	in Rubles			in % of workers' wages	
1950	69.0	122.9	64.3	178.1	93.2
1960	89.9	135.7	73.8	150.9	82.1
1965	101.7	148.4	85.8	145.9	84.4
1970	130.6	178.0	111.6	136.3	85.5
1971	135.4	181.4	114.4	134.0	84.5
1972	140.1	182.5	115.7	130.3	82.6
1973	145.6	184.9	118.5	127.0	81.4
1974	153.9	193.4	126.2	125.7	82.0
1975	160.9	199.2	131.3	123.8	81.6
1976	168.2	205.8	139.2	122.4	82.8

Table 10.10

Dispersion of earnings in Austria, Czechoslovakia and Poland, 1976

	$\frac{D_1}{Me}$	$\frac{Q_1}{Me}$	$\frac{Q_3}{Me}$	$\frac{D_8}{Me}$	$\frac{Q_3}{Q_1}$	$\frac{D_8}{D_1}$	$\frac{D_8}{D_2}$	$\frac{P_{85}}{D_1}$
Poland	0.57	0.74	1.33	1.45	1.79	2.54	2.12	2.85
Austria[1)]	0.65	0.78	1.32	1.42	1.69	2.19	1.93	2.40
Czechoslovakia[2)]	0.64	0.78	1.25	1.33	1.60	2.09	1.80	2.23

1) Adjusted data

2) 1977

References

Askanas B., Askanas H., Levcik F. (1976) 'Entwicklung und Niveau der Löhne in den RGW-Ländern. Mit einem Lohnvergleich mit Österreich', *Monatsberichte des Österreichischen Institutes für Wirtschaftsforschung,* no. 1, Vienna.

Atkinson A. B. (ed.) (1973) *Wealth, Income and Inequality,* Part Three, 'The Distribution of Earnings' Harmsworth, Middlesex: (Penguin Education).

Batkaev R. (1971) 'Rost zarabotnoy platy v vosmoy pyatiletke', *Socialisticheskiy trud,* no. 3, Moscow.

Berényi J. (1974) *Lohnsystem und Lohnstruktur in Österreich und Ungarn,* Studien über Wirtschafts- und Systemvergleiche, Wiener Institut für Internationale Wirtschaftsvergleiche, vol. 6 (Wien—New York: Springer-Verlag).

Chaloupek G. (1977) 'Die Verteilung der persönlichen Einkommen in Österreich. Die hohen Einkommen', *Wirtschaft und Gesellschaft,* no. 1 (Vienna: Europa Verlag).

Chaloupek G. (1978) 'Die Verteilung der persönlichen Einkommen in Österreich. II. Die Arbeitsverdienste', *Wirtschaft und Gesellschaft,* no. 2 (Vienna: Europa Verlag).

'Eine Einkommensschichtung in Österreich von 1953 bis 1970 im Lichte der Steuerstatistik', *Statistische Nachrichten,* no. 10, 1975, Vienna.

Farberova E., Shyutte G. (1972) 'Struktura zarabotnoy płaty v stranakhchlenakh SEV', *Socialisticheskiy trud,* no. 4, Moscow.

Füsser A., Unger P. (1976) 'Vergleich der tariflichen Lohn- und Gehaltsdifferenzierung in der UdSSR und der Bundesrepublik Deutschland', *Osteuropa Wirtschaft*, no. 1, Deutsche Gesellschaft für Osteuropakunde.

Kabaj M. (ed.) (1976) *Wartośeiowanie pracy jako metoda doskonalenia systemu płac,* Instytut Pracy i Spraw Socjalnych, Warsaw.

Kirsch L.J. (1972) *Soviet Wages: Changes in Structure and Administration since 1956* , (Cambridge, Massachusetts: The MIT Press).

Kordos J. (1973) *Metody analizy i prognozowania rozkładów płac i dochodów ludności,* Panstwowe Wydawnictwo Ekonomiczne, Warsaw.

Krajewska A. (1974) *Wykształcenie a zrożnicowanie płac,* Panstwowe Wydawnictwo Ekonomiczne, Warsaw.

Krajowicz T. (1978) 'Zróżnicowanie płac w CSRS', *Polityka spoleczna*, no. 1, Warsaw.

Krencik W. (1972) *Podstawy i kierunki polityki płac w PRL,* Państwowe Wydawnictwo Ekonomiczne, Warsaw.

Lecaillon J. and Germidis D. (1975) 'Economic Development and the Wage Share in National Income', *International Labour Review*, vol. 111, International Labour Office, Geneva.

Levcik B. (1969) *Wage Policy and Wage Planning in Czechoslovakia,* International Labour Office, Geneva.

Levcik F. (1975) 'The Distribution of Income in Centrally Planned Economies', in Fallenbuchl Z. (ed)., *Economic Efficiency in the Soviet Union and Eastern Europa*, (New York: Praeger Special Studies).

Lydall H. (1968) *The Structure of Earnings,* Oxford.

Lydall H. (1977) *Income Distribution and Employment Programme,* International Labour Office, Geneva.

Matthews M. (1975) 'Top Incomes in the USSR: Towards a Definition of the Soviet Elite', *Survey, a journal of East & West studies,* Summer vol. 21, no. 3 (96) (Oxford: Oxford University Press).

McAuley A. (1977) 'The Distribution of Earnings and Incomes in the Soviet Union', *Soviet Studies*, vol. XXXIX, no. 2, April.

McAuley N.D. (1976) *Wage Determination in the USSR,* The Seminar Series on Major Social and Economic Problems of the U.K. in the Light of East European Experience, London.

Michal J.M. (1971) *Size Distribution of Incomes under Socialism in Czechoslovakia,* Research Memorandum Nr. 57, June (Vienna: Institut für Höhere Studien und Wissenschaftliche Forschung).

Michal J.M. (1973) 'Size Distribution of Earnings and Household Incomes in Small Socialist Countries', *Review of Income and Wealth,* December.

Michal J.M. (1975) 'An Alternate Approach to Measuring Income Inequality', in Fallenbuchl Z. (ed), *Economic Efficiency in the Soviet Union and Eastern Europa,* (New York: Praeger Special Studies).

Mikulskiy K. (1975) 'Sovershenstvovanie raspredeleniya po trudu v stranakh SEV', *Voprosy ekonomiki,* no. 1, Moscow.

Mehran F. (1975) 'Dealing with Grouped Income Distribution Data', *Income Distribution and Employment Programme,* W.P. 20, International Labour Office, Geneva, August.

Melich A. (1973) *Podstawy teorii płac w socjalizmie,* Państwowe Wydawnictwo Ekonomiczne, Warsaw.

Morecka Z. (1971) 'System płac w gospodarce socjalistycznej', *Ekonomista*, no. 9, Warsaw.

Morecka Z. (1974) 'Problematyka płac w XXX-leciu PRL', *Ekonomista,* no. 3, Warsaw.

Paukert F. (1973) 'Income Distribution at Different Levels of Development' A Survey of Evidence', *International Labour Review,* vol. 108, nos. 2–3, August-September, International Labour Office, Geneva.

Pawlukiewicz M. (1975) 'Struktura i dynamika wynagrodzenia za pracę na Węgrzech 1968–1972', *Biuletyn Instytutu Gospodarstwa Spolcznego* no. 2, Szkola Głowny Planowania i Statystyki, Warsaw.

Pietsch A.J. (1972) 'Die Differenzierung der Arbeiterlöhne in der UdSSR und der Bundesrepublik Deutschland', *Osteuropa Wirtschaft*, no. 3, Deutsche Gesellschaft für Osteuropakunde.

Podgórski Z. (1976) 'Działowe i gałęziowe priorytety płacowe w Polsce w latach 1960–1975', *Wiadomosci Statystyczne*, no. 7, Warsaw.

Pryor F.L. (1971) *Economic System and the Size Distribution of Income and Wealth*, The International Development Research Center, Indiana University, Bloomington, Indiana USA.

Rabkina N.E. and Rimashevskaya N.M. (1972) *Osnovy differentsiatsii zarabotnoi platy i dokhodov naseleniya*, (Moscow).

Rzhanicyna L. (1971) 'Obespechenie vysokogo urovniya zhizni vsem trudyashchimsya', *Socialisticheskiy trud*, no. 8, Moscow.

Saunders C., Mukherjee S., Marsden D., Donaldson A. (1977) *Winners and Losers: Pay Patterns in the 1970s*, Centre for Contemporary European Studies and Political and Economic Planning (PEP) Series, vol. XLIII, no. 570, September.

Sawyer M. (1976) 'Income Distribution in OECD Countries', *OECD Economic Outlook. Occasional Studies*, July, Paris.

Schriftenreihe der Wiener Kammer für Arbeiter und Angestellte (1963) *Die langfristige Entwicklung von Löhnen und Gehältern in Wien*, Verlag des Österreichischen Gewerkschaftsbundes, Vienna.

Sekanina V. (1977) 'Vyvoj Miezd v krajinach RVHP v rokach 1950–1975', *Prace a mzda*, no. 6, Prague.

Shurko S. (1975) 'Novye usloviya otplaty truda', *Voprosy ekonomiki*, no. 10, Moscow.

Shvyrkov V.V. and Aidina L.K. (1968) 'Model raspredeleniya naseleniya po dokhodu', in *Opyt primeneniya matematicheskikh metodov i EVM v ekonomiko-matematicheskom modelirovanii potrebleniya* (Moscow).

Strińska Z. (1973) 'Zróżnicowanie i koncentracja płac w gospodarce uspołecznionenj w latach 1960–1970, *Wiadomości statystyczne*, no. 3, Warsaw.

Sukharevskiy B. (1975) 'Socialno-ekonomicheskie osnovy form zarabotnoy platy v promyshlennosti stran-chelnov SEV, *Socialisticheskiy trud*, no. 6, Moscow.

Tichý J. (1977) 'Odvetvové mzdové relace v cs. národním hospodárství', *Plánované hospodarství*, no. 6, Prague.

United Nation, Economic Commission for Europe (1967) *Incomes in Postwar Europe: A Study of Policies, Growth and Distribution.* (Economic Survey of Europe in 1965, Part 2), Geneva.

Vogel H. (1975) *Einkommens- und Sozialpolitik der UdSSR im Jahre 1974*, Berichte des Bundesinstitutes für Ostwissenschaftliche und Internationale Studien, no. 19, Cologne.

Volkov A.P. (ed) (1974) *Trud i zarabotnaya plata v SSSR*, Izdatelstvo 'Ekonomika', Moscow.

Volkov A.P. (1974) 'Trud, zarabotnaya plata i narodnoe blagostoyanie v SSSR', in Volkov A.P. (ed.) *Trud i zarabotnaya plata v SSSR.*

Weissel E. (1974) 'Die Lohnentwicklung in der Wiener Industrie in den sechziger Jahren', *Beiträge zu Wirtschaftspolitik und Wirtschaftswissenschaft,* VI., Schriftenreihe der Wiener Kammer für Arbeiter und Angestellte, Vienna.

Wilczyński J. (1972) 'Differentiation of Income under Modern Socialism', *Jahrbuch der Wirtschaft Osteuropas,* Band 3, Osteuropa-Institut (München–Wien: Olzog Verlag).

Wiles P. (1974) *Distribution of Income: East and West,* Amsterdam, Oxford, New York.

Yanowitch M. (1977) *Social and Economic Inequality in the Soviet Union*, (London: Martin Robertson & Co.).

Statistical Sources

Bulgaria: *Statisticheski godishnik na NRB* 1960, 1971, 1972, 1975, 1976, 1977

Czechoslovakia: *Statistická rocenka ČSSR 1967, 1972, 1975, 1976, 1977*
Statistické prehledy Nr. 12, 1977

Hungary: *Statisztikai évkönyv* 1957, 1971, 1974, 1975, 1976

Poland: *Rocznik statystyczny* 1971, 1972, 1975, 1976, 1977

Romania: *Annarul statistic al RSR* 1973, 1976, 1977

USSR: 1970 *Narodnoe khozyaystvo za* 60 let, 1975

International Labour Office: *Yearbook of Labour Statistics,* 1969, 1970, 1975, 1976, 1977

Austria: *Statistisches Handbuch der österreichischen Sozialversicherung* 1960, 1965, 1970–1976

Chapter 11

MACROECONOMIC PLANNING OF OIL REVENUE IN INDUSTRIALISED COUNTRIES: THE BRITISH CASE*

H. Motamen**

Introduction

The objective of this paper is to provide a framework for analysing the expenditure policies of oil revenue in industrialised countries. It is a case study of the United Kingdom, covering the twenty-five year period from 1976 – the commencement of the generation of the UK petroleum sector – to the year 2000.

The economic effects of North Sea oil on the British economy are indeed large and much underestimated. Although the revenue from this sector is generally regarded as relatively small, it can affect a series of variables ranging from the exchange rate, exports of manufactured output and the balance of payments to the level of investment and the growth of national income. In order to plan the proceeds of the resource, it is important to measure the impact of the oil sector on all these variables simultaneously. For this purpose the methodology of optimal control is found to be most suitable.

The long-run macroeconomic model presented here is basically applicable to an industrialised economy with both a flexible exchange rate system and an exhaustible resource. The model is solved numerically to study the intertemporal planning strategy for the utilisation of the North Sea oil income of the UK.

The form of optimal control applied here falls into the category of deterministic control. The algorithm used is based upon Zoutendijk's 'method of feasible directions'. It is devised to handle discrete-time problems with fixed horizons and inequality constraints. The technique of computation is one of gradient methods. The routine is set in a way to make a given policy first feasible, and then optimal. The computations have been carried out at the University of London on a CDC 7600 machine.

The problem is formulated with a terminal objective, subject to both terminal and intertemporal constraints. The system is optimised in conjunction with a macroeconomic model, where the latter is a rather aggregate (sixteen equations) model, featuring the main characteristics of the UK economy.

* Finance for this research was provided by the Social Science Research Council. Roger Strange and Stephen Hall worked as research assistants on this project.

** The writer is grateful to Stephen Frowen for his useful comments and suggestions.

The solutions reached through the computations are then compared with the actual policies adopted in Britain, and the differences between the two are shown where appropriate. Finally, some simulations are carried out and the sensitivities of the solutions are shown against changes in the parameter values; there follows a discussion of the time paths of the exogenous variables and their policy implications.

The Model

This section describes briefly the structure of the model, and presents the values for its parameters. The guiding principles behind the construction of the model were first that it should be well-based in terms of economic theory: second that it should include all the main aggregate economic variables; and third that it should reasonably fit past economic data associated with the UK economy.

The basic structure of the economy is explained by a set of self-evident identities, together with some behavioural relationships comprising sixteen equations. The notation used throughout the model to denote the economic variables and parameters is shown below.

Notation of variables and parameters

A. Variables

N_t = Net national income

D_t = Value-added in the non-oil sector at factor cost

P_t = Value-added in the oil sector, market prices

F_t = Income from abroad

K_t = Fixed capital stock net of depreciation

I_t = Net non-oil fixed capital formation

L_t = Labour input

R_t = Raw material input

π_t = International price of crude oil (index)

Q_t = Stock of oil reserves

q_t = Quantity of crude oil extracted annually from the North Sea

ℓ_t^I = Total government take from North Sea oil which includes petroleum revenue tax, royalties and corporation tax

ℓ_t^{II} = Expenditure tax

ℓ_t^{III} = Personal income tax

p_t^c = Company share of value-added of oil

E_t = Stock of assets abroad

C_t = Personal consumption

B_t = Current account balance (changes in reserves)

G_t = Government expenditure

X_t = Total exports

V_t = Non-oil exports

S_t = Exchange rate

B. Parameters

g = Scale variables in the production function

β = Rate of technical progress

α = Elasticity of response for capital

γ = Elasticity of response for labour

ρ = Elasticity of response for raw materials

ξ = Raw material used as a proportion of current output

θ_o = Scale variable in the external income function

θ_1 = Elasticity of response for portfolio of assets overseas

η = Average propensity to consume

ϵ = Coefficient of personal income tax

ω = Proportion of oil exported

σ = Coefficient of expenditure tax

m_o =
m_1 = Parameters of the export equation

Ω_o =
Ω_1 = Parameters of the exchange equation
Ω_2 =

ϕ = Essential imported share of raw material used in non-oil production

μ = Essential imported share of aggregate consumtion.

The macroeconomic model

$$N_t = D_t + \ell_t^{II} + P_t + F_t \tag{1}$$

$$D_t = g\,(1+\beta)^t\, K_{t-1}^{\alpha}\, L_{t-1}^{\gamma}\, R_{t-1}^{\rho} \tag{2}$$

$$\beta > o \quad o < \alpha < 1 \quad o < \gamma < 1 \quad o < \rho < 1$$

$$R_t = \xi D_t \tag{3}$$

$$P_t = \pi_t q_t \equiv \ell_t^I + p_t^c \tag{4}$$

$$q_t = Q_{t-1} - Q_t \tag{5}$$

$\ell_t^I = f(q_t)$ The formula for total government take from the oil sector is applied (6)

$$I_t = K_t - K_{t-1} \tag{7}$$

$$F_t = \theta_o E_{t-1}{}^{\theta_1} \tag{8}$$

$$\theta_o > 0 \quad 0 < \theta_1 < 1$$

$$B_t = E_t - E_{t-1} \tag{9}$$

$$C_t = \eta\,(D_t - \ell_t^{III} + F_t) \equiv \eta\,(1-\epsilon)\,(D_t + F_t) \tag{10}$$

$$1 > \eta > 0$$

$$\ell_t^{III} = \epsilon(D_t + F_t) \tag{11}$$

$$\ell_t^{II} = \sigma C_t \tag{12}$$

$$B_t = N_t - C_t - I_t - G_t \tag{13}$$

$$M_t \equiv X_t - B_t = V_t + \omega P_t - B_t \tag{14}$$

$$V_t = m_o S_{t-1}{}^{m_1} \tag{15}$$

$$\frac{dV_t}{dS_{t-1}} < 0$$

$$S_t = \Omega_o + \Omega_1 (\pi_t q_t)^{\Omega_2} \tag{16}$$

$$\frac{dS_t}{dq_t} > 0 \qquad \frac{d^2S_t}{dq_t^2} < 0$$

The first equation of the model brings out the role of the newly-developed oil sector by disaggregating domestic output into an oil and a non-oil sector. The non-oil output is determined by means of a production function (Equation 2), and the oil output is determined as a control variable. The impact of the oil sector on the balance of trade is captured through the exchange rate equation (Equation 16) and the export function (Equation 15). Foreign investment is determined by the income expenditure identity (Equation 13) in such a way that total investment determines the split between private and foreign investment. Equations 7 and 9 are simply the first difference equations which determine the stock of assets (domestic and overseas) in each period.

Private consumption is postulated as a function of the non-oil income generated domestically and abroad. Oil receipts contribute indirectly to private consumption through investment at home and overseas, the level of non-oil output and in turn consumption.

The actual level of private consumption in a country such as the UK does not bear a direct relation to the size of the oil revenue.

Among the variables of the model, L_t, G_t and π_t are exogenous, and the remaining variables are endogenous. Given this set of structural relations characterising the economy, the question posed in this exercise is: how can the oil revenue be recycled into a non-replenishable resource by the time the oil resource is exhausted? To provide an answer to this question one needs to set out an explicit economic target. As a starting point in our study, the following objective function is specified: what is the maximum global wealth that can be achieved through the intertemporal allocation of the petroleum revenue by the time the resource is exhausted? By global wealth we imply wealth both outside and within the UK.

$$\text{Max} \sum_{t=1}^{T} I_t + \sum_{t=1}^{T} B_t$$

It is important to note that this objective is interchangeable with maximising national income or aggregate consumption. The functional relationships of the model are such that domestic output is a function of the domestic non-oil capital stock (Equation 2), and income from abroad is a function of a portfolio of assets held overseas (Equation 8). Furthermore, private consumption is a function of the size of the two incomes less taxes, i.e. disposable income. Given the positive relationships among these variables, maximising the sum of global assets would be the same as maximising global income or maximising aggregate consumption. The variables thus become substitutable as arguments of our objective function.

The macroeconomic model defined here is optimised subject to two constraints: a balance-of-payments constraint and a total oil-stock constraint where the latter acts as a terminal constraint and the former as an intertemporal constraint imposed in each time period.

The balance-of-payments constraint postulates a minimum import requirement. In each time period the economy needs to import a certain amount which is necessary for domestic production and consumption. Such imports are categorised as *essential*. Total imports may well exceed essential imports, in which case the additional imports are regarded as *non-essential*. The purpose of introducing this constraint into the model is to illustrate that there is an upper limit to the maximum surplus the country can enjoy at any given time, or alternatively, a lower limit below which imports cannot fall. The constraint is expressed as an inequality constraint whereby the balance of payments on current account is less than, or equal to, total exports less *essential* imports. *Essential* imports are presented as a proportion, ϕ, of total raw materials and intermediate goods used in domestic non-oil production plus a proportion, μ, of private consumption. Thus the constraint is stipulated as:

$$B_t \leqslant X_t - \phi R_t - \mu C_t \tag{17}$$

where $o < \phi < 1 \qquad o < \mu < 1$.

The other constraint states basically that the size of the oil reservoir is finite and cannot be further expanded. The country can use up all the oil over the time-horizon considered, or have some left in the ground by the end of the planning horizon. The constraint is quantified as:

$$Q_T \geqslant 0 \tag{18}$$

The model has two control variables: the depletion rate of North Sea oil and the rate of domestic investment. The latter is defined as net non-oil domestic fixed capital formation. There are three state variables: the stock of non-oil domestic capital, the stock of overseas assets, and the stock of oil reserves in the North Sea.

Finally, the optimal control problem is stated as:

$$\text{Max} \sum_{t=1}^{T} I_t + \sum_{t=1}^{T} B_t$$

subject to

$$B_t \leqslant X_t - \phi R_t - \mu C_t \tag{19}$$

$$Q_T \geqslant 0$$

$$I_t \geqslant 0 \quad q_t \geqslant 0$$

where T is postulated as the terminal time period to coincide with the final exhaustion date of the resource. This date can of course become variable, depending on the number of new discoveries made in the North Sea or the development of technology to the extent that the wells in deeper waters become accessible.

To arrive at numerical solutions for the model, the following values of the parameters were used:

$g = 4.309$	$\theta_o = 0.1$	$\mu = 0.17$	$m_o = 65{,}000.0$
$\beta = 0.0$	$\theta_1 = 0.96$	$\xi = 0.4$	$m_1 = -1.0$
$\alpha = 0.32$	$\eta = 0.78$	$\Omega_o = 2.0$	$a = 0.5$
$\gamma = 0.31$	$\omega = 0.5$	$\Omega_1 = 0.0063$	$\epsilon = 0.15$
$\rho = 0.46$	$\phi = 0.22$	$\Omega_2 = 0.5$	$\sigma = 0.2$

Table 11.1

The time paths for the exogenous variables of the model

Year	Government expenditure (£ million)	Real price of oil (£ per barrel)	Labour force (million)
	G_t	w_t	L_t
1976	23,581	6.05	24.8
1977	23,334	5.71	24.8
1978	23.865	4.69	24.9
1979	24.334	5.63	25.0
1980	24.820	7.50	25.0
1981	25,317	7.90	25.0
1982	25,823	8.40	25.0
1983	26,339	8.90	25.0
1984	26.868	9.50	25.0
1985	27.404	10.00	25.0
1986	27,952	10.60	25.0
1987	28,511	11.20	25.0
1988	29.081	11.90	25.0
1989	29,663	12.60	25.0
1990	30,256	13.40	25.0
1991	30,861	14.20	25.0
1992	31,478	15.10	25.0
1993	32.108	15.90	25.0
1994	32,750	16.90	25.0
1995	33,405	18.00	25.0
1996	34,703	19.00	25.0
1997	34,754	20.20	25.0
1998	35,450	21.40	25.0
1999	36,159	22.70	25.0
2000	36,882	24.10	25.0

Sources:

– Government Expenditure, G_t:

1976–1979: *National Income and Expenditure* (London: HMSO, 1980, p.17).
1980–2000: Increase at two per cent p.a. on 1979 level.

– Real Price of Oil, π_t:

1976–1980: Sterling prices converted from dollar prices published in *Wood-McKenzie: North Sea Monthly Reports,* June 1979 to April 1981.
1981–2000: Increase at six per cent p.a. on 1980 level.

– Labour Force L_t:

1976–1979: *Employment Gazette* (London: Department of Employment, December, 1980) O.S7.
1980–2000: Constant at 1979 level.

The values of these parameters were determined by means of economic reasoning(1). They were not estimated through econometric estimation techniques.

The year 1975 was chosen as our base year. The values of the state variables for these years are:

K_{1975} = £ 474,000 million

E_{1975} = –£ 1,789 million

Q'_{1975} = 10,576 million barrels

The value for the initial oil stock is derived from the total of proven oil reserves only.

Initially these values were used to run the model. Changes in the values of the parameters were then considered. Subsequently we provide simulations against variations in the value of these parameters as well as the time path of the exogenous variables.

The projected paths of our three exogenous variables are given in *Table 11.1.* These variables are government expenditure, the price of oil and the quantity of labour in the economy. Since all the model solutions are in real terms, the values of our exogenous variables G_t and π_t are also expressed in real 1976 prices. The deflator used for this purpose is the UK wholesale price index. Government expenditure is set initially as being equal to actual figures for 1976–79 and then a 2 per cent growth rate has been postulated from 1980 onwards. The path for the price of oil uses international prices (in sterling) for the period 1976–1980. For the subsequent years it is projected on the basis of an average of six per cent per year growth in oil prices. Prices have risen substantially more in some of the years over the period under consideration. Basically they rose in the form of alternative platforms, i.e. sharp rises followed by periods of low growth. An assumption of six per cent is, therefore, subject to variation but we consider it to be fairly conservative. The labour force is also set at realistic total employment figures for 1976–79 and for the subsequent years it is assumed to remain constant.

The optimisation algorithm

For the purpose of our research, we made use of the Zoutendijk method of feasible directions (see Polak, 1972). This method was found to be suitable for fixed time problems with inequality constraints on the state and control variables, as well as constraints on the terminal states.

The algorithm is designed to solve problems of the general class that may be written as:

$$\text{Max } \left\{ f^o(z) \mid g^j(z) \leqslant 0, j = 1 \ldots m \right\}$$

where f^o (·) is the value of the objective function over the whole period, g^j (·) are the constraints; m being their total number. z is a vector of control variables, the number of elements of which will depend on the number of control variables as well as the length of the time interval representing the control horizon(2).

Without going into too much technical detail, we will explain below those features of the algorithm that would throw light upon its working and help understand the mechanism.

The algorithm computes a solution to the problem in two parts. It first finds a feasible solution that satisfies all the constraints and then finds an optimal feasible solution. Thus, for the purpose of applying the algorithm, one has first to introduce a control strategy as a possible solution to the problem. The programme then considers the strategy. As a result of this examination, two situations can arise:

Either (a) the strategy satisfies all the constraints, in which case the initial values are said to be feasible.

Or (b) some of the constraints are violated, making the control strategy infeasible.

The latter is a condition that happens more frequently, since a feasible solution may not be known initially. At this point, the algorithm's first task is, therefore, to find a feasible solution. If there exists a feasible solution to the objective function, then it can be found by solving:

$$\text{Min}\left\{z^o \mid g^j(z) - z^o \leqslant 0, j = 1,\ldots,m\right\}$$

where z^o is the feasible control vector, g^j (·) still remain as the constraints, and z as the vector of the control variables. Once this sub-problem is solved and a feasible starting point is obtained, the algorithm finds a local maximum of f^o (z) within the feasible solution. Reaching an optimal solution is quite cumbersome, and involves going through a large number of small steps.

The optimal feasible solution is reached by calculating a search direction which, near to the initial point, lies within the set and along which the value of f^o (z) is guaranteed to maximise. Therefore, the search direction is carried out by first calculating what is called the 'ϵ-binding' constraints. (These are constraints that are binding or within a distance ϵ of the initial feasible point.) Then the search direction is calculated using a linear programme.

Each time the estimate of the vector z is updated, an iteration occurs. Maximisation, therefore, takes place by a series of iterations and a local maximum is arrived at by a convergent sequence, the limit point of which is also the local maximum(3).

The numerical solutions

A convenient way for the examination of the results seemed to be summarising the solutions. *Tables 11.2a* to *11.2d* were constructed to show the time profiles of all the variables, reached by solving our non-linear control problem.

Table 11.2 a

Model solutions for the trajectories of the state variables

Year	Domestic non-oil capital stock (£ million) K_t^*	Overseas assets (£ million) E_t^*	Reserves of oil (million barrels) Q_t^*
1975	474,200	−1,789	10,576
1976	494,024	− 299	10,532
1977	516,584	999	10,335
1978	542,295	258	10,028
1979	570,042	396	9,516
1980	601,774	−18	8,841
1981	631,184	4,130	8,071
1982	667,807	3,629	7,193
1983	709,031	209	6,315
1984	748,904	182	5,415
1985	790,662	−91	4,537
1986	833,688	−26	3,692
1987	877,837	421	2,889
1988	921,798	3,587	2,045
1989	967,202	5,039	1,391
1990	1,012,605	4,171	1,060
1991	1,058,009	1,977	936
1992	1,103,413	775	840
1993	1,148,816	1,215	725
1994	1,197,073	−133	629
1995	1,245,345	0	525
1996	1,286,752	8,156	433
1997	1,329,247	16,870	332
1998	1,373,463	25,375	226
1999	1,419,291	33,815	114
2000	1,466,743	42,083	0

Value of Objective Function = 1,508,826
Value of Terminal Constraint = 0

Note: Solutions reached after eighty-five iterations of the algorithm when the system has converged.

Table 11.2 b

Model solutions for the trajectories of the control variables

Year	Domestic non-oil investment (£ million) I_t^*	Rate of oil extraction (mill. barrels per year) q_t^*	Rate of oil extraction (mill. barrels per day)	Overseas investment (£ million) B_t^*
1976	19,824	43.7	0.12	1,490
1977	22,560	197.7	0.54	1,298
1978	25,711	306.7	0.84	–741
1979	27,746	512.2	1.40	138
1980	31,733	674.5	1.85	–415
1981	29,410	770.3	2.11	4,148
1982	36,622	877.8	2.40	–501
1983	41,225	877.8	2.40	–3,421
1984	39,872	900.7	2.47	–27
1985	41,759	877.6	2.40	–273
1986	43,026	844.8	2.31	65
1987	44,148	803.1	2.20	447
1988	43,961	844.1	2.31	3,165
1989	45,404	653.7	1.79	1,452
1990	45,404	331,6	0.91	–868
1991	45,404	123.3	0.34	–2,194
1992	45,404	96.6	0.26	–1,202
1993	45,404	115.0	0.32	440
1994	48,256	95.3	0.26	–1,348
1995	48,272	104.5	0.29	133
1996	41,407	92.3	0.25	8,156
1997	42,495	100.7	0.28	8.714
1998	44,217	105.5	0.29	8,505
1999	45,827	112.3	0.31	8.440
2000	47,453	114.1	0.31	8,268

Note: Solutions reached after eighty-five iterations of the algorithm when the system has converged.

Since the optimal point is reached through a process of convergence, it is necessary for us to specify the desired degree of accuracy. Here we have imposed a maximum limit of 85, as it was found that good convergence was reached well within this number. *Figure 11.1* illustrates how the value of the objective function has changed as the iterations proceed. This figure clearly shows that the algorithm has quickly converged towards the solution. Most of the computations are clearly carried out in the first thirty iterations and very little further improvement occurs after this point.

To capture the impact of technological restrictions on the extraction of oil, it was necessary to impose certain constraints in the early years. During these years actual oil output

Table 11.2 c

Model solution for the trajectories of gross domestic product, oil revenue, private consumption and the exchange rate

Year	Gross domestic product (£ million) D_t^*	Oil revenue (£ million) $\pi_t q_t^*$	Private consumption (£ million) C_t^*	Exchange rate (US$/£) S_t^*
1976	95,486	264	63,010	2.102
1977	98,166	1,129	65,034	2.212
1978	100,855	1,439	66,917	2.239
1979	105,037	2,884	69,653	2.338
1980	108,741	5,059	72,116	2.448
1981	112,420	6,085	74,532	2.491
1982	115,911	7,374	77,045	2.541
1983	119,694	7,813	79,530	2.557
1984	123,826	8,557	82,108	2.583
1985	127,996	8,776	84,871	2.590
1986	132,237	8,955	87,658	2.596
1987	136,530	8,995	90,515	2.598
1988	140,859	10,045	93,411	2.631
1989	145,147	8,236	96,404	2.572
1990	149,446	4,444	99,320	2.420
1991	153,705	1,751	102,105	2.264
1992	157,906	1,458	104,789	2.241
1993	162,041	1,829	107,473	2.269
1994	166,109	1,610	110,191	2.253
1995	170,241	1,881	112,848	2.273
1996	174,368	1.753	115,606	2.264
1997	178,155	2,034	118,494	2.284
1998	181,805	2,259	121,295	2.299
1999	185,441	2.549	124,069	2.318
2000	189,114	2,749	126,860	2.330

Note: Solutions reached after eighty-five iterations of the algorithm when the system has converged.

could not be determined by purely economic factors, but rather by technological factors. In other words, there was an upper limit on the maximum amount of oil which was technically feasible to be uplifted. Therefore, we imposed a constraint on the years 1976–79 by restricting optimal oil output not to be greater than nine per cent in the first two years, seven per cent in the third and two per cent in the fourth year of the actual values of output shown in Table 11.3 below.

Before examining the optimal paths as a whole it is useful to compare the early observations with the actual statistics for these variables as shown in *Table 11.3.* This is done to

Table 11.2 d

Model solutions for the trajectories of income tax, expenditure tax, oil taxes, exports of oil and non-oil exports

Year	Income tax (£ million) ℓ_t^{III*}	Expenditure tax (£ million) ℓ_t^{II*}	Oil taxes (£ million) ℓ_t^{I*}	Exports of oil (£ million) $\omega\pi_t q_t^*$	Non-oil exports (£million) V_t^*
1976	14,256	12,602	185	132	32,500
1977	14,714	13,007	790	564	31,535
1978	15,140	13,383	1,007	719	30,577
1979	15,759	13,931	2,019	1,442	30,808
1980	16,316	14,423	3.541	2.529	30,089
1981	16,862	14,906	4,260	3,043	29,315
1982	17,431	15,409	5,162	3,687	29,381
1983	17,993	15,906	5,469	3,906	29.384
1984	18.576	16,422	5,990	4,279	29,786
1985	19,202	16,974	6,143	4,388	30,077
1986	19,832	17,532	6,269	4,478	30,590
1987	20,479	18,103	6,297	4,498	31,130
1988	21,134	18,682	7,032	5,023	31,737
1989	21,811	19,281	5,765	4,118	31,954
1990	22,471	19,864	3,111	2,222	33,349
1991	23,101	20,421	1,225	875	36,150
1992	23,708	20,958	1,021	729	39,420
1993	24,315	21,495	1,280	914	40,621
1994	24,930	22,038	1,127	805	40,907
1995	25,531	22,570	1,317	940	42,033
1996	26,155	23,121	1,227	877	42,489
1997	26,809	23,699	1,424	1,017	43,519
1998	27.442	24,259	1,581	1,129	43,994
1999	28,070	24,814	1,784	1,274	44,576
2000	28,701	25,372	1,924	1,374	45,102

Note: Solutions reached after eighty-five iterations of the algorithm when the system has converged.

ensure that (a) the model itself can be checked so that it is not generating wildly unreasonable figures, and (b) to see how the real world has departed from the optimal path.

The first four optimal oil depletion figures are, of course, constrained because of technological barriers. The initial investment figure is very close to the actual figure, and the fact that all the figures are fairly near to the correct order of magnitude demonstrates that the model is simulating the real world fairly closely. It is true that by 'normal modelling'(4) standards the investment figures are not very close but these standards cannot be applied to optimisation models. In this type of model the control variable is not restricted and it can take any positive value from between zero to infinity. The achievement of such

Figure 11.1

Convergence of the objective function as the algorithm approaches a solution

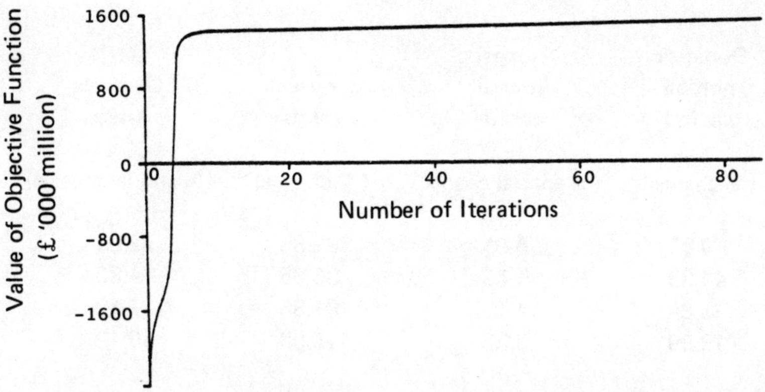

Table 11.3

Comparison of the actual and optimal figures for the control variables: non-oil domestic investment and the quantity of oil extracted

Year	Actual domestic non-oil investment † (£ million)	Optimal domestic non-oil investment (£ million)	Actual rate of oil extraction* (mill. barrels per year)	Optimal rate of oil extraction (mill. barrels per year)
1976	18,806	19,284	87.2	43.7
1977	18,462	22,560	276.8	197.7
1978	19,259	25,711	394.9	306.7
1979	19,604	27,746	587.4	512.2
1980	19,532	31,733	746.6	674.5

† *Source: National Income and Expenditure* (1981) (London: HMSO) p. 17 and 73.
* See Table 11.1

a close approximation to the real world is an indication that the model is, in fact, simulating the economy quite satisfactorily.

Table 11.4 illustrates how the domestic and foreign capital stocks have changed over a seven-year cycle. Ignoring the last four years, which is reasonable as the oil stock will be

Table 11.4

The rates of growth of the domestic and overseas capital stocks over seven-year periods*

Time Period	Domestic non-oil capital stock (% change)	Domestic non-oil capital stock (% annual change)	Overseas assets (% change)	Overseas assets (% annual change)
1975–1982	40.83	5.01	302.85	22.03
1982–1989	44.83	5.43	38.85	4.80
1989–1996	33.04	4.16	61.86	7.12
1996–2000	13.99	3.33	415.98	50.12

* Calculated on the basis of the solutions presented in Tables 11.2 a-d

virtually depleted by 1996, foreign assets will grow at a faster rate in the early years and at a much lower rate in the second and third seven-year cycles. There is a close relationship between the oil revenue, the exchange rate and the level of non-oil exports. Table 11.2c shows that as the size of the oil revenue increases, the optimal value of the US dollar/sterling exchange rate rises from an initial figure of US $ 2.10 in 1976 to a figure of US $ 2.44 in 1980. The actual average September exchange rate figure for 1976 was US $ 1.80(5) rising to US $ 2.40 by September 1980. Therefore, the model does seem to have somewhat captured the effect of oil revenues on the exchange rate. The effect of the rise in the exchange rate on non-oil exports is to cause a slump (as shown in Table 11.2d), which lasts from 1976 until the mid-1980s. When the exchange rate begins to fall in 1989, non-oil exports begin to expand again. This is shown in *Figure 11.6.* The decline in the exchange rate is due to the decline in oil revenue after its peak is reached in 1988. This illustrates that a loss of export markets is likely to accompany a rise in oil revenue even when the economy is acting optimally.

An important determinant of the optimal time paths of investment is the relationship between the rates of return generated by, on the one hand, the domestic output function and, on the other, the foreign asset function. Now in completely unconstrained conditions, one would expect that the optimal solution would exhibit equality between the rates of return (at the margin) in each time period. If, however, any of the state constraints on the balance of payments were binding (as is here the case), such a symmetrical relationship would not be obtained.

Figure 11.2

Optimal paths for non-oil domestic and overseas investment

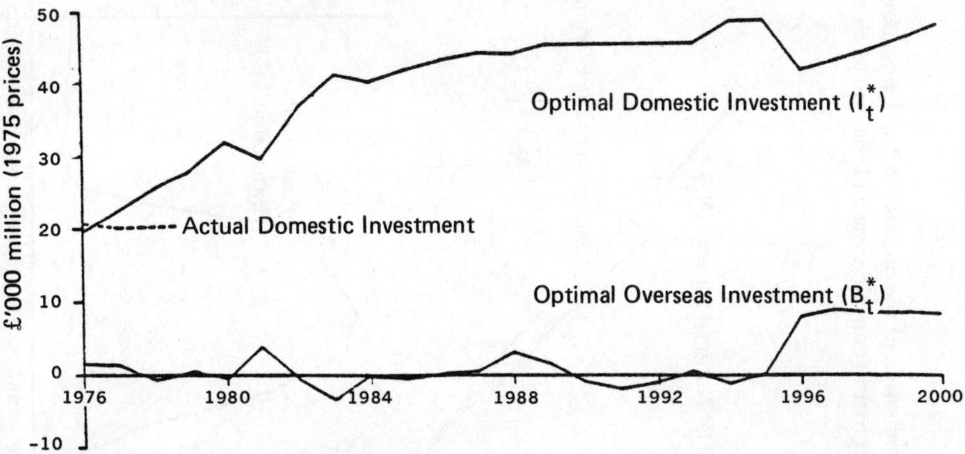

Figure 11.3

Comparison of the optimal paths of domestic non-oil capital stock and overseas assets

(£ '000 million; 1975 prices)

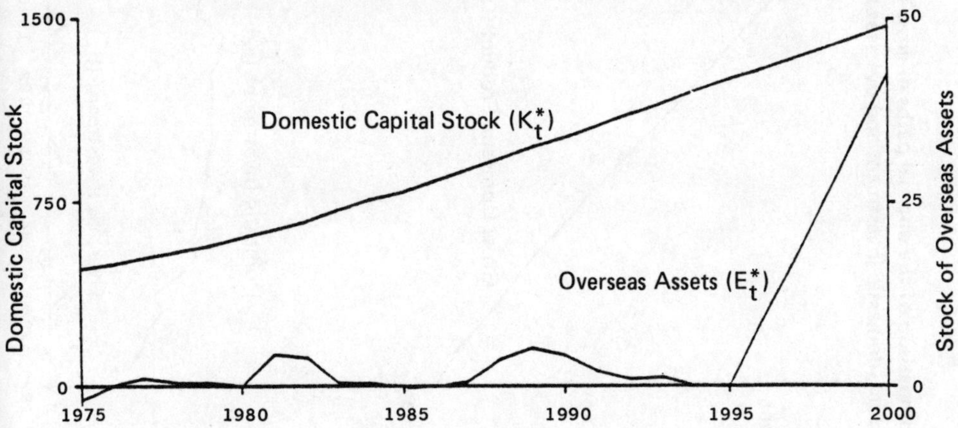

Figure 11.4

Comparison of the optimal paths of gross domestic product, domestic investment and overseas investment

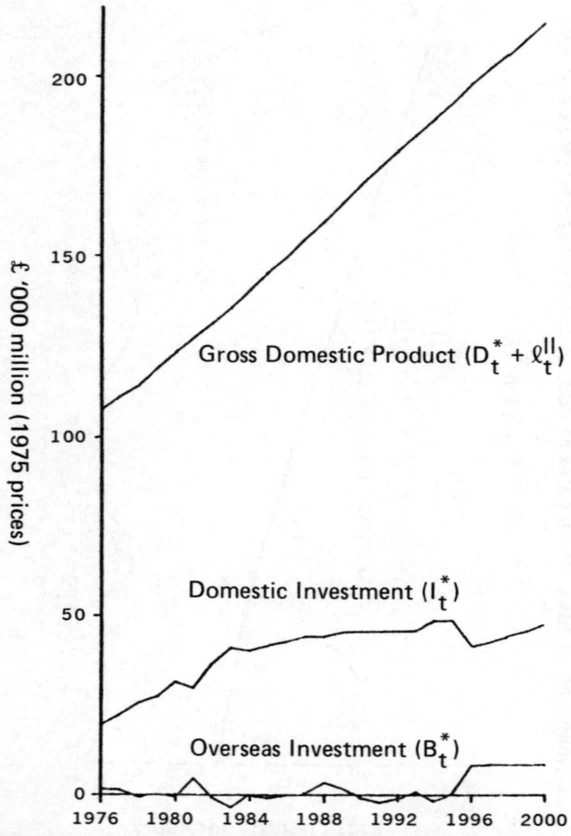

Figure 11.5

Comparison of the optimal paths of gross domestic product, net national income and the rate of oil extraction

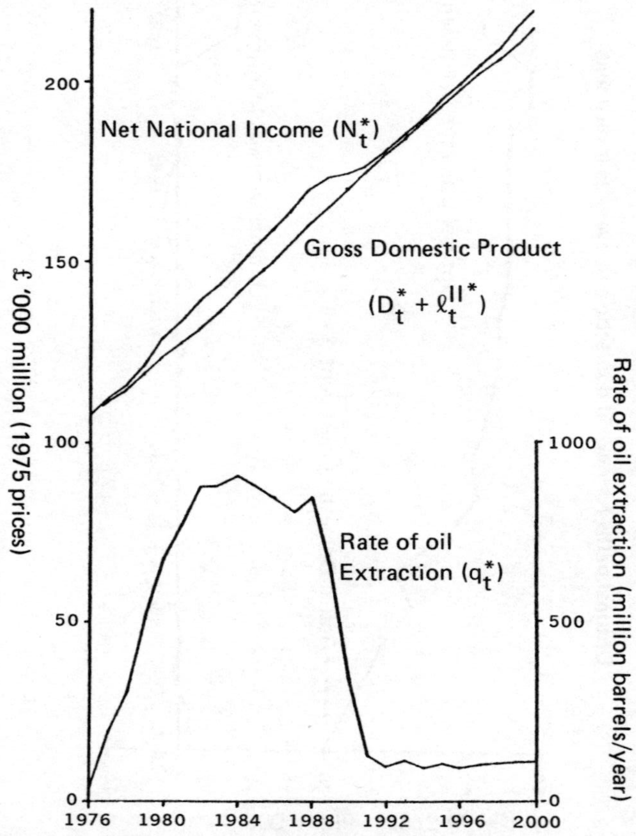

Figure 11.6

Comparison of the optimal paths of the exchange rate and non-oil exports

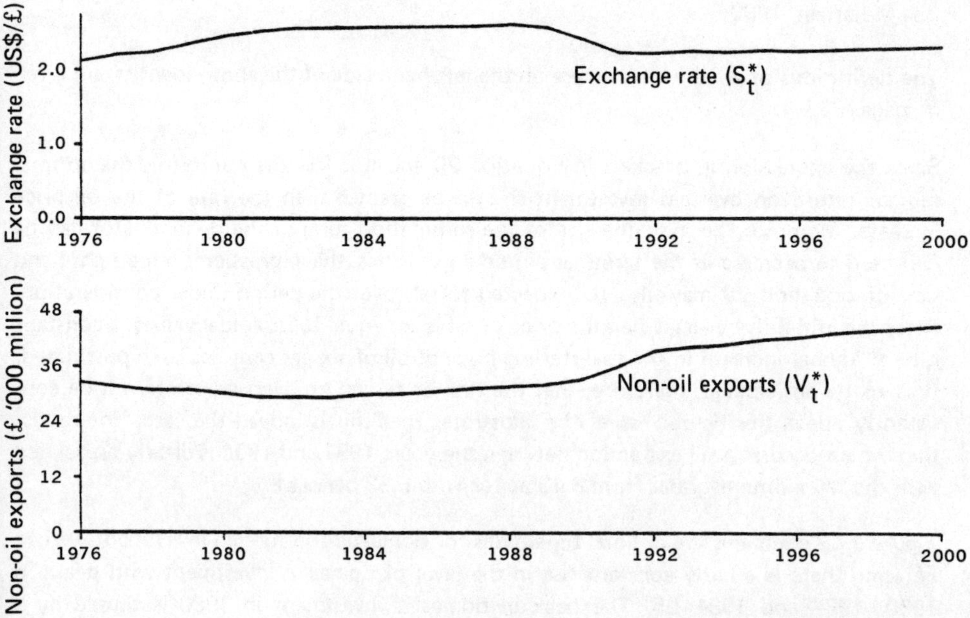

As specified in the model, overseas investment is allowed to take positive or negative values, implying either investment expenditure overseas or borrowing abroad. It can be seen in *Table 11.2a* that the size of overseas assets, E_t, is much smaller than its domestic counterpart, K_t, and for the most part of comparable size to the absolute level of overseas investment, B_t, as shown in *Table 11.2b.*

The basic determinant of the rate of oil depletion is the relationship between the rate of change of the price of oil and the rate of return on overseas assets weighted by a set of parameters defined as υo. In the unconstrained case, the relationship has already been shown to be:

$$\frac{\Delta\pi_{T-j}}{\pi_{T-j}} = \left(\frac{\upsilon_o}{1 + \sum_{k=T-j+2}^{T} F_k'}\right) F_{T-j+1} \qquad (20)$$

where for convenience we have defined:

$$(1 + \sigma\eta - \epsilon\sigma\eta - \eta + \epsilon\eta) \equiv \upsilon_0$$

(see Motamen, 1982).

The definitions of all the parameters on the left-hand side of the above identity are given on pages 233–4.

Since the expression in brackets in Equation 20 above is less than unity(6), the optimal rate of return on overseas investment should be greater than the rate of the oil price increase. Moreover, because the size of the summation term in the denominator can be expected to decrease as the terminal period approaches, the expression on the right-hand side of Equation 20 may also be expected to fall over the period under consideration. After the initial five years, when the price of oil is set equal to its actual values, a constant rate of annual increase in the real sterling price of oil of six per cent has been postulated. It is to be anticipated, therefore, that the rate of return on overseas assets will be consistently above this figure. *Table 11.5* illustrates that this is indeed the case. The reduction which occurs in oil extraction between the years 1987 and 1990 is clearly associated with the fall in interest rates from 8.43 per cent to 6.83 per cent.

Figure 11.2 compares the optimal time paths for domestic and foreign investment. As can be seen, there is a fairly constant rise in the level of domestic investment with peaks in 1980, 1987 and 1994–95. The peak in domestic investment in 1980 is caused by a sudden rise in foreign interest rates in 1981. The peak in 1987 is not in the true sense a peak; it is rather a change in the trend of investment. In fact, it is due to a fall in interest rates which continues between 1987 and 1990. Between 1981 and 1988 investment grows under a steady stream of oil revenues; in 1988 this trend of high oil revenues suddenly changes, and in 1989 there is a sudden drop in the extraction rate. This fall in oil revenues causes a drop in domestic revenue which declines in both 1989 and 1990. Figure 11.2 shows the paths for domestic and foreign investment. It also includes the historical data for these variables during these years. It can quickly be seen that the path produced by the algorithm is very close to the real world path.

What impact has the oil depletion path had on the overall economy? This is an interesting and important question and it can perhaps be most easily answered by examining the direct effect of oil revenues on gross domestic product. The GDP growth rate adjusts gradually to the sudden decline in oil depletion in 1989. In essence the total effect of North Sea oil on GDP will be a permanent increase of some twelve per cent from the year 2000 onwards. This would be the equivalent of increasing the rate of growth of GDP by a constant figure of 0.45 per cent per year over the whole period.

So far we have analysed the numerical results for the model with the basic set of parameters specified above (see p. 237 above). However, it is useful to ask the question: how

Table 11.5

The rates of return on domestic and overseas assets

Year	Rate of return on domestic assets (%) D′	Rate of return on overseas assets (%) F′
1976	6.44	7.11
1977	6.36	7.64
1978	6.25	7.28
1979	6.20	7.69
1980	6.10	7.56
1981	5.98	8.55
1982	5.88	6.88
1983	5.74	6.92
1984	5.59	7.75
1985	5.47	7.80
1986	5.35	8.02
1987	5.24	8.43
1988	5.13	7.54
1989	5.04	6.92
1990	4.94	6.83
1991	4.86	6.88
1992	4.78	7.09
1993	4.70	7.36
1994	4.63	7.23
1995	4.55	7.89
1996	4.48	9.60
1997	4.43	6.70
1998	4.38	6.50
1999	4.32	6.40
2000	4.26	6.33

Note: Solutions reached after eighty-five iterations of the algorithm when the system has converged.

might the optimal solutions change if some of the basic parameters were varied? This question is particularly useful when considering such variables as government expenditure, the income tax rate, the expenditure tax rate or the levels of private consumption. All these variables are to some extent under government control, and changes in them

Table 11.6

Model solution when there are no technological constraints imposed on oil production

Year	Domestic non-oil capital stock (£ million)	Overseas assets (£ million)	Reserves of oil (mill. barrels per year)	Domestic non-oil investment (£ million)	Rate of oil extraction (mill barrels per year)
	K_t^*	E_t^*	Q_t^*	I_t^*	q_t^*
1975	474,200	−1,789	10,576		
1976	497,740	−61	9,879	23,540	697.3
1977	522,177	2,243	9,200	24,437	678.3
1978	548,511	379	9,055	26,334	145.1
1979	577,521	−906	8,623	29,011	432.8
1980	607,277	3,160	7,645	29,756	977.8
1981	642,253	4,233	6,614	34,976	1,031.1
1982	678,505	6,667	5,485	36,252	1,128.5
1983	719,652	6,430	4,324	41,147	1,159.2
1984	759,916	4,886	3,620	40,264	706.2
1985	799,413	4,277	3,070	39,497	549.3
1986	842,337	−191	2,722	42,925	348.7
1987	882,146	−13	2,367	39,809	354.4
1988	922,026	137	2,144	39,880	223.1
1989	962,542	173	1,994	40,516	150.5
1990	1,003,058	1,248	1.867	40,516	126.6
1991	1,045,497	2,458	1,689	42,439	177.6
1992	1,089.714	2,480	1,565	44,217	124.0
1993	1,137,084	1,168	1,410	47,371	155.7
1994	1,185,321	−30	1,278	48,237	131.9
1995	1,231,779	4,076	1,027	46,458	250.5
1996	1,276,453	11,414	787	44,673	240.8
1997	1,322,441	18.491	577	45,988	210.1
1998	1,369,073	25,384	419	46,632	157.4
1999	1,416,367	33,269	255	47,295	163.7
2000	1,470,665	37,905	0	54,298	255.5

Value of objective function = 1,508,570
Value of terminal constraint = 0

Note: Solutions reached after eighty-five iterations of the algorithm when the system has converged.

could affect depletion policies and investment of the revenue. These questions can be answered fairly easily by conducting simulations against the model and comparing them with the solutions outlined in the last section. In each simulation we vary only one parameter or relationship at a time. This will allow us to investigate the effect of these changes as well as studying how robust the solutions are to variations in the model structure.

First we can study the impact on the overall solutions if we removed the technological constraints on the oil extraction which were imposed previously (see pp. 242–3 above). While this is undoubtedly a correct approach for arriving at the optimal solutions, it is interesting to discover how oil depletion would be affected if the depletion rate was constrained only by the terminal constraint. The results for this simulation are outlined in *Table 11.6.* The solutions generate an optimal oil depletion path which completely disregards the technologically possible levels of oil depletion, but which generates a rate of depletion that is based solely on economic factors and the price mechanism. As expected, the optimal depletion figures in the first two years are much higher than in the constrained case, while in the third year they are much lower. The reason for this sudden fall in depletion lies in the path of oil prices as shown in *Table 11.7.*

The results of this simulation provide a good test of the behaviour of the model, for it shows that the oil depletion path is determined in relation to the price of petroleum. This sensitivity is clearly manifested in the values of p_t^* compared to π_t as shown in Table

Table 11.7

Comparison of the rate of oil extraction and the price of oil (in real terms) with no technological constraints on depletion during 1976–1980

Year	Actual oil extracted † (mill. barrels per year) q_t	Optimal rate of oil extraction (mill. barrels per year) q_t^*	Oil* prices in real terms π_t
1976	87.2	697.3	6.5
1977	276.8	678.3	5.71
1978	394.9	145.1	4.69
1979	587.4	432.8	5.63
1980	746.6	977.8	7.50

† See Table 11.3 above.
* Prices are in real 1975 prices.

11.7. The real price of oil falls in 1977 and 1978 and rises thereafter. Accordingly, the values of q_t fall in the first two years and rise in 1979 and 1980. These results indicate that if the British economy had the choice to determine the amount of crude oil pumped out by the oil companies, it would have been optimal to extract substantially more than what was actually extracted in 1976 and 1977, and extract less in 1978 and 1979. These optimal values could not be attained by the British economy in earlier years due to the fact that oil platforms under construction were not all complete to allow any further extraction at that time, which is basically a question of technological constraints. Also, depletion could not have been reduced in 1978 and 1979 when the price fell because the oil companies had the policy of recovering their investments as fast as possible and were lifting the maximum amount of oil they could, irrespective of movements in petroleum prices. Nevertheless, this was a useful exercise to conduct in order to show the sensitivity of the model solutions to changes in the price of petroleum.

The next simulation we have conducted is against a change in the path of government expenditure which is an exogenous variable in the model. The growth of G_t is increased to three per cent from the original two per cent which was used in the solutions outlined in Tables 11.2a to 11.2d. Here again actual government expenditure figures are used for the years 1976–80 and a three per cent growth per year is projected thereafter (*Table 11.8*). Compared with the solutions shown in Table 11.2b, oil extraction is delayed and the overall path of depletion is flattened. This is true especially of the years 1978 to 1988; during the remaining years the path of depletion lies above these figures. Oil production peaks at a lower level amount to 817.7 million barrels per year in 1988, compared with the previous level of 900.7 million barrels in 1984. The economic solution to this result is as follows: if the government anticipates a higher growth in its expenditure, it is optimal to leave the oil in the ground in the earlier years and extract it later. This is because the higher expenditure will require an increased oil revenue to finance it, and more oil should be extracted in later years.

The solutions indicate, *ceteris paribus,* that with a lower government expenditure, i.e. two per cent per annum, it would be optimal to extract more in the late 1970s and the early 1980s, reaching a peak in 1984. Under these conditions the peak is determined more in relation to the price of petroleum and the rates of return on investment. The need to finance a higher government expenditure means that the effect of the price and the yield on investment becomes less important. As far as domestic investment is concerned, its optimal values are consistently lower than the solutions with lower government expenditure, which is to be expected. This will in turn involve a reduction in the value of capital terminal stocks implying a lower value of the objective function.

In the next simulation we raise the average propensity to consume by a small amount, say four per cent and find that the oil depletion path is quite sensitive to this parameter. The higher APC calls for a slowing down in depletion in the earlier years. During the years

Table 11.8

Model solution when 3% growth rate in real government expenditure is assumed

Year	Domestic non-oil capital stock (£ million) K_t*	Overseas assets (£ million) E_t*	Reserves of oil (mill. barrels per year) Q_t*	Domestic non-oil investment (£ million) I_t*	Rate of oil extraction (mill. barrels per year) q_t*
1975	474,200	–1,789	10,576		
1976	493,858	16	10,508	19,658	68.4
1977	517,767	1	10,309	23,909	198.5
1978	542,311	215	10,047	24544	262.3
1979	566,747	3,507	9,565	24,436	481.8
1980	600,337	435	8,967	33,590	598.0
1981	632,877	1	8,309	32,540	657.7
1982	666,885	0	7,576	34,008	732.9
1983	701,007	1,199	6,844	34,122	732.9
1984	737,751	907	6,139	36,744	704.5
1985	775,113	1,254	5,437	37,362	701.7
1986	815,515	0	4,728	40,402	708.8
1987	855,958	44	4,021	40,443	707.4
1988	898,580	678	3.203	42.622	817.7
1989	941,202	1,862	2.466	42,622	737.4
1990	982,994	1,613	2,015	41,792	451.3
1991	1,023,091	1,585	1,753	40,097	261.2
1992	1,064,880	205	1,536	41,789	217.5
1993	1,106,662	44	1,296	41,782	240.1
1994	1,149,420	3	1,044	42,757	251.4
1995	1,192,242	297	821	42,823	223.0
1996	1,234,027	2,170	613	41,785	208.2
1997	1,270,848	9,164	438	36,821	175.2
1998	1,306,529	17,364	296	35,680	142.1
1999	1,342,173	26,375	148	35,644	147.9
2000	1,378,441	35,354	0	36,268	147.9

Value of objective function = 1,413,795
Value of terminal constraint = 0

Note: Solutions reached after eighty-five iterations of the algorithm when the system has converged.

1977 to 1991, the values of the optimal quantities of oil extracted lie below those with a lower propensity to consume and above them in subsequent years. This implies that the higher level of aggregate consumption has to be financed by increased oil revenue.

As our next simulation, we lower the rate of income growth or expenditure taxes. A reduction in income tax from fifteen to thirteen per cent causes investment to be reduced and the oil depletion path to be flattened, i.e. more oil depletion is left for later years to finance a higher consumption level. The value of the criterion function is also reduced. We find the same overall solution when expenditure tax is also reduced from twenty to eighteen per cent.

Changes in the marginal productivity of capital has been examined by considering a reduction in the value of α, the exponent of capital, from thirty-two to thirty per cent. To maintain consistency, g has been increased from 4.309 to 5.598. The reduction in α reduces the rate of return, and we find domestic investment to be reduced.

When the rate of technical progress β is increased, the solutions show a higher overall domestic investment, compared to the original set of solutions. The overall result is that the terminal capital stock increases.

Finally, we tried to measure the overall impact of North Sea oil by conducting the optimisation with no oil revenue. This was done by assigning zero values to the petroleum prices projected over the planning horizon. With no oil the results show that domestic investment in the UK would be lower; the terminal value of the criterion function would also decrease by twelve per cent. Compared to the situation where there is oil revenue, the value of capital increases by about one half per cent per year, and the national income increases by about ten per cent over the life of the resource.

Footnotes

(1) Details of the specification of the parameters are given in Motamen, (1982) ch. V.

(2) Details of the algorithm can be found in Motamen (1979).

(3) A graphical exposition is provided by Motamen (1979), which can be consulted by the interested reader.

(4) By 'normal modelling' we mean simulation models.

(5) *Financial Statistics,* no. 215, (London: HMSO) March 1980, p. 130.

(6) It can be shown that $o < v_o < 1$, and therefore any positive number (which is the case in Equation 20 above) would be less than unity.

References

Forsyth, P.J. and Kay, J.A. (1980) 'The Economic Implications of North Sea Oil Revenue', *Fiscal Studies,* vol. 1, no. 3, July.

Motamen, H. (1979) *Expenditure of Oil Revenue, an Optimal Control Approach* (New York: St. Martin's Press; London: Frances Pinter Publisher).

Motamen, H. (1982) *Macroeconomics of North Sea Oil in the UK* (in collaboration with Strange, R.) (London: Heineman Educational).

Motamen, H. and Strange, R. (1981) 'UK Oil Revenue: the Medium-Term Outlook, *Energy Policy,* vol. 9, no. 1, March.

National Income and Expenditure (1980) (London: HMSO).

Polak, E. (1971) *Computational Methods in Optimization: A Unified Approach* (New York: Academic Press).

Polak, E. (1972) 'A Survey of Method of Feasible Directions for Solutions of Optimal Control Problems', *IEEE Transactions on Automatic Control,* vol. AC-17, no. 5, October.

PART IV

STABILISATION POLICIES

Chapter 12

POST-MORTEM ON BRITISH ECONOMIC POLICY 1960–1976*

F. Blackaby

Introduction

In 1960, real national product per head in the United Kingdom (estimated at purchasing power parities) was rather higher – perhaps about five per cent higher – than in either France or West Germany (Paige, 1961). By 1976, it was some twenty-five per cent lower (Kravis, Heston and Summers, 1978)(1). No other industrial country, in the last twenty years or so, has changed so many places in the rank order of standards of living. This is the main measure of the British economy's lack of success. Nor is the record better, measured by other indicators of economic performance – the movement of retail prices or the level of unemployment. The UK's price record is significantly worse than the industrial world's average, over this twenty-year period, and its unemployment record is no better than average.

Since the purpose of economic policy is to improve economic performance, the immediate and obvious judgement is that the various economic policies adopted in the United Kingdom have failed; in so far as their object was to bring about an improvement which did not occur, this judgement is certainly correct. However, there is no easy way of drawing conclusions from this failure. First of all, there was no great consistency of policy: it could legitimately be argued that certain policies would have succeeded had they been pursued systematically. Secondly, because a certain line of policy appears to have failed, it does not follow that an exactly opposite line of policy would necessarily have succeed-

* Mr. Blackaby's assessment of British economic policy was written in 1977. The author sees no need to alter the main gist of his conclusions. – ED.

ed. Thirdly, it is always possible that some of the policies made the best of a bad job: that the British economy's lack of success was mainly due to factors which were relatively unamenable to policy. This article asks five questions arising from the conduct of British economic policy since 1960. First, was the general practice of 'demand management' throughout this period a mistake? Secondly, was the doctrine of 'export propelled growth', which inspired certain lines of economic policy in the early 1960s, a total mistake? Thirdly, should the Government abandon the idea of using the exchange-rate as an instrument of policy? Fourthly, were Governments wrong in their sporadic pursuit of incomes policies? Fifthly, what are the lessons to be drawn about industrial policy?

Demand management

One of the main lines of criticism has been that the whole policy of demand management in the United Kingdom has been misconceived. The criticism can be summed up in the following syllogism:

a) British economic policy has been a failure.
b) That policy has consisted of Keynesian demand management.
c) Therefore Keynesian demand management has been a failure.

It is true that in the early post-war period economic policy was considered to be more or less synonymous with demand management — that is with 'the practical application of . . . the broad rule — to stimulate demand when it is deficient and to restrain it when excessive . . .' (Hall, 1964). However, certainly since the early 1960s the practitioners and advocates of demand management have recognised its limitations. They were well aware that it was not possible, simply by moving the level of demand up or down, to produce an economic situation which combined full employment and stable prices; and they were also well aware that it might not be possible to find a level of demand which combined full employment and an adequate balance of payments. To this extent, there is common ground between the advocates and the critics. Those critics who suggest that demand management has failed to deal with the problem of inflation, and that it has also failed to deal with the problem of the inadequate competitiveness of British manufacturing industry, are attacking a straw man. The defenders of demand management do not allege that it can deal with these problems. Their claim is rather that demand management makes it possible to 'make the best of a bad job'. They argue that in the absence of any demand management policies, the outcomes would have been worse than they actually were. However, they fully accept that other policies are needed in addition to demand management both to deal with inflation and to remedy the lack of international competitiveness.

The issue here is whether or not, with fiscal policy 'neutral' in some sense, the British economy has self-righting properties. The basically Keynesian models of the British economy which have been constructed in the Treasury and at the National Institute, do not have any tendency automatically to right themselves. For example, after some deflationary shock from the outside world, such as the oil-price rise, the economy could continue in depression with rising unemployment for a long time, in the absence of corrective fiscal action. If these models correctly represent the behaviour of the British economy, there is no inbuilt tendency for the economy to move automatically towards some 'natural' rate of unemployment.

The critics argue that these models do not properly represent the working of the British economy: in particular, that they do not give sufficient weight to the effects of changes in the rate of interest. Thus they claim that any change in the Government's fiscal stance tends to be ineffective because any stimulus from the public sector simply crowds out the private sector. The sequence is described as follows. Any public sector stimulus implies an increase in the borrowing requirement; the increased borrowing will force the Government to raise the rate of interest. This will reduce not only investment spending but consumer spending as well through a wealth effect: and the reduction in private spending will neatly offset the public sector's increase. The effects of changes in fiscal policy are thus negatived by its monetary consequences.

It is certainly possible to conceive of the sequence of economic events which is described in this counter-hypothesis. But it is not enough to describe a possible sequence of effects. The important question is the size of the effects – and whether or not they are more powerful than other sets of possible effects working in the contrary direction – such as the effect on investment of the higher expectations of demand, or the direct effect on consumer spending of tax reductions. What are the supposed numerical relationships between an increase in the public sector borrowing requirement and the rate of interest, and what in turn are the numerical relationships between changes in the rate of interest and consumer or investment expenditure?

If private investment is crowded out as a consequence of public reflationary action, then this should, of course, be observable. So we can look at two of the major reflations of recent years – 1963 and 1972 – and observe whether, as a consequence, private sector investment rose or fell. Between 1963 and 1965, investment in manufacturing industry, at constant prices, rose twenty-five per cent; between 1972 and 1974, it rose seventeen per cent. The post-war experience appears to be much more consonant with the view that reflation leads to upswings in demand and output, and private investment responds as output moves up more closely to capacity.

There was, further, a period – from 1970 to 1972 – when the Government of the day deliberately did not concern itself particularly with demand management; it was much more concerned with structural fiscal reform than with calculations of the reflationary or deflationary change required. The main consequence was that unemployment proceeded to climb throughout the period up to the beginning of 1972. By then, the Government decided that it had waited long enough for self-righting properties to appear, and it reverted to a policy of vigorous demand management.

It is certainly right to draw the lesson from the experience of the last twenty years that demand management — adjusting the level of demand up or down by fiscal policy — does not deal with the underlying problems of the British economy. However, this conclusion had effectively been drawn a long time ago. Because demand management cannot do everything, it does not follow that it can do nothing: it can make a potential bad outcome rather less bad.

Export-propelled growth

In the early 1960s, when policy-makers began to realise that the UK's growth rate compared poorly with the growth rates of its Continental neighbours, the suggestion was put forward that the essential ingredient of rapid economic growth was 'export-propulsion'. In particular, it was argued that the rapid rate of economic growth in Western Germany was based on her export success. The argument went as follows. Businessmen invest in an ambitious way only when they see the prospect of a long-continued rise in demand for their products. It is an increase in export demand, much more than an increase in home consumer demand, which will bring this confidence about; they will expect a rise in home demand alone to be shortlived, because it would lead to balance of payments difficulties; a rise in export demand on the other hand, could continue indefinitely. So an initial upsurge in exports could lead to confident expectations for the future, and so lead on to large-scale investment. This new investment in turn would improve productivity; the improved productivity would help to keep export prices competitive; and so the initial export success would be continued. Thus there was a virtuous circle of rapid economic growth, triggered off by initial export success.

Many of those who put forward this view of 'export-propelled growth' envisaged that the initial stimulus of export propulsion could come about by a devaluation of the pound. Some added, as an additional policy prescription for influencing businessmen's expectations, 'indicative planning'. This was an idea borrowed from the experience of the French. If the Government prepared a National Plan, based on an accelerated rate of growth, which embodied target figures for individual industries, businessmen — so long as they believed that the National Plan was credible — would adjust their own investment plans to the faster rate of growth, and by doing so they would help to bring that faster rate of growth about. These were the ideas which lay behind the four per cent growth targets set for the UK economy by the National Economic Development Council in 1962, and which was endorsed in the National Plan two years later.

In spite of the adoption of indicative planning, and in spite of the — admittedly belated — devaluation of the pound in 1967, there was no acceleration in the United Kingdom growth rate. Was the whole idea of export-propelled growth a mirage? Its proponents probably underestimated the difficulties of preserving price competitiveness, once it had been obtained by a devaluation. The advantage gained by the 1967 devaluation was eroded within two or three years, as the rate of UK inflation exceeded that of her competitors. For a devaluation to be effective, it had to be accompanied by policies which prevented the rise in import prices from accelerating the rate of internal inflation; that is, it had to be accompanied by policies which effectively restrained the increase in money earnings. This was something which proved very difficult to achieve. Further, the advocates of devaluation perhaps underestimated the importance of non-price factors in international competitiveness. Simply to give firms a price advantage in international trade might indeed discourage them from intensive efforts to improve their performance in other respects – such as design, delivery dates, after-sales service, and so on. A devalued currency was of much greater assistance to exporters of relatively simple, homogeneous products than to exporters of products which incorporated high technology. So the United Kingdom failed to keep a price-competitive advantage for any length of time; however, even if it had done so, it is not at all certain that British industry would have enjoyed the export success which West Germany and Japan experienced in the 1950s and 1960s.

It would be surprising, however, if these various ideas which were put forward in the early 1960s proved to be totally invalidated.

For instance, it would probably not be disputed that it is businessmen's expectations of the course of future demand which largely determine their investment plans – although there is now a good deal more doubt about whether the construction of a National Plan is an effective way of influencing those expectations. Secondly, the idea of 'virtuous and vicious circles' is still widely used in discussions of reasons for different rates of economic growth – though the label in current use is more often that of 'cumulative causation'. Within countries, it is observed that once the economy of a particular region begins to decline, a number of forces are set in motion which will tend to perpetuate that decline. As the Western industrial world during the last twenty years has increasingly become a free trade area for manufactured goods, then the same kind of forces which tend to perpetuate a relative decline, once begun, for a region within a country can reasonably be expected to be observed in the relative decline of individual countries in the industrial world. The importance of expectations, and the possibility of cumulative causation, are the ideas which have survived from the studies of relative economic growth of the early 1960s.

The exchange rate

During the last twenty years there have been major swings of fashion in the views held about the desirability of using the exchange rate as an instrument of policy. In the late

1950s and early 1960s those in the United Kingdom who advocated its use were widely regarded as irresponsible. Different groups rejected the idea of using the exchange rate for different reasons. Within the Labour Party, there was a certain suspicion of monetary manipulations – devaluation 'watered the weeds as well as the flowers' (Wilson, 1964). There was, at the other end of the political spectrum, the City argument that devaluation was dishonest: holders of sterling balances were robbed. There was also a City fear that devaluation would weaken London's position as a financial centre, and would destroy the City's invisible earnings.

After the 1967 devaluation, the time lags before the effects began to show in the trade flows were longer than expected; and as a consequence at the end of 1968 and the beginning of 1969, there was a fairly widespread belief that devaluation had failed to work. As 1969 went on, this changed; indeed by 1970 there was probably something approaching a consensus that devaluation had been successful; that it was a desirable addition to the instruments of economic policy; and that the mistake had been to delay it for too long. The high point of approval for devaluation, as an instrument of policy, was in the early 1970s.

The next swing in fashion was to take these conclusions further, and to assert that if only the exchange rate were allowed to float freely, the balance of payments would disappear as an economic problem. In floating rates, the Government had an automatic balance-of-payments regulating mechanism. So in 1972 the Government allowed the exchange rate to float freely, believing that in this way (together with an incomes policy) it would be possible to prevent expansionary policies from leading to a balance-of-payments deterioration.

The third swing in fashion has followed world experience since mid-1972. There have been very substantial changes in exchange rates since then; however, these do not appear to have been an effective equilibrating mechanism in the international payments system. Countries whose exchange rates have appreciated very substantially – Japan and West Germany – were still, in 1978, running large balance of payments current surpluses; countries whose currencies had depreciated considerably – such as the United Kingdom and Italy – had still not established strong balance-of-payments positions. The question at issue was not so much whether the elasticities of response of import or export volume to price changes were adequate: most studies still suggested that an 'effective' devaluation would eventually improve the balance of payments of the devaluing country. The argument was rather that the competitive advantage obtained by a downward movement of the exchange rate was rapidly eroded, so that any benefits lasted only for a very short time.

There were two separate lines of thought leading to the conclusion that the exchange rate was an ineffective instrument of policy. One line of thought used the 'law of one price'.

There could not for any length of time be any great divergence in the prices of goods traded on the world market: manufacturers in a devaluing country would soon move up their prices to the world price. This might give them a temporary increase in profits on export sales; however, wages would soon rise to reduce those profits to normality. So there was no way that a country could move its prices for tradeable goods significantly away from world prices for any length of time.

The other line of thought comes to the same conclusion – that the competitive advantage gained by a devaluation would be rapidly eroded – by a different route. The centre piece of this particular transmission mechanism is a wage equation which has in it a strong price term. Devaluation raises import prices; this moves up the general level of prices in the devaluing country, and this in turn will push up the figure for money earnings, with second-round effects on prices. So devaluation sets off a process in the devaluing country of a price-wage-price spiral which erodes the competitive advantage.

The first of these methods of erosion depends on wages responding to a rise in profits on export sales; the second depends on wages responding to the rise in import prices. The question at issue here is whether the Government can effectively prevent wages and earnings reacting in this way. If the movement of wages and earnings is precisely determined, so that no Government can affect it for any significant length of time, the arguments that erosion is inevitable are much stronger. If, on the other hand, it appears that the rise in wages or earnings is not so precisely determined, so that a Government may for example persuade a Trade Union movement not to demand full compensation for past price rises, then the case for the possible use of the exchange rate is much stronger.

Incomes policy

The argument about exchange rates is therefore closely linked with the argument about incomes policies. Here again, conflicting conclusions can be drawn from the experience since 1962. There is no doubt that successive incomes policies failed to meet the objectives which had been set – the rise in money earnings was nearly always significantly higher than the 'norm'. To that extent, they failed. On the other hand, it is an open argument whether or not the rise in money earnings would have been greater in their absence. Further, it can be argued that the country has been moving very gradually towards some necessary institutional changes in the system of wage bargaining; because the early attempts at such institutional change were not successful, it does not follow that a change is not needed, nor does it follow that all further attempts must also be unsuccessful. The question then is whether these early moves were along a road with a dead end. If incomes policy proves to be an idea with no future, then the early experiments were a waste of time; if, on the other hand, they were steps towards an eventual and necessary acceptance of some form of intervention in free collective bargaining, then the judgement has to be different.

For the term 'incomes policy' covers a very wide range of different forms of intervention; there is very little in common between the form of intervention which the then Prime Minister Mr. Macmillan attempted in 1962 – the National Incomes Commission – and the Labour Government's attempt to agree a social contract in the period from mid-1975 to mid-1978. Whether there was an evolution – in the sense that the attempts at institutional change at the end of the period had a greater chance of success than those attempted at the beginning of the period – is obviously a matter of debate; what is not a matter of debate is that the forms of intervention attempted were radically different.

The assessment of this period is, of course, bedevilled by the constant chopping and changing of policy. Each successive Government in turn abolished the institutions of its predecessor, and then in a number of instances was forced to recreate them, though in a different form and with a different name. There is the further complication that parties which supported incomes policies when in power, opposed them when out of power. The history of the period, therefore, is a history of spasmodic, interrupted interventions. The general impression given by an examination of the figures for the rise in money earnings over the period from 1962 to 1975 is of a rising trend, which is checked from time to time by periods of incomes policy – though only reversed for very short periods of freeze – but which then resumes the upward movement when the periods of incomes policy end.

The main conclusion is that it is perhaps rather jejune to ask: 'Do incomes policies work?' – as if incomes policy were a single instrument, like VAT or investment allowances. The variation in the types of incomes policy attempted is too great for there to be a general conclusion of this kind. It may be more sensible to ask: 'Are we moving towards some desirable kind of institutional change?' It is possible that the move towards some form of 'social contract' is such a change. First of all, the successive 'social contracts' since mid-1975 have at least succeeded in bringing down the rise in money earnings from the catastrophic figure of thirty per cent, which it reached between mid-1974 and mid-1975. Secondly, the trend towards some kind of social contract in now a general trend among European countries; in most of them there is some kind of discussion between the Government, the Trade Union movement, and (usually) the employers' organisations – either annually or more frequently – about the desirable size of the next wage-round. The methods of consultation are sometimes formal, sometimes – as in the United Kingdom – informal; but once the practice has been established of some annual consultation of this kind, it is unlikely to be dropped. It is one way of confronting the Trade Union movement with the aggregate consequences of its actions: in its absence, there is a tendency for each negotiating group to ignore the economic consequences which would follow if every other negotiating group were to act in the same way as itself. The idea of some kind of annual discussion of the 'norm' for each annual wage-round may well be here to stay.

This is perhaps small progress to have made in over fifteen years of institutional experimentation. We have discovered the need to try to reach some kind of social consensus about the 'norm' for what have now clearly become annual wage-rounds. But we have got nowhere in devising any satisfactory institutional procedure for arriving at some judgement about exceptions to the norm. Further, in the United Kingdom there are a great number of difficulties which arise from the multiplicity of bargaining units, and from the fact that bargaining is spread right round the year (with a short break for the summer holidays). The progress which has been made is still very fragile. The United Kingdom is still saddled with a wage bargaining system which tends to deliver figures for the average rise in money earnings which are much too high.

Industrial policies

Over the past fifteen years there has been an increasing number of international comparisons of British industries and British firms with comparable industries and firms in competing countries. These studies tend to suggest a certain 'generalised inefficiency' in British manufacturing industry. This particular approach has a long history: comparisons between British industries and their competitors, to the detriment of the British, date back to the turn of the century and beyond, with comments on Britain's excessive reliance on coal and textiles, on her failure to achieve economies of scale in the iron and steel industry and on her relative weakness in electrical, chemical and metallurgical industries. There is a very large number of facets of firms' performance which have been considered in these comparisons: comparisons have been made of innovative ability and of design; of research and development expenditure; of capital stock by worker and of the age of installed equipment; of the organisation and manning of the productive processes; of the proportions of management to other staff; of delivery dates; of the effort put into the study of markets, and into salesmanship and after-sales service. The general picture that emerges from such comparisons is of an average British firm which is a less effective competitor in world markets than its counterpart in other industrial countries. There is statistical confirmation for this picture in the UK's falling share in world trade in manufactures, in the fast-rising share of imports in home consumption of manufactures, and consequently in the UK's falling share in the total output of manufactured goods in the industrial world.

There has been no consensus about what policies — if any — might be appropriate: there have been sharp ideological divisions both between the main parties and within those parties as well. At one extreme, there have been those who argued that the main requirement was to reduce the degree of Government intervention and to provide greater post-tax rewards to managers and entrepreneurs. If this were done, the free enterprise system itself would solve the problem. At the other extreme were those who argued that the Government had insufficient power over private firms' decisions — particularly over their investment and export decisions — and that consequently the Government should equip itself with more sticks and carrots which could be used to influence the behaviour of individual firms. The policies actually adopted lay in a somewhat uncertain area between these two extremes.

This uncertainty was also apparent in Governments' competition policy. The non-interventionist view was that the promotion of efficiency should be left to the forces of competition. The interventionist view was that this might simply lead to the disappearance of large sectors of British industry. It was common ground that restrictive practices should in general be outlawed – but it is doubtful whether this made much difference to British industry's competitive performance in world markets. The uncertainty was most marked in policy towards mergers. In the 1960s they were encouraged in various ways – though policy was probably pushing against an open door in this matter, since there was a very strong 'natural' merger movement in British industry. The dominant view then was that in many industries British firms were not large enough to compete effectively in world markets. In the 1970s there was a reaction against this view. It appeared that many mergers had been financial exercises: only, with no change in the size of actual plants – and an alternative view began to be advanced, that medium-sized firms might well be more efficient, and also might well have better industrial relations, than large firms.

The main general measure which every Government adopted, to a greater or lesser extent, was the encouragement of investment – though there was some difference of opinion about whether tax allowances or grants were more appropriate. Otherwise, Governments found themselves, in their industrial policies, largely pre-occupied with the problems of failing firms or failing industries. It was unsuccessful firms and industries which were forced to appeal to the Government for assistance. Governments, after looking at the consequences for unemployment of doing nothing, usually came to the rescue. Thus industrial policy in practice consisted quite largely of rescue operations.

There were attempts at more positive policies. The Labour Government in 1966 set up the Industrial Reorganisation Corporation; in line with the thinking of the time, its remit was mainly to promote mergers and rationalisation schemes. The IRC was abolished by the Conservative Government which came to power in 1970; when a Labour Government was returned to power four years later, it set up a rather different institution for intervention in industry – the National Enterprise Board. This was indeed saddled with a number of rescue operations; otherwise, it was required to 'invest in success'. The Government also continued to use the National Economic Development Council for discussing industrial strategy; this Council was one of the few new economic institutions devised during this period which survived changes of Government. The Council had a number of sector working parties to discuss the problems of particular industries; these working parties only had the powers of providing information and attempting persuasion.

The Labour Government had intended to introduce 'planning agreements' with individual firms. During its period in opposition, it came to the conclusion that what was needed was not so much a National Plan, but an effective means of intervening in the decision-making of individual major firms. The idea of planning agreements was borrowed from French practice, in much the same way as the idea of indicative planning had been borrowed in the early 1960s. In a planning agreement, the Government would offer investment subsidies and other assistance in exchange for specific commitments about investment plans and export intentions. However, this idea was virtually still-born because of the opposition from British industry.

One school of thought which came to prominence in the mid-1970s came to the conclusion that the only hope for an effective reconstruction of British industry was to protect it from foreign competition for a considerable number of years. This school of thought rejected devaluation as a possible way of making British industry more competitive, because of the problems of engineering a 'real' devaluation. They argued that in the absence of import controls, British manufacturing industry would be reduced even further in relative size, and Britain would be faced with massive unemployment. However, the proponents of import controls tended to be less explicit about the precise policies which would be used to revitalise British industry behind the suggested barriers which kept out foreign competition.

Thus, at the end of this period, there was no consensus about the policies which might be appropriate in face of the apparent lack of competitive power of British manufacturing industry; and indeed it seemed possible that during the period when oil output was increasing, Governments would not be under any strong pressure to concern themselves overmuch with this problem. Certainly there were few signs of the development of that symbiotic relationship between industry and Government which appeared to exist in, for example, Japan. The problem of industrial policy remained unresolved.

Footnote

(1) The 1974 figures given in Kravis, Heston and Summers (1978) were roughly adjusted to 1976 by estimates of the movement of real national product in those three countries between 1974 and 1976.

References

Hall, R.L. (1964) Foreword to J.C.R. Dow *The Management of the British Economy 1945–50* (Cambridge: Cambridge University Press), pp. XV–XVI.

Kravis, I.B., Heston, A.W. and Summers, R. (1978), 'Real GDP *Per Capita* for More than One Hundred Countries', *Economic Journal*, vol. 88, June, pp. 215–242.

Paige, D.C., Blackaby, F.T. and Freund, S. (1961) 'Economic Growth: The Last Hundred Years', *National Institute Economic Review*, no. 16, July, pp. 24–49.

Wilson, H. (1964) Paper presented at the Bonnington Conference, Autumn 1964.

Chapter 13

IMPACTS OF FISCAL ACTIONS ON AGGREGATE INCOME AND THE MONETARIST CONTROVERSY: AN EMPIRICAL INVESTIGATION

S.F. Frowen and P. Arestis*

Introduction

In recognition of the pioneering work on economic planning and in developing national accounts and economic forecasting techniques undertaken by Christopher Saunders, to whom the present study is dedicated, it may not be inappropriate to devote this essay to a further analysis of the Keynesian contention that an increase in government expenditure induces repeated rounds of spending and thereby results in a multiple increase in national income. This contention has been severely challenged by a number of economists who argue that an increase in government spending financed by either taxes and/or borrowing from savings of the general public may reduce private sector spending to an extent that there will be little, if any, net increase in total spending. In other words, increases in government expenditure, which are not accompanied by money creation, cannot do more than induce temporary increases in national income with no net effect over a longer period of time. Or expressed yet differently, government spending financed by either taxation or borrowing from the public is nothing but a resource transfer from the private to the public sector, with little net effect on total spending.

Clearly, this debate is scarcely new. As early as 1776, Adam Smith was arguing that government labour was unproductive and was condemning the transfer of resources from the private to the public sector. The origins of the recent debate, and the interest over the impact of fiscal actions on aggregate income, can be traced primarily to the empirical results published by Andersen and Jordan (1968) and by Keran in two supporting studies (1969 and 1970). These results have been taken as an indication that monetary policy actions have a strong and lasting impact on aggregate income, with fiscal policy actions having no impact at all. It has been suggested, in fact, that the initially positive effect of expansionary fiscal actions is followed in later quarters by a negative effect of an approximately equal size. This negative effect is so rapid as to yield a zero cumulative impact within only one year.

The response to this proposition has been quite substantial, especially at the empirical level. Corrigan (1970) argued that the results reached by Andersen and Jordan appear to have overstated the case against fiscal policy(1), particularly with regard to the impact of

* We are indebted to Michael Artis for helpful comments and criticisms.

tax changes on aggregate income; this, Corrigan suggested, was entirely due to the unsatisfactory indicator of fiscal policy utilised by Andersen and Jordan, which was endogenous to a very large extent. Davis (1969) suggested that the main weakness of the Andersen-Jordan study was the absence of a detailed transmission mechanism and the channels through which instruments of policy were supposed to influence ultimate goals of economic policy. Gramlich (1971) demonstrated that the reduced-form type of analysis employed by Andersen and Jordan provided no internally consistent description of the various relationships involved, which inevitably meant that the reduced-form technique did not seem to be very conclusive. B. Friedman (1977) showed that, using updated series which included the 1969–76 period, even the St. Louis equation now 'believes in' fiscal policy. However, Carlson (1978) was sceptical about this latter result on statistical grounds, in that there was evidence of 'non-constant error variance'. To correct for this statistical problem, Carlson re-estimated the St. Louis equation in rate-of-change form which implied constancy in the error variance, to conclude that the evidence did not support the claim that the Andersen and Jordan equation *now* 'believed in' fiscal policy. For the Federal Republic of Germany, Läufer asserts that, despite econometric pitfalls in his study, 'the effects of fiscal policy on economic activity are about equally strong and at the same time they are faster and more reliable than those of monetary policy' (Läufer, 1977, p. 203). However, his work seems to demonstrate that there is a need for thinking in terms of a fully specified macroeconomic model, and that the short-cut used by Andersen and Jordan can be fallacious (Hennings, 1977, p. 212).

The studies that have attempted to avoid the criticisms referred to above, have in fact done so through the use of large models by examining the impact of fiscal actions through simulation results which show the implied government expenditure and tax multipliers over time. These model simulations, in general, do provide support to the proposition that 'government spending does matter' over a certain time period. This is clearly shown in the case of the US economy where most models reveal that real expenditure multipliers approach positive asymptotes. It is perhaps best summarised in the passage stating that 'such multipliers reach a peak in two or three years and then decline thereafter in fluctuating paths. At the end of five to ten years, some of the models show that continued sustained fiscal stimulus has ever-increasing perverse impacts' (Fromm and Klein, 1973, p. 393). The picture is pretty much the same for the UK, although it is true to say that less disagreement prevails in the case of the latter economy in terms of the pattern of fiscal policy impacts (Laury, Lewis and Ormerod, 1978)(2). What is particularly discouraging for the crowding-out thesis is the fact that it takes a considerable length of time in some of the models for the government spending multiplier to approach zero or turn negative, and policy makers historically have shown little concern for the long run (Klein, 1973).

The response to the Andersen-Jordan results has also taken place at a theoretical level. The critics have argued that the study by Andersen and Jordan must be assuming a demand for money which is nearly perfectly inelastic with respect to interest rates, a theoretical proposition, which does not have any empirical backing. The majority of empirical work has produced estimates that do not support a zero interest elasticity of money demand. Milton Friedman (1972) has responded to this particular attack arguing that the slope of the demand-for-money function is completely irrelevant to this debate(3). What is of vital importance for Friedman is the distinction between initial and subsequent effects of fiscal actions. For an 'expansionary' fiscal action might first be reflected in a rise in output, but the financing of the deficit would set in motion contractionary forces, which would eventually offset the initial stimulative effect(4). The contractionary subsequent effects will continue as long as a deficit exists; eventually the stock of private wealth will be reduced relative to what it would otherwise be because of private investment being crowded out, and also because of the rise in interest rates, which reduces the market value of the existing stock of government bonds(5). Blinder and Solow (1973) nevertheless directed a rigorous theoretical attack on these monetarist propositions through an IS-LM model properly extended to incorporate wealth effects in both the consumption and demand-for-money functions – a government budget constraint providing for government debt interest payments was also postulated. They concluded that fiscal policy was more effective than monetary policy, since their model was stable only when government expenditure was financed through borrowing and was more expansionary than in cases where government expenditure was financed through money creation. Otherwise the model was unstable(6).

The purpose of this paper is to study empirically the dynamic impacts of different modes of financing budget deficits on the level of aggregate income in the case of the UK economy for the period 1963 to 1975. Our approach is to build a small dynamic macroeconomic model including the monetary sector, estimate it, and then simulate it so that the dynamic impacts of different ways of financing an increase in government expenditure can be studied and evaluated(7).

The model and its empirical performance

The model used here consists of the following eleven equations:

(1) $$Y_t = C_t + I_t + S_t + G_t + X_t - Q_t - E_t$$

(2) $$C_t = c_o + c_1 r_t + c_2 Y_t^d + c_3 C_{t-1} + c_4 L_{pt}$$

(3) $$Y_t^d = Y_t - T_t$$

(4) $$T_t = t_o + t_1 Y_t$$

(5) $I_t = i_o + i_1R_t + i_2Y_t + i_3I_{t-1}$

(6) $S_t = s_o + s_1R_t + s_2Y_t + s_3S_{t-1} + s_4L_{ct}$

(7) $Q_t = q_o + q_1Y_t + q_2Q_{t-1} + q_3Q_{ct}$

(8) $R_t = p_o + p_1r_t + p_2Y_t + p_3R_{t-1} + p_4P_t + p_5(\Delta G_d)_t$

(9) $M^s_t = m_o + m_1r_t + m_2M_{t-1} + m_3r_{dt} + m_4P_t + m_5B_t + m_6B_{t-1}$

(10) $M^d_t = d_o + d_1r_t + d_2Y_t + d_3M_{t-1} + d_4P_t$

(11) $M^s_t = M^d_t = M_t$

where:

Y_t = gross national product

Y^d_t = disposable income

$T_t = Y_t - Y^d_t$ = taxes on income

C_t = consumption expenditure

I_t = gross private investment expenditure

S_t = stockbuilding

G_t = government expenditure

X_t = exports

Q_t = imports

E_t = adjustment to factor costs, representing taxes on expenditure less subsidies

L_{Pt} = selected real liquid assets of the personal sector (beginning of period)

P_t = GDP price deflator

L_{ct} = company sector's real liquid assets (beginning of period)

Q_{ct} = import credit

M_t = money stock (M_1-definition)

R_t = long-term interest rate (consol rate)

r_t = short-term interest rate (local authority rate)

r_{dt} = rediscount rate

B_t = monetary base (notes and coin held by banks and non-banks plus bankers' deposits with the Bank of England).

(ΔG_d) = changes in private sector's holdings of government bonds.

We now turn to the discussion of the above-mentioned equations, beginning with the consumption function (8). Although we include the C_{t-1} variable in this function, the specification does not allow us to differentiate between the two alternative hypotheses, i.e. the permanent-income hypothesis where permanent income is approximated by a distributed lag function of current and past values of disposable income, and the lagged adjustment hypothesis advanced by Brown (1952). However, an attempt is made to discover the role of wealth as suggested by Modigliani and Ando (1957) with one important difference: instead of total wealth we have used liquid assets for three reasons:

(i) Liquid assets can be more reliably measured than total wealth; and

(ii) Liquid assets are supposed to play a greater role in expenditure decisions than any other form of wealth.

(iii) The non-availability of satisfactory wealth series.

The short-term interest rate is included as a proxy for the unobservable implicit rate of discount applied to stocks of consumer durables (9). If it could be established that interest rates were important in influencing consumers' expenditure, it would provide an alternative to both the Keynesian and the Chicago views concerning the channels through which monetary policy operates. Contrary to the Keynesian income-expenditure approach, it would imply that monetary policy has a more direct effect on consumer behaviour. This more direct link is recognised in the alternative approach expounded by Friedman and Meiselman (1963), but they argue that it is neither very useful nor illuminating to view the effects of monetary policy as operating through interest rates.

Equation 3 is simply the definition of disposable income, and Equation 4 clearly states that the level of taxes is determined by the level of national income.

The investment function, the stockbuilding function, and the import function are all quite straightforward; the three of them are assumed to follow a stock-adjustment hypothesis for the desired levels.

The long-term rate of interest is postulated to be a function of the short-term rate of interest via a simple term structure of interest rates. The level of income through its impact on the demand for loans influences the long-term rate of interest positively: as the level of economic activity is stimulated and the demand for loans increases, one would expect an increase in the long-term interest rate. The (ΔG_d)-variable, i.e. changes in private sector bond holdings, is inversely related to the long-term interest rate; as the holdings of bonds by the private sector change and the demand for these securities expands, the long-term rate of interest is expected to fall. We also assume a lag-adjustment hypothesis for this variable.

The demand for and supply of money are fairly straight-forward. However, we should like to stress the way the supply of money is postulated (10). In fact, we assume it to be endogenously and not exogenously determined, although some exogenous variables also enter this function. The latter are the rediscount rate (11), base money and the price level. The endogenous element is the short-term rate of interest, which itself is determined by both the demand for and supply of money. As the short-term rate goes up, it does pay the banks to increase their holdings of earning assets, and to decrease them when the short-term rate declines. We thus expect the interest rate coefficient in this function to be positive but, perhaps, not significant; this last proposition may be explained by referring to the period under investigation which is from 1963 to 1975. Whereas before September 1971, i.e. prior to the introduction of 'Competition and Credit Control' (CCC), the authorities were principally concerned with stabilising interest rates implying a demand-determined money stock(12), this policy was subsequently abandoned implying greater variations in interest rates, and therefore greater variability in the holdings of earning assets by banks. Consequently, it makes more sense to talk about a money-supply function since September 1971 than for the pre-CCC period. We may also note that the money market plays a central role in this model, for it provides the mechanism through which the real sector feeds back on the financial markets, thereby contributing to the determination of market rates.

We note finally that since our data(13) are all in 1970 constant prices, wherever an income variable appears we include the P_t variable too, so that nominal and real changes can be distinguished. Preliminary empirical work showed that it made sense, statistically speaking, to include such a variable in the monetary sector only.

When data were collected and the technique of Two-Stage Least Squares (TSLS) was employed, the following results were obtained:

T.S.L.S. – ESTIMATES
(1970 Prices – 't' statistics in brackets)

1. $Y_t = C_t + I_t + S_t + G_t + X_t - Q_t - E_t$

2. $C_t = 0.387 - 0.020 r_t + 0.502 Y_t^d + 0.301 C_{t-1} + 0.034 L_{pt}$
   (1.93) (2.97) (6.84) (2.87) (4.17)
   S.E.E.* = 0.077 D.W.** = 2.403

3. $Y_t^d = Y_t - T_t$

4. $T_t = -7.007 + 0.652 Y_t$
   (1.73) (4.41)
   p*** = 0.981 S.E.E. = 0.154
   (29.61)

5. $I_t = -0.176 - 0.010 R_t + 0.086 Y_t + 0.718 I_{t-1}$
   (1.20) (2.21) (2.87) (9.75)
   p = –0.357 S.E.E. = 0.051
   (2.61)

6. $S_t = -0.396 - 0.031 R_t + 0.047 Y_t + 0.361 S_{t-1} + 0.050 L_{ct}$
   (1.24) (2.54) (1.24) (2.81) (1.97)
   S.E.E. = 0.112 D.W. = 2.076

7. $Q_t = -0.776 + 0.142 Y_t + 0.735 Q_{t-1} + 1.165 Q_{ct}$
   (2.14) (2.54) (8.25) (3.22)
   S.E.E. = 0.085 D.W. = 2.119

8. $R_t = -2.085 + 0.148 r_t + 0.188 Y_t + 0.796 R_{t-1} + 0.876 P_t - 0.378 (\Delta G_d)_t$
   (2.02) (4.42) (1.48) (11.20) (1.70) (3.19)
   S.E.E. = 0.387 D.W. = 1.976

9. $M_t^s = -0.048 + 0.017 r_t + 0.737 M_{t-1} - 0.109 r_{dt} + 1.239 P_t + 1.304 B_t - 0.814 B_{t-1}$
   (0.22) (0.30) (10.82) (1.50) (2.15) (3.67) (2.30)
   S.E.E. = 0.169 D.W. = 2.904

10. $M_t^d = -1.140 - 0.055 r_t + 0.177 Y_t + 0.746 M_{t-1} + 2.238 P_t$
    (2.27) (3.82) (2.51) (11.10) (5.64)
    S.E.E. = 0.179 D.W. = 2.744

11. $M_t^s = M_t^d = M_t$

* S.E.E. = standard error of estimate
** D.W. = Durbin-Watson statistic
*** p = autocorrelation coefficient

These results are quite acceptable and justify some of the points raised earlier. In particular, there are three comments worth making:

(i) The interest rate coefficient in the consumption function bears the right sign and is significant. Thus, it is true that monetary policy has a more direct effect on consumer behaviour and does provide an alternative to both the Keynesian and the Chicago views on the channels through which monetary policy operates.

(ii) The interest rate coefficient in the money-supply function does have the right sign, i.e. a positive sign, justifying our claim, perhaps, that the post-1971 period is more important for our money supply hypothesis.

(iii) The discount rate coefficient, too, has the right sign in the money-supply function, but it insignificant. This can be explained of course by the fact that during the estimation period the monetary authorities in the UK never attempted to control the money supply consciously via interest rate changes but instead used the discount rate for other purposes, in particular for influencing short-term capital movements(14).

We may now use the above model for simulation purposes which will enable us to derive so-called 'dynamic multipliers'; these multipliers are the basis of our conclusions on the dynamic impacts of fiscal actions on the level of income in the case of the UK economy.

Policy simulations and crowding out

The model outlined above has been simulated over the period under investigation. The simulated values of the endogenous variables can be compared with their actual time paths, which enables us to formulate some judgement as to how well the model performs as an interdependent way of tracking the movements of certain strategic economic variables. We employ the so-called 'root mean squared errors', defined as

$$\text{RMSE} = \sqrt{\frac{1}{T} \cdot \sum_{t=1}^{T} (Y_A - Y_S)^2}$$

where Y_A = actual values and

Y_S = simulated values,

to judge the performance of the model when simulated. In addition, the RMSE measure may serve to indicate the confidence that can be attached to the results of 'policy simulations' designed to estimate the typical time path of response of endogenous variables to changes in policy variables.

In Table 13.1 we have tabulated the RMSE measure for all the endogenous variables of our model. The root mean squared errors reported in this table suggest that our model

Table 13.1

Root mean squared errors

Endogenous variables	RMSE	Endogenous variables	RMSE
Y_t	1.49	S_t	0.14
C_t	1.71	Q_t	0.79
Y^d_t	2.54	R_t	0.39
T_t	1.17	M_t	0.28
I_t	0.33	r_t	0.37

Table 13.2

Dynamic multipliers

Initial conditions 1963 (1st quarter)

Impact on Y_t of £ 1 million change in G_t

Quarter	Dynamic multipliers	Cumulative multiplier effects	Quarter	Dynamic multipliers	Cumulative multiplier effects
0	1.10	1.10	19	1.36	−0.63
1	1.09	2.19	20	1.33	0.70
2	1.03	3.22	21	1.23	1.93
3	0.98	4.20	22	1.12	3.05
4	0.94	5.14	23	1.04	4.09
5	0.90	6.04	24	0.98	5.07
6	0.88	6.92	25	0.94	6.01
7	0.87	7.79	26	0.90	6.91
8	0.85	8.64	27	0.88	7.79
9	−1.36	7.28	28	0.87	8.66
10	−1.32	5.96	29	0.85	9.51
11	−1.23	4.73	30	0.85	10.36
12	−1.12	3.61	31	0.84	11.20
13	−1.04	2.57	32	0.84	12.04
14	−0.98	1.59	33	0.83	12.87
15	−0.93	0.66	34	0.83	
16	−0.90	−0.24	35	0.83	
17	−0.88	−1.12			
18	−0.87	−1.99			

performs reasonably well in terms of tracking down the movements of the endogenous variables. They also suggest that a reasonable degree of confidence may be attached to the results of 'policy simulations' reported in Tables 13.2 and 13.3.

The results of 'policy simulations' are the so-called 'dynamic multipliers', and are derived as follows: First, a 'control solution' is established using actual values of the exogenous variables. We then make a new simulation corresponding to different specific values of the exogenous variables (or parameter estimates) to see how much influence on the system, measured by departure from the control solution, they have. We compare the control solution,

$$y_{i,t_1},\dots,y_{i,t_1+1},\dots,y_{i,t_1+2},\dots y_{i,t_1+s}$$

corresponding to the exogenous variables

$$x_{i,t_1},\dots,x_{i,t_1+1},\dots x_{i,t_1+2},\dots,x_{i,t_1+s}$$

with the disturbed solution,

$$y^+_{i,t_1},\dots,y^+_{i,t_1+1}\dots y^+_{i,t_1+2},\dots,y^+_{i,t_1+s}$$

corresponding to the exogenous variables,

$$x^+_{i,t_1},\dots,x^+_{i,t_1+1}\dots x^+_{i,t_1+2},\dots,x^+_{i,t_1+s}$$

We use the ratio of the relative distances between y^+_{i,t_1+s} and y_{i,t_1+s} on the one hand, and x^+_{i,t_1+s} and x_{i,t_1+s} on the other, to derive multiplier effects after s periods of dynamic simulations. These are what one might call the 'dynamic multipliers'(15). We have estimated dynamic multipliers for thirty-six quarters; these register the impact of changes in government expenditure on the level of economic activity, as measured by the level of national income, of different modes of financing government expenditure. Four different modes are assumed here: changes in taxes (changes in t_o, i.e. the intercept, and changes in t_1, i.e. the slope of the tax line), bond-financed changes in government expenditure, and changes in the monetary base. These dynamic multipliers appear in Table 13.3.

The dynamic multipliers given in Table 13.2 also show the impact on the level of income of a change in government expenditure, but without distinguishing between different modes of financing government expenditure. The most cursory comparison of the two tables suggests that the two sets of results can differ dramatically. This important result

Table 13.3

Dynamic multipliers

Initial conditions 1963 (1st quarter)

Impact on Y_t of a £1 million change in G_t financed as indicated

Quarter	Tax financing $\Delta G \equiv \Delta T$ (for Δt_0) Dynamic multipliers	Cumulative multiplier effects	Tax financing $\Delta G \equiv \Delta T$ (for Δt_1) Dynamic multipliers	Cumulative multiplier effects	Bond financing $\Delta G \equiv \Delta G_d$ Dynamic multipliers	Cumulative multiplier effects	Money financing $\Delta G \equiv \Delta B$ Dynamic multipliers	Cumulative multiplier effects
0	0.55	0.55	0.42	0.42	1.12	1.12	1.30	1.30
1	0.38	0.93	0.19	0.61	1.12	2.24	1.38	2.68
2	0.30	1.23	0.09	0.70	1.09	3.33	1.38	4.06
3	0.26	1.49	0.05	0.75	1.05	4.38	1.36	5.42
4	0.25	1.74	0.05	0.80	1.02	5.40	1.35	6.77
5	0.24	1.98	0.05	0.85	1.00	6.40	1.34	8.11
6	0.24	2.22	0.07	0.92	0.99	7.39	1.33	9.44
7	0.24	2.46	0.08	1.00	0.98	8.37	1.33	10.77
8	0.24	2.70	0.06	1.06	0.97	9.34	1.32	12.09
9	−1.97	0.73	−2.08	−1.02	−1.24	8.10	−0.89	11.20
10	−1.93	−1.20	−2.02	−3.04	−1.20	6.90	−0.85	10.35
11	−1.83	−3.03	−1.92	−4.96	−1.10	5.80	−0.75	9.60
12	−1.72	−4.75	−1.82	−6.78	−1.00	4.80	−0.64	8.96
13	−1.64	−6.39	−1.75	−8.53	−0.92	3.88	−0.56	8.40
14	−1.57	−7.96	−1.69	−10.22	−0.85	3.03	−0.49	7.91
15	−1.53	−9.49	−1.66	−11.88	−0.81	2.22	−0.45	7.46
16	−1.50	−10.99	−1.63	−13.51	−0.77	1.45	−0.41	7.05
17	−1.48	−12.47	−1.60	−15.11	−0.75	0.70	−0.39	6.66
18	−1.46	−13.93	−1.58	−16.69	−0.74	−0.04	−0.38	6.28
19	0.76	−13.17	0.56	−16.13	1.48	1.44	1.85	8.13
20	0.73	−12.44	0.51	−15.62	1.46	2.90	1.82	9.95
21	0.63	−11.81	0.41	−15.21	1.36	4.26	1.72	11.67
22	0.53	−11.28	0.31	−14.90	1.25	5.51	1.61	13.28
23	0.45	−10.83	0.24	−14.66	1.17	6.68	1.54	14.82
24	0.38	−10.45	0.18	−14.48	1.11	7.79	1.47	16.29
25	0.34	−10.11	0.14	−14.34	1.07	8.86	1.43	17.72
26	0.30	−9.81	0.10	−14.24	1.03	9.89	1.39	19.11
27	0.29	−9.52	0.08	−14.16	1.01	10.90	1.37	20.48
28	0.27	−9.25	0.07	−14.09	0.99	11.89	1.36	21.84
29	0.26	−8.99	0.06	−14.03	0.98	12.87	1.34	23.18
30	0.25	−8.74	0.05	−13.98	0.98	13.85	1.34	24.52
31	0.24	−8.50	0.02	−13.97	0.97	14.82	1.33	25.84
32	0.24		0.01	−13.96	0.97	15.79	1.33	27.17
33	0.24		0.00		0.96	16.75	1.33	28.50
34	0.24		0.00		0.96		1.32	29.82
35	0.24		0.00		0.96		1.32	

justified our attempt to try and distinguish between different modes of financing government expenditure. Taking now the results of the two tables together one cannot help noticing that the values of the dynamic multipliers are rather low. The major explanation for this seems to be the high degree of built-in stability which is provided by the tax structure. Indeed, we find that within the first quarter, the net tax going to the government is about 65 per cent of the increase in national income.

We now concentrate on Table 13.3 and try to explain the reasons behind the differences in the values of the dynamic multipliers reported there.

In a general way the impact of changes in government expenditure on the level of income can be studied in terms of direct impacts and feedback responses to government expenditure changes. Direct impacts refer to the initial or first round impact of the change in government expenditure and of the associate changes due to the way government expenditure is financed. In our model, these initial impacts can be on consumption (via changes in the short-term rate of interest associated with the operation(16), and via changes in the L_{pt}-variable), on investment (via changes in interest rates directly associated with the operation), and on stockbuilding (via changes in interest rates directly associated with the financing of government expenditure, and via changes in the L_{ct}-variable). Feedback responses arise in response to the initial change in income. The following feedback responses prevail in our model: a positive feedback response on consumption, investment and stockbuilding, but also a negative feedback response on the same variables due to the income-induced rise in interest rates(17).

One may distinguish three types of direct impacts(18). First, the direct fiscal impact which is the impact of a change in government expenditure on the level of income in view of the fact that government expenditure is a component of aggregate expenditure. This impact is present in all three cases of Table 13.3. Second, the direct wealth impact which is the increase in consumption and stockbuilding induced by the increase in wealth associated with the increase in the supply of government bonds or the money supply. Third, the direct portfolio impact which is the decline in investment associated with the direct impact of an increase in the supply of government bonds on the rate of interest; it is obvious that this effect arises only in the case where government expenditure is financed by issuing bonds.

These distinctions may now be used to explain the differences in the values of the dynamic multipliers that appear in Table 13.3. These multipliers follow a common path as far as the direction of the impact on the level of national income is concerned. For the first eight quarters income increases, for the next ten quarters it decreases, and for the next fifteen quarters or so it increases again; by then convergence takes place in all three cases. The cumulative multiplier effects are positive in all cases, except when government expenditure is financed through taxation. In this case the only direct effect present is the direct fiscal impact which is positive due to the increase in government expenditure, but its value is reduced by the increase in taxes. With a small increase in income the subsequent positive income feedback effects are more than outweighed by the negative interest rate feedback effect.

The other two cases where the financing of government expenditure is done through issuing bonds and money are more interesting. The values of the dynamic multipliers arising from financing the change in government expenditure are higher than those where we have bond-financing. This is a result that can be explained by the fact that in the case of money financing, the negative direct portfolio impact is absent; present are only the other two, while in the case of bond-financing all three are operative(19). Consequently, the feedback responses will be stronger in the case of money-financed government expenditure rather than in the case of bond-financing.

The results reported in Table 13.2 may be usefully compared with the results obtained in the case of the US economy. A full-fledged comparison of the effects of budget deficits under alternative forms of financing in the case of the latter economy can be made by referring to the Wharton Mark III and the DHL III models. The dynamic multipliers of a $ 1 billion increase in government expenditure financed through taxation, bonds or money are reported in Table 13.4. In both models, as in our model also, the money-financed government expenditure multipliers for real national income are uniformly higher than bond-financed multipliers; and the latter are uniformly higher than the tax-financed multipliers. The result of these models as well as the results of our model clearly imply that the ranking of multiplier magnitudes under bond-financed and money-financed deficits does not support the theoretical results of Blinder and Solow (1973) referred to above. There is, however, an important difference between the results reported in Table 13.4 and our results. In none of the cases of Table 13.4 does the sign of the dynamic multipliers change from positive to negative. In our case this occurs uniformly after the elapse of eight quarters. The size of our multipliers tend to be smaller than those reported in Table 13.3 even when they are both positive. These differences, of course, are due to a number of reasons. Our model is a distinctly small model when compared with the Wharton and DHL models. Consequently differences of specification of equations become of crucial importance. There are also differences in the variables involved as well as in the period under investigation. Lack of standardisation of the exogenous variables employed and initial conditions do cause the results to differ significantly.

However, although the results reported in Tables 13.3 and 13.4 differ in the way we have just indicated, they are nevertheless of some importance in terms of the controversy between Kaynesians and monetarists, evolving around the values of the dynamic multipliers in the case of bond-financed government spending. Clearly there is no controversy over government spending financed through money creation since both sides agree that it will be expansionary. The only difference is that one group likes to call it fiscal policy,

Table 13.4

Dynamic multipliers
(Based on US data; in constant 1958 US dollars)
Impact on Y_t of a $ 1 billion change in G_t

Quarters of change	Bond financing: Wharton Mark III	Bond financing: DHL III	Money financing: Wharton Mark III	Money financing: DHL III	Tax financing: Wharton Mark III	Tax financing: DHL III
1	1.3	0.8	1.4	0.8	0.9	0.6
2	1.6	1.4	1.8	1.4	1.1	1.0
3	1.8	1.7	2.1	1.7	1.2	1.0
4	2.0	1.9	2.3	1.9	1.2	0.9
5	2.1	2.1	2.5	2.1	1.3	0.9
6	2.2	2.2	2.6	2.2	1.3	0.9
7	2.3	2.2	2.7	2.3	1.4	0.8
8	2.4	2.1	2.8	2.3	1.4	0.8
9	2.4	2.0	2.9	2.3	1.4	0.7
10	2.4	1.9	3.0	2.2	1.4	0.6
11	2.5	1.7	3.0	2.1	1.4	0.5
12	2.5	1.4	3.0	1.9	1.4	0.4
16	2.2	0.7	2.7	1.3	1.3	0.2
20		0.8		1.1		0.3
24		1.2		1.3		0.4
28		1.3		1.6		0.4
32		1.0		1.7		0.3
36		0.6		1.6		0.2
40		0.5		1.5		0.2

Sources: Vijaya G. Duggal, Lawrence R. Klein, and Michael D. McCarthy, 'The Wharton Model Mark III: A Modern IS-LM Construct', *International Economic Review,* Vol. 15, October 1974, Table 12, p. 589; Saul H. Hymans and Harold T. Shapiro, 'The Structure and Properties of the Michigan Quarterly Econometric Model of the US Economy', *International Economic Review,* Vol. 15, October 1974, Tables 7–9, pp. 644–47.

while the other prefers to call it monetary policy. We call it 'policy-mix'. Nevertheless, when the financing is undertaken by issuing bonds the two sides arrive at different conclusions. Keynesians would argue that bond-financed government spendig has a *net* expansionary impact on the level of income, a tenet supported by our results. Monetarists, on the other hand, argue that bond-financed government spending is completely impotent in terms of its impact on the level of income, since the cumulative long-run value of the dynamic multipliers is approximately zero(20). This conclusion is completely rejected by our results.

Our overall conclusion would seem to be that it makes a considerable difference in terms of the impact on the level of economic activity how the increased government expenditure is financed. Moreover, our findings appear to disprove the monetarist proposition that increases in government expenditure induce only temporary increases in national income if unaccompanied by money creation.

Summary and conclusions

This pilot study is concerned with the dynamic impact of fiscal actions in the case of the UK economy for the period 1963 to 1975. We started with a brief summary of the theoretical and empirical foundations of this area of substantial controversy amongst economists and proceeded to the construction, estimation and simulation of a small dynamic model for the UK economy, which enabled us to derive what is usually termed dynamic multipliers. The latter have been derived by assuming different modes of financing government spending. These dynamic multipliers were then compared with those derived when the way of financing government spending is ignored. Our major results may be summarised as follows:

It is important to spell out clearly how government expenditure is financed. Failure to do so introduces a bias in the derived dynamic multipliers. Our results clearly indicate that the extent of the impact of changes in fiscal actions on the economy strongly depends on the way they are financed; when the financing is through taxation it takes about two and a half years for the initial positive impact to be completely outweighed by subsequent negative impacts. If the government finances its budget deficit by means of the sale of bonds or by money creation, a positive cumulative impact can be observed throughout.

These results obviously depend on the faith one has in the type of small dynamic model applied in our study to determine the dynamic multipliers. But however tentative our conclusions may be, it is hoped that they will throw some light on a number of issues related to some crucial aspects of the 'Keynesian versus monetarist' debate.

Footnotes

(1) Further studies confirming this particular result are those by de Leeuw and Kalchbrenner (1969) and Artis and Nobay (1969).

(2) See also the paper by Arestis and Karakitsos (1980) using the UK model of the National Institute of Economic and Social Research, London. For studies using smaller models, see Frowen and Arestis (1976), Arestis, Frowen and Karakitsos (1978) and Arestis (1979).

(3) The contribution of Brunner and Meltzer (1972) is also relevant here.

(4) Meyer (1975) provides a numerical example in an IS-LM framework, showing the expansionary initial effects and the subsequent contractionary effects.

(5) Floyd and Hynes (1978) – see also Butkiewicz (1979) – provide similar results, although their argument suggests that even the initial positive effects of deficit financing are associated with some crowding-out, due to the wealth effect operating in the demand for money.

(6) For a critique of the Blinder and Solow (1973) analysis, see Infante and Stein (1976), but also consult Blinder and Solow (1976).

(7) The model presented here is a fixed exchange rate model, and most of our estimation period belongs to such a regime. Theory suggests, of course, that the effects of fiscal policy may look very different under a flexible exchange rate system; what evidence we have from the big models confirms that there is indeed a significant difference.

(8) The justification of this equation as well as the remaining equations of the model may be found in the study by Arestis (1979).

(9) An alternative explanation could be that the rate of interest is in fact picking up some wealth (revaluation) effects.

(10) The MI definition of the money supply has been used in our model. This reflects the fact that we wish to stress the transactions function of money.

(11) There has been some change in the rules relating to the UK rediscount rate. Since 20 August 1981, the Bank of England no longer continuously posts a minimum lending rate but reserves the right, in some circumstances, to announce in advance the minimum rate which, for a short period ahead, it would apply in any lending to the market.

(12) It must also be remembered that especially prior to the introduction of CCC, periods of increasing short-term interest rates often coincided with severe restrictions on the expansion of bank credits.

(13) The data on all variables were collected from *Economic Trends* (various issues), except for the data on M_t, r_t, r_{dt}, B_t and $(\Delta Gd)_t$, which were collected from the *Bank of England Quarterly Bulletin* (various issues). The period under investigation is 1963 (1st qtr.) to 1975 (4th qtr.).

(14) This situation changed markedly with the introduction of monetary targets for the UK in 1976 – see Artis and Lewis (1981) and Foot (1981). By switching from a monetary to an exchange rate target (see Artis and Currie, 1981), the original situation could be restored.

(15) For a detailed exposition of all these, see Klein (1974), ch. 6, pp. 226–280.

(16) This is particularly valid in the case of financing the increase in government expenditure by issuing bonds, which can of course be of a short-term nature as well as long-term nature. Some increase in the rate of interest is bound to come about in order to persuade bondholders to take up the increased volume of bonds.

(17) Our model is fix-price as far as the simulations are concerned. There is of course the possibility of feedback responses via inflation, which would tend to crowd out any price elastic private expenditures. In addition inflation implies a reduction in the real value of total wealth.

(18) For a similar discussion on the types of direct impacts as well as the feedback responses, see Meyer (1975) and Arestis (1979).

(19) The L_{pt} and L_{ct} terms would of course have to change appropriately during the course of the simulations.

(20) Indeed, some have argued that it can be negative (Silber, 1970, p. 467); see also Rasche (1973).

References

Andersen L.C. and Jordan J.L. (1968) 'Monetary and Fiscal Actions: A Test of Their Relative Importance in Economic Stabilisation', Federal Reserve Bank of St. Louis *Review,* vol. 50, no. 11, November, pp. 11–24.

Arestis P. (1979) 'The "Crowding-Out" of Private Expenditure by Fiscal Actions: An Empirical Investigation', *Public Finance,* vol. XXXIV, no. 1, pp. 36–50.

Arestis P., Frowen S.F. and Karakitsos E. (1978) 'The Dynamic Impacts of Government Expenditure and the Monetary Base on Aggregate Income: The Case of Four OECD Countries, 1965–1974', *Public Finance,* vol. 33, nos. 1–2, pp. 1–22.

Arestis P. and Karakitsos E. (1980) 'Fiscal Actions, Optimal Control and "Crowding Out" within the NIESR Model', *Greek Economic Review,* December, pp. 220–240.

Artis M.J. and Currie D.A. (1981) 'Monetary Targets and the Exchange Rate: A Case for Conditional Targets', *Oxford Economic Papers,* vol. 33, July, pp. 176–200, reprinted in Eltis W.A. and Sinclair P.J.N. (eds.) *The Money Supply and the Exchange Rate* (Oxford: Clarendon Press, 1981).

Artis M.J. and Lewis M.K. (1981) *Monetary Control in the United Kingdom* (Oxford: Philip Allan) pp. 38--60.

Artis M.J. and Nobay A.R. (1969) 'Two Aspects of the Monetary Debate', *National Institute Economic Review,* August, pp. 33–51

Artis M.J. and Nobay A.R. (1972) 'The Attempt to Reinstate Money', in Johnson H.G. (ed). *Readings in British Monetary Economics* (Oxford: Oxford University Press).

Blinder A.S. and Solow R.M. (1973) 'Does Fiscal Policy Matter?', *Journal of Public Economics,* November.

Blinder A.S. and Solow R.M. (1976) 'Does Fiscal Policy Still Matter? A Reply', *Journal of Monetary Economics,* November.

Brown T.M. (1952) 'Habitat Persistence and Lags in Consumer Behaviour', *Econometrica,* July.

Brunner K. and Meltzer A.H. (1972) 'Money, Debt and Economic Activity', *Journal of Political Economy,* September, pp. 951–977.

Butkiewicz J.L. (1979) 'Outside Wealth, the Demand for Money and the Crowding Out Effect', *Journal of Monetary Economics,* vol. 5, April, pp. 249–258.

Carlson K.M. (1978) 'Does the St. Louis Equation Now Believe in Fiscal Policy?', Federal Reserve Bank of St. Louis *Review*, vol. 60, no. 2, February, pp. 13–14.

Corrigan E.G. (1970) 'The Measurement and Importance of Fiscal Policy Changes', Federal Reserve Bank of New York *Monthly Review,* June.

Davis R.G. (1969) 'How Much Does Money Matter? A Look at Some Recent Evidence', Federal Reserve Bank of New York *Monthly Review,* June, pp. 119–31.

de Leeuw F. and Kalchbrenner J. (1969) 'Monetary and Fiscal Actions: A Test of their Relative Importance in Economic Stabilisation: A Comment', Federal Reserve Bank of St. Louis, *Review,* vol. 51, no. 4, April, pp. 6–11.

Floyd J.E. and Hynes J.A. (1978) 'Deficit Finance and "First-Round" Crowding Out: A Clarification', *Canadian Journal of Economics,* February.

Foot M.D.K.W. (1981) 'Monetary Targets: Their Nature and Record in the Major Economies', in Griffiths B. and Wood G.E. (eds.) *Monetary Targets* (London: Macmillan).

Friedman B.M. (1977) 'Even the St. Louis Model Now Believes in Fiscal Policy', *Journal of Money, Credit and Banking,* vol. IX, no. 2, May, pp. 365–367.

Friedman M. (1972) 'Comments on the Critics', *Journal of Political Economy,* September/October.

Friedman M. and Meiselman D. (1963) 'The Relative Stability of Monetary Velocity and the Investment Multiplier in the USA, 1897–1958', Research Study TWO, *Commission on Money and Credit: Stabilisation Policies* (Prentice Hall).

Fromm G. and Klein L.R. (1973) 'A Comparison of Eleven Econometric Models of the USA', *American Economic Review,* May.

Frowen S.F. and Arestis P. (1976) 'The Dynamic Impacts of Government Expenditure and the Monetary Base on Aggregate Income: The West German Case', *Kredit und Kapital,* vol. 9, no. 3, pp. 368–383.

Frowen S.F., Courakis A.S. and Miller M.H. (eds.) (1977) *Monetary Policy and Economic Activity in West Germany* (London: Surrey University Press; New York: Halsted Press; Stuttgart: Gustav Fischer Verlag).

Gramlich E.M. (1971) 'The Usefulness of Monetary and Fiscal Policy as Discretionary Stabilisation Tools', *Journal of Money, Credit and Banking,* (May).

Hennings K.M. (1977) 'Further Evidence on the Relative Importance of Fiscal and Monetary Actions in the Federal Republic of Germany – a Comment', in Frowen S.F. et al (eds.) *Monetary Policy and Economic Activity in West Germany* (London: Surrey University Press; New York: Halsted Press; Stuttgart: Gustav Fischer Verlag), pp. 207–212.

Infante E.P. and Stein J.L. (1976) 'Does Fiscal Policy Matter?', *Journal of Monetary Economics,* April.

Keran M.W. (1969) 'Monetary and Fiscal Influences on Economic Activity – The Historical Evidence', Federal Reserve Bank of St. Louis *Review,* November.

Keran M.W. (1970) 'Monetary and Fiscal Influences on Economic Activity: The Foreign Experience', Federal Reserve Bank of St. Louis *Review,* vol. 52, no. 2, February, pp. 16–28.

Klein L.R. (1973) 'Commentary on "the State of the Monetarist Debate" ', Federal Reserve Bank of St. Louis *Review*, vol. 55, no. 9, September, pp. 9–12.

Klein L.R. (1974) *A Textbook of Econometrics,* Second Edition (Prentice Hall, Inc.: Englewood Cliffs, N.J.).

Läufer N.K.A. (1977) 'Further Evidence on the Relative Importance of Fiscal and Monetary Actions in the Federal Republic of Germany' in Frowen F.S. et al. (eds.) *Monetary Policy and Economic Activity in West Germany* (London: Surrey University Press; New York: Halsted Press; Stuttgart: Gustav Fischer Verlag) pp. 195–206.

Laury J.S.E., Lewis G.R. and Ormerod P.A. (1978) 'Properties of Macroeconomic Models of the UK Economy: A Comparative Study', *National Institute Economic Review,* February.

Lewis G.R. and Ormerod P.A. (1979) 'Policy Simulations and Model Characteristics', in S.T. Cook and P.M. Jackson (eds.), *Current Issues in Fiscal Policy.*

Meyer L.H. (1975) 'The Balance Sheet Identity, the Government Financing Constraint, and the Crowding Out Effect', *Journal of Monetary Economics,* January.

Modigliani F. and Ando A. (1957) 'Tests of the Life Cycle Hypothesis of Savings'. *Bulletin of the Oxford University Institute of Economics and Statistics,* vol. 19, May, pp. 99–124.

Rasche R.H. (1973) 'A Comparative Static Analysis of Some Monetarist Propositions', Federal Reserve Bank of St. Louis *Review*, vol. 55, no. 12, December, pp. 15–23.

Silber W. (1970) 'Fiscal Policy in IS–LM Analysis: A Correction', *Journal of Money, Credit and Banking, November.*

Chapter 14

FISCAL POLICY IN WEST GERMANY: ANTICYCLICAL VERSUS EXPENDITURE-REDUCING POLICIES

N. Kloten and K.H. Ketterer

1

Fiscal policy is in a dilemma in the Federal Republic of Germany. Net borrowing by central, regional and local authorities (Federal Government, Länder governments and local authorities) amounted to approximately DM 77 billion in 1981 (1) – the highest new borrowing by the public sector in the history of the Federal Republic. The high debts and particularly the rapid increase in new public sector borrowing since 1977 have caused great anxiety in West Germany. Evidence of this is the fear of many of a possible government bankruptcy or the need to carry out yet another currency reform, although there is absolutely no objective reason for this. However, even scientifically based analyses, as for instance those carried out by the German Council of Economic Experts, show that it is essential to decrease the public sector deficit in order to restore a satisfactory rate of real growth of the economy emanating from the private sector.

The first steps in this direction seem to have been made. When in the middle of 1981 it became obvious that the record deficit of 1981 would be considerably exceeded in 1982, the coalition partners decided on cuts in public sector spending for the years 1982–85 (2). This was, however, only the first step. These cuts reduced the budget deficits of the central, regional and local authorities by DM 19 billion, which is a relatively large sum. The total deficit in 1982 will therefore be slightly below the 1981 level. It is, however, obvious that despite the cuts this deficit would have been higher if the Federal Republic's central bank, the Deutsche Bundesbank, had not transferred a profit of DM 10 billion to the Federal Ministry of Finance.

Consolidating the public sector budgets has become the need of the moment and will remain so for the next few years. This is against a background of a highly unsatisfactory economic development. In 1981 the German economy moved into a recession and the prospects for the coming years are not good. In 1982 unemployment will reach a level which was only exceeded in the Federal Republic during the initial post-war period (for details see Table 14.1). At the same time it has become clear that a high rate of unemployment will continue to be a problem for years to come. This should be the time for an expansionary fiscal policy and for programmes to increase employment. However, the pressure to reduce deficits has become so great that there is no possibility of fiscal policy being sufficiently expansive to counteract the effects of the recession by expenditure programmes. That is the dilemma.

Table 14.1

Trends on growth, unemployment and investment in Germany

Year	Gross national product at constant prices, change on year	Unemployment rate	Machinery and equipment at constant prices change on year	Building at constant prices change on year
1951	+ 10.4	10.4	+ 9.5	+ 2.4
1952	+ 8.9	9.5	+ 7.0	+ 9.9
1953	+ 8.2	8.4	+ 10.0	+ 21.9
1954	+ 7.4	7.6	+ 18.2	+ 9.1
1955	+ 12.0	5.6	+ 25.0	+ 17.9
1956	+ 7.3	4.4	+ 5.4	+ 11.0
1957	+ 5.7	3.7	− 2.3	+ 1.4
1958	+ 3.7	3.7	+ 6.2	+ 2.9
1959	+ 7.3	2.6	+ 12.0	+ 11.6
1960	+ 9.0	1.3	+ 17.6	+ 5.2
1950–1960	+ 8.0	5.7	+ 10.6	+ 9.1
1961	+ 4.9	0.8	+ 12.0	+ 4.9
1962	+ 4.4	0.7	+ 8.0	+ 2.9
1963	+ 3.0	0.8	+ 0.5	+ 1.6
1964	+ 6.6	0.8	+ 8.0	+ 12.9
1965	+ 5.5	0.7	+ 7.7	+ 3.5
1966	+ 2.5	0.7	− 1.2	+ 2.4
1967	− 0.1	2.1	− 7.4	− 6.5
1968	+ 6.5	1.5	+ 7.3	+ 2.5
1969	+ 7.9	0.9	+ 23.0	+ 4.3
1970	+ 5.9	0.7	+ 17.7	+ 6.7
1960–1970	+ 4.7	1.0	+ 5.8	+ 5.5
1971	+ 3.3	0.8	+ 5.9	+ 6.8
1972	+ 3.6	1.1	− 1.0	+ 6.3
1973	+ 4.9	1.2	+ 0.8	− 0.2
1974	+ 0.4	2.6	− 10.2	− 9.8
1975	− 1.8	4.7	+ 0.4	− 6.9
1976	+ 5.3	4.6	+ 6.5	+ 3.6
1977	+ 2.8	4.5	+ 7.7	+ 1.3
1978	+ 3.6	4.3	+ 8.2	+ 2.9
1979	+ 4.4	3.8	+ 9.5	+ 7.6
1980	+ 1.8	3.8	+ 2.9	+ 4.4
1970–1980	+ 2.8	3.1	+ 2.9	+ 1.4
1981	− 0.2	5.5	− 3.4	− 4.2
1982[1)]	− 1.0	7.5	− 6	− 6.5

1) Joint diagnosis of the economic research institutes, October 22, 1982.

There are those who argue in favour of postponing yet again the task of consolidating the budgets of the public sector and instituting new employment programmes which could be financed by borrowing.

On the other hand, it is argued that neglecting the problem and postponing the introduction of renewed programmes will eventually make the need to consolidate the budget so great that the skill of politicians may not be sufficient to overcome it. The decision to save DM 19 billion taken on September 2–3, 1981 brought the governing coalition to the brink of collapse; the opposition was already deeply divided when its proposals for cuts had not even reached the DM 10 billion mark.

This article is devoted to weighing up the arguments for and against an immediate and consistent attempt to solve the problem of consolidation. The procedure followed will be to give in Part 2 a description of the facts, i.e. the development of the debt position and the net borrowing of the central, regional and local authorities in West Germany during the post-war period; Part 3 provides an investigation of what importance should be placed on the need to consolidate the budget; in Part 4 there will be an investigation of how the need to consolidate the budget arose; in Part 5 the means of consolidating the budget will be dealt with and in Part 6 a conclusion will be drawn for policy.

2

The extent of the fundamental change in the position of government indebtedness which took place in the mid 1970s becomes clear if one considers the net borrowing of the central, regional and local authorities in the post-war period. The figures are shown in Table 14.2.

The table shows that the debts of the central, regional and local authorities in the Federal Republic rose from DM 18.7 billion in 1950 to DM 466.3 billion in 1980. The size of the debt position on its own does not give a true picture of the government's real debt operations, i.e. the budget deficits. It is clear that up to the 1960s the greatest part of total borrowing was composed of those debts which did not arise from government borrowing. These are, first, the so-called old debts which were taken over from the time of the Third Reich. Second, foreign debts were added to this in the 1950s after the arrangements for the repayment of German pre-war debts had been agreed upon at the London Debt Agreement of February 27, 1953.

The DM 18.7 billion of Government debt with which the story of debts begins in 1950 consists almost entirely of that sum of debts which the Federal Republic was prepared to take over from the Third Reich. The Debt Administration of the Reich had concluded its activity on April 21, 1945. When the register of debts of the Third Reich was closed

Table 14.2

Indebtedness, net borrowing and financial balances of public authorities[1)]

Year	Indebtedness[2)]		Net borrowing		Financial surplus or deficit (–)	
	All public authorities[3)]	of which Federal Government	Total	of which Federal Government	DM billion	in % of GNP
	DM million		DM million			
1950	18 743	6 068	604	196	– 1.7	– 1.7
1951	21 625	7 584	573	– 11	– 1.3	– 1.1
1952	24 314	8 601	1 751	682	– 0.1	– 0.0
1953	33 694	15 591	2 293	504	+ 0.4	+ 0.2
1954	38 967	17 933	1 328	– 245	+ 0.7	+ 0.4
1955	41 444	18 143	1 383	– 304	+ 2.6	+ 1.4
1956	43 011	20 639	759	– 660	– 1.3	– 0.6
1957	44 717	20 000	1 747	– 538	– 4.3	– 1.9
1958	47 552	20 762	2 034	– 410	– 3.9	– 1.6
1959	50 490	21 883	1 753	490	– 1.8	– 0.7
1960	51 892	22 285	596	– 61	+ 0.9	+ 0.3
1961	56 417	25 887	– 8	– 936	+ 2.4	+ 0.7
1962	59 140	26 402	2 163	297	– 1.9	– 0.5
1963	64 885	28 307	5 415	1 965	– 5.3	– 1.4
1964	72 503	30 497	5 396	583	– 5.6	– 1.3
1965	80 679	31 119	6 917	113	– 9.4	– 2.0
1966	88 616	32 677	5 815	218	– 7.7	– 1.6
1967	104 433	40 763	12 964	6 642	– 12.1	– 2.5
1968	114 136	45 652	10 711	5 757	– 7.4	– 1.4
1969	115 767	45 238	2 460	1	+ 2.5	+ 0.4
1970	123 174	47 746	6 494	1 107	– 5.8	– 0.9
1971	137 095	49 833	13 926	1 441	– 11.9	– 1.6
1972	154 187	54 465	15 380	3 976	– 18.8	– 2.3
1973	165 312	57 114	11 398	2 677	– 7.1	– 0.8
1974	188 811	69 420	22 459	9 475	– 24.7	– 2.5
1975	253 142	107 094	53 627	29 925	– 63.8	– 6.2
1976	292 253	125 344	46 749	25 783	– 48.0	– 4.3
1977	325 217	147 903	31 685	21 819	– 31.2	– 2.6
1978	365 457	176 202	40 672	26 088	– 40.3	– 3.1
1979	409 102	201 517	43 455	25 658	– 46.1	– 3.3
1980	466 288	228 294	55 198	26 797	– 56.5	– 3.8

1) Fiscal years up to 1959: April 1 to March 31; 1960 trunk fiscal year of 9 months; since 1961 fiscal year coincident with calendar year.

2) The date of the survey of debt statistics was up to 1959 March 31 of the following year; since 1960 it is December 31.

3) Federal Government, Länder Governments, Local authorities, ERP Special Fund and Equalisation of Burdens Fund, but excluding Social Security Funds.

Source: BMF

on that day, German government debt totalled RM 400 billion (3). These debts remained formally in existence, but no further interest payments were made and so they had become worthless.

By far the greatest part of the Third Reich's debts were held by the Reichsbank (the Central Bank of the Third Reich), the banks and the financial intermediaries such as the building and loan associations and the insurance companies. These institutions had maintained correspondingly large deposits as balancing entries on their liabilities side. On June 21, 1948 the Deutschmark took over from the Reichsmark by means of the so-called Currency Reform. As a result of the Currency Reform the claims of the debtors of the Third Reich were also declared null and void.

The deposits with the banks, building and loan associations and insurance companies were reduced to a level corresponding to an adequate supply of money. After the contraction of their liabilities, which were from now on calculated in DM, these institutions' needs for balancing items on the asset side of their balance sheets were supplied by so-called 'equalisation claims' on the public purse. DM 16.9 billion of these 'claims' (4) were distributed at this time. This was the starting point of government indebtedness at the beginning of the Federal Republic's history. In the early 1950s the central, regional and local authorities, primarily the Federal Authorities, were burdened with a further DM 13.7 billion in foreign debts as a result of the London Debt Agreement.

The foreign debts and the old debts formed by far the greatest part of the central, regional and local authorities' debts until well into the 1960s. For a long time no significant budget deficits were covered by resources borrowed in the market (5). The proportion of debts from resources borrowed in the market for the Federal Government amounted to approximately 12 per cent in 1955 and 15 per cent in 1960.

In the 1950s and 1960s the government had therefore never contracted significant new debts. In fact, the population was accustomed to this and was content with it. From 1953 to 1955 the Federal Government had even accumulated reserves to the tune of approximately DM 7 billion – the so-called 'Julius tower' (6).

The accumulation of this surplus is nowadays occasionally praised as a symbol of what a virtuous Finance Minister can do, although on closer inspection it can be seen that this hoarding was probably nothing but the result of bad planning (7). Throughout the 1950s and 1960s there were only two years – 1967 and 1968 – when public sector borrowing reached a level worth mentioning, but even then it was minimal compared with the current level of borrowing. In 1967 the German economy entered the first recession of the post-war period. The Federal Government then attempted to move the economy out of the depths of the depression by the use of two expenditure programmes to support investment and building which were financed by borrowing. The experts certainly had to use considerable persuasion to make the government finally indulge for once in some borrowing and not adjust it's expenditure in a recession to the shrinking tax revenue (8). By 1969 the government's net borrowing had once again been reduced to practically nothing.

The public was therefore accustomed to a government which did not incur debts of any consequence and which basically balanced its budget. It is understandable that they reacted with considerable concern when the situation underwent a fundamental change and the government suddenly became a large borrower. The extent of this concern becomes understandable if one considers certain figures. From 1970 to 1974 the regional authorities borrowed more from the capital markets than in the whole of the previous 20 years. There was a further jump in 1975. The new borrowing of the year was 2 1/2 times as large as that of 1974. Just during the 3 years 1975–77 the central, regional and local authorities incurred more new internal debts than in the whole of the previous 25 years. The increase in Federal borrowing was more rapid than that of the regional and local authorities. The new borrowing by the Federal Government in 1975 almost equalled the total borrowing in the previous 25 years.

Public sector borrowing in the capital markets as a proportion of its total indebtedness was also increasing rapidly. For the Federal Government it amounted to 58 per cent in 1975 and reached 95 per cent by 1980. Similar proportions apply to the borrowings by Länder governments: 18 per cent in 1955, 35 per cent in 1960, 90 per cent in 1975 and 96 per cent in 1980.

The public could not fail to remember that twice this century government borrowing had risen sharply – admittedly as a result of war financing. On both occasions the government was unable to keep its promise that its securities were of lasting value. Such worries could equally be reawakened by a large increase in government indebtedness, which is caused by factors other than rearmament and war. And there is certainly some reason for this.

The reasons for the large increase in the financial deficits of the public sector in 1975 could perhaps still be made to appear plausible. In that year the Federal Republic, like other industrialised countries, had moved into a deep recession. The lessons of anti-cyclical fiscal policy suggest that falls in tax revenue caused by the recession should be compensated for by borrowing. It was also advisable to set in motion government programmes to support investment and to increase employment, which should also be financed by borrowing. The same lessons also suggest that these budget deficits should be cut back when the economic situation improves again. Initially this was also attempted. In 1977 the budget deficit of the regional authorities was only half as high as in 1975. However, it is possible, but not certain, that the public authorities proceeded too quickly in consolidating their deficits. The Council of Experts calculated that in 1977 fiscal policy exerted a contractionary effect on economic development. Problems also developed in that year with the movement out of the recession and it seemed reasonable to connect this with the course of fiscal policy, even though the evidence for this is not conclusive. There was sharp criticism of the public authorities which certainly may have been responsible for the governments' subsequent expenditure behaviour.

In the years since 1977 continually higher deficits were incurred in good years and bad years alike. The government did not even use the prosperous economic conditions of 1979 and 1980 to slow down the speed of its new borrowing. If politicians explained that even in 1980 the need of public authorities for credit is determined by the needs arising from economic conditions, this may show great courage but certainly not a great deal of insight into matters. Occasionally the high deficits were also justified by the argument that the government had to prepare for growth in the 1980s. But as far as we know the prospects for growth in the 1980s have not been improved by large government borrowing. On the contrary, strong doubts must be raised as to whether 'forced' government expenditure can still exert an expansionary effect on private industry under prevailing conditions, a consideration to which we shall return later. We shall therefore concentrate on an economic evaluation of the high level of debt and, connected with this, the question of what should be consolidated.

3

It is certainly a difficult task to answer the question of how high the 'right' level of government indebtedness should be. There are, however, a few reliable clues which may help to answer this question.

It is a characteristic of a growing economy that individuals' monetary resources increase continuously. This means that the supply of money looking for investment opportunities to economic entities which demand credit, will also increase continuously. The government can and should make use of this. If private individuals have got used to holding a certain proportion of their growing wealth in the form of claims on the government, then government indebtedness can increase at approximately the same rate as that of private sector wealth. The Council of Experts expressed this as follows: If monetary assets are increasing and if the government increases its indebtedness at the same rate, then by selling claims against itself it is only making use of just that part of monetary resources which, as it were, was intended for it anyway (9). There is therefore no objection to the mere fact that government indebtedness increases continuously and also that the annual new indebtedness, that is the public sector borrowing requirement, is also increasing continuously. The aim of consolidation is therefore *not* the complete elimination of budget deficits and certainly not the *net repayment* of existing government debts. The decisive question is that of the *speed* of the increase in government indebtedness; this is where the task of consolidation starts.

The Council of Experts has introduced the concept of structural deficits into the discussion of the need for consolidation in the government budgets (10). It has become clear that this concept gives a solid analytical basis for quantifying the need for consolidation and it has therefore been widely used.

The concept is based on two main ideas:

(i) That part of the central, regional and local authorities' budget disequilibria which is cyclically induced is not considered part of the need for consolidation because it automatically disappears with the normalisation of economic conditions and a return to normal use of productive capacity.

(ii) Normal indebtedness which accrues to the government because of an upward trend of monetary assets is not considered part of the need for consolidation either. Based on calculations of the average debt behaviour of the West German public sector in the 1960s and 1970s, the Council of Experts considered as normal borrowing an annual borrowing by the government which amounted to approximately 1 per cent of overall productive capacity, measured at current prices (capacity orientated borrowing). There is, of course, an element of arbitrariness in this figure, and so the Council of Experts expressly talks of it as a contribution to the discussion (11).

The concept therefore assumes that at times of normal use of overall productive capacity, the outstanding debt and the public sector deficit should grow at the some rate as nominal productive capacity. When capacity is under-utilised there is a cyclically induced decrease in tax revenue which should be compensated for by additional borrowing and not by adjustment on the expenditure side of the public authorities' budgets. Extra cyclically induced expenditure is also considered as belonging to the part of the budget disequilibrium determined by economic conditions. The Council of Experts here includes the extra expenditure which arises as a result of higher payments for unemployment benefits. If normal indebtedness and cyclically induced components are deducted from the actual budget deficit of the central, regional and local authorities, one obtains the structural deficit.

This can usefully be clarified by a calculation which is shown in Table 14.3. Structural deficits for all the central, regional and local authorities of the Federal Republic of Germany have been calculated for the years 1974 to 1982. Let us take 1981 as an example. The financial deficit of the central, regional and local authorities amounted to approximately DM 72.5 billion in that year (12). It is made up as follows:

The capacity orientated borrowing, that is the normal new borrowing, which, based on the Council's assumptions, is DM 16.3 billion.

The cyclical component of the budget deficit is DM 15.1 billion and is a result of the West German economic recession. This figure is the sum total of the fall of DM 11.1 bil-

Table 14.3

Structural deficit of all public authorities in the Federal Republic of Germany

DM billion

	1974	1975	1976	1977	1978	1979	1980	1981	1982
(1) Financial balance	– 21,0	– 56,9	– 37,0	– 21,8	– 31,0	– 39,3	– 54,0	– 72,5	– 63,5
(2) Additional (+) tax revenues or shortfalls (–) due to changes in capacity utilisation	– 5,3	– 17,3	– 11,7	– 10,6	– 6,2	+ 1,5	– 0,2	– 11,1	– 15,5
(3) Potential oriented borrowing	5,5	7,8	10,8	13,1	13,4	14,2	15,3	16,3	17,5
(4) Additional expenditures due to changes in capacity utilisation	–	9,2	–	–	–	–	1,8	4,0	5,5
(5) Correction item[1)]	–	–	–	–	–	–	–	–	7 0
(6) Structural deficit	– 10,2	– 22,6	– 14,5	+ 1,9	– 11,4	– 26,6	– 36,7	– 41,1	– 32,0

1) The Council of Economic Experts assesses a 'normal' distribution of the profit of the Bundesbank at DM 3 billion. A higher distribution does not reduce the structural deficit. Therefore 7 billion of the planned distribution of DM 10 billion have to be added to the financial balance.

Source: Council of Economic Experts and authors' calculation.

lion in tax revenue (actual tax revenue is this figure less what would have been collected if there had been normal utilisation of 97.25 per cent of the productive capacity) and DM 4 billion arising from cyclically induced extra expenditure (which is that part of the Federal Government's grants to the Federal Labour Office explainable by the increase in unemployment benefits because of an increase in underemployment). If the normal new indebtedness of DM 16.3 billion and the cyclical component of DM 15.1 billion are deducted from the actual budget deficit of DM 72.5 billion, we obtain the structural deficit of DM 41.1 billion. The task of consolidation is to reduce this structural deficit.

The purpose of the operation is to regain some freedom of action for the government and also to improve general conditions for the private sector in respect of more investment and more innovation. The very size of the central, regional and local authorities' budget deficits for 1981 suggests that they had a highly expansive effect on the economy – the Council of Experts estimated it to be almost DM 50 billion (13). In previous years government budgets had never contained anything approaching such a high impulse. The very fact that the West German economy still moved into a deep recession proves that the conditions, under which government expenditure financed by borrowing actually has an expansionary effect, hardly exist any more, or perhaps do not exist at all. The government has itself contributed significantly to this situation. Economic recovery is handicapped by growing doubts about the solidity of government finances. The extensive use of finance, as well as the expectation of future increases in taxes and painful stabilisation measures have a depressing effect; these repercussions of fiscal policy reduce the expansionary effect and can even more than compensate for it. This seems to characterise the present situation. The government's scope for action has been exhausted and this has happened at a time when it is more needed than ever. The question is, how did this happen?

4

As the figures show, there can hardly be any doubt that the present need for consolidation has been building up since 1977.

The development was greatly affected by government programmes to improve – as it was called – economic conditions and growth. From 1977 to 1980 no less than five such programmes were adopted. The programmes consisted of extra expenditure and reductions in tax revenue because of tax relief. The total burden on the government's budgets resulting from these programmes from 1977 to 1980 amounts to DM 61.4 billion. Their success has been disappointing; the actual effect on the economy and economic growth lagged far behind expectations, and the programmes have led to structural deficits which have become an increasing burden. The programmes will not be described in detail here, but it is worth mentioning a few characteristics.

The story begins on March 23, 1977 when a programme to help growth and the environment was adopted, the so-called 'Programme for Future Investment'. This programme provided for expenditure of DM 16 billion distributed over the years 1977 to 1981 to be used primarily for government building projects. By far the greatest part of the expenditure took place between 1978 and 1980. This was a period when private demand for building was also extremely high. The existing capacity in the construction industry was clearly overstretched. But not even price increases by the construction companies, which were an attempt to ward off demand, succeeded in making the government temporarily withhold expenditure from the programme or at least provisionally cut their expenditure markedly. The effects on the exceptionally large increase in construction prices are plain to see and the real economic effect was undermined.

In 1977 the tax burden on private individuals and companies was decreased twice, by the Tax Amendment Act of June 16, 1977 and the Tax Relief Bill and Investment Promotion Aid of October 27, 1977. The effect of the relief was intended to be DM 8.8 billion for private individuals (including the increase in child benefit) and DM 2.7 billion for companies. The main concern, particularly of the second act, was to reduce the government's share of the national product and to create more room and incentives for the activities of private individuals. This concern was widely accepted. If, however, it had been carried through to its logical conclusion the government would have had to reduce its claims on productive capacity and carry out corresponding cuts on the expenditure side of its budget. This did not happen.

It was even more serious for the budgetary position of the central, regional and local authorities when a 'Package to increase demand and to improve economic growth' was passed on November 17, 1978. This law provided for a further burden on government budgets totalling DM 16.8 billion. This programme consisted of a mixture of reductions of direct taxes, increases of indirect taxes, measures to assist families and additional public expenditure. This certainly did not take place without a certain amount of pressure by the most important industrialised countries. At the World Economic Summit in July 1978 the Federal Government had made the concession that it would enact an anticyclical programme of approximately 1 per cent of GNP ('Locomotive Concept') as its contribution to the recovery of the world economy. It would probably have been very difficult to oppose the wishes of our most important trading partners, but it certainly came at a most untimely point for the German economy. In mid 1978 economic conditions had started to improve of their own accord, and this resulted in the boom conditions of 1979.

On July 4, 1980 the Federal Government also passed a Tax Relief Law, from which private households benefited by DM 14.5 billion and firms by DM 1.9 billion. The majority of the relief fell in 1981, and this is added to the large decrease in tax revenue caused by the recession.

If one looks retrospectively at the above-mentioned measures to improve economic conditions and growth, then it is clear that from the point of view of individuals there is probably very little cause to criticise the way the income side of the government budget was formed. The various tax relief measures have partly counteracted the increase in tax revenue caused by inflation and have made the progressive effects of the tax system appear more tolerable. There has been no decisive change in the tax quota, that is, the proportion of the tax revenue of the overall budget to GNP. It has declined from 24.9 per cent in 1977 to 24.1 per cent in 1981 but it is still higher than at the beginning of the 1970s when at times it was less than 23 per cent.

It is clear that the fall in the tax quota occurred partly as a result of tax relief measures which were in themselves contradictory and caused further anomalies in the tax system. This certainly had something to do with the fact that social matters were given higher priority. This also does not correspond to what would have been advisable from the point of view of achieving stability. For the idea of supporting economic conditions would have suggested changing the tax system so as to provide for greater economic growth. On the other hand, it is clear that these tax relief measures contributed to an easing of tension in wage negotiations. A larger increase in deductions would probably have led to higher wage demands by wage and salary earners, and would not have allowed an easing of the conflict over distribution.

It is the expenditure side of the budget that should be criticised. The tax relief measures should logically have been followed by corresponding adjustment of expenditure. This would have required that rates of increase of the central, regional and local authorities' expenditure would have been less than the growth of GNP, at least while favourable economic conditions prevailed. It would certainly be very laborious to investigate the validity and urgency of the justification for every single type of expenditure. But the increasing complaints about the misuse of the government's supply of services and the many indications of opportunities for cuts in the important subsidised areas may show that the government did not fully exploit its potential for restraint or at least considered these rather timidly.

Whatever the case may be, a neutral and objective observer cannot concern himself with being right or having been right. Nevertheless those observers may feel vindicated who in earlier years pointed out that the government would not have the scope to incur debts in exactly those years in which it would be particularly necessary if it did not attack the problem of reducing the deficit in time. At any rate as a result of the course of fiscal policy in past years the need for consolidation has now moved into the centre of discussion at a time when the pure lesson of fiscal policy must actually suggest the opposite of a reduction of budget deficits. This makes the path to consolidation particularly stony and raises the question of how we can get out of an exceptionally unfortunate situation.

5

The structural deficit can be reduced both by cutting expenditure and by increasing taxation. Both ways admittedly have different consequences for the economy. Increases in taxes reduce individuals' incentives for achievement. The tax quota, as already mentioned, is approximately 24 per cent; contributions to social and pension insurance funds are approximately 15 per cent of GNP. Together with the burden on incomes arising from quasi-governmental special taxes, of which there are many, there is a tax quota for the whole economy of approximately 40 per cent (14). In addition there are the contributions to health insurance companies which have already been increased considerably in recent years and which will increase still further in the future, as the increase in expenditure in the health sector itself cannot be strictly controlled. The great majority of the population is of the opinion that the limits of the tax burden have been reached. The majority of experts as well as the Federal Government also believe that taxes should not be increased again. Consolidation will therefore have to start on the expenditure side of the government budget.

The Council of Experts has put up a plan for consolidation for discussion (15). Starting from its concept of the structural deficit it suggests reducing the deficit of the total government budget by DM 40 billion. In consideration of the economic situation the consolidation should be spread over four years. It considers the cuts of September 1981 to be sufficient consolidation for 1982 as they will cause a reduction of the structural deficit in 1982 of approximately DM 9 billion to approximately DM 32 billion. For the years after that the Council of Experts suggests that there should be further consolidation of DM 8 to 10 billion per year up to and including 1985. In order to achieve this the expenditure of the total government budget should rise each year by 2 per cent less than the growth in nominal productive capacity which is estimated to be 5.5 per cent. The government quota, i.e. the proportion of expenditure in the total government budget to productive capacity measured at prevailing prices will decrease every year by approximately 0.6 per cent from 33 per cent in 1981 to 30.6 per cent in 1985. It would then have reached the 1974 level.

The quantitative aspects of this proposal may seem very plausible. The Council of Experts has admittedly not expressed an opinion on what kinds of expenditure should be reduced and by what extent. Neither are there any indications of how the reduction in the deficit should be distributed between the individual regional authorities. The distribution of the burden of consolidation is a real problem in a federal state in which budget deficits are made at all levels – Federal Government, Länder governments and local authorities. Furthermore, it remains uncertain whether success will be achieved in fixing government budgets four years in advance. Certainly nothing like this is foreseen in present budget law. Because of these objections some observers do not hold out much hope that the Council of Experts' proposal will be realised.

There still remains the question of how, in concrete terms, the situation will progress. A first round of consolidation has been started with the cuts of September 2–3, 1981 after the pressure of circumstances had become overwhelming. In the middle of 1981 it became obvious that the Federal Government's deficits for 1982 could reach the DM 50 billion level and the deficit for the total budget could be around DM 80 billion. One major contributory factor was that, contrary to expectations, the tax reductions in 1981 had not been accompanied by compensatory reductions in expenditure. Another factor was that in the planning of the budget for 1981 some expenditure estimates had been too low. The really dramatically deteriorating budgetary situation therefore necessitated the immediate introduction of counter-measures.

The package of measures of September 2–3, 1981 consists of reductions in expenditure, increases in taxes and some measures in the area of employment policy. The reductions in expenditure, in so far as they require changes to laws, amount to approximately DM 9.5 billion. They provide for significant reductions in the provisions of the Labour Promotion Act. (Unemployment benefit was admittedly not touched.) Furthermore, child benefit is reduced (child benefit had been raised again with effect from January 1, 1981; this increase is now dropped). There was further relief when contributions to the Federal Labour Institute were increased from 3 per cent to first 3.5 per cent and then, by a decision of October 26, 1981, to 4 per cent of the incomes liable for calculation of contributions. In return the contributions to pension insurance were reduced by half a per cent, restricted to the years 1982 and 1983.

The tax increases should bring about a reduction of the Federal budget deficit of approximately DM 2.5 billion in 1982. The largest contribution is made by the increase in the tax on tobacco and there are also some tax advantages which have been reduced or cancelled. The employment policy measures in the package consist of an improvement in depreciation opportunities and of further grants to companies in the steel industry. There were serious arguments within the coalition government about the financing of the additional expenditure. Influential forces wanted to finance the employment policy expenditure of the programme by an addition to income tax, the so-called supplementary tax. Others pointed out that the course of budgetary policy had not exactly been consistent, if, as had happened, incomes were relieved of taxes in 1981, then subjected to extra taxes in 1982 and simultaneously a promise was made that there would be a reduction in taxes to offset the progressive effect. These forces eventually prevailed, but perhaps only temporarily. There is still discussion of passing an employment programme even though it will be an extra burden on the budgetary situation. It will therefore probably be a question of finding measures to promote employment which do not affect expenditure directly.

It is an integral element of the decisions of September 2–3, 1981 that the Federal Budget will be topped up by using more than DM 10 billion of the Bundesbank's profit. No objections will be made to transferring the profits *per se*; the important question, however, is the amount. The fact that despite all the apparently so painful and far-reaching cuts the Federal budget deficit would in 1982 have once again been larger than in 1981 if the Finance Minister had not been able to include approximately DM 10 billion profits from the Bundesbank as a receipt on his books, shows once again how serious the dilemma is. In this connection it must be admitted that cyclically determined expenditure which is not included in the concept will account for the largest part of the expected deficit for 1982.

The cuts of 1981 are basically designed so as to continue to have an effect up to 1985, but they certainly do not bear witness to a consistent strategy of consolidation. There is as yet no concrete evidence that any success has been achieved. The expenditure of the Federal Government should therefore, according to the fiscal plan, only grow at 4 per cent per year, that is 1.5 to 2 per cent less than the expected nominal national product. At present there has been no indication of which expenditure the government can cut correspondingly strongly in order to achieve this goal. There is widespread scepticism at present (16) even in the Fiscal Planning Council that the growth in expenditure, particularly of the Federal Government, will once again be out of control by 1982. For this reason there are many indications that by the autumn of 1982 the pressure of circumstances will become so great that cuts will again be on the agenda.

6

A sober and objective view of the situation leads to the judgement that the problems would only be made worse if we fail to make a substantial contribution to the consolidation of the government budgets.

If the government cannot regain the confidence that it will overcome its problems, it will continue to have to fear that because of counter-productive repercussions, budget deficits will not have those effects which text-books lead us to expect. It does not suit the economic climate, *per se,* but the intention may well be helped by the unpleasantness of the general economic situation; if the government is compelled to take action because the coffers are empty it can justify restraint in expenditure to the citizens more convincingly than if it waits until revenue is received in greater quantities. If sufficient money is available, there is more than enough resistance against being thrifty with money. There is therefore no way round preparing to approach the task of consolidation in a way that inspires confidence. This also includes creating the expectation that the precept of restraint in expenditure will not be forgotten as soon as tax revenue becomes more plentiful. The qualitative aspects are also important; the structure of government expenditure and the creation of resources has an important contribution to make to satisfactory growth of the private sector.

Translated from the German by Bruce Gibbons

Footnotes

(1) This figure is based on the classification of the financial statistics. The net borrowing according to the classification of the National Accounts can differ from the financial statistics; however, the differences are small.

(2) See Part 5 for the details of the cuts.

(3) Pfleiderer (1978), 14.

(4) The 'equalisation claims' increased later as the process of finally confirming the converted balance sheets of a number of financial institutions took more than 10 years. Repayment stretched over 25 to 47 years according to the quantity of equalisation claims. As a result of the Act on the Redemption of Equalisation Claims of 1956 a fund was set up at the Bundesbank (the Central Bank of the Federal Republic) to buy Equalisation claims. According to paragraph 27 of the Bundesbank law DM 40 billion up to 1979 and from 1980 DM 30 billion of the net profit of the Bundesbank were paid into this fund. Up to the end of 1980 DM 5.3 billion of the equalisation claims have been redeemed. It is expected that all the equalisation claims will have been redeemed by 1992–93.

(5) German financial statistics show the public sector's domestic debts under the item 'debts from resources borrowed in the market' which have been incurred since June 21, 1948, the date of the Currency Reform.

(6) The Julius Tower is situated in Berlin-Spandau. It was used as a depository for compensation payments made by France to the German Government after the 1870-71 war.

(7) On May 1, 1955 the Federal Republic became a member of NATO and this meant that it had to create its own army. In 1953 and 1954 the Federal Government had created special reserve funds totalling DM 4 billion in order to be prepared for unforeseen expenditure arising from the building up of the Federal Army. Considerable sums had already been included in the budget plan for 1955 for armed forces. The schedule for building up the Federal Army could not, however, be adhered to. The budgetary expenditure therefore lagged behind what had been calculated, and reserve funds were created involuntarily. The accumulation of these funds did not only cause praise. The then Finance Minister was succeeded by Etzel, who used the slogan of the 'dictate of the empty coffers' (Etzel, 1959, 114). Today something completely different would be understood by empty coffers.

(8) See Sachverständigenrat (1967/68), 74 ff.

(9) Sachverständigenrat (1974/75), 162.

(10) Sachverständigenrat (1975/76), 166 f.

(11) Sachverständigenrat (1981/82), 124.

(12) In the classification of the National Accounts. The Council of Experts has based its calculations on this classification since 1979.

(13) Sachverständigenrat (1980/81), para 370.

(14) Sachverständigenrat, special report (1981), 6.

(15) Sachverständigenrat (1981/82), 160 ff.

(16) The manuscript was completed in the Spring 1982.

References

Etzel, F. (1959), *Gutes Geld durch gute Politik,* Stuttgart.

Pfleiderer, O. (1978), *Von der Reichsmark zur Deutschen Mark.* Mittlerer Neckar, Mitteilungen der Industrie- und Handelskammer 6, 11–14.

Sachverständigenrat zur Begutachtung der gesamtwirtschaftlichen Entwicklung, Jahresgutachten (Annual Report) 1967/68. *Stabilität im Wachstum,* Stuttgart and Mainz 1967.

ibid, Jahresgutachten (Annual Report) 1974/65. *Vollbeschäftigung für Morgen,* Stuttgart and Mainz 1974.

ibid, Jahresgutachten (Annual Report) 1975/76. *Vor dem Aufschwung,* Stuttgart and Mainz 1975.

ibid, Jahresgutachten (Annual Report) 1977/78. *Mehr Wachstum – Mehr Beschäftigung,* Stuttgart and Mainz 1977.

ibid, Jahresgutachten (Annual Report) 1980/81. *Unter Anpassungszwang,* Stuttgart and Mainz 1980.

ibid, Sondergutachten vom 4. Juli 1981 (Special Report of 4th July 1981). *Vor Kurskorrekturen – Zur finanzpolitischen und währungspolitischen Situation im Sommer 1981,* Stuttgart and Mainz 1981.

ibid, Jahresgutachten (Annual Report) 1981/82. *Investieren für mehr Beschäftigung,* Stuttgart and Mainz 1981.

Chapter 15

OPTIMAL STABILISATION POLICIES IN WEST GERMANY AND THE NETHERLANDS*

P. Arestis, S. Holly and E. Karakitsos

1. Introduction

Most western industrialised countries experienced high inflation rates and substantial unemployment in the 1970s. This has led to questions being asked about the appropriateness of using conventional stabilisation policies. The aim of this paper is to consider, in the context of the Fed. Rep of Germany, and the Netherlands, whether it would have been possible to design stabilisation policies which would have attenuated, if only to a limited extent, the rapid rise in the rate of inflation and the level of unemployment during the period under investigation (1973–77), but especially so in the shorter period 1974–76. However, it must be emphasised that, although both countries' inflation and unemployment rates during this period were lower – perhaps more so in the case of the F.R.G. – than those experienced by some of the other industrial countries, they were, nevertheless, higher than those experienced in the 1960s.

To design such a stabilisation policy, an optimisation technique is used to find the minimum of a quadratic cost function subject to the constraints of a nonlinear econometric model. The tentative conclusion of this study is that in both countries a more discretionary monetary policy, used at the right time, would have made it possible to reduce substantially the rise in unemployment while at the same time achieving a lower rate of inflation.

The theoretical underpinnings of two econometric models of the West German and the Netherlands economies are outlined in Section 2. The problem of designing optimal stabilisation policies for the two countries is posed formally in Section 3. In Section 4, the results of a number of optimisation exercises are reported and discussed. Finally, some brief conclusions, drawn from our investigations, are summarised in Section 5.

2. The Models for the Fed. Rep. of Germany and the Netherlands

The two models (1) (listed in Appendices B and C) follow the standard income-expenditure approach to model building with additional sectors for incomes, money, employ-

* The work described here was carried out as part of the joint Programme of Research into Optimal Policy Evaluation at Imperial College of Science and Technology and the London Graduate School of Business Studies. The financial support of the Social Science Council is gratefully acknowledged.

ment, wages and prices. They differ slightly in their degree of disaggregation and in the definitions of certain variables because of differences in the data available for each country.

Given the purpose of this paper it is important to spell out clearly the channels through which policy instruments affect targets and in particular how changing financial conditions affect the behaviour of the private sector. Two main channels can be identified.

The first, which has come to be known as the 'cost of capital' channel, works through changes in the terms upon which credit can be obtained. These terms can of course be altered by changes in financial conditions. The cost of capital is approximated by either the nominal rate of interest or the real rate of interest defined as the nominal rate minus the expected rate of inflation; the expected rate of inflation is approximated for the purposes of this study by the previous period's annualised rate of inflation on the assumption that past experience heavily influences economic agents' expectations about the future (2). The cost of capital, nominal or real, affects all forms of expenditure (investment in plant and machinery, investment in construction, and consumer durable expenditure), so that the two models resemble in this respect the Keynesian paradigm of how the economy works. Changes in the money supply affect interest rates which in turn affect all the types of expenditure referred to above. The second channel is what has been termed in the literature the 'wealth effect' channel. To the extent that wealth influences expenditures, policy-induced changes in the volume or value of wealth would provide a way of 'channelling' the impact of policies. Changes in the stock of money, for example, affect the volume of outstanding liquid assets — used as a proxy for wealth — which influences consumption; changes in the stock of money also affect interest rates which in turn alter the value of wealth, thus again affecting consumption. The channels of fiscal policy are quite conventional. In the West German model government expenditure contributes directly to aggregate demand, while taxes on wages and salaries and taxes on other personal incomes bring about changes in aggregate demand through real disposable income. In the model of the Dutch economy the same effects are recognised. However, as we do not have consistent series on taxes, their disaggregation differs from that of the West German model.

Where the data permitted, consumers' expenditure has been disaggregated into durable and non-durable expenditure. The structure of the consumption equation for non-durable goods and services reflects the life-cycle hypothesis. The basic idea underlying this theory is that the consumption of a representative household 'reflects a more or less conscious attempt at achieving the preferred distribution of consumption over the life cycle, subject to the constraint imposed by the size of the resources occurring to the household over its lifetime' (Modigliani, 1966). This hypothesis expresses consumption as a linear function of expected real disposable income and of net worth, the latter being proxied by 'real liquid assets' (3).

The specification of the equation for durables is substantially different from that of non-durables. The reason is that durables provide a stream of services over a period of time and therefore are more like capital goods. Thus consumers' expenditure on durables is treated along the lines of investment expenditure, which means a stock adjustment or flexible accelerator model. In particular, expenditure on durables is proportional to the difference between the desired (or optimum) and actual stock of durables. The optimum stock is in turn a function of the real rental rate (defined as the price of durables times the user cost of durables). Finally, the real rental rate is a function of expected real disposable income, a measure of the opportunity cost of capital, the expected rate of change of consumers' durables prices and the relative price of durables to that of non-durables.

The disaggregation of consumption into durables and non-durables was possible only in the case of the Netherlands where the results (4) for both equations are satisfactory. We may note, though, that the estimated form for non-durables indicates that the approximation of real net worth by using real liquid assets might be a valid approach to adopt in as much as the influence of real liquid assets is very close to that obtained for real net worth in the case of the USA (chiefly Modigliani, 1975). Furthermore, the unconstrained Almon (see Almon, 1965) long-run consumption response to income confirms that consumers attach more importance to the more recent rather than the more distant past, and also that the 'horizon' turns out to be of the order of sixteen months. The most important channel through which relative prices influence consumers' durables is the expected rate of inflation, with the cost of capital being of secondary importance. Nevertheless, one should bear in mind the fact that the period under investigation is dominated by high inflation rates which partly explains this result. The estimated consumption function in the case of the F.R.G. is equally satisfactory, and notably the 'horizon' turns out to be the same as in the Netherlands.

The specification of the investment-in-dwellings equation follows the work of Kalchbrenner (1972). Investment is assumed to be a function of the profitability of building houses which, in turn, depends upon the relation between the market price of houses and the construction cost. The current price of houses depends on the gross 'rental rate' which is derived by equating the demand for housing stock with the existing stock. The modelling of investment in plant and machinery follows the modified neo-classical approach which takes account of the putty-clay technological constraints (Bischoff, 1971). This hypothesis allows *ex ante* substitution between capital and labour, but recognises *ex post* fixed factor proportions. Investment thus depends on output and relative prices (as in neo-classical theory) but the effect of the latter works gradually as capital wears out, and not as in Jorgenson's (1963) case where the effect of relative prices equals that of output because of an assumed Cobb-Douglas production function.

The results obtained for these equations are satisfactory and suggest the existence of a cost-of-capital channel. They also confirm, in the case of investment in housing, where the response to changes in relative input prices is rapid, that the technology is implicitly putty-putty. For investment in plant and machinery, however, the empirical results support a putty-clay technology. The response to changes in relative prices is slow and of less importance than output.

Changes in stocks are treated as a residual in the income identity in the case of the Dutch economy. This is entirely due to the unavailability of data on this particular variable.

In the case of the West German model the changes in stocks are simply made a function of changes in GNP, the lagged long-term interest rate, and lagged changes in stocks.

The specification of the imports function is also straight-forward. Expenditure on imports depends upon the level of demand and the relative price of imports. Furthermore, because of the consumer durables and capital goods content of imports a partial adjustment hypothesis is introduced.

The sum of the demand components determines GNP which in turn feeds back on various components of the demand for output. The various income categories along with tax rates and transfers determine disposable income. This feeds into consumption and in the case of the Netherlands into investment in dwellings. We should note at this stage an important difference between the two models dictated by the unavailability of data. In the F.R.G. disposable income is defined as in Equation 26 (App. B). Since for the Netherlands this disaggregation was not possible it was decided to determine disposable income via Equation 33 (App. C), where it is simply made a function of the current price value of GDP.

A special feature of the determination of the money stock is that the money supply is assumed to be determined jointly by the combined behaviour of the monetary authorities, the banks and the non-bank public. It is thus hypothesised to be an endogenous variable linked to the monetary base via a multiplier. The monetary base itself is assumed to be at least partly under the control of the authorities. As is well known, the money multiplier is determined by the reserve ratio observed by the banking system, and the ratio between currency and deposits held by the public. Since these two ratios reflect optimum portfolio selection, banks are assumed to respond to changes in the return from lending, as well as the cost of borrowing (i.e. the discount rate). The behaviour of the public is assumed to be influenced by the rate of return paid on bank deposits and on other financial assets, and constrained by the level of income or wealth. When these assumptions are combined and the additional assumption is made that banks as well as the public take time to rearrange their asset portfolio to a change in financial conditions, the money supply equation is finally obtained.

The demand for money equation is based on portfolio theory. The problem of the individual economic unit is to optimally allocate his given wealth among alternative assets, with money being one of them. Thus the demand for money depends on the returns on alternative assets considered and upon income or wealth. Furthermore it is recognised that the adjustment of an individual's portfolio to equilibrium does not occur in any single time period, for it takes time for money holders to become aware of changed conditions and therefore to rearrange their assets. In particular, it is assumed that in any single period only a fraction of the desired difference is in fact adjusted. The demand-for-money equation which this analysis produces can be used, in combination with the money supply equation, to determine the equilibrium rate of interest as that rate which clears the money market. Alternatively, the reduced form for the rate of interest can be estimated directly. This is in fact the method applied here. Thus the monetary sector of the model has an equation for the supply of money and an equation for the rate of interest.

The equation for the term structure of interest rates follows from the 'preferred habitat' theory. The expected return from all bonds, regardless of the term of maturity, will be identical for any given holding period. The return is defined as the sum of cash payments plus expected capital gains; changes in the expected capital gains will then reflect changes in the expected long-term rate which is assumed to depend on the long-run historical long-term rate plus the expected rate of inflation.

The wage rate is derived through a conventional Phillips-type mechanism and it is a function of unemployment, productivity and inflation. The latter variable stands for the effect of anticipated inflation. In other words, anticipated changes in prices lead to an increase in wages independently of any excess demand for labour. On the other hand, any effect of unanticipated inflation on wages is captured through the excess demand for labour; that is, an unanticipated rise in the price level lowers the real wage rate, raises excess demand and through a Phillips curve leads to a rise in wages.

The price equation is derived by assuming a mark-up pricing theory (Lipsey and Parkin, 1970) and a measure of excess demand proxied by the money stock. The main components are therefore labour cost, prices of imported materials, and changes in the money supply. We have also directly estimated an unemployment equation (5) which captures the dynamics of the excess demand in the labour market through the effects of the rate of inflation and the excess demand in the goods market as well as through the feedback effect of wages on unemployment.

Turning now to the results obtained for the price, wage and unemployment equations, an important point has to be stressed regarding the definition of the 'wage' variable, which may well explain some of the differences in the estimation results for the two countries. For the F.R.G. the variable CWSC stands for 'changes in average earnings' whereas for the Netherlands the corresponding variable is 'changes in hourly wage rates' (CWRH). Finally, although the long-run response of wages to prices is smaller than unity, the results cannot reject a vertical long-run Phillips curve.

3. A problem in optimal stabilisation policy

Given the two dynamic non-linear models described in the previous section, the general problem is to choose the values for the policy instruments that minimise the value of a specified cost function for a given period of time (usually finite). For the sake of simplicity the cost function is assumed to be quadratic in deviations of the policy instruments and targets from present desired paths over time.

Formally, representing each of the non-linear models as

$$f_i\,[\underline{y}(t)\,,\,\underline{y}(t-1),\ldots,\underline{y}(t-s),\,\underline{u}(t),\,\underline{u}(t-1),\ldots\underline{u}(t-r)\,] = 0$$

$$i = 1,\ldots,\ell\ ;\ t = 1,\ldots,N \tag{3.1}$$

where there are a maximum of s lagged values of the ℓ endogenous variables and a maximum of r lagged values of the m exogenous variables, the aim is to minimise the quadratic cost function

$$J = \tfrac{1}{2}\sum_{t=1}^{N}\,[\delta\underline{y}(t)^T A(t)\delta\underline{y}(t) \;+\; \delta\underline{u}(t)^T B(t)\delta\underline{u}(t)] \tag{3.2}$$

by choosing the vector of instruments $\{\underline{u}(t),\ 1 < t < N\}$ subject to equation (3.1). The deviations, $\delta\underline{y}(t)$, $\delta\underline{u}(t)$ are defined as

$$\delta\underline{y}(t) = \underline{y}(t) - \underline{y}^d(t)\ ;\ \delta\underline{u}(t) = \underline{u}(t) - \underline{u}^d(t)$$

where the superscript d denotes desired values and

$$A(t) \geqslant 0\ ;\ B(t) > 0 \qquad\qquad t = 1,\ldots,N$$

are the weighting matrices on the targets and instruments respectively. The algorithm used to achieve this is described briefly in Appendix A.

Optimisation techniques have considerable advantages over simulations in uncovering the dynamic structure of an econometric model (Holly et al, 1979, ch. 8). It is important to be aware, however, of the conditional nature of what is calculated as the 'optimal' policy (6). For 'optimal' policy to be better than all other policies, prior specification of the desired paths and the weights in the cost function are necessary because different settings for these will generate different 'optimal' policies.

Despite this important qualification, useful information can be obtained from the model by choosing the desired paths and the weights so as to keep the values of the policy instruments and the targets within broadly acceptable regions.

The results reported in this paper are for a given set of weights (7) and a given set of desired paths covering the period 1973 (Q1) to 1977 (Q4). Needless to say, the sensitivity of the optimal policies to variations in these initial conditions would be of interest. However, in order to keep the results reasonably clearcut comparatively simple optimal control techniques have been applied.

Firstly, monetary policy, represented by the monetary base and the discount rate, has been assigned for both countries to the target 'unemployment' only. This was achieved by placing a zero weight on all the target variables except unemployment, and placing a very large weight on all the instruments except the monetary base and the discount rate. Secondly, the rate of inflation has been included as an additional target. As in Run 1 the monetary base and the discount rate were the policy instruments. Thirdly, fiscal policy (represented by government expenditure) has been used as well as monetary policy. As in the second exercise both inflation and unemployment were the targets.

The period over which the exercises were carried out is of particular interest. Both the F.R.G. and the Netherlands, in line with the majority of industrialised countries, experienced a rapid rise in the level of unemployment combined with high rates of inflation (relative to the preceding twenty-five years). Admittedly, the rise in both the level of unemployment and the rate of increase of prices did slow down during 1977, but only to gain momentum again during the following years. Many explanations have been offered to account for this, ranging from the deflationary consequences of the increase in oil prices by OPEC, the deep structural changes accruing in industrial societies and the increases in the power of Trade Unions to changes in conditions in the labour market. Irrespective of the relative importance of each one of these factors the question we are concerned with is to establish whether the authorities could have made more extensive use of the instruments at their disposal in order to reduce the rate of inflation and unemployment or whether what happened was an inevitable price to pay for previous policy errors.

4. The results

The numerical results reported in this section have to be interpreted with care. The models are being used to study a particular period. In order to set up an exercise to design optimal stabilisation policies for the F.R.G. and the Netherlands, a number of more or less arbitrary assumptions must be made about (i) what is and what is not inincluded in the optimisation and (ii) what are reasonable desired paths for the policy instruments and the targets. For instance, by including the monetary base, the discount rate and government expenditure only as policy instruments we have to assume that other possible instruments, for example taxes, remain on their historical path. Furthermore, the assumption that the desired paths for the policy instruments should be the actual historical paths may inject a strong bias into the results in favour of what actually happened.

Similar problems arise with the choice of the weights in the quadratic objective function. Having constant weights over time does not allow for the possibility that policy makers discount the future, or for the fact that if there is a trend, a weight at the beginning of the period would have a smaller impact (measured at constant values) than at the end of the period.

Bearing in mind these qualifications, the results do provide a useful insight into the structure of the two models, and by implication throw some light upon the kind of policies the West German and Dutch governments might have benefited from during the period 1973 to 1977. The runs reported were designed to ask some fairly straightforward questions about how fiscal and monetary policies could have been better orchestrated in order to achieve certain desirable paths for inflation and unemployment.

In the first run (Run 1 in Figures 15.1–6 for the F.R.G., and Figures 15.7–12 for the Netherlands) the only instruments used were the monetary base and the discount rate, with the level of unemployment as the only target. The desired paths for unemployment are shown in Table 15.1. For the F.R.G. the level of unemployment was allowed to rise until the end of 1975. From there onwards it was required that it be held at a constant 500,000 until the end of the period of optimisation.

For the Netherlands the desired path rises until the end of 1973 after which it was required that it be held at 135,000. Initially the desired value for the level of unemployment for both countries was set at a constant value much closer to the value of the level of unemployment at the beginning of the period (250,000 for the F.R.G., and 110,000 for the Netherlands), but this tended to generate unacceptable paths for the policy instruments. Thus the desired paths actually used for Runs 1 to 3 were chosen so as to allow for the possibility that there were factors other than those represented by the model which were tending to push the level of unemployment up during this period.

From Figures 15.6 and 15.12 we see that the optimal path for unemployment compares well with the simulated path for unemployment (by simulated we mean the path generated by the model when all the exogenous variables are set to their historical values). This, however, is not very surprising since we are assigning our instruments to a single target. The important question is what will be the consequences for the rate of inflation of having unemployment as the sole target. Given that the two models have been constructed on lines common to many income-expenditure models it is reasonable to suppose that a lower level of unemployment would be achieved by monetary expansion and lower interest rates, which would increase aggregate demand and in turn raise employment. However, a consequence of this would be to raise the rate of inflation. In terms of the conventional Phillips curve higher employment can only be obtained by having a higher rate of inflation.

Fed. Rep. of Germany

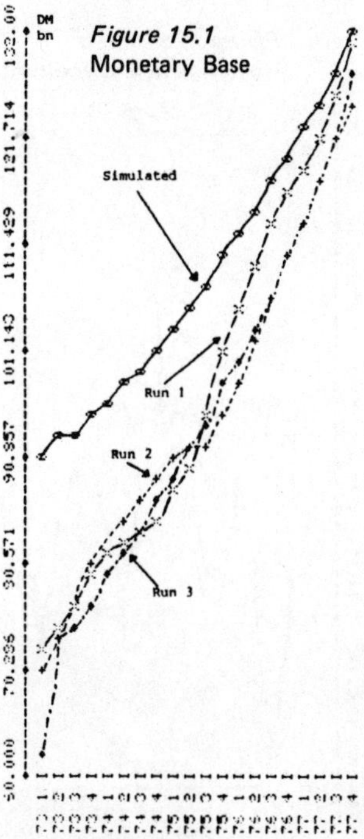

Figure 15.1
Monetary Base

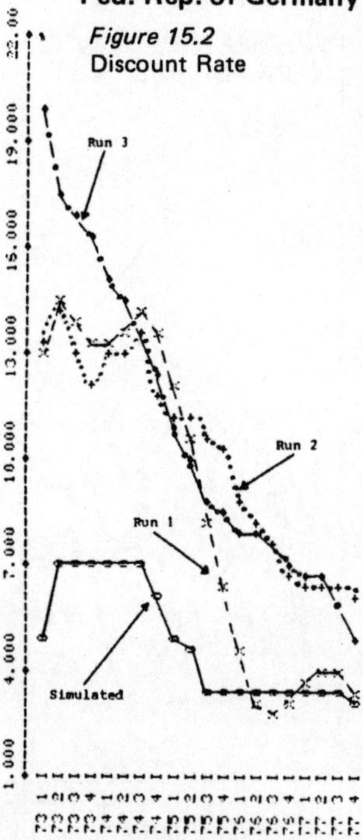

Figure 15.2
Discount Rate

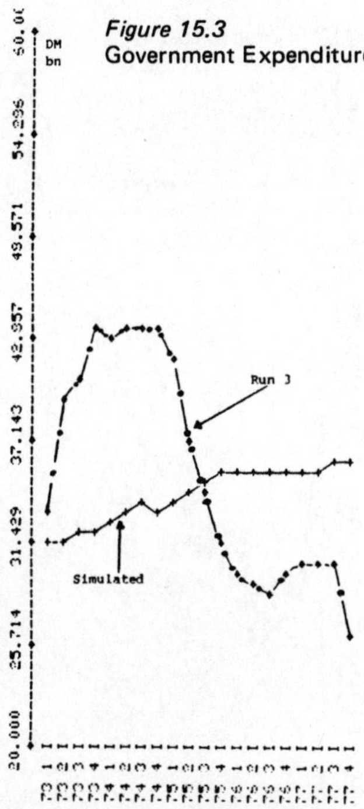

Figure 15.3
Government Expenditure

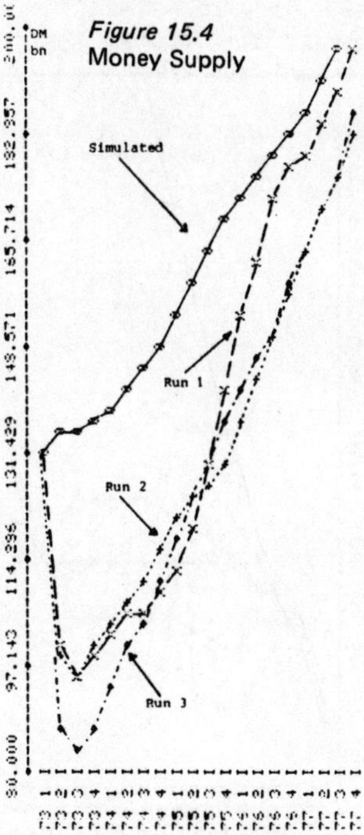

Figure 15.4
Money Supply

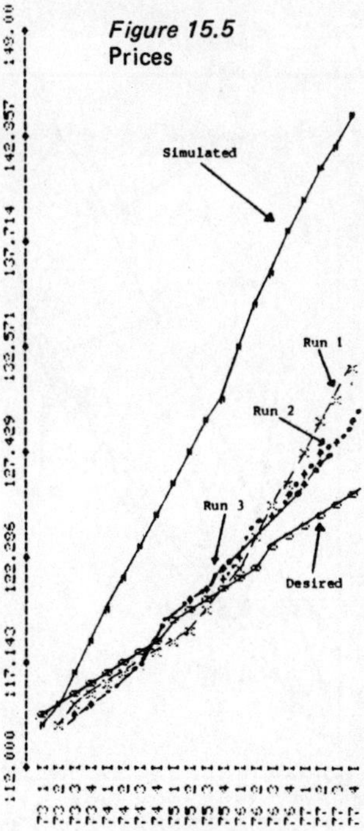

Figure 15.5
Prices

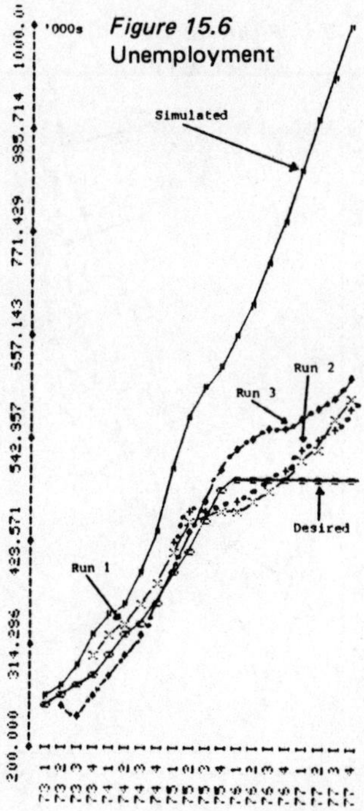

Figure 15.6
Unemployment

Netherlands

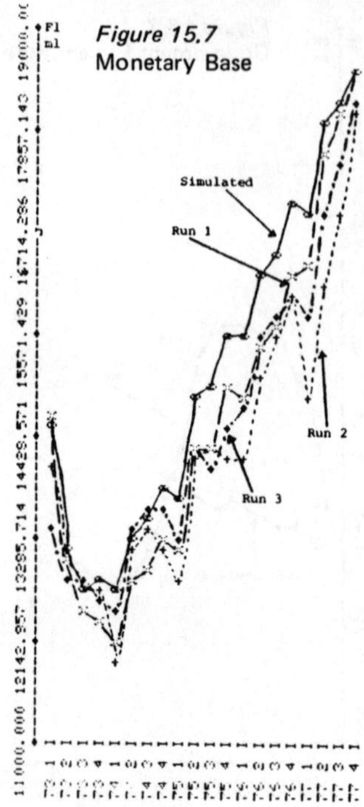

Figure 15.7
Monetary Base

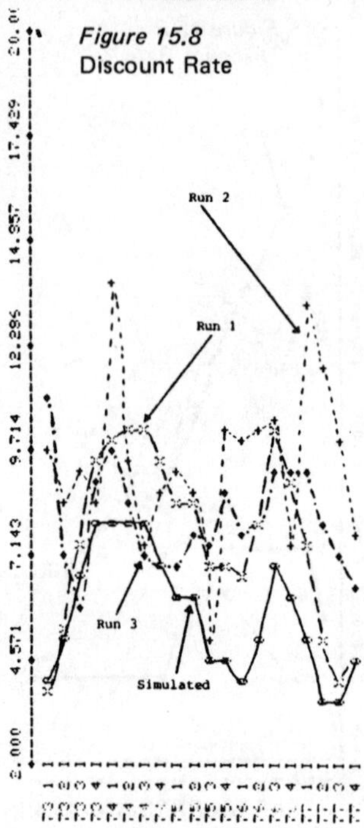

Figure 15.8
Discount Rate

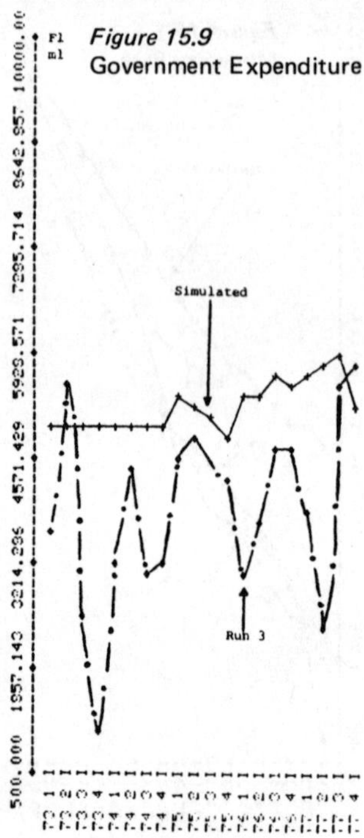

Figure 15.9
Government Expenditure

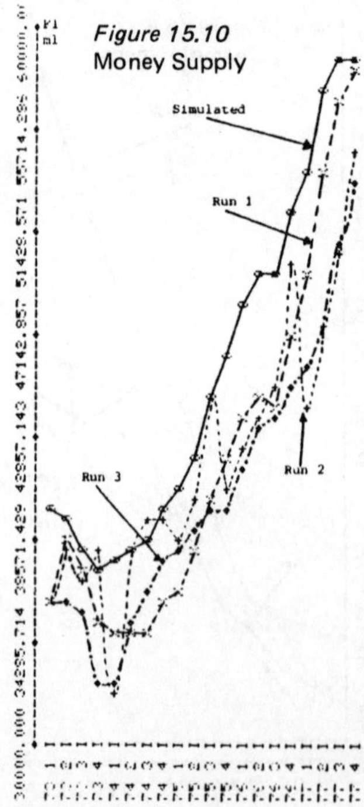

Figure 15.10
Money Supply

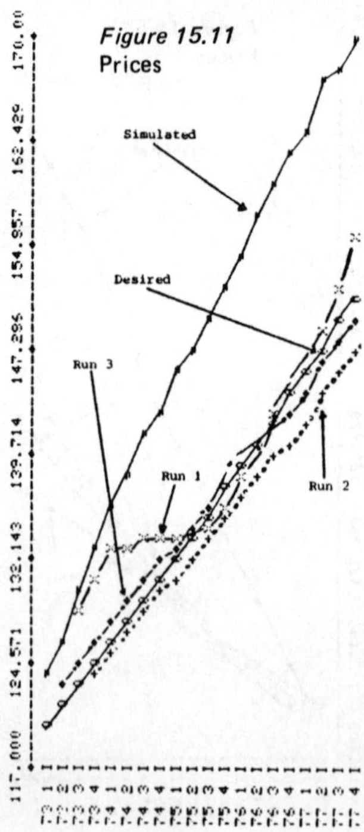

Figure 15.11
Prices

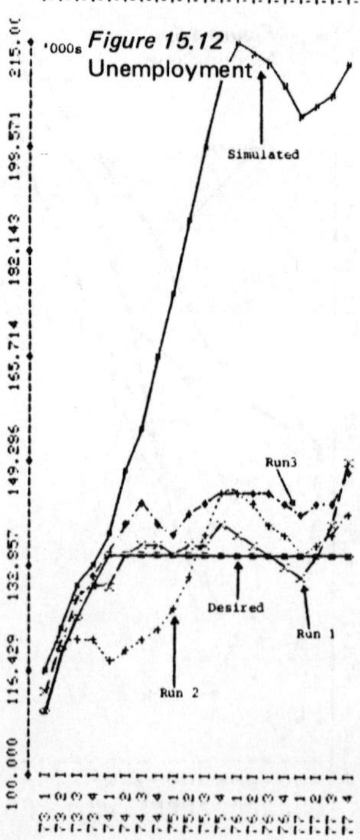

Figure 15.12
Unemployment

Detailed specification of the Objective Function

Fed. Rep. of Germany

Target variables	Prices, %				Unemployment, '000s						
	Desired path	Weights			Desired path				Weights		
		Run 1	Run 2	Run 3					Run 1	Run 2	Run 3
Horizon	I–IV	I–IV	I–IV	I–IV	I	II	III	IV	I–IV	I–IV	I–IV
1973	2	0	5×10^6	5×10^6	250	260	270	280	0.15	0.15	0.15
1974	2	0	5×10^6	5×10^6	300	320	340	360	0.15	0.15	0.15
1975	2	0	5×10^6	5×10^6	390	420	450	480	0.15	0.15	0.15
1976	2	0	5×10^6	5×10^6	500	500	500	500	0.15	0.15	0.15
1977	2	0	5×10^6	5×10^6	600	500	500	500	0.15	0.15	0.15

Policy instruments	Monetary base, bn			Discount rate, %			Government expend., bn		
	Weights			Weights			Weights		
	Run 1	Run 2	Run 3	Run 1	Run 2	Run 3	Run 1	Run 2	Run 3
Horizon	I–IV	I–IV	I–IV	I–IV	I–IV	I–IV	I–IV	I–IV	I–IV
1973/77	0.2	0.2	0.2	1	1	1	10^4	10^3	0.12

1973/77 Desired paths for policy instruments are the corresponding historical paths.

(continued)

Netherlands

Target variables	Prices, %				Unemployment, '000s						
	Desired path	Weights			Desired path				Weights		
		Run 1	Run 2	Run 3					Run 1	Run 2	Run 3
Horizon	I–IV	I–IV	I–IV	I–IV	I	II	III	IV	I–IV	I–IV	I–IV
1973	5	0	5×10^6	5×10^6	110	120	125	130	0.15	0.15	0.15
1974/77	5	0	5×10^6	5×10^6	135	135	135	135	0.15	0.15	0.15

Policy instruments	Monetary base, bn Weights			Discount rate, % Weights			Government expend., bn Weights		
	Run 1	Run 2	Run 3	Run 1	Run 2	Run 3	Run 1	Run 2	Run 3
Horizon	I–IV	I–IV	I–IV	I–IV	I–IV	I–IV	I–IV	I–IV	I–IV
1973/77	10^{-5}	10^{-5}	10^{-5}	1	1	1	10^3	10^3	8×10^{-6}

1973/77 Desired paths for policy instruments are the corresponding historical paths.

It was nevertheless found that the paths for the monetary base, the discount rate, the money stock and the rate of inflation all pointed to an entirely different conclusion. In both countries, even though the individual time profiles differ, the paths for unemployment are brought closer to that desired by a restrictive monetary policy early on in the period (Figures 15.2, 4, 8, 10). This applies particularly to the F.R.G. Given these counter-intuitive results some explanation in terms of the structure of the two models is required. During the construction of the models the only way the rise in the level of unemployment could be accounted for was by including the rates of wage and price inflation as explanatory variables. Moreover, the rate of change of the money stock enters directly into the equation for consumer prices. Any expansion in employment as a result of a monetary expansion is quickly choked off by the effects of higher inflation on employment. To this extent the implications of the model are quite classical. The lags between monetary expansion and higher prices are rather short so that the optimisation results reveal that in the context of these two models, the best way to reduce unemployment over time is to reduce the rate of inflation. The lower rates for both the F.R.G. and the Netherlands are shown in Figures 15.5 and 15.11.

One further qualification ought to be noted here. The optimisation is carried out over twenty time-periods, but the world does not cease to operate after that. With a dynamic model, there are effects of policy changes made during the period of optimisation which are felt afterwards but which are not costed in the quadratic objective function. This means that depending upon the dynamic lag structure of the model, things may be occurring in the latter part of the period of optimisation which make it difficult to draw clear inferences. Apart from extending the period of optimisation, which really only postpones the problem, the only solution is to ignore the final four to eight quarters and to concentrate on the earlier part. Nevertheless, this proviso does not affect the main thrust of the results which flow from the behaviour of the models in the first eight quarters or so.

To explore some other dimensions of the two models a second run is reported in which the rate of inflation is included as a target together with the level of unemployment. A desired annual rate of inflation of 2 per cent was chosen for West Germany and a rate of 5 per cent for the Netherlands. As can be seen from Figures 15.5 and 15.11 this desired path is tracked closely for both countries. In the case of F.R.G. this is achieved by a slightly less contractionary monetary policy early in the period and a more contractionary policy in the second half. In the Netherlands monetary policy becomes more variable as a result of the rate of inflation in this country varying more over this period than in West Germany.

In the final run reported government expenditure was included as a policy instrument. In contrast to the results for monetary policy, this run does not allow us to draw any particulary strong conclusions about the effectiveness of fiscal policy. The most noticeable feature is the much higher degree of variation of government expenditure, (Figures 15.3 and 15.9) when compared with its historical path. In the F.R.G. the path is distinctly cyclical while in the Netherlands the level of government expenditure oscillates quite rapidly. At the same time its use as a policy instrument does not appear to allow the desired paths for inflation and unemployment to be tracked any better. For the Netherlands the average tracking of the two targets is actually worse. In the case of the F.R.G. the tracking of the rate of inflation is little different while for unemployment, the tracking in the first half of the period is better but deteriorates during the second half. Moreover, if fiscal policy is included as an instrument the variation of monetary policy increases, especially in the early part of the period. In both countries optimal monetary policy is more contractionary than when government expenditure is constrained to its historical path.

5. Conclusions

It is important to bear in mind the usual qualifications about the fallibility and incompleteness of econometric models, and the relative ease with which judgements of hindsight can be made. Nevertheless, the results reported in the previous section may have some implications for the conduct of economic policy in the F.R.G. and the Netherlands during the period 1973–1977. They imply that a more discretionary policy, designed to reduce the rate of inflation during the early part of the period, would have made a major contribution towards reducing the rapid rate at which unemployment rose from 1974 to 1976. This unusual conclusion is a result of the particular specification of the sectors of employment and prices in the two models. Although the wages equation by itself implies a conventional trade-off between unemployment and inflation, the Phillips curve relationship is dominated by the fact that a higher inflation rate increases unemployment. Moreover, the rate of increase in the money stock has a direct impact upon the rate of inflation through a change in expectations. The dynamic behaviour of the two models is consequently dominated by monetary influences, with fiscal policy being assigned a comparatively subsidiary role.

An even more important qualification which we should bear in mind is the role of discretionary policy under rational expectations. The importance of rational expectations for the conduct of macroeconomic policy is widely recognised. But there is still not widespread agreement on the extent to which rationally formed expectations vitiate any role for discretion. It is certainly true that in the kinds of model which Sargent and Wallace (1975) have used, anticipated monetary policy has no role to play. However, it is now accepted that in more realistic models there is scope for discretionary policy even when expectations are rational (see Pagan (1980) and Minford (1980) for a rational expectations model of the UK economy in which there is potential scope for policy). However, establishing that discretionary policy is feasible under rational expectations does not mean that we can then proceed as if expectations were adaptive. The reason for this is that if expectations are forward-looking the dynamic responses of the model to both anticipated and unanticipated disturbances – even in the absence of discretionary policy – are going to be quite different.

The incorporation of rational expectations in the two models we have used would be a desirable feature but it would take us well outside the scope of this paper. However, we can mention briefly some work which has been done on formulating macroeconomic policy in a model of the Netherlands in which *consistent* one-step ahead expectations were imposed. By consistent we mean that expectations of inflation and interest rates one step ahead had actually to be consistent with the outturn of the model. This was achieved with a penalty function method (Holly and Zarrop, 1980). The main finding – not unexpectedly – was that although there was room for discretionary policy, the actual form the policy took was quite different from a policy calculated – as in this paper – on the assumption that expectations were adaptive.

Footnotes

(1) See Appendix D for definition of variables and sources of data

(2) However, recent theoretical developments in macroeconomics emphasise the importance of forward-looking, or rational, expectations. The effects on the Netherlands model of having future terms in inflation and interest rates are examined in Holly and Zarrop (1980).

(3) 'Real liquid assets' may be a better variable than net worth in any case. This is so since 'This historical path of household wealth results from (a) planned accumulation, the consequence of the very saving behaviour that wealth is supposed to help explain, (b) unexpected gains or losses due to changes, actual or expected, in the capital stock to earn income for the owners and (c) unexpected gains or losses due to changes in the discount rates at which the market capitalises prospective earnings. These sources of change in wealth should not be expected to have identical effects on consumption' (Tobin and Dolde, 1971, p. 102). One would expect, though, that the impact of 'real liquid assets' on consumption would be more clear-cut.

(4) The period of estimation is 1967 (Q1) to 1978 (Q2). The estimation technique is 'Generalised Least Squares'.

(5) Ideally one would have liked to have derived unemployment as a residual of a demand for, and supply of, a labour model. However, a specification of the demand for labour apart from the well known problems in estimating an employment equation (Henry, 1979) would also require an aggregate capital-stock series which is both unavailable and conceptually vulnerable.

(6) For a fuller discussion of the conditional nature of optimality see Westcott et al (1979).

(7) The process of arriving at this set of weights is usually quite drawnout. To produce 'sensible' results, we start with a set of normalised weights so that each target and instrument is weighted equally. This, however, will not take into account the relative impact of each instrument on each target so that a further process of 'tuning' the cost function has to be followed.

References

Almon S. (1965), 'The Distributed Lag between Capital Appropriations and Expenditures', *Econometrica*, (January).

Bischoff C. W. (1971), 'Business Investment in the 1970s: A Comparison of Models', *Brookings Papers on Economic Activity*, (no. 1).

Henry S.G.B. (1979), 'Employment Equations for the UK', Paper presented to the SSRC Modelling Group, London School of Economics (February).

Holly S. and Zarrop M.B. (1980), 'Calculating Optimal Economic Policies when Expectations are Rational', *Economic Forecasting Unit Discussion Paper no. 58*, London Business School.

Holly S., Rustem B., Westcott J.H., Zarrop M.B. and Becker R. (1979), 'Control Exercises with a Small Linear Model of the UK Economy', Chapter 8 in Holly S., Rustem B. and Zarrop M.B. (eds.) in *Optimal Control for Econometric Models: An Approach to Economic Policy Formulation* (London: Macmillan).

Jorgenson D. W. (1963), 'Capital Theory and Investment Behaviour', *American Economic Review*, (May).

Kalchbrenner J.G. (1972), 'A Model of the Housing Sector', in Gramlich, E.M. and Jaffee D.M. (eds.) *Savings Deposits, Mortgages, and Housing* (ch. 6) (London: D.C. Heath and Co.).

Lipsey R. G. and Parkin J. M. (1970), 'Incomes Policy: A Reappraisal', *Economica* (May).

Minford A.P.L. (1980), 'A Rational Expectations Model of the United Kingdom under Fixed and Floating Exchange Rates', in *The State of Macroeconomics,* Carnegie-Rochester Conference Series on Public Policy.

Modigliani F. (1966), 'The Life Cycle of Saving, the Demand for Wealth and the Supply of Capital', *Social Research* (vol. 33, no. 2, Summer).

Modigliani F. (1975), 'The Channels of Monetary Policy in the Federal Reserve – MIT – University of Pennsylvania Econometric Model of the United States', in Renton G. A. (ed.) *Modelling the Economy,* (London: Social Science Research Council).

Pagan A. (1980), 'Rational Expectations and the Theory of Policy' *Australian National University Working Paper,* no. 24, February.

Rustem B. and Zarrop M. B. (1978), 'Newton-type Methods for the Optimisation and Control of Nonlinear Econometric Models', *PREM Discussion Paper no. 25,* Department of Computing and Control, Imperial College (London).

Sargent T. J. and Wallace N. (1975), 'Rational Expectations, the Optimal Monetary Instrument and the Optimal Money Supply Rule', *Journal of Political Economy,* vol. 83.

Tobin J. and Dolde W. (1971), 'Wealth, Liquidity and Consumption', in *Consumer Spending and Monetary Policy: The Linkages,* Federal Reserve Bank of Boston, Conference Series, no. 5 (June).

Westcott J. H., Zarrop M. B., Holly S., Rustem B. and Becker R. (1979), 'A Control Theory Framework for Policy Analysis', chapter 1 in Holly S., Rustem B. and Zarrop M. B. (eds.) *Optimal Control for Econometric Models: An Approach to Economic Policy Formulation* (London: Macmillan).

Zarrop M. B., Holly S., Rustem B. and Westcott J. H. (1979), 'Control of Large Non-linear Econometric Models: Two Possible Approaches' chapter 7 in Ormerod P. (ed.) Economic Modelling (London: Heinemann).

APPENDICES

Appendix A – An algorithm for the optimisation of nonlinear econometric models

The algorithm used to compute the optimal policies described in the main part of this paper is briefly sketched in this appendix. A much fuller treatment and exposition can be found in Rustem and Zarrop (1978) and Zarrop, Holly, Rustem and Westcott (1979).

A nonlinear deterministic econometric model can be written as

$$f_i(\underline{y}(t), \ldots \underline{y}(t-s), \underline{u}(t), \underline{u}(t-1), \ldots, \underline{u}(t-r)) = 0 \qquad \text{(A.1)}$$
$$i = 1, \ldots, \ell, t = 1, \ldots, N$$

There is a maximum of s lagged values of the ℓ endogenous variables and a maximum of r lagged values of the m policy instruments. There are a total of N time periods over which economic policy is to be analysed. For compactness, define

$$\underline{Y} = (\underline{y}(1)^T, \underline{y}(2)^T, \ldots, \underline{y}(t)^T, \ldots \underline{y}(N)^T)^T \qquad \text{(A.2)}$$

$$\underline{U} = (\underline{u}(1)^T, \ldots, \underline{u}(N)^T)^T \qquad \text{(A.3)}$$

where $\underline{Y}$ is the N-vector of endogenous variables and $\underline{U}$ is the mN-vector of policy instruments throughout the period [1,N]. The model equations can be written

$$\underline{F}(\underline{Y},\underline{U}) = 0 \qquad \text{(A.4)}$$

Given the quadratic objective function (assuming time constant weighting matrices for simplicity)

$$J(\underline{Y},\underline{U}) = ½(\underline{Y}-\underline{Y}^d)^T Q_{\underline{Y}}(\underline{Y}-\underline{Y}^d) + ½(\underline{U}-\underline{U}^d) Q_{\underline{U}}(\underline{U}-\underline{U}^d) \qquad \text{(A.5)}$$

where the superscript d denotes the desired values, the symmetric matrix $Q_{\underline{Y}}$ is assumed to be positive semi-definite and the symmetric matrix $Q_{\underline{U}}$ is assumed to be strictly positive definite, the basic optimisation problem is to choose the endogenous variables $\underline{Y}$ and policy instruments $\underline{U}$ such that (A.5) is minimised subject to the equations of the econometric model throughout the period [1, N].

Thus the problem is

$$\min \left\{ J(\underline{Y},\underline{U}) \mid \begin{bmatrix} \underline{Y} \\ \cdots \\ \underline{U} \end{bmatrix} \in F \right\} \qquad \text{(A.6)}$$

where $F \subset R^{(\ell + m)N}$ is the feasible set of paths defined by (A.4). For any nonlinear econometric model a solution program computes values for the endogenous variables given values for the exogenous variables, such that

$$\underline{Y} = g(\underline{U}) \tag{A.7}$$

The constrained problem (A. 6) can be reformulated as an unconstrained one in the policy instruments only by substituting (A.7) into (A.6).

$$\min \left\{ G(\underline{U}) \mid \underline{U} \in R^{mN} \right\} \tag{A.8}$$

where

$$G(\underline{U}) = J(\underline{g}(\underline{U}),\ \underline{U})$$

The minimum of (A.8) can be found interactively by successively generating suitable descent directions. An algorithm to achieve this has been proposed by Rustem and Zarrop (1978) which is a modified Gauss-Newton of the form

$$\underline{U}_{k+1} = \underline{U}_k - \alpha H^{-1} \nabla G(\underline{U}_k) \tag{A.9}$$

where $\nabla G(\underline{u})$ is an approximation to the gradient of (A.5) und $H_{\underline{u}}$ is an approximation to the Hessian. The subscript k refers to succesive values of the instrument vector. It is assumed that the Hessian is positive definite and the scalar α equal to unity. Since $G(\underline{U})$ is not generally quadratic, α can be chosen to ensure $G(\underline{U}_{k+1}) < G(\underline{U}_k)$. The gradient and approximate Hessian can be written explicitly:

$$\nabla G(\underline{U}_k) = N^T Q_{\underline{Y}}(\underline{g}(\underline{U}_k) - \underline{Y}^d) + Q_u(\underline{U}_k - \underline{U}^d); \qquad H_{\underline{U}} = N^T Q_{\underline{Y}} N + Q_{\underline{U}}$$

where

$$N = \begin{bmatrix} M(o) & o & \dots o \\ M(1) & M(o) & \dots o \\ \cdot & \cdot & \cdot \\ \cdot & \cdot & \cdot \\ \cdot & \cdot & \cdot \\ M(N-1) & M(N-2) & \dots M(o) \end{bmatrix}$$

where $M(\tau)$ is the 1xm matrix of dynamic multipliers at lag τ calculated from the first interval of the period over which policy is to be optimised.

Appendix B – Model of the West German Economy

(1) GNP = COE + INC + INE + CHS + TGEX + EXL – IMP

(2) $$COE = \underset{(2.62)}{10.0930} + \sum_{i=o}^{3} b_{1i}\ RLA\ (t-i) + \sum_{i=o}^{4} d_{1i} RDI\ (t-i)$$

$$- \underset{(2.70)}{0.4838} RLB + \underset{(4.34)}{0.5615} u(t-1)$$

$\sum_{i=o}^{3} b_{1i} = 0.1540$ (2nd d.p. constrained zero at both ends)

$$b_{10} = \underset{(1.89)}{0.0308},\ b_{11} = \underset{(1.89)}{0.0462},\ b_{12} = \underset{(1.89)}{0.0462},\ b_{13} = \underset{(1.89)}{0.0308}$$

$\sum_{i=o}^{4} d_{1i} = 0.6461$ (2nd d.p. constrained zero at t = 5)

$$d_{10} = \underset{(3.42)}{0.2904},\ d_{11} = \underset{(7.95)}{0.1873},\ d_{12} = \underset{(3.24)}{0.1067},\ d_{13} = \underset{(1.04)}{0.0486},\ d_{14} = \underset{(0.36)}{0.0131}$$

$\bar{R}^2 = 0.9961$, D. W. = 2.01, S.E. = 0.6457

(3) $$RLA = \frac{NLA(t-1)}{PCE} * 100$$

(4) $$CHS = \underset{(5.57)}{0.5800}\ CHS\ (t-1) - \underset{(2.96)}{0.4377} RLB(t-3) + \underset{(3.35)}{4.1761} CGNP$$

$\bar{R}^2 = 0.55$, D.W. = 2.01, S.E. = 1.1631

(5) $$CGNP = \frac{GNP}{GNP(t-1)}$$

(6) $$INC = \underset{(1.83)}{3.1916} + \sum_{i=o}^{3} b_{2i} GNP(t-i) + \sum_{i=o}^{4} d_{2i}\ RRB(t-i) + \underset{(11.56)}{0.8033} INC(t-1)$$

$\sum_{i=o}^{3} b_{2i} = 0.0110$ (2nd d.p. unconstrained):

$$b_{20} = \underset{(5.53)}{0.2845},\ b_{21} = \underset{(3.65)}{-0.1670},\ b_{22} = \underset{(4.98)}{-0.2230},\ b_{23} = \underset{(2.23)}{0.1165}$$

$$\sum_{i=o}^{4} d_{2i} = -0.0962 \text{ (2}^{nd}\text{ d.p. constrained zero at both ends):}$$

$$\underset{(3.03)}{d_{20} = -0.0137}, \quad \underset{(3.03)}{d_{21} = -0.0220}, \quad \underset{(3.03)}{d_{22} = -0.0247}, \quad \underset{(3.03)}{d_{23} = -0.0220}, \quad \underset{(3.03)}{d_{24} = -0.0137}$$

$\bar{R}^2 = 0.8839$, D.W. = 2.05, S.E. = 0.7295

(7) RRB = RLB – PPIC(t–1)

(8) PPIC = (PIC/PIC(t–4) –1)∗ 100

$$\text{(9) INE} = \underset{(2.58)}{-17.7853} + \sum_{i=o}^{2} b_{3i}\text{RRB}'(t-i) + \underset{(2.87)}{19.0364}\frac{\text{GNP}}{\text{GNP}(t-1)} + \underset{(25.87)}{0.9403}\,\text{INE}(t-1)$$

$$\sum_{i=o}^{2} b_{3i} = -0.0634 \text{ (2}^{nd}\text{ d. p. constrained zero at both ends)}$$

$$\underset{(1.62)}{b_{30} = -0.0190}, \quad \underset{(1.62)}{b_{31} = -0.0254}, \quad \underset{(1.62)}{b_{32} = -0.0190}$$

$\bar{R}^2 = 0.9439$, D.W. = 1.84, S.E. = 0.4975

(10) RRB′ = RLB – PPIE(t–1)

(11) PPIE = PIE/PIE(t–4)–1)∗ 100

$$\text{(12) IMP} = \underset{(1.55)}{-17.4287} + \sum_{i=o}^{4} b_{4i}\,\text{GNP}(t-i) \underset{(2.25)}{-20.4165}\,\text{IPIM} + \underset{(7.52)}{0.7464}u(t-1)$$

$$\sum_{i=o}^{4} b_{4i} = 0.4352 \text{ (2}^{nd}\text{ d.p. constrained zero at } t = 5\text{):}$$

$$\underset{(2.54)}{b_{40} = 0.1823}, \quad \underset{(7.03)}{b_{41} = 0.1235}, \quad \underset{(3.64)}{b_{42} = 0.0759}, \quad \underset{(1.15)}{b_{43} = 0.0394}, \quad \underset{(0.52)}{b_{44} = 0.0141}$$

$\bar{R}^2 = 0.9846$, D.W. = 2.23, S.E. = 1.1031

(13) IPIM = CPIM/CPCE

(14) CPIM = PIM/PIM(t–1)

(15) PCE = CPCE∗PCE(t–1)

$$MS1 = \underset{(0.99)}{3.2570} + \sum_{i=2}^{4} b_{6i} RTB(t-i) + \underset{(2.59)}{0.6154} REM - \underset{(3.46)}{1.3133} DIS + \underset{(3.87)}{0.6093} MS1(t-1) \quad (16)$$

$$\sum_{i=2}^{4} b_{6i} = 0.4770 \text{ (2}^{\underline{nd}} \text{ d.p. constrained zero at both ends)}$$

$$b_{62} = \underset{(1.29)}{0.1431},\ b_{63} = \underset{(1.29)}{0.1908},\ b_{64} = \underset{(1.29)}{0.1431}$$

$\bar{R}^2 = 0.9948$, D.W. = 2.22, S.E. = 2.5939

$$RTB = \underset{(0.53)}{4.2755} + \sum_{i=o}^{3} b_{5i}\, CMS1(t-i) + \underset{(26.38)}{0.9206} DIS + \underset{(2.99)}{11.7843} CGNP(t-1) \quad (17)$$

$$\sum_{i=o}^{3} b_{5i} = 15.8560 \text{ (2}^{\underline{nd}} \text{ d.p. constrained zero at both ends)}$$

$$b_{50} = \underset{(2.66)}{-3.1710},\ b_{51} = \underset{(2.66)}{-4.7570},\ b_{52} = \underset{(2.66)}{-4.7570},\ b_{53} = \underset{(2.66)}{-3.1710}$$

$\bar{R}^2 = 0.9650$, D.W. = 1.68, S.E. = 0.2957

$$CMS1 = \frac{MS1}{MS1(t-1)} \quad (18)$$

$$RLB = \underset{(2.39)}{-55.5704} + \sum_{i=o}^{2} b_{7i} CPCE(t-i) + \underset{(4.80)}{0.2170} RTB + \underset{(7.88)}{0.6786} RLB(t-1) \quad (19)$$

$$\sum_{i=o}^{2} b_{7i} = 56.500 \text{ (2}^{\underline{nd}} \text{ d.p. constrained zero at both ends)}$$

$$b_{70} = \underset{(2.41)}{16.9500},\ b_{71} = \underset{(2.41)}{22.6000},\ b_{72} = \underset{(2.41)}{16.9500}$$

$\bar{R}^2 = 0.9247$, D.W. = 1.60, S.E. = 0.3745

$$LUNE = \underset{(0.87)}{-4.3370} + \underset{(2.22)}{2.2178} LPCE + \underset{(1.99)}{1.3253} LWSC(t-1) \quad (20)$$

$$\underset{(2.44)}{-2.6800} LGNP(t-1) + \underset{(2.48)}{0.4109} LUNE(t-1) + \underset{(7.06)}{0.7984} u(t-1)$$

$\bar{R}^2 = 0.9790$, D.W. = 2.12, S.E.=0.669

(21) $CWSC = -0.3296 - 0.000008UNE + 0.8710CPCE + 0.4697CPRD$
(0.77) (1.93) (2.30) (3.00)

$\bar{R}^2 = 0.4379$, D.W. = 2.55, S.E. = 0.0073

(22) $PRD = \frac{GNP}{EMP}$

(23) $CPRD = \frac{PRD}{PRD(t-1)}$

(24) $WSC = CWSC * WSC(t-1)$

(25) $CPCE = -0.1542 + 0.04397CMS1 + \sum_{i=o}^{2} b_{27i}CWSC + \sum_{i=o}^{4} d_{27i}CPCE(t-i)$
(1.08) (1.67)

$\sum_{i=o}^{2} b_{27i} = 0.27402$ (2nd d.p. constrained zero at both ends)

$b_{270} = 0.08221, b_{271} = 0.1096, b_{272} = 0.08221$
(4.25) (4.25) (4.25)

$\sum_{i=o}^{4} d_{27i} = 0.8308$ (2nd d.p. constrained zero at both ends)

$d_{270} = 0.1187, d_{271} = 0.1899, d_{272} = 0.2136$
(7.19) (7.19) (7.19)

$d_{273} = 0.1899, d_{274} = 0.1187$
(7.19) (7.19)

$\bar{R}^2 = 0.6149$, D.W. = 1.95, S.E. = 0.00304

(26) $DIN = TWS + OPI + TRP - TXW - TOI - ECS$

(27) $TWS = WSC * EMP$

(28) $EMP = LAS - UNE$

(29) $RDI = \frac{DIN}{PCE} * 100$

Note: Numbers in parentheses indicate t-statistics. An L before a variable means the natural logarithm of the variable.

Appendix C – Model of the Dutch Economy

(1) GDM = CND + CDE + IND + INI + INO + ING + GEX + CHS + EXL – IMP

(2) $CND = \underset{(3.48)}{2394.2} + \underset{(1.93)}{0.0595}RLA(t-1) + \sum_{i=o}^{4} b_{1i}RDI(t-i) + \underset{(2.92)}{0.4427}u(t-1)$

$\sum_{i=o}^{4} b_{1i} = 0.51$ (2nd d.p. constrained zero at t = 5)

$b_{10} = \underset{(2.02)}{0.1903}, b_{11} = \underset{(5.62)}{0.1404}, b_{12} = \underset{(3.02)}{0.0964}$

$b_{13} = \underset{(1.21)}{0.0583}, b_{14} = \underset{(0.69)}{0.0262}$

$\bar{R}^2 = 0.9797$, D.W. = 2.03, S.E. = 199.93

(3) RLA(t–1) = (NLA(t–1)/PCE)*100

(4) NLA = MS1 + OLA(t–1)

(5) $CDE = \underset{(1.68)}{998.81} + \sum_{i=o}^{2} b_{2i}RDI(t-i) - \underset{(1.53)}{5.7397}\,RRL - \underset{(1.63)}{8.4955}\,RPD$

$-\underset{(2.72)}{12.2076}\,CPD + \underset{(7.75)}{0.7033}\,CDE(t-1) - \underset{(6.25)}{0.7141}u(t-1)$

$\sum_{i=o}^{2} b_{2i} = 0.03$ (2nd d.p. constrained zero at both ends)

$b_{20} = \underset{(3.06)}{0.009}, b_{21} = \underset{(3.06)}{0.0121}, b_{22} = \underset{(3.06)}{0.009}$

$\bar{R}^2 = 0.9453$, D.W. = 1.65, S.E. = 73.16

(6) RRL = RLB – CPD(t–1)

(7) CPD = (PCD/PCD(t–4) –1)*100

(8) RPD = (PCD/PCE)*100

$$(9)\ IND = \underset{(1.82)}{494.64} + \sum_{i=o}^{5} b_{3i}\ RDI(t-i) - \underset{(2.40)}{60.5433}\ RLB - \underset{(1.37)}{2.2662}\ CSH + \underset{(5.74)}{0.6405} IND(t-1)$$

$\sum_{i=o}^{5} b_{3i} = 0.413$ (2nd d.p. constrained zero at both ends)

$b_{30} = \underset{(1.96)}{0.004425}$, $b_{31} = \underset{(1.96)}{0.007376}$, $b_{32} = \underset{(1.96)}{0.008851}$

$b_{33} = \underset{(1.96)}{0.008851}$, $b_{34} = \underset{(1.96)}{0.007376}$, $b_{35} = \underset{(1.96)}{0.004425}$

$\bar{R}^2 = 0.6574$, D.W. = 2.21, S.E. = 95.01

$$(10)\ INI = \underset{(4.13)}{1128.09} + \sum_{i=o}^{2} b_{4i} DRL(t-i) + \underset{(2.20)}{0.43860}\ INI(t-1) + \sum_{i=o}^{7} d_{4i} DGD\ (t-i)$$

$\sum_{i=o}^{2} b_{4i} = -10.466$ (2nd d.p. constrained zero at both ends)

$b_{40} = \underset{(1.45)}{-3.14}$, $b_{41} = \underset{(1.45)}{-4.186}$, $b_{42} = \underset{(1.45)}{-3.14}$

$\sum_{i=o}^{7} d_{4i} = 0.3484$ (2nd d.p. constrained zero at both ends)

$d_{40} = \underset{(3.59)}{0.02323}$, $d_{41} = \underset{(3.59)}{0.04065}$, $d_{42} = \underset{(3.59)}{0.05226}$

$d_{43} = \underset{(3.59)}{0.05807}$, $d_{44} = \underset{(3.59)}{0.05807}$, $d_{45} = \underset{(3.59)}{0.05226}$

$d_{46} = \underset{(3.59)}{0.04065}$, $d_{47} = \underset{(3.59)}{0.02323}$

$\bar{R}^2 = 0.6558$, D.W. = 1.79, S.E. = 83.87

(11) $DRL = RLI - RLI(t-1)$

(12) $RLI = RLB - CPI(t-1)$

(13) $CPI = (PII/PII(t-4) - 1) * 100$

(14) $DGD = GDM - GDM(t-1)$

(15) $INO = \underset{(2.16)}{606.205}, + \sum_{i=4}^{7} b_{5i} RLB(t-i) + \sum_{i=o}^{5} d_{5i}\, GDM(t-i) + \underset{(3.40)}{0.5427}\, INO\,(t-1)$

$\underset{(1.72)}{-0.2787}u(t-1)$

$\sum_{i=4}^{7} b_{5i} = -45.43$ ($2^{\underline{nd}}$ d.p. constrained zero at both ends)

$b_{54} = \underset{(1.24)}{-9.085}, b_{55} = \underset{(1.24)}{-13.63}, b_{56} = \underset{(1.24)}{-13.63}, b_{57} = \underset{(1.24)}{-9.085}$

$\sum_{i=o}^{5} d_{5i} = 0.02268$ ($2^{\underline{nd}}$ d.p. constrained zero at both ends)

$d_{50} = \underset{(2.33)}{0.002430}, d_{51} = \underset{(2.33)}{0.004049}, \; d_{52} = \underset{(2.33)}{0.004859}$

$d_{53} = \underset{(2.33)}{0.004859}, d_{54} = \underset{(2.33)}{0.004049}, d_{55} = \underset{(2.33)}{0.002430}$

$\bar{R}^2 = 0.42$, D.W. = 1.80, S.E. = 143.873

(16) $IMP = \underset{(2.05)}{2001.66} + \underset{(2.38)}{0.2128}GDM + \sum_{i=o}^{2} b_{6i} RPM(t-i) + \underset{(4.67)}{0.6272}\, IMP(t-1)$

$- \underset{(2.00)}{0.3009}u(t-1)$

$\sum_{i=o}^{2} b_{6i} = -29.582$ ($2^{\underline{nd}}$ d.p. constrained zero at both ends)

$b_{60} = \underset{(2.43)}{-8.876}, b_{61} = \underset{(2.43)}{-11.83}, b_{62} = \underset{(2.43)}{-8.876}$

$\bar{R}^2 = 0.9541$, D.W. = 1.90, S.E. = 517.812

(17) $RPM = (PIM/PGM) * 100$

(18) $RTB = \underset{(3.70)}{16.5983} + \underset{(5.96)}{1.0193}\, DIS - \underset{(4.27)}{17.2909}\, CMS1 + \underset{(1.28)}{0.07682}\, PGDM + \underset{(3.93)}{0.543}u(t-1)$

$\bar{R}^2 = 0.8016$, D.W. = 2.18, S.E. = 0.8028

(19) CMS1 = MS1/MS1(t–1)

(20) PGDM = (GDM/GDM(t–4) – 1)*100

(21) $RLB = \underset{(10.73)}{5.2446} + \sum_{i=o}^{8} b_{7i} RTB(t-i) + \sum_{i=o}^{5} d_{7i} CPGM(t-i)$

$\sum_{i=o}^{8} b_{7i} = 0.2706$ (2nd d.p. constrained zero at t=9)

$b_{70} = \underset{(9.22)}{0.1875}$, $b_{71} = \underset{(8.42)}{0.1222}$, $b_{72} = \underset{(6.06)}{0.06803}$, $b_{73} = \underset{(2.42)}{0.02497}$

$b_{74} = \underset{(0.66)}{-0.006978}$, $b_{75} = \underset{(2.63)}{-0.02781}$, $b_{76} = \underset{(3.83)}{-0.03753}$,

$b_{77} = \underset{(4.60)}{-0.03614}$, $b_{78} = \underset{(5.12)}{-0.02363}$

$\sum_{i=o}^{5} d_{7i} = 0.1405$ (2nd d.p. constrained zero at both ends)

$d_{70} = \underset{(4.49)}{0.01505}$, $d_{71} = \underset{(4.49)}{0.02508}$, $d_{72} = \underset{(4.49)}{0.03010}$

$d_{73} = \underset{(4.49)}{0.03010}$, $d_{74} = \underset{(4.49)}{0.02508}$, $d_{75} = \underset{(4.49)}{0.01505}$

$\bar{R}^2 = 0.7098$, D.W. = 1.90, S.E. = 0.3850

(22) CPGM = (PGM/PGM(t–4) – 1)*100

(23) $MS1 = \underset{(4.02)}{-9892.48} + \underset{(4.55)}{1.1840}\,REM - \underset{(5.44)}{934.104}\,DIS + \underset{(3.78)}{401.308}\ RTB(t-1)$

$+ \underset{(3.24)}{0.4157}\,GDM + \underset{(7.92)}{0.5870}\,MS1(t-1) + \underset{(2.66)}{0.3803}\,u(t-1)$

$\bar{R}^2 = 0.9967$, D.W. = 1.77, S.E. = 678.207

(24) $CWRH = \underset{(1.47)}{0.1113}\,CPRD\,(t-1) + \sum_{i=o}^{4} b_{8i} CPCE(t-i) + \sum_{i=o}^{4} d_{8i} UNE(t-i)$

$\sum_{i=o}^{4} b_{8i} = 0.9105$ (2nd d.p. constrained zero at both ends)

$$b_{80} = \underset{(11.96)}{0.1301}, \; b_{81} = \underset{(11.96)}{0.2081}, \; b_{82} = \underset{(11.96)}{0.2341}$$

$$b_{83} = \underset{(11.96)}{0.2081}, \; b_{84} = \underset{(11.96)}{0.1301}$$

$$\sum_{i=o}^{4} d_{8i} = -0.0000945 \text{ (2}^{\underline{nd}} \text{ d.p. constrained zero at both ends)}$$

$$d_{80} = \underset{(3.62)}{-0.0000135}, \; d_{81} = \underset{(3.62)}{-0.0000216}, \; d_{82} = \underset{(3.62)}{-0.0000243}$$

$$d_{83} = \underset{(3.62)}{-0.0000216}, \; d_{84} = \underset{(3.62)}{-0.0000135}$$

$\bar{R}^2 = 0.2632$, D.W. = 1.65, S.E. = 0.009180

(25) PCE = PCE(t−1)∗CPCE

(26) WRH = WRH(t−1)∗CWRH

(27) CPRD = PRD/PRD(t−1)

(28) PRD = GDM/EMP

$$\text{(29) CPCE} = \underset{(1.00)}{0.0025} + \underset{(5.14)}{0.7490}\text{ CWRH(t−1)} + \underset{(1.00)}{0.03675}\text{CPIM}$$

$$+ \sum_{i=o}^{4} b_{9i}\text{CMS1 (t−i)} - \underset{(2.27)}{0.3458}\text{u(t−1)}$$

$$\sum_{i=o}^{4} b_{9i} = 0.15239 \text{ (2}^{\underline{nd}} \text{ d.p. constrained zero at both ends)}$$

$$b_{90} = \underset{(1.88)}{0.0293}, \; b_{91} = \underset{(1.88)}{0.04689}, \; b_{92} = \underset{(1.88)}{0.05275}$$

$$b_{93} = \underset{(1.88)}{0.04689}, \; b_{94} = \underset{(1.88)}{0.0293}$$

$\bar{R}^2 = 0.2980$, D.W. = 2.04, S.E. = 0.01323

(30) CPIM = PIM/PIM(t−1)

(31) $CUNE = \underset{(1.97)}{2.1452}CWRH + \underset{(2.83)}{2.3262}CPCE(t-1) + \sum_{i=o}^{4} b_{10i}CGDM(t-i)$

$\sum_{i=o}^{4} b_{10i} = -3.4981$ (2nd d.p. constrained zero at both ends)

$b_{100} = \underset{(3.13)}{-0.4997}$, $b_{101} = \underset{(3.13)}{-0.7996}$, $b_{102} = \underset{(3.13)}{-0.8995}$

$b_{103} = \underset{(3.13)}{-0.7996}$, $b_{104} = \underset{(3.13)}{-0.4997}$

$\bar{R}^2 = 0.2323$, D.W. = 1.54, S.E. = 0.08988

(32) CGDM = GDM/GDM(t−1)

(33) $DIN = \underset{(2.99)}{-1362.8537} + \underset{(71.51)}{0.7080}\ VGM + \underset{(4.58)}{0.62798}u(t-1)$

$\bar{R}^2 = 0.9890$, D.W. = 1.92, S.E. = 314.2108

(34) VGM = GDM*PGM/100

(35) $PGM = \underset{(2.58)}{4.9340} + \underset{(67.18)}{0.9481}\ PCE + \underset{(3.80)}{0.5317}u(t-1)$

$\bar{R}^2 = 0.9870$, D.W. = 1.93, S.E. = 1.2322

(36) LAS = EMP + UNE

(37) UNE = UNE(t−1)*CUNE

(38) RDI = (DIN/PCE)*100

Appendix D

1. List of variables

GDM = GDP at market prices
COE = total consumers' expenditure
CND = non-durables consumption
CDE = durables consumption
INC = investment in construction (public and private – includes both business and residential)
IND = investment in dwellings (residential)
INE = investment in plant and machinery
INI = investment in manufacturing industry (both construction plus plant and machinery)
INO = other investment
ING = government investment
GEX = government expenditure (other than investment)
TGEX = total government expenditure (including investment)
CHS = changes in stocks
EXL = exports
IMP = imports
RLA = real liquid assets
RDI = real disposable income
NLA = nominal liquid assets (end of period)
PCE = CDE price deflator
MS1 = money stock (M_1-definition)
OLA = other liquid assets (other than MS1)
RRL = real long-term interest rate
RPD = relative prices of consumers' durables
CPD = changes in RPD
RLB = nominal long-term interest rate
PCD = price of cosumers' durables
CSH = cost of housing
RLI = real user-cost of capital
DRL = changes in RLI
DGD = changes in GDP
CPI = changes in prices of investment
PII = INI-price deflator
PIM = IMP-price deflator
RPM = relative import prices
PGM = GDP-price deflator
RTB = Treasury bill rate
DIS = discount rate
CMS1 = changes in MS1
PGDM = GDM-rate of growth
CPGM = PGM-rate of inflation
REM = reserve money
DIN = nominal disposable income
WRH = hourly wage rate
CWRH = changes in WRH
CPCE = changes in PCE
UNE = unemployment
CUNE = changes in unemployment
CPIM = changes in PIM
CGDM = changes in GDM
VGM = nominal GDM
LAS = labour supply
PRD = productivity
CPRD = changes in productivity
EMP = employment
GNP = gross national product
VGN = nominal GNP
TRP = transfer payments
ECS = personal contributions to social security
TWS = total wages and salaries
WSC = wages and salaries per capita
CWSC = changes in WSC
CGNP = changes in GNP
PIE = price-deflator of INE
PIC = price-deflator of INC
SAV = savings
IPIM = $\left(\frac{CPIM}{CPCE}\right)$

PPIE = $\left(\frac{PIE}{PIE\ (t-4)} - 1\right) * 100$

PPIC = $\left(\frac{PIC}{PIC\ (t-4)} - 1\right) * 100$

RRB = real rate of interest on government bonds (see text)

RRB' = real rate of interest on government bonds (see text)

OPI = other personal incomes

TOI = taxes on OPI

TXW = taxes on TWS

u = stochastic errors

2. List of Sources

(i) All data for the Netherlands were obtained from two sources:
  (1) Central Bureau of Statistics, *Monthly Bulletin,* various issues
  (2) The Netherlands Bank, *Quarterly Bulletin,* various issues

(ii) All data for the Federal Republic of Germany were obtained from the following source:
  (1) Deutsche Bundesbank, *Monthly Report,* various issues and statistical supplements.

For consistency of data practically all issues covering the 1970s were used.

Chapter 16

NATIONAL INSTITUTE FORECASTING*

G. D. N. Worswick

This paper is about the experience of twenty years of short-term forecasting at the National Institute of Social and Economic Research (NIESR), London, but I shall attempt to place the narrative in the setting of developments of economic forecasting generally.

Full Employment

All the major industrial countries witnessed massive unemployment in the 1930s and at the end of the Second World War many of their governments undertook commitments of one kind or another to secure high or full employment, commitments which implied that governments understood the causes and disposed of the remedies for unemployment. In the British case, according to Lord Roberthall: 'Both Labour and Conservative ministers had doubts about whether it would be technically possible to maintain high employment, which was the one thing that seemed to me and to many economists at the time, and turned out to be, the easiest of all the problems' (1). The Keynesian revolution in economic theory, the construction of national accounts and the experience of managing the war economy were the foundations of post-war stabilisation, or 'demand management', policies.

At different times governments have given highest priority to a variety of economic and social objectives: first, the making good of war damage, and in later years the development of social services. For more than twenty years the 'easiest' objective, full employment, was for most of the time at the top of the list, but on occasions the fear of inflation, and more commonly the emergence of deficits in the balance of payments, caused temporary abandonment of *the full* employment objective.

With the benefit of hindsight the question whether, in fiscal and monetary policy, demand management disposed of sufficient instruments to secure continuous achieve-

* This article was completed in May 1978. Since then a number of further studies of different aspects of National Institute forecasting have been published. In the *National Institute Economic Review,* May 1979, there are two studies: D.R. Osborn, 'National Institute Gross Output Forecasts: A Comparison with US Performance', and F. Teal and D.R. Osborn, 'An Assessment and Comparison of Two NIESR Econometric Model Forecasts'. *NIESR Discussion Paper,* no. 41, 1981, is a study by S. Brooks and K. Cuthbertson of 'Economic Models and Economic Forecasts'. A condensed version of this paper was published in the *National Institute Economic Review,* February 1981.

ment of full employment, price stability and external balance seems only to admit of a negative answer. But in the 1950s the sceptics were in the minority. Moreover, when doubt was expressed it was usually accompanied by a recommendation that the armoury of weapons at the disposal of governments should be increased by the addition of exchange rate adjustment and incomes policy.

National Income Forecasts

National Income Forecasts were prepared inside the Treasury from the early post-war days and for a decade or so these were the only systematic and regular forecasts being produced in Britain. They were not made public and the Treasury economists became concerned that there was no technical comment on their work by professional economists; it was from the Treasury economists that the suggestion came in the middle-1950s that the National Institute of Economic and Social Research might make similar forecasts for publication. It was hoped that the Institute would also be able to undertake some of the research into the structure of the economy which the Treasury economists knew was needed but had not the opportunity themselves to carry out.

It was always intended that the Institute's analysis should be independent of that of the Treasury but, given its origins, there was bound to be similarity, especially in the earlier years. Both the Directors who planned and started the *National Institute Economic Review,* Bryan Hopkin and Christopher Saunders, were seconded to the National Institute from the Treasury and the Central Statistical Office respectively. The original team also included several members with previous Treasury experience. Movements of staff from the Treasury to the National Institute and vice versa have continued to occur from time to time, but in the past ten years and more the intellectual input has been wholly independent.

The Methods of Early Forecasts

Table 16.1 is a shortened version of one of the tables which appears in every issue of the *Economic Review,* and it illustrates the position at the beginning of 1978 when a quarterly forecast was being prepared until the end of 1979. At that date the main figures for the national product were available up to the third quarter of 1977 but for the fourth quarter it was still necessary to make estimates using the partial information provided by such indicators as retail sales or visible exports and imports which are published within a month or less of their collection. To make a forecast is to fill in numbers in all the empty squares in the table. While an indefinite number of alternative forecasts may be conceived, any figures put down are subject to two different kinds of constraint. Firstly, they have to be consistent with accounting principles: this requires in Table 16.1, that reading across every row, columns (2 + 3 + 4 + 5 + 6) = column 7 and, columns (7 – 8 – 9) = column 1. Secondly, they must be consistent with any behavioural relationships which

Table 16.1

Framework of a national income forecast

		GDP (1)	CE (2)	PAC (3)	GFI (4)	Exports (5)	Stockbuilding (6)	Total final demand (7)	Imports (8)	AFC (9)
1977	I	11,941	8761	2737	2248	3954	207	17,907	3715	2251
	II	19,777	8665	2768	2231	4126	130	17,920	3748	2198
	III	11,958	8796	2754	2262	4204	−97	17,919	3705	2256
Estimate	IV	12,004	8840	2770	2255	4105	−20	17,950	3696	2270
Forecasts										
1978	I	x	x	x	x	x	x	x	x	x
	II	x	x	x	x	x	x	x	x	x
	III	x	x	x	x	x	x	x	x	x
	IV	x	x	x	x	x	x	x	x	x
1979	I	x	x	x	x	x	x	x	x	x
	II	x	x	x	x	x	x	x	x	x
	III	x	x	x	x	x	x	x	x	x
	IV	x	x	x	x	x	x	x	x	x

(1) Gross domestic product at factor cost.
(2) Consumers' expenditure at market prices.
(3) Public authorities' current consumption.
(4) Gross fixed investment.
(5) Exports of goods and services.
(6) Value of physical increases in stocks.
(7) Total final demand.
(8) Imports of goods and services.
(9) Adjustment to factor cost (indirect taxes less subsidies).

have been observed for the past and which, it is believed, will continue into the future, subject to any specific modification, whether for a single quarter or for a longer period, which may be introduced. Table 16.1 includes only the main components of final demand, all expressed in constant prices; other tables show the generation of personal incomes and expenditure, the main items of investment and the balance of payments. Various index numbers of price change are included. However many variables are introduced, the forecast values must continue to satisfy the two kinds of constraint illustrated for Table 16.1.

Experience will show that some of the variables are in the main determined outside the system and may be classified as *exogenous;* for instance, it may be postulated that public expenditure (current or capital) on goods and services will go ahead according to plan, whatever is happening to the private sector; on the other hand, some other elements of public expenditure, e.g. unemployment benefits will change if there is a change in the private sector. *Endogenous* variables are those whose value is clearly seen to depend upon the values of other variables under consideration. The interaction between variables may go both ways: higher consumers' expenditure may cause employers to lay down more plant, i.e. to stimulate higher investment, but the construction of plants generates incomes which will be spent on more consumption. The interaction may be simultaneous or there may be delays such that a change in A causes a change in B at some later period which feeds back upon A again in a later period still.

The forecasting procedure can be carried out at widely different levels of sophistication. The behavioural relationships can be roughly judged by inspecting graphs, or they may be estimated more systematically by elaborate statistical techniques requiring considerable calculation. The forecast values can be filled in by a process of successive approximation, whereby an initial set of numbers is written in for some of the variables, the remainder being calculated according to the behavioural relationships. If one or more of the accounting identities is then found to be infringed, a new set of numbers is tried. This iterative process can be continued to get nearer and nearer to sets of numbers which both satisfy the behavioural relationships and the accounting identities.

An econometric model is an assemblage of mathematical equations, in which the variables are those economic magnitudes in which the modellers are primarily interested, or which have a bearing upon them, there being in both cases available statistical time series. The form of the equation is chosen to be as simple as possible – a linear equation is most common. The coefficients of the equations may be imposed using prior information, or they may be estimated directly from the available data. However obtained, it is still an open question whether an equation which has fitted the data in the past will continue to do so in the future.

In the early days of the *Economic Review* very few equations between variables had been formally estimated. The procedure was informal and contained substantial elements of discretionary judgement; as already mentioned, this approach came very close to that being used in the Treasury at that time. In 1961 Robert Neild, the first Editor of the *Economic Review,* and E. A. Shirley made an assessment of forecasting performance in the first two years, comparing it with the few other forecasts then available (Neild and Shirley, 1961). The details need not detain us, the more so, in that we shall be giving information about forecasting errors covering longer periods later in this article. The *Economic Review* forecasts compared quite favourably with other forecasts made by similar methods and one conclusion was that the greatest scope for improvement appeared to lie in making better forecasts of the exogenous variables, notably exports. The forecasts which had been made with the Oxford econometric model turned out to be distinctly poorer. The concluding observation was: '. . . those using the model, as was to be expected, ran into many of the same troubles as the rest of us. The model could do nothing to foretell what was going to happen to the variables which caused us most trouble in 1959 and 1960 – conditions in export markets or the effect of changes of hire purchase terms. Added to that, they appear to have fared worse because of the rigid and restricted framework of their model. The trouble with attempting to produce a complete system of equations is that reality has to be too heavily sacrificed for the sake of simplicity.' Forecasting with a formal model was not, the authors observed, so different from the less formal type practised at NIESR: 'The model codifies some relationships, but it still leaves a large number for judgement.' Moreover, they thought that the formal equations did not capture reality very well – allthough this was less a criticism of principle than a comment on the limitations of the particular specifications.

In the next five years much work was done at the Institute to develop good equations for strategic variables. Besides Neild's own work on prices and employment (Neild, 1963), articles were published on 'output and employment', 'imports' and 'taxes' by J. R. Shepherd, W. A. H. Godley, and W. A. B. Hopkin of the Treasury, and there was continuous working and re-working of the wage-price relationships following on work by J. C. R. Dow and I. A. Dicks-Mireaux in the late 1950s. A feature of all this work was the increasing importance attached to time lags in the transmission of changes through the economy.

Econometric Models

My own association with forecasting began when I succeeded Christopher Saunders in 1965. After a period to learn the procedures, it seemed fairly clear what the next stage of development should be. We had a small number of what we believed to be fairly robust equations for various sectors of the economy. We had, potentially, the framework of a complete model, consisting of some formal struts (the aforesaid equations) joined by less formal methods. There was no reason, in principle, why formal equations should not be written to replace these informal struts. The programme which suggested itself, therefore, was:

(i) to review all existing equations, either endorsing or revising them;
(ii) to write new ones to close the 'informal' gaps; and
(iii) to extend research to make estimates of coefficients hitherto chosen by rough guesswork.

At that time I had two ideas which I have since been obliged to revise substantially. The advantage of equations is that they set out explicitly ideas about systematic behaviour in the past; in addition, the knowledge is public and not dependent on the presence of particular individuals carrying that piece of information in their heads. The disadvantage of a formal model, as I then thought, was that the forecast generated would be restricted by the assumptions of unbroken continuation into the future of past trends. It was only later that I appreciated that the discretionary adjustment of such extrapolations, to allow for special factors and for announced change in policies, was not merely conceivable but, with the aid of electronic computers, very easy to make without requiring lengthy recalculations of all the other variables so as to ensure conformity with the other accounting identities. The other idea was that one could normally find relationships which were not only stable for the past, but would remain stable in the future. Thus, with limited research resources, one could build the model step by step, getting a good equation for imports, then going on to consumption and then to investment and so on. Greater experience indicates that no sooner is a 'really good' equation estimated and put into forecasting operation than it begins to wilt. Sometimes bad old equations come back on course when new and 'better' equations are beginning to perform especially badly. Each new generation of researchers arrives fresh from the econometric training camps armed with the latest techniques which will surely avoid the mistakes of the past. One day, perhaps, they may be right. But the longer one has experience of econometric estimation, the more elusive seems the final solution.

A model was used in the forecast for the first time in 1969 and it consisted of approximately ten behavioural equations and ten identities (2). In 1973 and early 1974 this model was extended to some twenty-four behavioural equations with fifty identities and thirty-eight exogenous variables; the model, though larger, was in many respects similar to the original one and is conveniently referred to as Model I. The advantages of evolutionary development of a model, which has to be called into operational service every quarter, are plain enough. New research into particular sectors, when it yields better equations, can be taken on board between forecasts as time permits. The disadvantage is that the equations gradually accumulating may lack a consistent body of economic theory. Consequently, a new and more ambitiously structured model was built independently during the period 1973–75. The novelty was that output, pricing, investment and employment should all be consistent with the same production function. This Model II, as it came to be called, had some fifty behavioural equations and seventy identities; (it is fully described in National Institute Discussion Papers 10A, 10B, 10C and 10D, October 1977).

While Modell II was under construction, Model I continued to be operated and developed by the then Editor of the *Economic Review,* John Bispham. By chance, both he and the majority of members of the team which had built Model II left the Institute during 1975 and at the end of that year a largely new forecasting team found itself with a choice of two models. Model I had evolved by piecemeal extension; the theory behind each equation was relatively simple, and its properties were fairly well understood from regular operational use. Modell II could claim that the economic theory behind the equations was more consistent but the model was untried in practice. There followed a period of extensive study of the comparative properties of the two models. In the end, neither proved to be superior to the other on all the tests applied, and the upshot was the emergence of Model III which is the basis of current forecasting operations (3). The output, employment, stocks and financial sectors of Model II were integrated with the pricing and investment functions of Model I; if these modifications entailed some sacrifice of consistency of economic theory, they brought gains in ease of operation of the model and its short-term tracking performance.

This brief history suggests that in twenty years the techniques used by the National Institute have become continuously more sophisticated. A formal econometric model was introduced ten years ago, but it was very small; its present successor is considerably larger (4). Undoubtedly, part of this increase in sophistication is the direct result of research of the many people who have worked in the team. But, as was mentioned earlier, the idea that after so many months of research one could discover definitive equations for particular sectors which would continue to forecast well in the following years proved illusory. In the mid-1960s, for instance, the majority of applied economists thought that the Phillips Curve, with some modifications, was the last word in explaining the rate of increase in money wages. Nowadays, the Phillips Curve, even when it is modified out of all recognition, has very few staunch supporters. This erosion of equations from the moment they are first estimated is not confined to wages; it is encountered almost everywhere.

What has contributed most to the sophistication of technique has been the development of the electronic computer, and the emergence of a new generation of economists equipped to use it. Nowadays, the volume of calculation which goes into a single forecast far exceeds what was possible in a whole year of work twenty years ago. Not only is the calculation speedier, it is also more flexible. The model can be set up in such a way that the forecast values which it generates can be modified at will, while retaining adherence to accounting identities and the other behavioural relationships. Thus, the formal model turned out to be more flexible, and not less flexible, than the informal procedures which it replaced. Not only is it easier to exercise discretionary judgement in modifying a forecast, but it is possible to keep a clear record of such adjustments.

Testing Forecasts

It would be natural to enquire whether this sophistication of technique has been accompanied by an improvement in forecasting performance. However, the comparison of forecasts with events, or the comparison of different methods of forecasting the same events, on the face of it seemingly straightforward, turn out to be beset with difficulties of many kinds.

In the first place, nearly all macro-economic forecasts are implicitly or explicitly conditional upon the continuation of various institutions and policies throughout the forecast period. One has to ask what is being assumed, for instance, about fiscal and monetary policy. Will tax rates remain unaltered? Will the exchange rate float freely, or will the authorities intervene from time to time and, if so, what is being assumed about this intervention? Secondly, there are Acts of God. When is it legitimate, in testing a forecast, to make an adjustment for a particular event? The outstanding instance in recent years was the quadrupling of the price of oil at the end of 1973. Depending, of course, upon the forecaster's theory of the impact of that change upon the general level of prices and on economic activity, should he be permitted to 'correct' his forecast accordingly before comparing with the actual outturn? It is only human nature for forecasters to be more anxious to make such corrections when they improve the forecasts than when they make them worse. If they are allowed at all, they should be made consistently. Thirdly, the data available for the past, especially the recent past, at the time when a forecast is made are often provisional and subject to revision, sometimes months or even years later; such revisions can be substantial. For instance, the first official figures showing the change in exports between the second half of 1972 and the second half of 1973 became available in April, 1974. In the figures published in 1977, the change in exports had been revised by 3.8 per cent, an amount which is actually the same as the annual average growth rate of exports during the period 1971–75. This is a striking case though it was not the largest difference in recent years. It is not uncommon for the first published estimate of growth rates from half year to half year to deviate, in absolute terms, from the latest data by more than half the average growth rate of the period (5).

Finally, a forecast may refer to a single variable, such as the rate of inflation, but more commonly refers to a number of variables, such as GDP, unemployment, the balance of payments, the rate of price increase, and so on. If forecaster A gets all variables better than B, well and good; but what if A gets some items better and some worse? The judgement then depends, presumably, on the relative importance of the different variables. In recent years strong claims for the superiority of particular methods of analysis of the economy have frequently been made on the basis of a 'better' forecast for a single variable, such as the balance of payments, price increases, or the exchange rate.

The Committee on Policy Optimisation has lately published figures for forecasts made between 1970 and 1975 by the Treasury, the London Business School and the National

Institute of Economic and Social Research – all of whom use econometric models – which come to grips with some of the difficulties which I have just mentioned (Table 16.2). All three forecasts are normally made upon the assumption of unchanged government policies. In principle, the adjustment to each forecast should be derived from the model used in generating that forecast and, as we shall see a little later, the three models are by no means identical. This is a possible explanation of the tendency of forecasters to do relatively better by comparison with others when they themselves are in charge of the comparisons – just as football teams more often win at home than away. In this case, a common adjustment was made, but it had been agreed by all parties that it was a fair one. In the conduct of this exercise it was noticed both that the 'policy adjustment' makes a difference to the scale of error of particular forecasts, and that, in recent years, the average forecasting error had been quite sensitive to the inclusion or exclusion of a few forecasts.

The figures in Table 16.2 illustrate further the problems of the errors in data and subsequent revisions. The average errors in forecasting real GDP a year ahead were 1.2 per cent for the London Business School, 1.4 per cent for the Treasury and 1.6 per cent for the National Institute; all these compare with an annual average growth rate for the years 1970–75 of 1.7 per cent. The table does not, however, tell us whether there was any trend of improvement or deterioration in the accuracy of forecasts.

When reporting progress to the S.S.R.C. conference on 'Modelling of the UK Economy' in 1972 (Renton, 1975), I gave some figures of N.I.E.S.R. forecasting errors between 1959 and 1971 and ventured the conclusion that the record up to that time was 'consistent with the view that we have been getting slightly better in our forecasting in the most recent period'. Detailed tracking records of forecasting performance are hard to come by, but it is probably the case that the majority of US forecasters who make use of econometric models would have claimed a similar improvement in forecasting the US economy until 1972 or 1973. We do have evidence that things went badly wrong for virtually all forecasters in the recession following the oil crisis of end-1973.

Table 16.3 shows the error in forecasts of real output, GNP for USA and GDP for the UK, for four quarters ahead: that is to say, we are studying forecasts made during any quarter of the year for the change in GNP or GDP from that quarter to the corresponding quarter of the year following (6). Inspection of the table shows that in the eleven forecasts made from 1971 II to 1973 IV in the USA, the error in forecasting GDP for quarters ahead was small – less than 1 per cent in seven out of eleven instances; the best forecaster would have been even better still. N.I.E.S.R. does not do as well as this, going over 2 per cent on four occasions out of the eleven. But after the oil crisis things went awry for the US forecasters. If the scale of the rise in the price of oil is regarded as unforecastable, we can discount the fact that few forecasters during 1973 made correct forecasts for the corresponding quarter of 1974, but it is seen that the US error continues to rise in 1975;

Table 16.2

Average absolute errors of percentage growth forecasts by half years based on sixteen forecasts made between 1970 and 1975*

	Treasury	LBS	NIESR
Gross domestic product			
(Annual average growth 1.7%)			
First half year	1.12	1.62	1.30
Second half year	2.04	1.62	2.32
First full year	1.36	1.22	1.57
Third half year	2.88	2.54	(2.32)
Consumers' expenditure			
(Annual average growth 2.1%)			
First half year	0.72	0.60	0.82
Second half year	1.20	0.86	1.74
First full year	0.87	0.56	1.19
Third half year	1.87	1.61	(1.42)
Exports			
(Annual average growth 4.6%)			
First half year	2.52	2.64	3.40
Second half year	2.62	2.94	3.59
First full year	2.24	2.21	3.09
Third half year	4.52	4.04	(5.05)
Imports			
(Annual average growth 4.3%)			
First half year	2.14	2.25	2.59
Second half year	4.07	4.00	4.39
First full year	2.76	2.76	2.98
Third half year	4.88	4.89	(5.61)
Consumer price index			
(Annual average growth 12.5%)			
First half year	0.96	1.05	1.39
Second half year	1.82	1.78	2.75
First full year	1.38	1.32	2.06
Third half year	3.71	3.94	(3.53)

* Averages based on less than 16 observations are enclosed in brackets.

Source: Report of the Committee on Policy Optimisation, HMSO, Cmnd. 7148, March 1978.

Table 16.3

Comparative four-quarter percentage growth forecast errors

Four Quarters ending		U.S. real GNP* Median error	U.S. real GNP* Actual growth	U.K. real GDP NIESR error	U.K. real GDP Actual growth
1971	II	0.3	2.7	0.4	1.1
	III	0.4	2.7	0.3	1.9
	IV	−1.0	4.6	−0.9	2.0
1972	I	0.1	4.2	2.2	0.7
	II	−1.5	5.4	0.5	3.0
	III	−0.6	6.0	2.1	1.8
	IV	−1.2	7.3	−0.8	3.8
1973	I	−1.6	7.6	−3.6	9.5
	II	−0.4	5.6	−1.8	5.0
	III	0.4	5.0	−0.5	4.7
	IV	0.9	3.2	2.6	2.3
1974	I	4.1	0.1	6.9**	−0.2**
	II	3.8	−0.9	2.6	0.4
	III	4.3	−2.1	2.1	2.2
	IV	5.8	−4.4	0.0	1.9
1975	I	8.3	−5.7	0.9	3.4
	II	7.0	−4.0	3.0	−2.6

*The errors are taken from McNees (1976), while actual growth figures have been calculated from the *Survey of Current Business,* National Income Issue, 1976. The use of different sources implies that the two series may not exactly correspond.

** An adjustment has been made to allow for the effects of the miners' strike and the 3-day week in the first quarter of 1974.

that is to say, the US forecasters simply missed the onset of the US recession and it was some time before they picked it up. National Institute forecasts also got somewhat worse but not on anything like the same scale. After the shock of the oil crisis and the subsequent recession, forecasters seem to have recovered their poise, and errors in forecasts of annual changes in GDP, for instance, are back to the levels achieved before it. Even so, there is no guarantee that setbacks will not recur, and it may well be that forecasters have already come near to an irreducible minimum of forecasting error. Such a conclusion would have implications both for economic policy and for the direction of future research into forecasting and control.

Sources of Error

The errors in actual forecasts are not generated exclusively by the econometric models used in their preparation. In the first place, the data about the past on which the forecast was projected may have been revised by the time the end of the forecast period has been reached. Secondly, the exogenous variables may turn out differently from what they had been assumed to be; for instance, the export forecasts may have been too high simply because of an over-optimistic view about world trade, with the consequence that the final GDP forecast would be out, even if the model were an exact replica of the domestic economy. In the same way, the assumptions made about policy of government or the central bank may turn out to be wrong. This raises the interesting question of how far one should treat policy changes as essentially autonomous and how far one should attempt to predict policy changes by studying the reaction of the authorities to past situations of similar types. Then there is the fact that the model itself is not an exact replica of the economy but only an inexact one. The most recent observations from the past would not normally be those predicted by the equations, but deviate from them in either direction. Should the forecaster stick firmly to the expected values delivered by his equations for the future or should he notice that, for instance, the last three observations in the import equation have all been higher than predicted? Does this suggest that the next one will be higher also, or, indeed, does it imply that it will be lower? The forecaster may have additional information, not available at the time that the equation was estimated, which will account for recent positive deviations or might suggest that a positive or negative deviation should be expected in the future. In the nature of the case this information will not yet have been incorporated in any systematic estimations so that an element of judgement comes into the determination of the forecast values. Forecasting error, then, arises from many sources: data revision, errors in exogenous forecasts, unforeseen changes in policy, model errors and judgemental error. These sources of error are not necessarily additive: very often they may offset one another. It is pure luck if exogenous variable error and model error cancel out, but it is clearly the purpose of judgemental adjustments to offset what is believed to be model error, although the object may not always be achieved.

Although the National Institute has from the very beginning made a practice of recording and publishing its forecasting errors, there was until recently comparatively little work done on the decomposition of forecasting error. The reason for this is straightforward enough: first cook your goose. You have first to do some forecasts before you can start studying just where you go wrong. In the National Institute's case an additional stimulus to error decomposition was provided by the fact, referred to earlier, that at the beginning of 1976 a largely new team found itself confronted with the choice between two alternative models of the economy. It turns out that decomposition of error, even for a single forecast, is complex and intricate. So far, only two forecasts have been analysed in detail (Osborn and Teal, 1977), so that generalisations about the different kinds of error would be premature. However, there is already evidence that all the sources of error mentioned above turn up in significant amounts in one or other of the studies. One way to try to improve performance is to examine your own mistakes; another is to see how others are doing. The forecasting error itself is, of course, the acid test of the various teams of economists, but the fact that team A forecasts better than team B tells us nothing about how they have achieved this result. We have just seen how complex a task it is to decompose error in a single forecast; a systematic comparison of different forecasting teams would, on the face of it, be an even more complicated exercise and, so far as I am aware, has never been attempted. However, some work has been done, both in the United States and more recently in Britain, to compare the characteristics of various models used by different forecasters. We already knew, from inspection of their details, that models differed from one another both in the specification of individual equations and, in cases where they use similar specifications, in the value of the coefficients. A study of eight US econometric models was published by C.F. Christ in 1975 (Christ, 1975). His conclusion was that: 'Though the models forecast well over horizons of four to six quarters, they disagree so strongly about the effects of important monetary and fiscal policies that they cannot be considered reliable guides to such policy effects, until it can be determined which of them are wrong in this respect and which (if any) are right.' A similar study has lately been undertaken for three UK models, those of the Treasury, the London Business School and the National Institute (Laury, Lewis and Ormerod, 1978). The authors thought that their comparison produced less disagreement than might have been expected from Christ's study of the USA, though they pointed out that Christ had eight models while they compared only three. Their greater optimism stemmed, however, less from the similarity of the simulation results for the three models than from the fact that they felt able to put their finger on the sources of the differences in a number of instances.

So far, neither in USA nor in Britain, countries in which the volume of econometric model-building has been substantial in the past quarter of a century, has a 'consensus' model of the economy emerged. It is possible, indeed, that such degree of consensus as there is may be somewhat overstated because of the lack of articulated 'monetarist' models leading to tangible forecasts with which comparisons might be made.

Some Lessons

After more than twenty years there is no clear tendency for National Institute forecasts to get continously better, nor is there a tendency for economists in general to converge upon a consensus model of how the economy works. Has not the time come, as some have suggested, to abandon the whole exercise, or will, as others seem to imply, the adoption of even more sophisticated econometric techniques suffice to pull us into the clear? It may be doubted whether either extreme of pessimism or optimism is justified.

The most important lesson of the past two decades has been the change in the role of the econometric model. In the late 1950s the construction of such a model for the economy on even a modest scale was a major research enterprise, involving much time of economists and computing assistants in lengthy calculations. With the advances in computer technology and the increase in supply of economists and programmers, the econometric model has become an indispensable tool of quantitative economic analysis. Like all tools it needs to be designed in relation to its purpose or purposes. The National Institute is concerned both with research and with providing a service to those 'in business and elsewhere, who need to take a view of the general economic situation and prospects'. The object is not only to generate forecasts, but to study at the same time the scope and limitations of forecasting. But its views on the latter will only be of interest to those who need forecasts if it can show by its own performance that it has earned the right to present them.

The foundation of quantitative work in economics is a full understanding of the data, how it has been collected, classified and processed, what kinds of error are encountered in early estimates, how often it is revised, and so on. How many of the writers who so confidently warn of the danger of pushing the public sector borrowing requirement (PSBR) beyond some limit are aware that the average error made in recent years by the Treasury in forecasting PSBR at the beginning of the financial year has been over £ 3 billion, which can be as much as one-third of the PSBR itself. Time and again in editorials we are assured that keeping the money supply constant or moving it along some track will bring many benefits, but hardly ever are we told which is thought to be the relevant concept of money. Yet, as the Governor of the Bank of England pointed out in 1978, since 1970 the correlation between quarterly changes in M_1 and M_3 was +0.1 (Mais Lecture, 1978). Merely to keep up to date with data for national income and its components, for industrial production and employment, for wages and prices, and so on, is a task for several people.

Next there is the question of analysis. If consumption functions, investment functions and the like once found were to continue to perform reliably ever after then a single economist would be able to work his way round the entire economic system, estimating equations one at a time and eventually producing a fullyfledged model of the economy. Unfortunately, as we have seen, stable functions which stay stable are rarities. Watchers have to be posted round the economy to keep track of the performance of groups of equations. To be able to forecast regularly with the kind of error shown in Table 16.2 above is beyond the capability of a single economist; it requires a team. (One or two people can *operate* a model already built, but they cannot *maintain* it as well.) If a number of researchers are studying different parts of the economy, the results of their work must be co-ordinated. This is the key role played by the econometric model which at any point in time represents the pooled knowledge of the team concerning relationships between the different variables. This does not mean that the team is committed to accepting uncritically the predicted values of every variable delivered by the model. The model has been programmed in such a way that at any time equation values can be adjusted upwards or downwards at the behest of the proprietors. If an import equation has come under suspicion, one does not have to suspend all forecasting operations until a new equation has been found: the existing equation can be superseded and replaced by arbitrary values until such time as a better one is obtained. The team, in fact, need not even be committed to the view that there always must exist a good equation 'out there' if only the right trick to estimate it can be discovered. The system enables the team to avoid any doctrinaire position concerning the invariable superiority of econometric techniques over others. It allows the use of other systems of forecasting (e.g. intention surveys or guessing) where such methods have proven superior.

Obviously, improvement of econometric technique is always one of the potential directions of research, but there are many others. It must suffice here to touch on just a few of the questions which seem likely to come up in the next two or three years. Mention has already been made of the need to re-estimate the model when revisions of national accounts data are published. When these revisions are large, as sometimes happens, it may take time for ideas about the economy to be correspondingly revised.

Recently a number of exercises have been carried out jointly with other model proprietors: the study of errors for the Policy Optimisation Committee and the policy simulations of the Treasury, London Business School and National Institute models have both been mentioned; in addition, an exercise was carried out for a conference on 'demand management' by the proprietors of four models (L.B.S., Cambridge Department of Applied Economics, Professor David Laidler and the National Institute) in order to generate best policies for certain past periods and for the period ahead (Posner, 1978). It is clear that a number of other collaborative exercises will be worth undertaking before diminishing returns set in in this area of comparative study. One of the questions brought into sharp focus by the 'demand management' exercise was the use of the short-term forecasting model to generate medium-term projections for the economy. We are not satisfied that we know how to do this properly and what is the best way of presenting medium-term projections.

Finally, there is the question of the influence of the forecast itself upon future events. Treasury forecasts were developed precisely in order to give guidance to the Chancellor of the Exchequer on what to do. Thus, if a recession was expected, he should expand; if a boom was predicted, he should put the brakes on. The National Institute forecast was originally conceived as a shadow of the Treasury forecast so that a similar argument might apply: namely, that if the forecast is taken seriously, it may alter policy. But there is another way in which the forecast itself has consequences which has received more attention in recent years, namely the influence upon markets. A forecast of recession may be self-fulfilling if it induces businessmen to cancel investment plans, or a forecast of exchange rate movements might help to bring them about. There is a more complicated route whereby the forecast induces a change in government behaviour which in turn induces responses from the market to frustrate its intentions. These are intriguing possibilities.

The advantage of the division of labour is one of the profoundest ideas of economics and specialisation abounds in economics itself. But if the specialisation is to be rational, there has to be a product. Forecasting is the point of production of economics as a positive science.

There is no better way of getting a grasp on the quality of the data, of finding out what is known and what is not known. The quarter by quarter observation of the process of amendment and revision to National Accounts data has a most salutary effect. Economists not submitted to the discipline of regular forecasting are apt to take a time series from the nearest available statistical abstract as the truth, and not stay for any further question. Yet many ingenious hypotheses have been invented to explain behaviour which statistical revisions have indicated was not there after all.

Regular forecasters have to come to terms with the fact that, time and again, relationships which have a splendid record in fitting the past, fail to predict well into the real future. When this happens there are many places in which to look for trouble: Were the data appropriate? Was the economic theory sound? Was the econometric technique appropriate? But the trouble may lie in none of these places but in the fact that patterns of behaviour themselves may change. One notices that among economists it is the forecasters who are the most up to date, giving advance warning of the obsolescence of well-tried equations.

Forecasting is not so much a specialist activity as the assembly plant in which the specialisms of data collection and measurement and economic analysis are brought together. The good forecaster needs to know when and where to seek specialist advice to improve his performance; equally, the specialist should know the forecaster, for without him his own studies may sink into sterile scholasticism.

Footnotes

(1) National Institute Economic Review, November 1969, p.3.

(2) This model was described in *The Analysis and Forecasting of the British Economy* by M.J.C. Surrey, Cambridge University Press, 1971, and an updated version given to an econometric conference in 1972 by J.A. Bisphan. At this conference also a paper was given by the present author describing rather more fully the early years of experience with econometric modelling at the National Institute. Both papers were eventually published in *Modelling the Economy* edited by G.A. Renton, Heinemann, 1975.

(3) The most recent version of this model is described in *National Institute Discussion Paper* no. 7, 'A Listing of National Institute Model III, May 1977 Review', 1977. After this paper was written the Central Statistical Office published estimates of real national accounts data based on prices of 1975, to supersede previous estimates based on 1970 prices. As always when output and other series are rebased some changes occur in the profile of past years. On this occasion, because of the very large rise in the price of crude oil relative to other goods between 1970 and 1975 the effects on some items, such as the volume of imports, were quite substantial. Model III was estimated with the new data and brought into use as Model IV in February 1979. The re-estimation exposed areas of weakness in the model which required urgent attention.

(4) The size of an econometric model is not just a question of the number of variables but needs to take into account the structure of the model as well. A model with fewer variables which interact upon one another could be, in some sense, larger than one in which the variables occur in distinct groups. For instance, if a small model is used to forecast GDP, and then the production of different industrial sectors of the economy is forecast from functions of GDP alone and there is no feedback from these sector forecasts into the main model, then although more variables are being added, the effective size of the model is not being changed.

(5) See the *Report of the Committee on Policy Optimisation,* HMSO 1978, p. 39.

(6) The U.S. data in Table 16.3 have been obtained from a series of studies of U.S. forecasters by Stephen McNees which are published in the journal of the Federal Reserve Bank of Boston, the *New England Economic Review.* The particular figures quoted refer to the median error of eleven forecasters, which include all the best-known econometric ones. The table is drawn from *National Institute Discussion Paper no. 1* by Denise Osborn, 1977.

References

Ball, R.J., Hazlewood, A. and Klein, L.R. (1959) 'Econometric Forecasts for 1959', *Bulletin of the Oxford University Institute of Statistics,* vol. 21, no. 1.

Brooks, S. and Cuthbertson, K. (1981) 'Economic Models and Economic Forecasts', *NIESR Discussion Paper,* no. 41, 1981 and *National Institute Economic Review,* Feb. 1980.

Christ, C.F. (1975) 'Judging the Performance of Econometric Models of the US Economy', *International Economic Review*, vol. 16, no. 1.

Laury, J.S.E., Lewis, G.R. and Ormerod, P.A. (1978) 'Properities of Macro-Economic Models of the UK Economy', *National Institute Economic Review,* no. 83.

McNees, S.K. (1976) 'The Forecasting Performance in the Early 1970s', *New England Economic Review.*

Mais Lecture (1978) *Bank of England Quarterly Bulletin,* vol. 18, no. 1.

Neild, R.R. (1963) *Pricing and Employment in the Trade Cycle,* NIESR Occasional Paper XXI (Cambridge: Cambridge University Press).

Neild, R.R. and Shirley E.A. (1961) 'An assessment of forecasts, 1959–1960', *National Institute Economic Review,* no. 15.

Osborn, D.R. (1979) 'National Institute Gross Output Forecasts: A Comparison with US Performance', *National Institute Economic Review,* May 1979.

Osborn, D.R. and Teal, F. (1977) 'An Analysis of NIESR Forecasting Error in 1975', *NIESR Discussion Paper,* no. 2.

Osborn, D.R. and Teal, F. (1977) 'An Analysis of NIESR Forecasting Error in 1976' , *NIESR Discussion Paper,* no.6.

Posner, M.V. (ed.) (1978) Demand Management, *NIESR Economic Policy Papers 1* (London: Heinemann).

Renton, G.A. (ed.) (1975) *Modelling the Economy* (London: Heinemann).

Teal, F. and Osborn, D.R. (1979) 'An Assessment and Comparison of Two NIESR Econometric Model Forecasts', *National Institute Economic Review.*

Christopher T. Saunders: A BIBLIOGRAPHY

Books & booklets

a. 1934 *Social Survey of Merseyside,* part author; D. Caradog Jones, Director. 3 vols. (University Press of Liverpool)

b. 1934 *Elementary Education on Merseyside.* (University of Liverpool)

a. 1936 *Seasonal Variations in Employment.* (London: Longmans Green)

b. 1975 *From Free Trade to Integration in Western Europe?* (London: Chatham House and PEP; European Series, no. 22)

b. 1977 *Winners and Losers: Pay Patterns in the 1970s,* with D. Marsden et al. (Centre for Contemporary European Studies (University of Sussex) and Political & Economic Planning, London: PEP, vol. 43, no. 570, September)

b. 1978 *Engineering in Britain, West Germany and France: some Statistical Comparisons* (Sussex European Research Centre, Sussex European Papers, no. 3. University of Sussex)

b. 1979 *A Six-country Comparison of the Distribution of Industrial Earnings in the 1970s,* with D. Marsden. (Background paper to Report no. 8 of the Royal Commission on the Distribution of Income & Wealth. London: HMSO)

a. 1981 *Pay Inequalities in the European Community,* with D. Marsden. (London: Butterworth, European Studies)

a. = book, b. = booklet

Books edited

Conference volumes including introductions and/or summaries by C.T. Saunders.

For the International Association for Research in Income and Wealth:

1959 *Income and Wealth Series 8* with R. Goldsmith. (London: Bowes and Bowes)

For the Vienna Institute for Comparative Economic Studies, Workshops on East-West European Economic Interaction:

1977 *East-West Cooperation in Business: Inter-firm Studies* (Vienna: Springer-Verlag)

1977 *Industrial Policies and Technology Transfers between East and West.* (Springer-Verlag)

1978 *Money and Finance in East and West.* (Vienna: Springer-Verlag)

1980 *East and West in the Energy Squeeze.* (London: Macmillan)

1981 *East-West-South: Economic Interactions between Three Worlds.* (London: Macmillan)

For Sussex European Research Centre, University of Sussex:

1981 *The Political Economy of New and Old Industrial Countries.* (London: Butterworth, Studies in International Political Economy)

Articles and papers*

1931 'A Study of Occupational Mobility', *Econ. Jnl.*, vol. 41, no. 162, June

1932 'How Classes Choose their Churches', *Liverpool Post and Mercury,* 10 and 11 February

1933 'Overcrowding and Poverty: East London and Merseyside', *New Statesman and Nation,* 4 March

1934 'Benefit and "Needs"', *Manchester Guardian,* 17 January

'Future of Unemployment Pay', *Manchester Guardian,* 9 November

1935 'The Agricultural Worker and Insurance Benefit', *Manchester Guardian,* 17 January

'The Importance of Seasonal Variations in Employment in the UK', *Econ. Jnl.*, vol. 45, no. 178, June

1937 'Recent Trends in the Lancashire Cotton Industry', *Econ. Jnl.*, vol. 47, no. 185, March

1939 'Germany's Vulnerability', *The Economist,* 18 November (unsigned)

1946 'Manpower Distribution 1939–1945', *Manchester Statistical Society* (reprinted in *The Manchester School,* May 1946, vol. 4, no. 2)

1952 'Consumption of Raw Materials in the United Kingdom: 1851–1950' *JRSS (A)*, vol. 115, Part 3

1954 'The Pattern of Savings and Investment', *Manchester Statistical Society* (reprinted in *Review of Economic Studies,* 1955)

'National Income Statistics: are they accurate or useful?', *The Incorporated Statistician,* vol. 5, no. 1, March

* *Econ. Jnl.:* Economic Journal.
JRSS(A): Journal of Royal Statistical Society, Series A (General)

1955 'Current Trends in National Income Statistics', *Applied Statistics,* vol. 4, no. 3

1956 'Using National Income Statistics', *National Provincial Bank Review,* no. 36, November

'The Development of National Income Statistics', *The Bankers' Magazine,* vol. 182, no. 1348, July [reprinted in S.F. Frowen and H.C. Hillmann (eds.) *Economic Issues,* 1957, pp. 43–48]

'Economic Statistics in Business', *Manchester Guardian, Survey of Industry,* December

1957 'National Expenditure in the First Three Quarters of 1956', *The Bankers' Magazine,* vol. 183, no. 1355, February 1957

'Lancashire's Lot', *The Economist,* 4 May (unsigned)

1958 'Economic Instability in the West', *Foreign Trade Research Institute Monographs* (Belgrade)

'The Cohen Council's Report', *The Bankers' Magazine,* vol. 185, no. 1368, March (unsigned)

'Staatliche Wirtschaftspolitik und kurzfristige Konjunkturschwankungen', *Konjunkturpolitik,* nos. 5 & 6

1959 'Western Europe in the World Economy', *Westminster Bank Review,* February

'Cohen Council Mark III', *The Bankers' Magazine,* vol. 188, no. 1386, September

'Radcliffe under Scrutiny: the New Data – and their Uses', *The Banker,* December

1960 'A Neutral Budget?', *The Bankers' Magazine,* vol. 189, no. 1394, May

1961 'EEC/EFTA: and Future Marketing Research Problems', *Esomar/Wapor Conference,* Baden-Baden, September

1962 'The Kennedy Trade Plan', Europe House Paper 9

'A possible Ten-year Projection for the British Economy', in R.C. Geary (ed.) *Europe's Future in Figures* (Amsterdam: North Holland)

1963 'The GATT Negotiations: a Conflict of Aims', *Investors Chronicle Supplement,* 14 June

'Forecasting and Policy Projection for the Long Term', *The Malayan Economic Review,* vol. 8, no. 2, October

'Towards Free Trade?', *Woolwich Economic Papers,* no. 1.

'International Comparisons of Productivity Growth in the 1950s' (with R.E. Crum), *JRSS (A),* vol. 126, part 2

'Analyse Economique et Politiques d'Expansion', *Revue de la Société d'Etudes et d'Expansion* (Liège), no. 207, Sept–Oct

1964 'Public Expenditure in Perspective', *Daily Telegraph,* 3 April

'The Development and Problems of Economic Planning in Great Britain, *Weltwirtschaftliches Archiv,* vol. 92, no. 1

1964 'Britain's Competitive Achievement', *Investors Chronicle Special Survey,* 5 June

'Economic Tightrope', *Frontier,* vol. 7, no.4

'Can Britain Escape from her Balance of Payments Difficulties?', *Nationalekonomiska Forëningens* (Stockholm), December

1965 'Incomes Policy and Equity', *Westminster Bank Review,* February

'Income Policies', *Societe Royale d'Economie Politique de Belgique,* May

'Incomes Policy in Britain: with Special Reference to Considerations of Equity', *Probleme der Einkommenspolitik,* Institut für Weltwirtschaft, Kiel (Symposium), May

1968 'Economic Forecasting at the International, National and Business Level', *Kemp-Gee International Investment Symposium,* Wengen, June

'Macroeconomic Aspects of Incomes Policy', in A.D. Smith (ed.) *The Labour Market and Inflation* (London: Macmillan) (Symposium)

1970 'Incomes Policies: What are they an Instrument for?', *Japan Economic Research Bureau, Planning and Macroeconomic Policy,* Tokyo, September.

1972 'Incomes Policy: Lessons from European Experience', in F.T. Blackaby (ed.) *An Incomes Policy for Britain* (London: Heinemann) (Symposium)

'Problems and Policies for Inland Transport' (with G.F. Ray), in W. Beckerman (ed.) *The British Economy in 1975* (Cambridge: Cambridge University Press for NIESR)

1974 'Industrial Specialisation and Industrial Policies' in UN Economic Commission for Europe. *Factors and Conditions of Long-term Growth* (Symposium, Stockholm: UN Sales no. E.74.II.E.14)

'Entwurf einer Einkommenspolitik', *Brennpunkte,* no. 4 (Rüschlikon, Switzerland: Gottlieb Duttweiler-Institut) (translated)

1977 'New Structures in the World Economy', in H. Seidel and F. Butschek (eds.) *Die Rezession 1974/75*, Österreichisches Institut für Wirtschaftsforschung (Symposium, Vienna)

'Inflation, Incomes Policies and Pay Differentials', in R.T. Griffiths (ed.) *Government, Business and Labour in European Capitalism* (London: Europotentials Press)

'Welfare and the GNP', in C.A. van Bochove et al. (eds.) *Modelling for Government and Business,* Essays in honour of P.J. Verdoorn (Leiden: Martinus Nijhoff)

'The Economics of Advanced European Society' in P. Freeman (ed.) *Europe Today and Tomorrow* (London: Longman)

'Concentration and Specialisation in Western Industrial Countries' (translated into Magyar) in *Ipargazdasági Szemle,* 1977/2

'The Feasibility of Welfare-oriented Measures to supplement the National Accounts and Balances: A Technical Report', United Nations Statistical Office, *Studies in Methods* F 22

1978 'Towards Restructuring the World Economy', in F. Levcik (ed.) *Internationale Wirtschafts-Vergleiche und Interdependenzen,* Festschrift für Franz Nemschak (Vienna: Springer-Verlag)

1980 'Measures of Total Household Consumption', *Review of Income and Wealth,* Series 26, no. 4, December

'Household Surveys as an Instrument for Assessing Living Standards in Developing Countries', World Bank, *Living Standards Measurement Study, Working Paper* 10

'Changes in Relative Pay in the 1970s', in F. Blackaby (ed.) *The Future of Pay Bargaining* (London: Heinemann) (Symposium)

1981 'EEC-CMEA Cooperation', *Peace and the Sciences,* 2/81 (International Institute for Peace, Vienna) (Symposium, Varna)

'Pay Distribution and Differentials in Britain and other Western Countries', in E. Tarantelli and G. Willke *The Management of Industrial Conflict in the Recession of the 1970s* (Symposium of European University Institute, Fiesole)

1982 'Changes in the Distribution of World Production and Trade', in John Pinder (ed.) *National Industrial Strategies and the World Economy* (London: Croom Helm)

1983 'The Third World in the Industrial Slow-down', in *Market Economies, Planned Communism and the Third World: Strength and Dependence* (1983 Economics Symposium, University of the South, Sewanee, Tennessee; to be published by University of Pennsylvania Press, 1984)

Book Reviews*

1938 H. Mendershausen, Les Variations du Mouvement Saisonnier. *Weltwirtschaftliches Archiv* vol. 48, no. 2, September

1956 R.W. Goldsmith, D.S. Brady and H. Mendershausen, 'A Study of Saving in the United States'. *Economica,* vol. 23, no. 89, February

M. Gilbert and R. Stone (eds.), 'Income and Wealth, Series IV', *Econ. Jnl.,* vol. 66, no. 264, December

1957 A.O. Dahlberg, 'National Income Vizualised', *JRSS (A)* Part I.

United Nations, 'Statistics of National Income and Expenditure' (Statistical Papers H. 10). *The Bankers' Magazine,* vol. 184, no. 1360, July

Central Statistical Office, 'National Income and Expenditure 1957'. ('New Facts from the National Accounts') *The Bankers' Magazine,* vol. 184, no. 1362, September

Conference on Research in Income and Wealth (US), 'Problems of Capital Formation', *The Bankers' Magazine,* vol. 184, no. 1362, September

* *Econ. Jnl.:* Economic Journal
JRSS(A): Journal of the Royal Statistical Society, Series A (General)

1958 R. Robson, 'The Cotton Industry in Britain', *Economica,* vol. 25, no. 97, February
1959 H. Theil, 'Economic Forecasts and Policy. *The Economist,* (unsigned), 9 May
'Know Your Ministry', *The Bankers' Magazine,* vol. 187, no. 1383, June
1961 G.H. Moore (ed.) 'Business Cycle Indicators', *The Economist,* 9 September.
1962 Statistical Unit, Church of England, 'Facts and Figures about the Church of England', *JRSS (A)* vol. 125, part 4
1963 National Bureau of Economic Research, 'The Rate and Direction of Inventive Activity', *International Statistical Review,* vol. 31, no. 2
1964 R. Brech, 'Britain 1984: A Forecast for Unilever', *JRSS (A)* vol. 127, Part I
R. Stone (ed.) 'A Programme for Growth' and British Association for Commercial and Industrial Education; 'Economic Growth and Manpower'. *Econ. Jnl.,* vol. 74 no. 295, September
1966 G. Stuvel, 'Systems of Social Accounts', *Econ. Jnl.,* vol. 76, no. 303, September
O. Morgenstern, 'On the Accuracy of Economic Observations', *JRSS (A),* vol. 129, Part 1
1967 E. Coenen, 'La „Konjunkturforschung" en Allemagne et en Autriche 1925–1933', *Econ. Jnl.,* vol. 308
1969 A. Sampson, 'The New Europeans', *Frontier,* May
1971 Industrial Council for Social and Economic Studies (Stockholm), 'On Incomes Policy', *Econ. Jnl.,* vol. 81, no. 321, March
1972 A. Cairncross, 'Essays on Economic Management, *Econ. Jnl.,* vol. 82, no. 325, March
1976 K.D. George and T.S. Ward, 'The Structure of Industry in the EEC', *Econ. Jnl.,* vol. 86, no. 341, March
Lord Robbins, 'Political Economy Past and Present', *The Business Economist,* vol. 8, no. 2
1977 E. Kirschen (ed.), 'Economic Policies Compared – East and West', *Econ. Jnl.,* vol. 87, no. 345, March
1979 A. Shlaim and G. Yannopoulos, 'The EEC and Eastern Europe', *Econ. Jnl.,* vol. 89, no. 355, September
1981 J.M. van Brabant, 'Socialist Economic Integration', *Econ. Jnl.,* vol. 91, no. 362, June

Contributions (anonymous) to collective works

University of Liverpool
1932 *Industrial Survey of Merseyside* (London: HMSO)

Joint Committee of Cotton Trade Organisations (Manchester)
1935–1939 *Economic Service*

Central Statistical Office (London)
1956 *National Income Statistics: Sources and Methods* (London: HMSO)
1952–1957 *National Income and Expenditure* (annual 'Blue Books') (London: HMSO)

National Institute of Economic and Social Research (London)
1960 Evidence to (Radcliffe) Committee on the Working of the Monetary System, about The Improvement of Financial and Monetary Statistics. Principal Memoranda of Evidence, vol 3, Part II (London: HMSO)
1959–1964 *National Institute Economic Reviews*

Ministries of Labour and Transport
1964 *Report of the Committee of Inquiry to Review Pay and Conditions of Employment of Drivers and Conductors of the London Transport Board Road Services* (London: HMSO)

United Nations Economic Commission for Europe (Geneva)
1965–1973 *Economic Surveys of Europe* (annual)
1967 *Incomes in Post-war Europe: Policies, Growth and Distribution* (UN Sales no. 66.II.E.14)
1971 *Structural Trends and Prospects in the European Economy* (Economic Survey of Europe in 1969, Part 1. UN Sales no. E. 70. II. E 1)
1972 *The European Economy from the 1950s to the 1970s* (Economic Survey of Europe in 1971, Part 1. UN Sales no. E.72.II.E.1)
1977 *Structure and Change in European Industry* (UN Sales no. E.72.II.E.3)
1980 *The Economic Role of Women in the ECE Region* (UN Sales no. E.80.II.E.6)

LIST OF CONTRIBUTORS

P. Arestis — Thames Polytechnic, London, U.K.

M. J. Artis — University of Manchester, Manchester, U.K.

B. Askanas — Vienna Institute for Comparative Economic Studies, Vienna, Austria

F. Blackaby — Stockholm International Peace Research Institute, Solna, Sweden

G. Blazyca — Thames Polytechnic, London, U.K.

L. H. Dupriez — formerly University of Louvain, Louvain, Belgium (deceased)

C. Freeman — University of Sussex, Brighton, Sussex, U.K.

S. F. Frowen — University of Surrey, Guildford, Surrey, U.K.

S. Holly — London Graduate School of Business Studies, London, U.K.

E. Karakitsos — Imperial College of Science and Technology, London, U.K.

K. H. Ketterer — Landeszentralbank in Baden-Württemberg, Stuttgart, FRG

N. Kloten — Landeszentralbank in Baden-Württemberg, Stuttgart, FRG

F. Levcik – Vienna Institute for Comparative Economic Studies, Vienna, Austria

A. Maizels – University College London, U.K.; formerly UNCTAD, Geneva, Switzerland

Homa Motamen – Imperial College of Science and Technology, London, U.K.

L. Needleman – University of Waterloo, Waterloo, Ontario, Canada

G. F. Ray – National Institute of Economic and Social Research, London, and University of Surrey, Guildford, Surrey, U.K.

P. B. W. Rayment – Economic Commission for Europe, United Nations, Geneva, Switzerland

J. Townsend – University of Sussex, Brighton, Sussex, U.K.

Vivian H. Walsh – University of Manchester Institute of Science and Technology (UMIST), Manchester, U.K.

Nita Watts – formerly St. Hilda's College, Oxford, and the University of Oxford Institute of Economics and Statistics, Oxford, U.K. (retired)

G. D. N. Worswick – formerly National Institute of Economic and Social Research, London, U.K. (retired)

NAME INDEX*

References in *italics* indicate authorship of a paper in this volume.

* Complied by *Audrey Bamber*

SUBJECT INDEX*

* Compiled by *Audrey Bamber*